# Developing SGML DTDs
## From Text to Model to Markup

*Eve Maler*
*Jeanne El Andaloussi*

*For book and bookstore information*

**http://www.prenhall.com**

*Prentice Hall PTR*
*Upper Saddle River, New Jersey 07458*

© 1996 by Eve Maler and Jeanne El Andaloussi
Published by Prentice Hall PTR
Prentice-Hall, Inc., A Simon & Schuster Company
Upper Saddle River, New Jersey 07458

The publisher offers discounts on this book when ordered in bulk quantities. For more information, contact Corporate Sales Department, Prentice Hall PTR, One Lake Street, Upper Saddle River, NJ 07458.
Phone: 800-382-3419; FAX: 201- 236-7141. E-mail: corpsales@prenhall.com

Editorial/production manager: *Camille Trentacoste*
SGML conversion and formatting: *Soph-Ware Associates*
Cover design director: *Jerry Votta*
Cover designer: *Scott Weiss*
Cover illustration: *Charles Waller for The Stock Illustration Source, Inc.*
Manufacturing manager: *Alexis R. Heydt*
Acquisitions editor: *Mark L. Taub*
Editorial assistant: *Dori Steinhauff*

Printed in the United States of America
10  9  8  7  6  5  4  3  2  1

## ISBN 0-13-309881-8

Prentice-Hall International (UK) Limited, *London*
Prentice-Hall of Australia Pty. Limited, *Sydney*
Prentice-Hall Canada Inc., *Toronto*
Prentice-Hall Hispanoamericana, S.A., *Mexico*
Prentice-Hall of India Private Limited, *New Delhi*
Prentice-Hall of Japan, Inc., *Tokyo*
Simon & Schuster Asia Pte. Ltd., *Singapore*
Editora Prentice-Hall do Brasil, Ltda., *Rio de Janeiro*

# Contents

# Figures

←————————————————————————————————————————————→

# Tables

# Examples

# Preface

A document type definition (DTD) forms the foundation of an SGML edifice. The goal of *Developing SGML DTDs: From Text to Model to Markup* is to help individuals and organizations develop high-quality, effective DTDs.

We have been involved in a variety of Standard Generalized Markup Language (SGML) projects, including design and development of large DTDs, in computer companies and industry-wide forums. Through these efforts, we've refined a DTD development methodology that can help anyone embarking on SGML projects to develop DTDs that meet the goals of those projects. In this book we will describe our methodology and techniques for designing, implementing, and documenting DTDs.

## Audience

*Developing SGML DTDs* is intended to serve as a workbook for anyone who is, or might soon be, responsible for developing DTDs. The audience for this book includes people in the following roles:

- *Publications and MIS project managers and project leaders* responsible for the successful migration to and implementation of SGML-based systems in their environments. If you're a manager in this position, this book will show you how to make the DTD development phase of your SGML project successful through resource and project planning. Parts 1 and 4 are meant especially for people in this role.

- *Document authors, editors, and other subject matter experts* who create, edit, or assemble the targeted information. They are authorities in the required form and content of that information and are typically in the best position to describe many document type requirements. If you're a subject matter expert, this book will show you how to uncover, express, and justify your requirements in clear, usable document analysis reports. Part 2 is meant especially for people in this role.

- *DTD implementors, developers of document-processing applications, and system and database administrators* responsible for implementing and maintaining DTDs and the systems and software tools that process the targeted information. If you're a developer, this book will show you how to contribute to the DTD requirements work and how to design and implement DTDs for readability, maintainability, and flexibility. Part 3 and some notes in Chapter 5 are meant especially for people in this role.

If you're embarking on a relatively small SGML project or a pilot for a larger effort, you may find yourself filling all three roles; this is often the case for the "SGML champion" in an organization.

# Prerequisite Knowledge

If you're a subject matter expert participating in a document type design team or if you're a manager, you need no special knowledge before beginning to make use of this book. We'll teach the methodology, formalisms, and techniques you need to know for the design portion of the work, and Chapter 1 provides some basic information on SGML concepts. However, document type design team members will probably need additional training in SGML concepts to participate fully in the team's work.

If you're a DTD implementor, Part 3 is directed solely at you. Before reading these chapters, you need to be able to read and write SGML markup declarations, and you should be familiar with technical SGML terminology for common concepts, only a few of which are explained in the text. (Appendix A provides a quick reference to SGML syntax.) We strongly suggest that you have on hand one of the various SGML reference books and other hardcopy and electronic sources as you read and work (see Appendix E for information on sources).

# Scope of This Book

*Developing SGML DTDs* covers the breadth of the DTD development process for SGML (ISO 8879) applications, and it uses general-purpose examples in order to help you reach a beginning or intermediate level. For the most part, it doesn't discuss specific existing applications of SGML, such as industry-standard DTDs, or applications of the HyTime standard (ISO 10744) for hypertext and multimedia.

Our discussions and examples are based mostly on document production and publishing applications, that is, creation, processing, and delivery of documents in a business environment. Other types of applications, such as marking up documents for personal use or performing computerized analysis on documents written outside an organization's control, are not specifically covered. However, such projects can use our methodology and techniques with few modifications.

DTD development is an important part, but by no means the only part, of an SGML project. We stick closely to describing DTD-related tasks, leaving aside such topics as making the SGML decision in the first place, implementing conversion software and processes, and developing formatting stylesheets.

Appendix E suggests sources that address some of these additional topics.

# Organization of This Book

This book is organized into four main parts and also has five appendices and a glossary.

Part 1 introduces SGML and our methodology and discusses the management of a DTD development project.

Part 2 explains the basic steps for the document type design team to use in analyzing the target document class and developing design requirements and rationales, resulting in the production of a "document analysis report" that can be used by a DTD implementor.

Part 3 describes how to implement markup requirements in a high-quality SGML DTD that takes into account any needs for customization and maintenance. It also discusses how to test the results.

Part 4 explains how to document a DTD and train authors to apply markup correctly using it.

Appendix A provides reference information for DTD implementors on constructing DTDs and SGML declarations.

Appendix B provides reference information on the graphical tree diagram formalism we introduce for SGML information modeling.

Appendix C provides an extended example of DTD techniques for reuse and customization.

Appendix D summarizes the ISO character entity sets.

Appendix E suggests further reading and sources.

The Glossary explains phrases introduced in the text, including some terms that are defined in ISO 8879.

# Conventions Used in This Book

This book uses the following typographical conventions:

- In text, `element` type generic identifiers and `attribute` names are in fixed-width font, and attribute `"values"` are shown in the same font with quotation marks.

- In text, the general `&entity;` names and parameter `%entity;` names are in fixed-width font and are delimited as if they were references to the named entities.

- Computer-related `literal` strings that must be used exactly as shown are in fixed-width font; *variable* parts of computer strings are in fixed-width oblique font. SGML reserved name keywords, such as `ATTLIST`, are shown in all capitals.

- **New terms** are shown in boldface type where they are introduced and defined in text; these terms are also defined in the glossary.

- Checklists containing practical advice appear throughout this book. Items in checklists have this symbol next to them:

DTD implementors in particular should note the following conventions that we use for DTD examples, primarily in Part 3:

- Where real elements, attributes, and so on must be declared and used in DTD examples, we usually assume a straightforward structure-oriented book DTD and use simple descriptive names for the parts of the structure: `div` or `division` for a division element, `para` for a paragraph, and so on. These declarations don't correspond to any existing DTD, and any two examples are likely to be incompatible with each other.

- The DTD examples assume the reference concrete syntax and quantity set, with the exception of the `NAMELEN` quantity, which we assume is 32. We assume `OMITTAG` minimization is set to `YES`, so we generally include omitted-tag specification characters in element declarations. In order not to distract from whatever issue is under discussion, we usually provide hyphen (-) specification characters to indicate that tags cannot be omitted. SGML declarations are discussed in Section A.9.

- Ambiguous and otherwise invalid DTD and markup examples have the following symbol next to them, to remind you not to use them as templates for your own DTDs:

# Colophon

Drafts of this book were written in the DocBook DTD and variants thereof with the Soft-Quad Author/Editor™ and ArborText ADEPT•Editor™ products for Microsoft Windows™, and were formatted with ADEPT•Publisher for UNIX™ systems. The graphics were prepared with Visio™. The final typeset output was produced with FrameBuilder® and ADEPT•Publisher. OmniMark™ was used to validate the SGML examples.

# Acknowledgments

You always write the book you wish you'd had the first time around. A great many people were involved in the events that shaped our experiences, opinions, and working styles, and we owe them a large debt for their contributions to the methodology and this book. Of course, any errors herein are ours alone.

Many thanks to ArborText and SoftQuad for providing the software we used in writing the book. ArborText also gave permission for us to use the DTDs in Appendix C. We also gratefully acknowledge Berger-Levrault/Advanced Information Systems, and Dominique Vigneaud in particular, for introducing us to an early version of the tree diagram notation as a way to document DTDs. Thanks go to Andrew Rogers, creator of the `rcard` recipe-formatting program, for allowing us to use the `rcard` markup and output in examples in Chapter 4. Tim Allen kindly helped us validate the SGML examples in the book. Camille Trentacoste of Prentice Hall and the people at Soph-Ware Associates did a wonderful job turning our manuscript into a printed book.

The proposal and, later, the book were given attention by many thoughtful reviewers. We are especially grateful to Terry Allen, Steve DeRose, Lee Fogal, Charles Goldfarb, Kathy Greenleaf, Paul Grosso, Eduardo Gutentag, Dominique Péré, Russ Rauhauser, Yuri Rubinsky, and Rich Yampell for their helpful contributions. We would also like to thank Deborah Dormitzer for recipes and advice, and Earl Grey for inventing "writing juice."

Jeanne says:

> Many thanks go to Groupe Bull, for allowing me to use real-life examples gleaned from Bull projects; Jacques Rousseaux, for his help in modeling the project workflow tasks using the Mallet methodology; Christophe Lecluse, for technical advice; and Eve, for agreeing to do this project, as it provided the perfect excuse for me to spend some quality time with her in the States. Most of all, I thank Jean Charles Burou and our son Alexandre for their incredible patience. I fondly hope that they can forgive me for all the nights we missed going out on the town and for the succession of baby-sitters (respectively). Alexandre has heard SGML being spoken since before he was born; it's a wonder his first word wasn't "pee-cee-data."

Eve says:

> I owe much to Aidan Killian; Ludo Van Vooren; Aviva Bock; the many people at ArborText and Digital Equipment Corporation who gave me moral support; Jeanne and her family, for putting me up and putting up with me; my own family and friends, for being patient even when I got *really* boring; and especially my husband and true love Elias Israel, not only for coming up with the title, not only for providing an example of how one could write a book and survive, but for his ceaseless aid and comfort.

We dedicate this book to M'Hammed El Andaloussi and to the memory of Ned Maler.

# Part 1

←——————————————————————————————→

# Introduction
# and Overview

←——————————————————————————————→

We start by giving a broad overview of SGML concepts in Chapter 1, and of our DTD development methodology in Chapter 2. Chapter 3 describes the actions a project manager must take to launch a DTD development project and guide it to completion.

You don't need any special knowledge to read these chapters, though after reading them you may want to seek additional information on SGML concepts. Appendix E suggests other sources of information.

←——————————————————————————————→

2

# Introduction to SGML

With the advent of readily available computer publishing technologies, the world is awash in electronic documents. Companies create, deliver, and store ever-increasing numbers of manuals, journals, catalogs, and memos in the course of business, and these documents are becoming easier and easier to produce and print.

At the same time, because more and more computer users recognize the difficulties that arise from growing piles of documents, publishers are now offering software tools to search through documents for the desired information.

Unfortunately, because of the way these documents are usually created and stored, some of the information that would have been most valuable for using the documents in creative ways *never reaches the electronic files*. Instead, the files are usually just computerized versions of a single slickly formatted arrangement of words and pictures that comes out of the typesetting process.

As a result, it is often harder for producers and consumers of electronic documents to *find and use the information they want, when they want it, and in the form they want it*. Most of the potential of the information in these documents ends up being wasted.

What the files are usually missing is the right kind of "information about the information": facts about its organizational structure and its "meaning." The **Standard Generalized Markup Language**, or **SGML**, is a technology that provides a framework for providing this extra layer of information in your files so that you can maximize both the value of your electronic documents and your ability to manage and access them.

Computer systems can use this layer of added value in a variety of ways:

- Arranging, formatting, and excerpting the same electronic source files for different online and paper forms

- Searching for information based on characteristics of its context within a document

- Using hyperlinks to connect cross-references with the actual information to which they refer

- Treating archived documents as a database that can be searched and analyzed

SGML is a language for recording and storing document information—a computer language that nonetheless can also be read and understood by humans. You use SGML to write rules that a group of related documents should follow when they store your desired added value. The general process of figuring out the rules is called **modeling**, and when you're done modeling and expressing the model in SGML form, your set of rules serves as the "language" that these documents use to "speak" to computers. In SGML terminology, such a group of documents is described by the term **document type**, and a rule set for a document type is called a **document type definition**, or **DTD**.

For example, newspapers might be a document type, and your SGML rules for adding information to the newspapers' electronic files would be a newspaper DTD. Such information might include, for instance, the date each feature article was assigned to be written and the name of the news organization from which each photo was obtained.

For computer systems to find the added value in your files and act on it, you must have stored that added value in the files. But before you can add the value, you need to decide exactly what value you want stored and exactly what its expression in SGML form should be. To make these decisions, you need to encapsulate the desired value in a model and build an effective and cohesive DTD from it. And to build a high-quality DTD, you need a methodology—a system of principles, procedures, and tools that you can apply to the work. In this book we provide such a methodology, along with DTD development techniques and other information about both the business and the art of DTD development.

The rest of this chapter introduces SGML concepts. Chapter 2 gives some background on our DTD development methodology and some of its tools.

## 1.1    SGML, Document Types, and Documents

DTDs form the foundation for every SGML-based document production system by:

- Rigorously recording and enforcing your requirements for document intelligence and structure

- Controlling the text editors that insert and keep track of the added intelligence and structure, allowing some authoring functions to be automated

- Controlling the systems that manage whole and partial documents

- Providing information about the documents to the software that formats them, indexes them for retrieval, and otherwise processes them

The SGML language can be used to express any number of DTDs. Likewise, each DTD can be used as the basis for many documents of the same general type, with each document being an **instance**—an example—of the type described by its DTD. Any set of similar documents can be considered a document type to be modeled using SGML DTD rules: love letters, project plans, product catalogs, and so on.

Figure 1-1 shows the relationships of SGML, DTDs, and document instances.

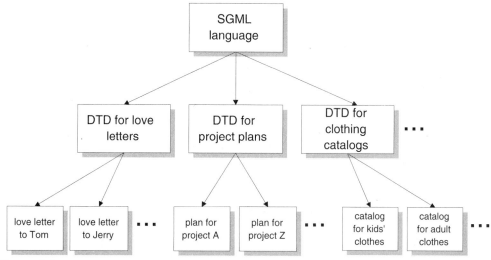

**Figure 1-1**  SGML, DTDs, and Document Instances.

All documents stored on computer systems, including SGML documents, have instructions or codes embedded in the text that indicate how the text should be processed. These instructions are called **markup**, after the handwritten instructions on document manuscripts indicating typefaces, margins, and other layout specifications, that were once the formal method of communication with human typesetters. SGML markup is what provides the added value to SGML document text, but it is typically used to emphasize what the text *represents* (that is, what the information actually *is*) rather than what it looks like or how it is to be processed, so one appearance or type of processing doesn't get "locked in" to the document files.[1] Each DTD can be said to form a unique markup language.

The idea of a DTD often seems foreign to people who have only used traditional word processors and desktop publishing systems, though a DTD simply makes explicit much of what you know intuitively when you write documents. For example, if you've ever used a Word for Windows Version 6.0 character style for "new terms" in a document so that you

---

1. In the case of DTDs that describe rules for the analysis of existing documents, what the text "means" might very well be connected to how it looks. For example, if you want to analyze a set of archived newspaper stories, it may be important to know that a story about a certain politician was "above the fold" on page 1 rather than buried deep in Section 2 somewhere. And in the case of DTDs such as the Hypertext Markup Language (HTML), much of the focus is on dictating appearance or browser behavior while still taking advantage of some of the other benefits of SGML.

don't have to keep putting those terms in boldface manually, you were engaging in applying markup—that is, **marking up** the document—using a construct of the same kind that a DTD would offer to authors of SGML documents.

In many ways, DTDs are closer to a database technology than a document-publishing technology in that they provide a "schema" for each "field" in a document that contains a unique kind of information that you'll want to access later. But DTDs add a new twist to this picture: Some fields can contain other fields. In other words, they're **hierarchical**.

Since it's a DTD rather than SGML itself that defines the model for acceptable markup within documents, SGML can be considered a **metalanguage**, a language in which other languages are written. Thus, it may be useful to think of the "Standard Generalized Markup Language" as a document markup *system* or *framework* rather than a markup *language* all by itself. However, when we're talking about SGML-based documents in the abstract without concern for the DTD with which they are associated, we use the phrases "SGML markup" and "SGML documents."

Because of the DTD layer between the SGML language and an SGML document, every SGML document must have at least two parts:

- A **document type declaration** containing (or pointing to one or more files that contain) the DTD rules to which the markup in this document is supposed to conform

  For example, the electronic file for a newspaper would point to the newspaper DTD in its document type declaration.

- A **document instance** containing all the content and embedded markup of the document

  For example, for a newspaper, the electronically stored document instance would consist of the newspaper's actual words and other content plus its DTD-conforming markup.

So far in this discussion, we've used the term "document" as if its meaning were clear and unambiguous. Certainly, it's easy to see that a letter, a book, or a newspaper, for example, constitutes a single document as most people understand the term. However, the definition of the term **document** in the SGML standard broadens its scope in an interesting way. Here is the definition:

> A collection of information that is processed as a unit. A document is
> classified as being of a particular document type.

An SGML document is any collection of information that gets processed *together*. So, for example, while a newspaper might be a document, a single article might also count as a document if you deliver individual articles to particular reading audiences. For another example, both cookbooks and recipes might be considered documents, depending on what you intend to do with them. Document types can model whatever level or size of document is appropriate for your needs.

There's another way in which SGML challenges the traditional understanding of a document. If you can hold a printed book in your hand and then view the same basic contents on a computer screen, how many documents do you have—one or two?

The usual view in the word processor world is that a document is made by its medium—that the same content, formatted two different ways, constitutes two documents. SGML takes the opposite view: It's the content and markup that make up an SGML document, and the precise presentation of the material (formatting characteristics, display or suppression of different pieces of content, and so on) happens apart from document creation.

The particular expression of an SGML document when it is presented to a reader is sometimes called a **presentation instance**, a term analogous to document instance. It might help to think of an SGML document as the source of a potentially infinite number of presentation instances—a "proto-document" as far as printing and delivery are concerned. Figure 1-2 shows the relationship between SGML documents and possible presentation instances.

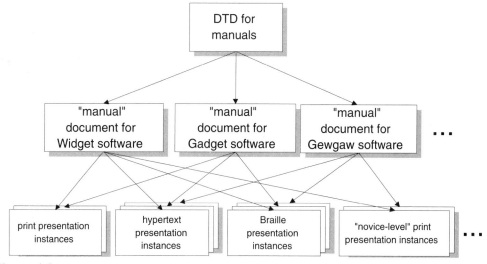

**Figure 1-2**     SGML Documents and Presentation Instances.

## 1.2   SGML and Other Markup Systems

It's useful to describe the characteristics of SGML markup by contrasting it with other types of markup. T$_E$X, `troff`, and Script are examples of traditional typesetting markup languages that use embedded codes which are visible to authors who are working on the files. Originally, word processor software also used visible markup codes in text files, but modern word processors and desktop publishing systems incorporate viewing software that instead shows authors only the formatting effect of the markup, simulating the formatted version of the document.

We'll examine SGML and various other markup systems along the following dimensions:

- Procedural versus declarative

- System-specific versus generic

- Noncontextual versus contextual

## 1.2.1   Procedural versus Declarative Markup

**Procedural** markup supplies detailed instructions for actions that software must follow in processing the data—it says, "Do $x$." For example, the text of each item in a bulleted list might be preceded with markup that provides the following instructions to the software:

> Output the bullet symbol "•" and tab over to 24 points from the original line length before you output the first line of text, and indent any subsequent lines of text 24 points.

The text of each item might be followed with markup providing this instruction.

> Restore the original line length.

The markup would have the following effect when the text is formatted:

- An apple is a fruit that is sweet-tasting, approximately round in shape, and red, yellow, or green in color.

- An orange is a fruit that is sweet-tasting, approximately round in shape, and orange in color.

By contrast, **declarative** (or **descriptive**) markup supplies only high-level logical descriptions of the data's role or purpose ("I am a $y$"), expecting that separate processing software will map the markup to the precise actions to be performed as well as actually perform the actions. For example, the text of the same bulleted list item might instead be surrounded with markup that says only

> This is the start of a bulleted list item.

and

> This is the end of a bulleted list item.

This markup puts the text in a "virtual container." A formatting system must apply rules for using this markup appropriately to change line lengths, add bullet characters, and generally manage the output of the item.

Traditional markup systems usually offer both a set of basic procedural requests and a way to define groupings of requests called "macros." Desktop publishing systems and word processors have a similar capability, usually called "styles." Such groupings of requests can be designed to be relatively declarative. For example, following is a list encoded with a hypothetical `troff` macro package:

```
.LS                              start of bulleted list
.Li                              start of list item (no end-macro)
An apple is a fruit that is
sweet-tasting, approximately
round in shape, and red, yellow,
or green in color.
.Li                              start of list item (no end-macro)
An orange is a fruit that is
sweet-tasting, approximately
round in shape, and orange in
color.
.LE                              end of bulleted list
```

The calls to the macros in the source file are highly declarative in that they don't mention the exact appearance the list will have. Thus, you can use different macro definitions with the same file to get different formatting results.

Procedural markup is efficient because it allows a computer to follow the supplied instructions without doing additional interpretive work. However, it binds the data closely to a single kind of manipulation, such as choosing one value for list-item indent over all other values.

Declarative markup requires an additional interpretation step, but allows document data that is stored in a single form to be formatted, analyzed, and manipulated many different ways, increasing the value of the data once it has been described thoroughly and abstractly. For example, if the "house style" changes, new interpretation rules could be substituted for the old ones to change the indents or bullet characters for list items. Of course, this flexibility is only an option wherever declarative markup has been used to the exclusion of procedural markup. Word processor users who have controlled all facets of formatting manually can't take advantage of changes in style definitions.

Purely procedural and purely declarative markup are actually two ends of a continuum. Typesetting markup languages and desktop publishing systems tend to use markup that is closer to the procedural end because they give authors a large degree of control over the formatted appearance. For example, systems like `troff` often come with sets of declarative macros, but allow authors to use procedural markup at any time. By contrast, SGML markup can be highly declarative because it does not "come with" any particular formatting system; if an SGML markup language is well designed and properly used, it is independent of procedures and processing and does not allow the data's value for multiple purposes to be compromised.

## 1.2.2    System-Specific versus Generic Markup

**System-specific** markup works only with particular electronic-publishing software applications that create and format the document data, and the packages are often limited to particular hardware platforms. For example, `troff` markup is intended to be processed by the `troff`-based formatting software common on UNIX™ systems and cannot be directly processed on PCs with desktop publishing software. The reverse is also true: Files produced by word processors and desktop publishing programs such as Word and WordPerfect® are useless in a UNIX `troff` processing environment. To make the systems share the documents, you must convert the documents to each target system's native markup, an expensive process with a high potential for loss of information through conversion, along with managing other difficult problems such as file storage formats and character sets.

**Generic** markup, however, is independent of the characteristics of any one system. SGML is a truly generic markup system for document text because it lends itself to being shared successfully among systems.

- It is stored in plain text files, typically ASCII, which are potentially able to be handled by any computer system.

- It provides a formal way to record the character sets used in the document files.

- It is the joint creation of a formal, worldwide process for building standards through consensus under the **International Organization for Standardization (ISO)**, rather than by any one software vendor. Thus, your choices for software tools that process your existing textual document files remain open if your current system ceases to meet your needs, and you can manage the same document files on heterogeneous platforms.

- Likewise, the design of DTDs is owned by document producers rather than by software or hardware vendors, thus reflecting the real needs of producers and protecting them from changes in the markup language that benefit vendors exclusively.

  In fact, many DTDs have already been developed for various vertical segments of the information-publishing market, such as the CALS (Continuous Acquisition and Life-cycle Support) DTDs for information produced by U.S. Department of Defense contractors, the ATA (Air Transport Association) DTDs for commercial aircraft maintenance information, and DocBook for software documentation.

Note that even if a markup language is declarative, it's not necessarily generic. For example, the style names in a Word for Windows template can be relatively free of references to appearance, but the styles must still be processed by Word software.

## 1.2.3    Noncontextual versus Contextual Markup

Most markup languages are **noncontextual**; that is, the data and markup occur in a stream on which particular relationships of order and hierarchy aren't explicitly imposed. For example, `troff` is a noncontextual markup language. In the example in Section 1.2.1, list items are shown as being "inside" a pair of macros representing the start and end of a list, which is helpful in making the markup declarative. However, nothing in the definitions of the `.LS`, `.Li`, and `.LE` macros specifies that a connection exists between lists and list items. Each definition just contains a series of formatting instructions, with the assumption that authors won't inappropriately put an `.LE` before the first `.LS`, or use chapter-heading macros inside pairs of list macros.

With a markup language that has the notion of **context**—the ordering and hierarchical containment of pieces of information—you can use context to your advantage by:

- Making explicit rules about how the pieces should interact

- Using computers to check the structural validity according to your rules

- Processing and searching for text based on its context

SGML markup has a built-in notion of hierarchical containers for information that allows you to ensure, for example, that "lists" contain "items" and that they don't contain "chapters." You can also test whether a bulleted list item is inside another bulleted list, and format it to have an introductory dash instead of a bullet and to have an additional indent level, or do the same for various levels of numbered lists so that the top level has Arabic numbers, the second level has lowercase letters, and so on. To achieve the same effect in a word processor, you must use a different style for each possible location in which a list item of each type occurs, with the result that you can end up with dozens of styles for a single logical kind of text.

## 1.2.4    SGML Markup Strengths

To summarize, SGML markup is unique in that it combines several design strengths:

- It is declarative, which helps document producers "write once, use many"—putting the same document data to multiple uses, such as delivery of documents in a variety of online and paper formats, and interchange with others who wish to use the documents in different ways.

- It is generic across systems and has a nonproprietary design, which helps make documents vendor- and platform-independent and "future-proof"— protecting them against changes in computer hardware and software.

- It is contextual, which heightens the quality and completeness of processing by allowing documents to be structurally validated and by enabling logical collections of data to be manipulated intelligently.

The characteristics of being declarative, generic, nonproprietary, and contextual make the Standard Generalized Markup Language "standard" and "generalized."

## 1.3    SGML Constructs

The grammar of every SGML markup language has four basic "parts of speech": elements, attributes, entities, and comments. In the following sections we'll use a hypothetical set of DTD rules for a very simple "recipe" document type, along with two real recipes, to illustrate these parts of speech.

### 1.3.1    Elements

Section 1.2 described the notion of nestable containers for collections of document information. In SGML, containers are called **elements**. The DTD rule for the occurrence and sequence of document data and other elements inside a particular *kind* of element, or **element type**, is called a **content model**. Our recipe DTD creates six element types, and declares their content models as follows:

- A "recipe" element must contain a "title" element, followed by an "ingredient list" element, followed by an "instruction list" element. All these inner elements are required.

- A "title" element contains characters.

- An "ingredient list" element must contain one or more "ingredient" elements.

- An "ingredient" element contains characters.

- An "instruction list" element must contain one or more "step" elements.

- A "step" element contains characters.

Figure 1-3 shows how these nested elements apply to a real document—a recipe for Hawaiian coconut pudding. The rectangles represent elements containing either the words of the recipe or smaller elements that ultimately contain words.[2]

If you scan the recipe from top to bottom, you cross the upper and lower boundaries of each rectangle in the same logical places at which you would come across SGML element markup in a document instance. Each upper boundary corresponds to an element

---

2. From this point on, we generally stick to the standard SGML terminology for document content and strings of characters. **Data** refers to strings of characters, whereas **text** refers to any combination of characters and markup that makes up the document content. When we use the word "text" in referring colloquially to the prose-based material that makes up the bulk of the passages in a document, we put it in quotation marks.

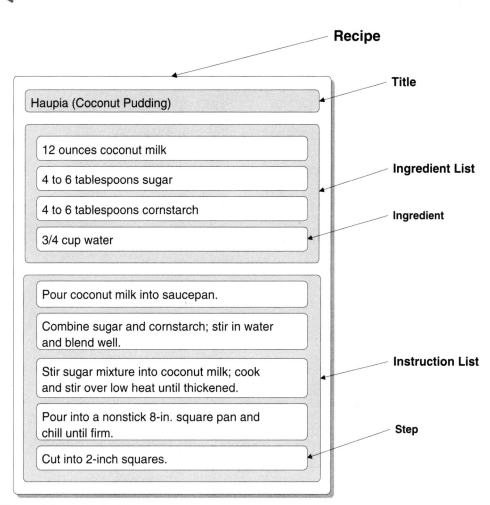

**Figure 1-3**     Recipe Elements.

start-tag, and each lower boundary to an element **end-tag**. By default, SGML tag markup consists of the name of the element type surrounded by angle brackets (<>), with the addition of a slash (/) before the name in the end-tag, as follows.

```
<recipe>                            recipe start-tag
<title>                             title start-tag
Haupia (Coconut Pudding)
</title>                            title end-tag
<ingredient-list>                   ingredient-list start-tag
<ingredient>                        ingredient start-tag
12 ounces coconut milk
</ingredient>                       ingredient end-tag
<ingredient>
4 to 6 tablespoons sugar
</ingredient>
<ingredient>
4 to 6 tablespoons cornstarch
</ingredient>
<ingredient>
3/4 cup water
</ingredient>
</ingredient-list>                  ingredient-list end-tag
<instruction-list>                  instruction-list start-tag
<step>                              step start-tag
Pour coconut milk into saucepan.
</step>                             step end-tag
<step>
Combine sugar and cornstarch;
stir in water and blend well.
</step>
<step>
Stir sugar mixture into coconut milk;
cook and stir over low heat until thickened.
</step>
<step>
Pour into a nonstick 8-in.
square pan and chill until firm.
</step>
<step>
Cut into 2-inch squares.
</step>
</instruction-list>                 instruction-list end-tag
</recipe>                           recipe end-tag
```

This example barely scratches the surface of SGML content-modeling possibilities. Following is a brief list of the major content model choices:

- An element can be required (as all the recipe elements are) or optional.

- An element can be repeatable (as the ingredient and step elements are) or nonrepeatable (as the recipe, title, ingredient list, and instruction list elements are).

- A group of several elements can be specified so that elements occur in a certain unchangeable order (as the elements inside the recipe element are); in an order left up to the discretion of the document creator; or mutually exclusive of each other.

- Like single elements, groups of elements can be specified to be required or optional and to have their occurrence controlled.

- A particular element can be allowed to appear anywhere directly within another element and further down within that element's contents. Conversely, an element can be banned from appearing anywhere within another element.

## 1.3.2   Attributes

A DTD can specify rules for special labels, called **attributes**, that can be attached to particular elements to further describe their content. Our sample DTD declares that the recipe and step element types have attributes as follows.

- A "recipe" element can optionally have values for the following attributes:

  o  Type of dish

     The value can be any character string (for example, "starter" or "main course").

  o  Number of servings it makes

     The value must be a number (for example, "10").

  o  Number of minutes it takes to prepare

     The value must be a number (for example, "30").

- A "step" element can optionally have a value indicating whether performing the step is necessary. The value can be either "yes" or "no"; if a value isn't supplied explicitly, the default value is "yes."

Figure 1-4 shows attribute values assigned to these elements; they appear near the top of their respective element rectangles. The attribute values on the steps use the default.

In an SGML document instance, attribute information, if there is any, is stored inside an element's start-tag. An attribute has two parts, a **name** and a **value**, separated by an equal sign (=). For example, for the pudding recipe instance, the markup would look as follows; the attributes are shown on separate lines for ease of reading, but they can all appear on the same line:

```
<recipe
   type="dessert"
   servings="6"
   preptime="10">          recipe start-tag with attributes
   ⋮
<step
   necessary="no">         step start-tag with explicitly set value
Thoroughly wash and dry    (step included only to show how to set attribute)
the pot you will use.
</step>
```

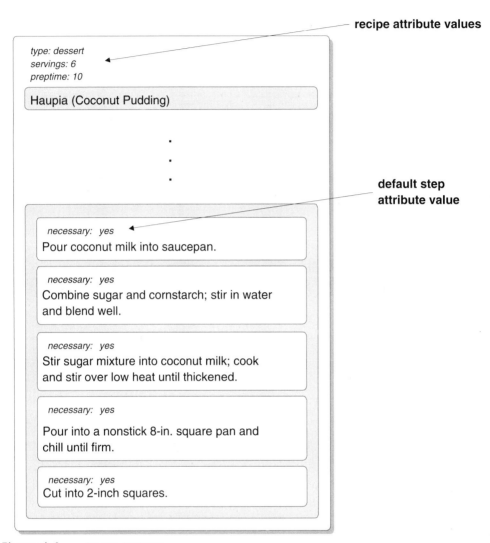

recipe attribute values

*type: dessert*
*servings: 6*
*preptime: 10*

Haupia (Coconut Pudding)

•
•
•

default step
attribute value

*necessary:  yes*
Pour coconut milk into saucepan.

*necessary:  yes*
Combine sugar and cornstarch; stir in water
and blend well.

*necessary:  yes*
Stir sugar mixture into coconut milk; cook
and stir over low heat until thickened.

*necessary:  yes*
Pour into a nonstick 8-in. square pan and
chill until firm.

*necessary:  yes*
Cut into 2-inch squares.

**Figure 1-4**        Recipe Attributes.

```
<step>                          step start-tag with default value
  :
  :
</step>
</instruction-list>
</recipe>
```

An attribute's allowable values can be controlled through its DTD rule. Requiring the value to be a number (a series of digits) is only one possibility; another, for example, is to require the value to be a "name" (a keyword beginning with a letter and containing only letters, digits, and a few special characters).

## 1.3.3    Entities

A DTD can identify fragments of document content, called **entities**, that are stored separately from the main content of the documents in which they're used. Storing such a fragment separately allows it to be used multiple times and to be updated easily through the changing of a single definition. Documents use **entity references** to include an entity's content everywhere it is supposed to appear.

Our sample DTD creates an entity called "pour-chill-cut" that contains all the data and all the markup for two sequential steps that are likely to occur in several recipes:

- A step with a default attribute value, containing the string "Pour into a nonstick 8-in. square pan and chill until firm."

- A step with a default attribute value, containing the string "Cut into 2-inch squares."

Figure 1-5 shows where the original document data and markup for the two steps are replaced by the entity reference.

In SGML markup, references to entities containing data and markup appear in the document wherever that text is desired, with the name of the entity surrounded by an ampersand (&) and a semicolon (;). For example, the "pour-chill-cut" entity reference looks as follows when placed at the end of all the other steps that are physically present in the file (remember that the entity reference includes both the words of the two steps and their <step> tag markup):

```
    ⋮
<step>
Stir sugar mixture into coconut milk;
cook and stir over low heat until thickened.
</step>
&pour-chill-cut;                    reference to entity
</instruction-list>
</recipe>
```

## 1.3.4    Comments

Any SGML document can contain **comments**, notes to the author or to other readers of the SGML data and markup, in nearly any location. The DTD can't control whether or where comments are used, and the logical SGML "view" of the document ignores comments entirely as if they weren't present; they appear in the SGML document instance, but they are disposed of during processing.

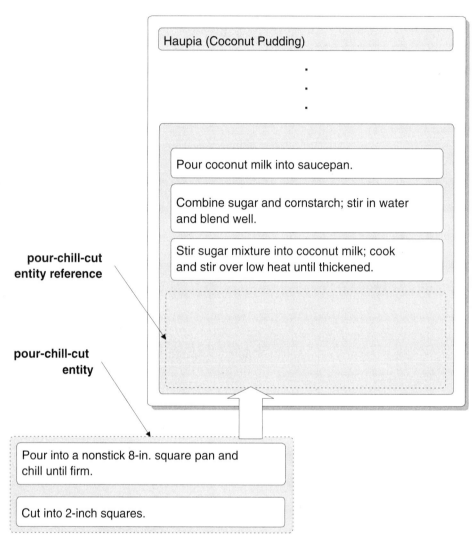

Haupia (Coconut Pudding)

Pour coconut milk into saucepan.

Combine sugar and cornstarch; stir in water and blend well.

Stir sugar mixture into coconut milk; cook and stir over low heat until thickened.

**pour-chill-cut entity reference**

**pour-chill-cut entity**

Pour into a nonstick 8-in. square pan and chill until firm.

Cut into 2-inch squares.

**Figure 1-5**    Recipe Entity and Reference.

In SGML document instances, comments are delimited by the strings < ! -- and -->. For example, the pudding recipe might contain the following comments:

```
<recipe
   type="dessert"
   servings="6"
   preptime="10">
<!--I wrote down this recipe                              comment
just as my grandmother told me
about it, but I have some doubts.
I need to test it in the kitchen.
-->
<title>
Haupia (Coconut Pudding)
</title>
<ingredient-list>
<ingredient>
12 ounces coconut milk
</ingredient>
<ingredient>
4 to 6 tablespoons sugar
</ingredient>
<ingredient> 4 to 6 tablespoons cornstarch<!--Is this    comment
amount correct??-->
</ingredient>
<ingredient>
3/4 cup water
</ingredient>
</ingredient-list>
    :
    :
</recipe>
```

## 1.3.5   Putting the Pieces Together

Figure 1-6 illustrates elements, attributes, and entities for the recipe all at once. (Remember that comments are not part of the logical SGML structure of a document; this is why they aren't shown here.)

Example 1-1 shows the actual SGML document corresponding to the entire pudding recipe in Figure 1-6. The first line contains the document type declaration, indicated by an exclamation point (!) and the DOCTYPE keyword. This is the part of the SGML document that points to the DTD rules to which this document instance conforms. In this case, the DTD rules are stored in a file on the system named recipe.dtd (shown in Example 1-2). The rest of the lines contain the content of the document instance.

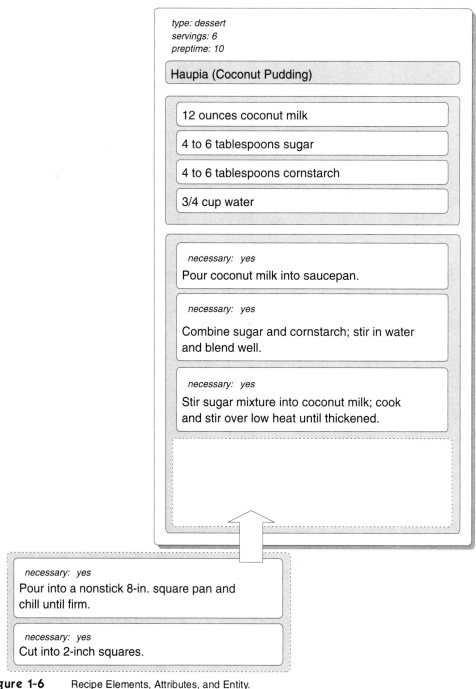

**Figure 1-6** Recipe Elements, Attributes, and Entity.

**Example 1-1**    SGML Document for Pudding Recipe.

```
<!DOCTYPE recipe SYSTEM "recipe.dtd">        pointer to DTD rules
<recipe
    type="dessert"
    servings="6"
    preptime="10">
<!--I wrote down this recipe
just as my grandmother told me
about it, but I have some doubts.
I need to test it in the kitchen.-->
<title>
Haupia (Coconut Pudding)
</title>
<ingredient-list>
<ingredient>
12 ounces coconut milk
</ingredient>
<ingredient>
4 to 6 tablespoons sugar
</ingredient>
<ingredient>
4 to 6 tablespoons cornstarch<!--Is this
amount correct??-->
</ingredient>
<ingredient>
3/4 cup water
</ingredient>
</ingredient-list>
<instruction-list>
<step>
Pour coconut milk into saucepan.
</step>
<step>
Combine sugar and cornstarch;
stir in water and blend well.
</step>
<step>
Stir sugar mixture into coconut milk;
cook and stir over low heat until thickened.
</step>
&pour-chill-cut;
</instruction-list>
</recipe>
```

Example 1-2 shows the actual recipe DTD, consisting of the SGML rules found in the `recipe.dtd` file. Lines in angle brackets (<>) and beginning with an exclamation point (!) can be thought of as "statements" in the SGML metalanguage; they are called **markup declarations** because they specify the rules that the markup must follow. The ELEMENT keyword begins a rule for an element type, the ATTLIST keyword begins a rule for the list of attributes available on an element type, and the ENTITY keyword begins a rule for an entity. The #PCDATA keyword indicates that the element type being declared can contain data characters. (It's possible for a content model to allow #PCDATA to be mixed in with elements, but none of the element types in the recipe DTD happen to allow this configuration.)

**Example 1-2**   Recipe DTD.

```
<!ELEMENT recipe          - - (title, ingredient-list,
                              instruction-list)>
<!ATTLIST recipe
         type             CDATA          #IMPLIED
         servings         NUMBER         #IMPLIED
         preptime         NUMBER         #IMPLIED >
<!ELEMENT title           - - (#PCDATA)>
<!ELEMENT ingredient-list - - (ingredient+)>
<!ELEMENT ingredient      - - (#PCDATA)>
<!ELEMENT instruction-list - - (step+)>
<!ELEMENT step            - - (#PCDATA)>
<!ATTLIST step
         necessary        (yes|no)       yes
>
<!ENTITY  pour-chill-cut
"<step> Pour into a nonstick 8-in.
square pan and chill until firm.
</step>
<step>
Cut into 2-inch squares.
</step>">
```

Using this DTD, you can create documents with different arrangements of elements and attributes as long as they adhere to the same rules. Example 1-3 shows a second recipe conforming to the recipe DTD. It has different numbers of ingredients and steps and uses some different values for attributes, but makes use of the same "pour-chill-cut" entity containing two steps.

**Example 1-3**    SGML Document for Fudge Recipe.

```
<!DOCTYPE recipe SYSTEM "recipe.dtd">
<recipe type="dessert" servings="6" preptime="15">
<title>Two-Minute Fudge</title>

<ingredient-list>
<ingredient>1 pound confectioner's sugar</ingredient>
<ingredient>1/2 cup cocoa</ingredient>
<ingredient>1/4 teaspoon salt</ingredient>
<ingredient>1/2 cup butter</ingredient>
<ingredient>1/4 cup milk</ingredient>
<ingredient>1 tablespoon vanilla</ingredient>
<ingredient>1 cup chopped nuts (optional)</ingredient>
</ingredient-list>

<instruction-list>
<step>In a 1-1/2 quart glass casserole,
blend the first five ingredients.</step>

<step>Microwave on HIGH 2 minutes.</step>

<step>Stir until smooth and
blend in the vanilla.</step>

<step necessary="no">Add the chopped nuts.</step>
<!--Consider suggesting raisins as an alternative?-->

&pour-chill-cut;
</instruction-list>
</recipe>
```

To make a point, we've slightly varied the appearance of the physical markup from that in Example 1-1, putting most of the start-tags and end-tags on the same line as the element's content and adding a few blank lines for readability. These changes to the markup make no difference to the logical SGML view of the document, and no difference to the final output of formatted recipes. In other words, the "formatting" of the actual markup is largely irrelevant.

Finally, Figure 1-7 shows a visual comparison of the structure of the two documents, side by side.

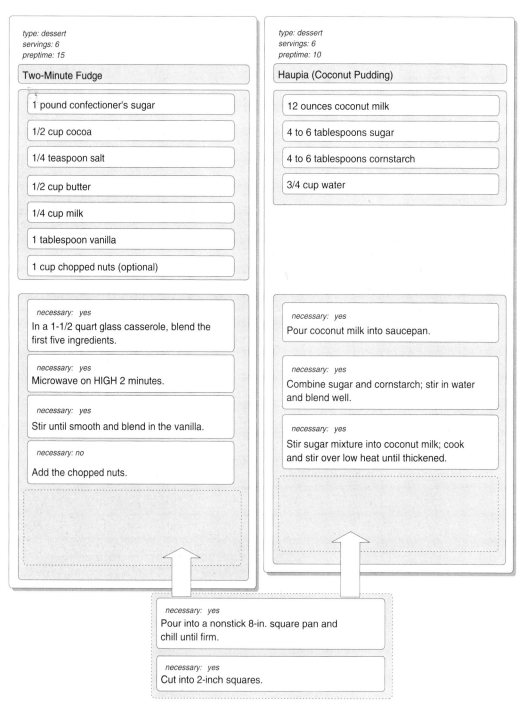

*type: dessert*
*servings: 6*
*preptime: 15*

Two-Minute Fudge

1 pound confectioner's sugar

1/2 cup cocoa

1/4 teaspoon salt

1/2 cup butter

1/4 cup milk

1 tablespoon vanilla

1 cup chopped nuts (optional)

*necessary: yes*
In a 1-1/2 quart glass casserole, blend the first five ingredients.

*necessary: yes*
Microwave on HIGH 2 minutes.

*necessary: yes*
Stir until smooth and blend in the vanilla.

*necessary: no*
Add the chopped nuts.

*type: dessert*
*servings: 6*
*preptime: 10*

Haupia (Coconut Pudding)

12 ounces coconut milk

4 to 6 tablespoons sugar

4 to 6 tablespoons cornstarch

3/4 cup water

*necessary: yes*
Pour coconut milk into saucepan.

*necessary: yes*
Combine sugar and cornstarch; stir in water and blend well.

*necessary: yes*
Stir sugar mixture into coconut milk; cook and stir over low heat until thickened.

*necessary: yes*
Pour into a nonstick 8-in. square pan and chill until firm.

*necessary: yes*
Cut into 2-inch squares.

**Figure 1-7**    Two SGML Documents Conforming to the Recipe DTD.

## 1.4   SGML Document Processing

A DTD is an essential part of an SGML-based document-processing environment.[3] However, it is only a small part. To convert, create, and format documents, build databases for search and retrieval, and otherwise manipulate your SGML documents effectively, you must use software applications. You can break down the kinds of software processing you need to perform into three major categories:

- Document creation

  This category might include, for example, writing and revising data and markup using an SGML-aware text editor or word processor; converting documents in non-SGML file formats to make them conform to a target DTD on a one-time or routine basis; and assembling whole documents from fragments.

- Document management

  This category might include, for example, storing and archiving documents and document fragments in a database; extracting document fragments for assembly; and controlling and tracking workflow, document revisions, and access to files.

- Document utilization

  This category might include, for example, formatting documents for printing and on-line viewing; indexing them for online retrieval; adding hyperlinks to them for online navigation; and interchanging them with business partners and customers in original SGML form.

Companies might have business requirements for only one or two of the three, or for only a few aspects of each one.

At the base of all SGML-aware software technology is a **parser** component, which reads SGML documents and recognizes the markup in them so that other software components can process the markup and data. Many products incorporate a **validating parser**, a special kind of parser that reads DTDs and document instances and finds any markup errors in them. Several public-domain validating parsers are available. Typically, documents are validated as they enter and exit each stage of their processing.

Applications that operate on SGML documents are often said to be "event-driven" because they search through the document looking for markup events: configurations of markup conditions that have been specified by an application developer. They can then process the document content that has been located.

---

3. It is possible (though not usually advisable) to create and use SGML documents in a way that never requires a DTD to be used by any software. However, a DTD is still advantageous in these cases as a specification that helps *humans* understand and apply the markup correctly.

A wide range of SGML-aware search capabilities is available in commercial and public-domain applications. All can detect elements, specific attribute values, and elements that appear inside certain other elements. Many can detect elements that occur in a certain position in a group. It is more rare to find applications that can detect elements whose *contents* include certain other elements, or any other situation that involves "lookahead" past the current point in the flow of the document. The more capable a system's SGML search capabilities, the more flexible and valuable will be the potential uses. Other factors are important as well; for example, it should be possible to locate data, save it, and output it in a different location.

Because each DTD contains a different set of markup rules, and each company has unique requirements for SGML document processing, each application typically requires customization in order to be usable.

Let's return to our recipe example to see what kinds of utilization might be possible. Once the recipes are marked up thoroughly and precisely (through the use of either an editor or a conversion program), you'll probably want to use processing software that treats them as more than just the antecedents of ink on paper. Certainly, you can format the documents consistently and professionally for a single chosen formatting style. For instance, you can use the value of the `necessary` attribute on step elements to generate an "Optional:" prefix on every unnecessary step, or process each recipe's preparation time information to output it in either "*n* minutes" form or "*n* hours *n* minutes" form, depending on whether the `preptime` attribute value is over 59.

However, you can also produce multiple styles of formatted output from the same source files, such as regular-print, large-print, and Braille editions of a cookbook, or several cookbooks that bring together different collections of recipes, or packets of index cards with a recipe on each one. Furthermore, you can use the identical files to build a hierarchical recipe database that users can query in interesting ways.

- I don't have much time to cook. Which *dessert* recipes take *less than 30 minutes* to prepare and have *fewer than eight required steps*?

- For my dinner party, what is the total shopping list of items necessary to make *spinach salad*, *steak*, and *chocolate mousse*?

- There's not much food left in the house. Which *vegetable* dishes require no more than *pickles*, *canned corn*, and *baking soda*? (It is to be hoped that this query won't return any hits!)

Chapter 2 introduces how you can develop DTDs that help your project meet its goals for document creation, management, and utilization.

# Introduction to DTD Development

The recipe DTD presented in Chapter 1 didn't come out of nowhere, of course. Its rules were *designed* through a process of applying knowledge of recipe structures and goals for recipe-processing applications.

If your document processing purposes would be better served by a different or more complex organization for recipes, you could define a different DTD. For example, you might find it useful to add an "amount" element to be used inside the "ingredient" element, so that users can query your recipe database more easily to find dessert recipes with minimum amounts of sugar when they're running low (or on a diet). Or, you might want to create markup for oven temperature settings and food measurements, to facilitate switching between Celsius and Fahrenheit values and volume and weight measurements for different country-specific editions of a cookbook.

DTD development is primarily an exercise in exactly this kind of value judgment. The list of design issues to be considered can be as long as you want to make it, given your own trade-offs of time and effort. In the case of the recipe document type, for example, one could ask:

- Should one general recipe element be defined, or several specific ones for desserts, meat dishes, and so on? Do the different recipe types have different internal structures?

- Is it useful to provide preparation time information in the first place? If so, should each step supply a breakdown of the preparation time?

- Should each ingredient element indicate whether the ingredient is optional?

The answers to these questions depend strongly on the intelligence and logical structure you want to put into your documents, which in turn depend on what you intend to *do* with the intelligence and structure.

Some design considerations have less to do with the innate organization of the documents than with workflow, software design, and human factors. You might need to ask yourself the following questions:

- We've discovered that instruction steps have a lot of internal structure. How complex can we make the design of step elements before recipe authors start having trouble marking up their recipes?

- We want to be able to make cross-references between recipes so that, for example, the recipe for an entrée can point the reader to any especially appropriate side dishes. To facilitate making these references into hyperlinks on our cookbook CD-ROM, we want recipe authors to build a unique identifying string into each recipe by supplying an attribute value. How can we ensure that all these attribute values are unique?

- Is there an existing recipe DTD used widely by the cookbook industry? If so, how well must the recipe DTD that we use match the industry-standard DTD? Must we submit our recipes in standard form to a testing kitchen for nutritional analysis?

- Can we assume that instruction steps will always be numbered by the formatting system? If so, it's probably nonsensical to have only *one* step in a set of instructions, and if there is only one instruction, it shouldn't be considered a "step." Do we want to require at least two steps in any one recipe and offer an alternative structure for very simple recipes?

This book naturally can't offer specific advice about the factors in the documents and environment of your individual company that might affect your DTD decisions, so we'll do the next best thing: provide a framework that helps you do the work of articulating the factors and making the design decisions yourself. The methodological approach that underlies this book is to treat each aspect with the appropriate perspective at the appropriate stage, deferring decisions until the time is ripe for them.

If you're a DTD implementor who's familiar with reading and writing DTDs, you might be wondering why a whole framework for developing DTDs is needed when you could just type everything into a text editor directly as you think of it. Or, if you're a project manager with severe resource constraints, you might think the amount of work involved in "doing the job right" seems prohibitive.

An important goal for us is to discourage "design at the keyboard"—inconsistent decisions made by a programming specialist for expediency, sometimes based on guesses about what the document specialists may want, as a DTD is implemented. No matter what the size of the project, it's best to use a cohesive philosophy in approaching the work, logical steps for executing it, tools for modeling, and formalisms for recording design decisions. In this way, you can maximize your ability to develop DTDs that are relevant to your goals, coherent, reliable, adaptable to changing needs, and reflective of the complexity of the information that you're modeling. You can also gain control over and reduce the overall costs of DTD development by increasing the quality of the result while reducing the need for later reengineering of software applications and document instances and the retraining of personnel.

Specifically, the methodology can help you do the following when it's properly applied:

- Clearly and completely formulate the problem, and base your solutions on objective criteria arising from it.

- Develop a DTD resulting from cooperation by document specialists, application developers, systems administrators, and users, rather than a system based on the personal preferences of one or a few developers.

- Apply empirical methods in solving information-modeling problems, rather than using "intuitive" solutions that fail.

- Make efficient progress in building the solution by prioritizing problems and getting input from people with the right skills at the right times.

- Evaluate the DTD you've developed, at any moment in its lifecycle, on its technical efficiency and its ability to satisfy users' needs.

Do you need to bother analyzing your needs and developing DTD design requirements in a formal process if you *know* you'll be using an industry-standard DTD? In a word, yes. First of all, just because there are dozens of industry-standard DTDs doesn't mean that using one of them is appropriate for your business, especially if interchange with customers or business partners is not a goal for you. Second, industry-standard DTDs tend to be too big, too complex, and too general for everyday use; for every industry-standard DTD, there are dozens or hundreds of efforts by companies and consultants to create subsets of and extensions to the standard DTDs for use in real document production environments.

Our focus in this book is primarily on the development of new DTDs, not on the customizing of specific existing DTDs. For advice about implementing customized versions of existing DTDs, you should consult their accompanying documentation, and from there determine the work that needs to be done. However, the steps for analyzing the suitability of an existing DTD have some similarities to those for doing original design work, and we cover these in some detail in Chapter 7. Also, the suggestions in Chapter 10 on implementing DTDs for modularity and customizability can help developers of variants of standard DTDs understand how to approach their work.

The following sections outline the steps, conceptual tools, and formalisms of the methodology.

## 2.1   DTD Development Phases

Developing a DTD has the following overall phases:

1.   Articulate the goals of your project (discussed in Chapter 3). Are you looking for better document validation, gains in author productivity, the ability to deliver documents on CD-ROM and through the Internet as well as on paper, enhanced online search capabilities, all of the above? What documents are in the scope of the project? What is the proposed document processing architecture?

2.   Analyze the needs of your document data (discussed in Chapter 4). What kinds of document intelligence must be considered for encapsulation in markup?

     In this phase, the core of the methodology begins. It has the following steps:

     a.   *Identify* and define the basic information components that the markup must encode.

     b.   *Classify* the components into logical groups.

     c.   *Validate* the analysis against other models that have already been developed.

3.   Design document type requirements based on your goals by modeling your document data with SGML (discussed in Chapter 5). What are your requirements for markup, based on the knowledge and experience of subject matter experts, processing application developers, and document users?

     This phase continues the core of the methodology. It has the following steps:

     a.   *Select* the components that the document type design should address.

     b.   *Build* the element and attribute models for the overall document hierarchy.

     c.   *Build* the element and attribute models for the mid-level elements.

     d.   *Build* the element and attribute models for low-level elements.

     e.   *Populate* the locations in the overall model where authors can choose from many elements.

     f.   *Make connections* within the model and from the model to the outside world.

     g.   *Validate* that the model is complete and that it has been informed by similar models already developed.

4.   Complete the design of the actual DTD and implement it (discussed in Part 3). What techniques should you use for easy maintenance? Should your DTD be modular, to allow for expansion? Should you create a set of interrelated DTDs for overlapping document types or divergent processing purposes?

     We use the term **markup model** to refer to those aspects of the DTD related solely to the design of the markup; the techniques for maintenance and customization could be considered the DTD's "architecture."

5. Test the outputs of the design processes and the DTD (discussed in Chapter 11). Have you met your goals?

6. Document the DTD and train people to use it correctly (discussed in Part 4). How can authors and application developers best understand and use the DTD?

## 2.2 Modeling Tools and Formalisms

In the course of describing the steps for DTD development, we introduce a number of conceptual tools for modeling document type requirements, as well as formalisms for recording those requirements. Sometimes, as in the case of a project glossary, the tool or formalism is simple prose. More often, sentences of description don't do the job as well as a nonprose version, such as a form, a graphical arrangement, or a matrix.

In addition, the graphical tools that we introduce have been designed to offer more precision in describing SGML requirements than does prose. Natural languages are notoriously ambiguous. For example:

> A recipe contains a title and either a recipe cross-reference or a list of
> ingredients and a list of instruction steps.

Are both lists *together* an alternative to a recipe cross-reference, or just the first kind of list? While adding some commas in appropriate places would help people interpret the sentence correctly, the fact is that it's easier to construct a grammatically correct description that's ambiguous than one that is crystal clear. By using a tool that's been designed specifically to convey such descriptions, you can avoid many more cases of logical ambiguity.

If precision is required, why not just do information modeling directly in SGML? There are several reasons:

- The tools provide a simple common language with which both subject matter experts and processing application developers can communicate. Getting the input of people who know the documents inside and out, but don't necessarily know the complexities or syntax of SGML, is essential to high-quality modeling results.

- The formalisms separate the content of a requirement from its form. If a modeling requirement goes directly from people's minds into SGML markup declaration form, you have no way to check whether the ultimate expression in SGML was faithful to the original intent. This separation is also useful for providing the raw material for DTD documentation, which must be produced anyway.

- The tools can offer *conceptual* modeling ideas that overlay the *formal* modeling abilities available in SGML. In this way, modeling techniques that have been refined over time to address many common characteristics of documents (such as the construction of element "collections" discussed in Chapter 5) can be applied immediately by novices.

One tool that we introduce uses the metaphors of "trees" and "ancestry" for information modeling. In computer science terms, every SGML document can be thought of as an inverted tree, with nodes representing elements that branch out to the elements found within them. The top-level element is the "root," the lowest-level elements containing only data characters are the "leaves," and any part of a tree terminating in a leaf is a "branch." A containing element is the "parent" of all the elements it directly contains and a more distant "ancestor" of all the elements contained within it at lower levels. The inner elements are its "children" (if directly contained) or more distant "descendants."

To use the recipe example, `recipe` is the root element for all recipe documents, the parent element of `title`, `ingredient-list`, and `instruction-list`, and additionally an ancestor of `ingredient` and `step`. The `ingredient-list` element is the parent of some number of `ingredient` child elements, and `instruction-list` is the parent of some number of `step` child elements. The `title`, `ingredient`, and `step` elements are all leaf elements containing only character data.

Figure 2-1 shows an informal representation of several document trees that our recipe DTD can potentially produce; the tree representing the Hawaiian pudding recipe is shown at the bottom of the figure.

Much of SGML information modeling involves generalizing a rule from examples of correct structure. There are a number of formalisms you can use to represent the generalization of individual document tree structures.

One formalism is an outline, where elements are simply indented according to their intended containment relationships. For example:

```
recipe
        title
        ingredient list
                ingredient
        instruction list
                step
```

Another formalism is a diagram that shows the same information, only in graphical form. While the diagram in Figure 2-2 looks very much like the simplest tree structure in Figure 2-1, it is meant to represent a generalization of the rules for all recipe documents.

The outline and containment-tree formalisms are useful for recording examples of structure in existing documents that are being analyzed; they show parent-child relationships between containers and can show multiple levels of nesting simultaneously. However, they don't capture the finer details of the content models, such as the fact that at least one ingredient element and at least one step element are required, and so they don't work very well as tools for developing precise requirements or as formalisms for recording decisions.

Another formalism often used for representing DTD rules is the "railroad diagram." In the diagrams in Figure 2-3, the boxes represent elements, and the boxes with black triangles indicate leaf elements (elements that contain only character data). The lines with arrows

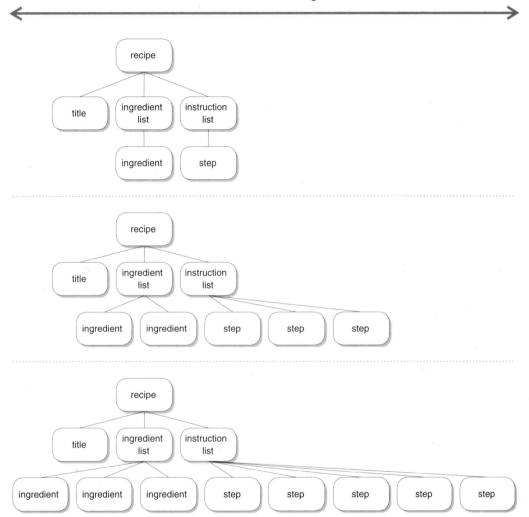

**Figure 2-1**    Some Potential Tree Structures for Recipe Documents.

represent the requirements for the order of the elements in the document file; as you follow the lines and arrows from left to right, you come across the valid order of elements
inside the element named at the left.

This formalism does show that at least one ingredient and one step are required because,
in following the lines and arrows, you must pass through the ingredient element or
step element at least once before being allowed to loop around and pass through it again.
Thus, railroad diagrams are more precise than the outline and containment-tree formalisms. However, each railroad diagram can describe the content model for only one element, a limitation that can obscure some useful details about nesting levels and structural
similarities among different elements; for example, you usually can't get a quick sense of

**Figure 2-2**    DTD-Level Graphical Description of Recipe Containment Rules.

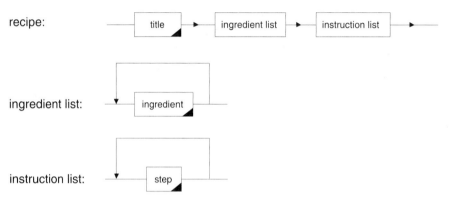

**Figure 2-3**    Railroad Diagrams for Recipe Content Models.

how "deep" an element's content model is when you look at its railroad diagram. Also, railroad diagrams are difficult for nontechnical people to use as a modeling tool, and the combinations of lines and arrows can quickly grow large and unwieldy.

We use a graphical formalism called an **elm tree diagram** ("elm" stands for "enables lucid models") for modeling information with SGML; we feel it combines the best features of the other formalisms. Figure 2-4 shows our elm tree diagram for the recipe DTD at a relatively late stage of the modeling work. (This example demonstrates only a few of the features of the tree diagram notation.)

Boxes represent elements, and ovals represent locations where collections of the items in the oval are allowed in a freely ordered mixture. Attributes are represented by single lines of descriptive text next to element boxes. The rules for an element's content are shown below its box, with various kinds of lines and symbols indicating various sequence and occurrence rules. For example, this diagram happens to use the following parts of the notation:

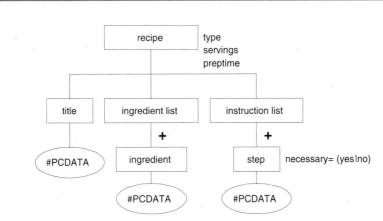

**Figure 2-4**     Recipe DTD Tree Diagram.

- A plus (+) on an element box means the element must occur one or more times.

- The ovals containing "#PCDATA" mean that zero or more characters can be supplied in the elements to which the ovals are attached.

- A horizontal bracket (⌐⌐) below an element box means that each box or oval attached to the bracket must appear in the left-to-right order shown.

Appendix B provides a complete reference description of all the features of the tree diagram notation.

This formalism offers an intuitive graphical form that allows people unfamiliar with SGML to express SGML-based modeling requirements with great precision. The tree diagrams grow along with the analysis and design process because they include special notations for representing decisions as yet unmade and pointers to expanded subdiagrams located elsewhere. A collection of complete diagrams also provides a powerful recording mechanism with which to document DTD design requirements for implementors, and is useful for documenting finished DTDs for authors. In working with groups of people who have varying levels of technical skill and SGML training, we have found that elm tree diagrams are a *lingua franca* that enhances DTD development productivity.

Several software tools are available for the graphical development and display of DTD rules, and they are generally regarded as useful adjuncts to developing DTDs, particularly for people who are new to application development. Don't feel, though, that you have to spend a lot of money on DTD development software to use our conceptual tools and formalisms; we and others have used them and developed DTDs quite successfully with pencils, paper, simple text editors, and validating parsers found in the public domain. Based on your SGML experience and budget, you may want to survey the state of the art in preparation for your own SGML effort.

Now that you have an idea of how the work will proceed, you can form a team for doing DTD development work and launch the project. Chapter 3 describes how.

# 3 DTD Project Management

In this chapter, we explain where DTD development takes place in the context of a global SGML project, listing all the issues you need to consider before a DTD development project can be started and describing how to run the project with a minimum of risk. We conclude by giving hints on how to handle the politics of such a project.

This chapter is primarily for the project leaders and their managers who are responsible for planning and executing a DTD development project. Other key people on the project, such as the facilitator of the DTD design team or the DTD implementor (roles we'll explain in Section 3.3.1), may find some useful information here about how the project is run and what is expected from them.

We won't cover in detail how a DTD development project is run on a daily basis, nor will we mention the traditional project management methods and tools that are handy to use if your project is large and complex.

## 3.1 The Global Picture

This section puts DTD development in perspective within the realms of document management and the setup of a complete SGML-based document production system. It should help you determine what must happen before the actual DTD project starts and what the DTD, once it is completed, is likely to be used for.

To design a useful and efficient DTD, you need to figure out how the documents will be created, how they will travel through their lifespan, and the uses to which they will be put. Because documents are created, controlled, and used by humans, we call their various states "interactions people have with documents."

Once you can articulate all the interactions people will have with your documents and their sequence, you will be able to define the features your information system will need to offer and to derive its probable architecture.

This section will therefore discuss:

- The three basic types of interaction people have with documents

- The typical components of an SGML-based document production system and their interdependencies

- The "reference DTD" and the variants on this DTD that are likely to be needed

## 3.1.1    Types of Interaction with Documents

Writing documents is usually not a self-justified activity, unless you are writing poetry or fiction. Most documents stored in SGML form are created for the purpose of conveying information or keeping track of information. These considerations delimit the three types of interactions people have with documents:

- Creation and modification

- Management, storage, and archiving

- Utilization

These interactions are, of course, strongly intertwined, but for the sake of clarity it is convenient to describe them separately. This classification system can be represented graphically, as shown in Figure 3-1. The question marks at the boundaries between classes represent document validation.

People involved in SGML projects tend to focus on document creation and modification needs because they are the first obvious activities in which the DTD is used, and also because it is their usual domain of activity. Limiting your horizon to these activities is usually a mistake; when designing your DTD, you must also take into account needs arising from management and storage activities and those arising from the various uses that will be made of the documents. This broader point of view not only has consequences for the DTD design and implementation, but also for the way you will build your SGML-based production system.

The following sections describe the goals to be achieved, the documents to be produced, and the hardware and software considerations to be resolved for each type of interaction.

### 3.1.1.1    Document Creation and Modification

Creation and modification consist of all the activities involving the input of up-to-date documents into the system. These include the obvious on-site creation and modification activities, as well as review, validation, input of untagged data, and all the other ways to import documents from other sources.

There are several cases of import. The documents to be imported may already follow the chosen standards of your information system, in which case we can call their insertion in the information system a plain "import." Then you simply need to ensure you have a reading device for the media on which the files are delivered.

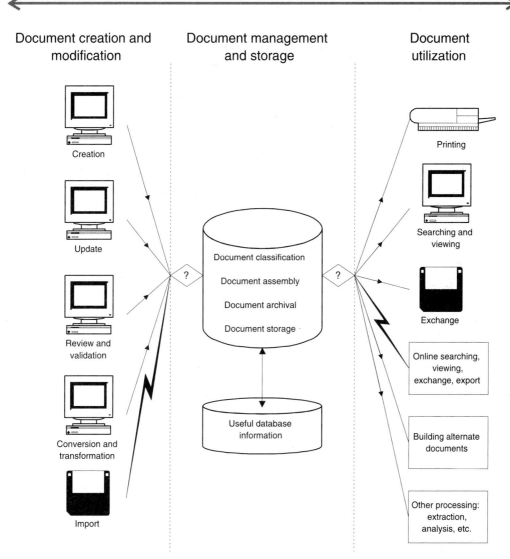

**Figure 3-1**     Document Interaction Classification.

In most cases, however, the documents to be imported into the system are heterogeneous, with different file formats, markup systems, and levels of consistency within types. They may even include SGML documents marked up according to a DTD other than the ones with which your system works. These documents will need to be processed before they can be imported. Following current industry practice, we'll use the term **conversion** for the processing of non-SGML source documents and **transformation** for the processing of SGML source documents, no matter what the target form.

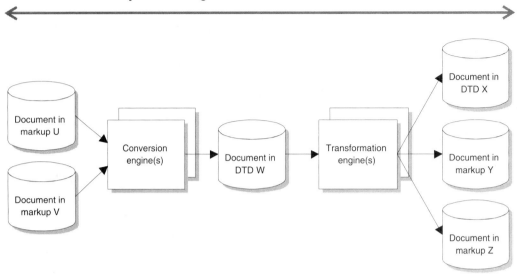

**Figure 3-2**    Conversion and Transformation Processes.

Conversion and transformation processes are illustrated in Figure 3-2.

The answers to the following questions can help you define your import, creation, and modification activities, and as such they will influence the specifications of your DTD and document production system. If you are building an entirely new production system, asking these questions and analyzing the answers will help you specify and prioritize your requirements. But this specification is an iterative process, because some answers are likely to change as the system is developed and the in-house culture evolves.

### Document Contents

What are the documents' contents: text, tables, illustrations, equations, video, other? In what proportions?

This answer helps you determine how many different types of objects you will have to handle, the human competence you will need to have in-house, and the number of different tools these people will have to master.

### Document Languages

In how many languages are the documents written? What character sets do they require? Do any documents need to contain text from multiple natural languages? Will any documents be translated by humans or software?

This answer helps determine certain technical aspects of the DTD and related setup information, and suggests special objects and markup that you may need to handle.

## Markup Consistency

Within the files, is the markup consistent (use of stylesheets, templates, DTDs)?

Whatever the original markup, if it has been used consistently and the rules have been checked regularly, then the conversion process can be largely successful (though it generally won't invent markup that wasn't there initially). If the markup hasn't been used consistently, then the results of conversion are usually insufficient and need to be manually controlled and enhanced.

## Sources of Documents

Do the documents come from one or several sources? On what media (paper, diskette, tape, online files, CD-ROMs)? By what means (online connection, up- and downloading, "sneakernet," other)?

As already mentioned, for a plain import of conforming material, you need to make sure your system knows how to make use of the delivery media. This is not as trivial as it may sound; if the markup of the documents is system-specific, it may require a particular hardware platform or operating system. If the import is from an online source, you need to make sure the network protocols are compatible and that your system knows how to read the downloaded result.

## Document Outputs

What is the expected output of the documents produced: books, magazines, catalogues, CD-ROMs, online databases, other? Under what circumstances will the contents and the writing style need to change?

There are three main ways for the content to differ according to the output:

- The document delivery media are so different that they require different ways of expressing the same content and different writing styles.

- There are various outputs based on extraction parameters from a single set of content.

- The content of the documents undergoes revision over time, and multiple chronological versions may need to be produced simultaneously.

If the content and writing style of your documents differ according to their output, you will probably have to support several variants of the same information simultaneously, each containing the editorial changes required by each form of output. For instance, in computer companies, there may be substantial content differences between the summarized documentation they offer on line with their software and the full-blown paper user documentation. The difficulty is to teach the authors to write coherent variants, then to implement a coherence control device in the system so as to ensure that the information contained in each output version does not diverge.

If you plan to support only one set of source files for each document and produce different delivered forms of the documents through processing that same source differently, you have to define the relevant processing parameters up front and consider them in your modeling process. Once the source documents are properly parameterized or marked up, you must be able, through an automated process, to produce all the expected outputs. For instance, from the same source document you could automatically produce different documents for different target populations (elementary, intermediate, advanced), for different models of the same equipment, and with different levels of confidentiality.

In addition, your documents will evolve over time, and you may need to keep track of the progression of versions. Information systems typically call this "version control."

You should plan to keep careful track of all the variants and versions that are important to your documents.

### Document Creators

Who creates the documents: subject matter experts, professional writers, secretaries, other people? Will authors type and mark up the documents themselves or have it done by others?

Most often, authors design the content and type their text themselves. In doing so, they also do some markup of their documents, but with traditional word processors the markup process is transparent. With an SGML-aware editor, they have to select and add the markup on top of their text. In this case, the authors are responsible for the design of the content, the choice of the markup, and the input of the data.

However, there are other possible divisions of the labor. We know of a legal publisher where consulting lawyers could not be convinced to learn a DTD and write in SGML. The publishing department had to accept jurisprudence discussions even in handwritten form, and therefore had secretaries type or retype the texts and then had legal experts mark up the electronic documents. In this case, the functions of content development, markup, and data entry were performed by three different categories of staff.

In another case, in a nuclear plant, where experts had to go into the field to do their work and produce their reports, it was decided that the troubleshooting teams would look over the equipment, analyze and fix the problems, and write the incident report on the spot. To avoid any ambiguity, they would hand-tag their handwritten report and would then give it to a secretary who would input the report content and markup electronically. The SGML-encoded report would then be reviewed by the author and signed by the troubleshooting manager before it could be entered in the database. In this case, the development of the content and the choice of the markup is made by the subject matter expert and the input by a tool specialist who has no knowledge of the content.

It is important to determine what the organization is going to be like in your company for two reasons. First, you need to ensure that you have representatives of both the people who design the content and the people who choose the markup on your design team. Their view of structure and content may be quite different, and you need to ensure that both points of view are accommodated by your final DTD. Second, your choice of editor or editing environment will depend on the amount of markup assistance the person at the keyboard will need and the speed at which that person will have to work. SGML-aware editors with a graphic interface provide the most markup assistance, but many data entry specialists feel that nongraphical editors are more efficient for straight input.

## Creation Locations

Where are the documents created: on the company site, off-site, at the authors' homes, at a subcontractor's site? Can the site be connected to the information system?

The answers are crucial to the architecture of your document production system. If you need authors to work on standalone systems on- or off-site, then you must provide standalone editing environments. This is especially difficult when you want your information system to provide file names, IDs, or database information such as copyrights or parts numbers. In this case, you may need to build an "antechamber" for the standalone documents so that every aspect of their validity can be checked before they can be added to the system.

## Creation Timeline

How are the documents created over time? Are they created all at once, or over a certain length of time? Are regular additions made? Do they require several passes and reviews?

This will help define how long each document will need to remain in unfinished form in the system and decide whether a software-based revision-tracking system or a full-fledged workflow system should be implemented. If the same document is reviewed and corrected several times before it is finally published, it will probably be necessary to keep track of its various revisions. If the process is well defined and can be modeled, then a full-fledged workflow system may be useful.

When documents are created over a period of time or are assembled from information modules of the same size (chapters, recipes, addresses), it is likely that people will edit only fragments of a document at one time. It is therefore important to determine what size of document fragment people feel is most practical to work on at a time, and use this fragment size as a basic level of information granularity. The answer will probably suggest an appropriate architecture for an authoring sub-DTD (discussed in Section 3.1.3.2).

If the documents are created by several authors and then assembled, or if they include pieces of information already created and stored in the information system, you need to define the extraction and assembly processes, each of which may use variant DTDs (see Section 3.1.3). If authors work on information modules, then the information system must check that the IDs are not duplicated and that the cross-references are satisfactorily resolved.

Above all, ensuring the quality of the final assembled documents (for example, sequence and transitions between chunks) will require careful thought. Contrary to common belief, information reuse is far from easy and risk-free. For example, reusing a graphic already designed in another document by a different author requires a very sophisticated control system to avoid blunders when the original author decides single-handedly to change the original graphic. The same goes for chunks of text, with the added difficulty of reusing text at the right structural level. Cutting and pasting is not always neutral in terms of meaning, and good writers do not write similarly at different hierarchical levels of a document. Reuse may imply some rewriting and adding transitional paragraphs to avoid producing awkward documents. (Section 6.5 discusses some of these issues further as they relate to document type modeling.)

### Deadlines

Are there specific deadlines in document creation and modification? What are their frequency and criticality?

Listing the constraints on document creation regardless of document production constraints allows you to adapt and dimension your creation environment and your information system and to choose feasible solutions that will automate and facilitate as many processes as possible to meet the deadlines.

### Revision and Reuse

Do the documents need to be revised and/or reused over time? If yes, how often, in what proportion to original material, and to what extent?

Your revision needs will affect your requirements for keeping at hand the editing and conversion environments that produced your documents in the first place. If your information system contains only nonrevisable (for example, scanned) documents, you don't need to maintain an editing environment over time. The more formats you intend to use for revisable text, vector graphics, raster graphics, and so on, the more expensive and complex your creation and modification tools must be.

To avoid the multiplication of tools and tool proficiency, you may want to standardize all the data to one format for each type, and then convert incoming documents to those formats. This approach becomes very efficient when the time comes to update the documents.

If your information system is only a repository of dead documents, the cheapest and simplest system might be in order. If you need to update most documents, if they come from various sources, and if the minimum annual update rate is about 35 percent, then it is worthwhile to build a powerful DTD, have an SGML-based information system, and work with conversions and transformations.

## Editing Culture

What is the editing environment like? Do authors use structure-aware tools, WYSIWYG tools, or plain text editors? What should they use in the future?

The answers help you understand the current authors' culture and figure out to what extent it should or should not be changed. The idea here is not to concentrate on tools, but on the authors' frame of mind. Are they happy with what they have? Do they see any limitations? Would they like to have more structure-aware tools? Are they already using tools with structural constraints, and would real-time markup assistance and validation be helpful? Are they aware of what more intelligent markup would help produce in editorial terms?

Once you have assessed the authors' willingness to change or improve their editing environment and depending on where you want to take them, you know what basic features your editing environment and tool should offer and how much training and "convincing" are ahead of you.

This survey should pay close attention to the editing and inclusion of nontextual objects and tricky textual objects such as tables, because they are just as important a part of documents as text is, and they easily become an issue, especially with authors used to WYSIWYG tools.

## Auxiliary Data

How do authors collect and include additional relevant information?

This kind of information covers technical specifications and marketing requirements for technical documentation, raw facts for an encyclopedia editor's remarks, or translation tips. It is often overlooked in the creation and modification activities. Ideally, you want to devise an efficient electronic system for this exchange of information rather than make merely cosmetic changes to any inefficient processes in place, such as oral tradition, sticky notes, and "sneakernet."

### Delivery Content

What is an author's delivery composed of?

The problem here is to define what to expect in terms of an author's handoff of material (content, form, media, metainformation about the delivery) and the ability to qualify a completed task. For instance, if authors are fully responsible for developing chapter content and marking it up in SGML but aren't responsible for producing illustrations, and if their authoring DTD doesn't accommodate the required higher levels of document division, then you need to define the "interface" between the authors' delivery and the next step in document production. Authors might be required to declare entities for illustrations, insert entity references into the files, store their chapters in the information system, provide metainformation about each chapter, and validate the chapters. If you want them to do all this, you need to provide them with the tools and training to safely achieve all these tasks and have a mechanism for checking that they've performed the steps correctly.

### 3.1.1.2    Document Management and Storage

The document management and storage classification covers many activities. Managing documents implies checking, naming, classifying, and indexing them in order to retrieve them. It includes the assembling of document pieces, the updated insertion of data extracted from various databases, and the resolution of links. Your management system may put in place safety devices such as providing unique file names and IDs, locking up files while they are edited, automatic saving of current work, version control, and enforcement of document workflow. The storage activities range from the basic save and backup to more elaborate archiving devices, such as automated destruction of obsolete documents and regeneration of previous editions of documents.

To evaluate your current system and define the system you need, the answers to the following questions might be useful. They will complement the answers to the questions in Section 3.1.1.1, since the creation and modification activities are closely linked to those of management and storage.

### Document Types

What types of documents are handled? Are they of the same kind (all recipes, all articles, or all standards) or of various kinds (research and development specifications, memos, marketing literature, and press reviews)?

If various types of documents are handled, you need an information system that can handle several DTDs (or models of other kinds), plus a way to retrieve a thematic grouping of different types of documents based on specific parameters. For instance, there may need to be a way to group and search through all the documents related to a specific piece of equipment, from design specifications to after-sale maintenance documentation. Such a requirement can put a heavy constraint on the DTDs you will build, such as providing some compatible content models and similar markup names for similar components in the various DTDs.

### Electronic Storage

Are all documents currently stored in electronic form?

If not, you will have to evaluate the real need for those documents to be stored in electronic form, and then evaluate the cost of finding the sources, or scanning and using OCR versus keying in the documents from scratch. Such a process is usually long and costly. In most projects where documents are not available in electronic form, people generally start to build the system with current documents that are available electronically and documents that have yet to be written, and just leave the legacy documents to be handled in the old way.

### Electronic Formats

What are the electronic formats being used? Are there multiple formats for text and for each kind of nontextual object?

The fewer the formats, the easier it is to handle them in your new system. Since this is not always the case, you need to choose the formats you want your system to support, and provide converters for all other formats. As already mentioned, any conversion process is a tricky and often disappointing one.

### Document Reuse

How are documents used or reused? By whom? How often? From where (the same network, the same site, or some unconnected location)? Is there any version control? How is it, or does it need to be, implemented? Are documents reused "as is" or after modification?

These questions are the same as some of those in Section 3.1.1.1, but need to be considered from the system administrator's point of view rather than that of the authors.

### Document Processing

What processing happens to the documents? At which stages? Can documents be built from other documents? Which ones, and how? Is workflow control necessary?

These questions will help define the applications you need to build within the document database management system to meet the needs of the users. You may be able to take advantage of commercial products for workflow and groupware, but may need to develop your own applications to meet specific company or department needs.

## Access Control

Is there access control to documents? For editing or consulting? How is it enforced?

This is just a sample of all the questions you need to ask in relation to the security features of the system. The answers to these questions may be irrelevant to your business, or they may be absolutely crucial.

## Storage and Archival

Which documents must be stored in the work process, and for how long (taking into account business and legal considerations)? Is there a need for a "hub" storage or archival format and, if so, what is it (for example, SGML or formatted files)? What are the security requirements for archived documents? Are documents destroyed after their "expiration date" and, if so, by whom?

These questions aim at automating the storing and archival process. One common mistake is to overlook the need to regularly destroy obsolete documents because they do not physically disturb the office environment. But documents do take up a lot of room on hard disks, and providing a device to regularly destroy old documents or make people clean up their files is rewarding in the middle term. Also, the ISO 9000 standard requires expiration dates on documents, which is helpful in automating the cleanup process.

If you need to archive source-form documents but want to retain some facts about their presentation, you might want to employ a special kind of presentation DTD that records portions of documents that have been generated for delivery, such as tables of contents and indexes.

In some organizations, the document management and storage activity is completely set aside and left to the discretion of authors. In this case, documents are written and the output is generated right after they are created. However, the uses of such documents are rather limited because all uses requiring large collections of data or documents (such as electronic publishing) imply some level of document management.

### 3.1.1.3    Document Utilization

If you are not limited by the architecture of your document production system, a whole range of uses is open to your documents: printing, searching, viewing, exporting, interchanging, extracting information and building alternate documents or subdocuments, and processing the contents to do all kinds of analysis.

It is essential to be able to describe precisely which uses are expected in the short and middle terms for your documents so as to specify DTD requirements and the necessary processing applications. To describe the uses, you need to answer the following questions.

**Reading and Viewing**

How can the documents be read or viewed? On paper, on screen, in Braille? Online or standalone? On-site or off-site, or both?

**Searching and Navigation**

How can the information be searched in each delivered form? By page, by table of contents, by table of illustrations, by index, by full-text search, by keywords, by browsing hyperlinks, by other methods?

**Delivery and Media**

How do you need to prepare for delivery? Which media will you use (paper, diskette, smart card, CD, Internet, other)?

**Required Processing**

Do you need to process the information first before actually using it?

The answer to this question leads to other issues:

- If the source files can be delivered as they are, such as when you exchange source files with business partners and subcontractors, you do not need to develop processing applications. Rather, you can just ensure that you can package the entire contents of an SGML document properly and that the recipients are equipped with a compatible environment.

- If you must process the information, what kind of processing is necessary (assembling, extracting, formatting, indexing, building links, transforming to a different DTD, content analysis processing)?

- Does the processing operate on whole documents or just fragments? In the latter case, what information from larger documents must travel with the fragments so as to render usage feasible?

## 3.1.2    Components of an SGML-Based System

With the three types of document interaction in mind, it is easier to define the potential components of an SGML-based document production system and their interactions.

Just like any other document production system, an SGML-based production system needs to offer tools to create or import documents, tools to store and archive them, and tools to publish or view them. Each of these activities corresponds to one or more components of the production system. Just as in the construction of a building, which has various parts (foundation, garage, ground floor, other floors) and logistical connections (stairs, elevators, electricity, plumbing), the pieces of a production system can't be assembled at random, though some pieces might be optional or might be added to the system later.

The components we have identified are as follows:

- Editing tools and environments
- Conversion engines and applications
- The document management system
- Formatting engines and applications for rendering on paper and screen
- Other transformation engines and applications
- Search and retrieval engines
- Additional processing applications
- The "document engineering toolbox"

In the following sections we describe each of the potential components of an SGML-based production system, their purpose, and some constraints that might apply to them. Section 3.1.2.9 describes the dependencies among these components. Not all systems need to include all of the potential components; you can pick the ones that are adapted to your company's needs.

### 3.1.2.1    Editing Tools and Environments

To create SGML documents, you need to provide an editing environment or other ways to acquire information.

It's common to have to build your document repository using a combination of tools:

- SGML-aware editors
- Traditional word processors and other existing editing tools
- Tools for one-time and/or routine conversions
- SGML-to-SGML transformation tools

The conversion and transformation tools are described in later sections.

For actually creating and modifying documents, either you can use one or more of the available SGML-aware editors or simple non-SGML-aware text editors, which can work directly on native SGML documents, or you can continue to use your existing word processor or desktop publishing system and provide ongoing batch conversion to SGML. If you plan to use an SGML-aware editor for your existing documents coded with traditional markup, you need to perform a one-time conversion to SGML first. If you need to import documents from external sources, you may need to convert them or perform various SGML transformations, depending on the markup they use.

The decision between SGML-aware editors and traditional editors is an important one. Following are some of the factors to consider.

An SGML-aware editor integrates several functions. Apart from being a text editor with its traditional functions, it includes parser-based software that first compiles or otherwise prepares a DTD to become resident in the system, and then controls the validity of the document instances being built with the selected resident DTD. It also offers markup assistance, as it lets the user see and use only valid markup in context, and can offer a variety of automated authoring functions, such as automatic insertion of required markup, building tables of contents, and management of boilerplate text stored in entities. SGML-aware editors generally have interfaces that take advantage of the hierarchical nature of SGML, which can have a positive effect on the processes of document planning, outlining, and revision. There are a variety of SGML-aware editing products available on the market with more or less sophisticated markup facilities, WYSIWYG features,[1] text-editing functions, accessibility from an external database, and availability on computer platforms.

As a result, when using such a tool, you can rely on the documents produced to conform to your DTD. Thus, you can concentrate your efforts on training authors to apply the markup correctly and thoroughly and using the features of the tool itself.

If you keep using a traditional word processor, the problems of hardware, software, training, and documentation are already solved. Nevertheless, this solution does not ensure consistent markup of the documents and usually does not allow the content to be sufficiently and unambiguously marked up. In order to facilitate and improve the quality of the conversion to come, you will have to build extremely detailed stylesheets or templates and build tools to enforce their constraints, and even so, the results may be unsatisfactory. (Section 3.1.2.2 discusses the reasons in more detail.) Thus, though it may seem like an inexpensive option at first, its ongoing costs can be quite burdensome.

---

1. Of course, a single SGML document usually produces several outputs. A WYSIWYG appearance may be misleading as to the final different forms the instance will have.

### 3.1.2.2   Conversion Engines and Applications

A mechanism for conversion is a component that can often be postponed in the setup of the production system but usually can't be ignored, because most projects have legacy documents to convert. Some projects start with conversion because of the need to have a huge document base from which to work; others start with creating new documents compliant with the new standard, and when they are sure the whole production line is operational, they turn to conversion to import all their legacy documents into the system.

However, conversion is absolutely unavoidable when you are planning to keep using a traditional tool for editing documents. In this case, the conversion process, whether in real time or in batch, is crucial to the editing of documents and therefore to the life of the system.

Commercial conversion engines that specialize in converting non-SGML documents to SGML usually work in two phases: the decoding of the source document, followed by its interpretation, resulting in an SGML instance conforming to the DTD for which you have parameterized it. Other character string manipulation tools can achieve the same result, but they are not sold as SGML-specific conversion engines, and they must be programmed specifically to achieve that task.

The first step is to read the source document and decode whatever pattern of markup there is. Some engines translate this markup into an internal language, and some translate it into a specifically designed or existing presentation DTD (for example, the Rainbow DTD, described in Section 3.1.3.3). For documents produced with some desktop publishing tools, multiple choices of markup can be used to produce the same presentation. In this case, the conversion engine must provide a capability that recognizes the various presentations just like a human eye would, regardless of the markup used to achieve the result. This feature helps to identify the relevant objects based on their presentation rather than recognizing patterns of electronic data and markup.

The second step is to interpret the results of the first step and generate an instance conforming to the selected DTD. This step consists of identifying the relevant objects, matching them with SGML markup, adding structure that wasn't originally present (for example, chapter containers and element end-tags), and taking care of reordering, removing what will later be added back as generated text, and so on.

To parameterize a conversion engine, you build rules based on markup, layout, and patterns that tell the engine what to do when it encounters a pattern or a relevant object. Some rules are quite simple, like the matching of paragraphs. Others, like lists, require some typographical information to define where the items start and stop and if they are lists within lists. Some rules generate several actions from one event, such as inserting a chapter start-tag before a chapter title start-tag when such a title is encountered. Some rules need to be sensitive to context in order to be efficient, for example, checking whether an apparent "chapter" title in the source document begins with a capital letter followed by a period before marking it up as a chapter or an appendix.

Some engines don't allow the building of sophisticated contextual rules, especially when the required context occurs after the event where the rule must be applied, a technique called "lookahead."

The quality of your conversion results is mainly based on the quality of the non-SGML source documents. If your source documents are all created with the same word processor and the same stylesheet with a consistent layout, the results are probably going to be very good. Conversely, if your documents were created with various tools, if no stylesheet or template or writing rules were imposed, or if authors were free to control the presentation and structure of their documents, then you are in trouble because it will be impossible to create rules which are applicable to all documents.

You must also be aware of the limits of conversion to SGML. Conversion of data formats has always been a necessary but difficult process. Converters are typically based on a set of filters that try to match the source format with the target format, trying to lose as little information as possible on the way; but how much is lost is difficult to evaluate. With SGML, the problem is slightly different. In most cases, the level of information that is marked up in the source documents is significantly inferior to the level of information that is expected to be marked up with the new DTD.

When you need to convert documents edited with a traditional word processor to SGML, you're likely to run into some common problems. Usually, converting the overall hierarchical structure of a document is a simple matter. The three main problems are the identification of boundaries of information blocks such as paragraphs, exercises, and notes; the identification of the end of each element when elements are nested; and the identification of in-line pieces of information. A more subtle problem is that authors may have used appearance cues to give each document a unique "feel," which is nearly impossible to capture in an automated conversion process.

With word processor styles, you usually mark up just the beginning of information blocks. Because the start of a new block is assumed to end the previous one, the end is never explicitly marked up. SGML can nest blocks of information inside other blocks, but automatic converters can have difficulty figuring where some blocks end unless this information is included in your original markup.

In-line information has a slightly different problem. Often, few of the significant words and phrases in a document are marked up at all, since they may look identical to other text. Even if the odd boldface, italicized, or underlined word appears, often the emphasis is inconsistently applied or has multiple meanings. Converters are often unable to mark up in-line information appropriately, since several possibilities are open.

To help solve these problems, you may need to create styles and codes to mark up material that has never been marked up before, teach authors to use them properly and consistently, and develop validating software to catch improper usage. If the authors don't have real-time markup assistance, the validator may find many errors.

It is therefore very important before you launch the conversion project that you thoroughly study your source documents, their homogeneity or heterogeneity, and the type of problems you are likely to encounter. If you can rely only on the presentation, you need to choose a type of engine based on visual recognition. If the patterns are very obvious and recurrent, you can choose a pattern-matching type of engine.

If you have made up your mind to use conversion on a regular basis as a way to let the authors keep writing with their favorite tool, then it is worthwhile that you standardize the way they write and the stylesheet they use, and that you make the markup as precise as possible—even to the extent of using hidden text codes representing SGML-like markup—in order to make the conversion process as easy and reliable as possible.

### 3.1.2.3    Document Management System

To manage and store SGML documents, it is convenient to have a database run by a database management system, complete with a version control device or a workflow system. Some database management systems are now specifically adapted to the handling of SGML documents. Setting up this system will be a whole task in itself, as you will have to define the user interactions, the document types and formats, the document flow, the documents status and lifespan, and so on. This component of the production line is crucial because it is the link between creation and utilization.

As of this writing, there is no one solution for SGML document management that can be unequivocally recommended. Commercial producers and consumers of document management systems are still wrangling over whether relational databases are sufficient or object-oriented databases are required to do a proper job.[2] Some software publishers are building SGML-aware layers atop hybrid object/relational database management systems, which may provide efficient solutions for managing SGML documents at the granularity of the individual elements.

What is more, experience shows that no document repository is as pure as we might wish it to be, so chances are that your system will have to handle both SGML and non-SGML documents.

Following are some basic requirements that may be useful in helping you to specify and choose such a system. The ideal document management system should at least offer the following features, even if you do not plan on implementing them all. Keep in mind, though, that the ideal system may not exist yet!

 **Handles All Documents**

Inputs, stores, and outputs all the documents you need to manage.

---

2. Some products that are touted as object-oriented turn out to be basic relational systems on further examination.

### Controls Access and Retrieval

Allows authors and system managers to log in, select work, and check out relevant documents. Allows authorized people to check documents back in after having done the necessary validation control (parsing or other).

### Controls Writing of Data

Locks up documents while they are being worked on.

### Handles SGML and Non-SGML Documents

Imports validated SGML documents, as well as non-SGML legacy documents, and provides at least a minimal management functionality for non-SGML documents (naming, storing, retrieving).

### Manages Nontextual Objects

Along with text, manages nontextual objects such as graphics, images, sound, video, animation, or other objects you have.

### Controls Workflow

Controls the workflow from creation through reviews, comments, modifications, approval, mastering, and archiving state, and provides a device to show the status of each document and route it accordingly.

### Manages Document Characteristics

Manages the formats, names, IDs, and locations of documents so as to store them safely and retrieve them reliably.

### Handles Version Control

Offers ways to master and keep track of the versions and variants of documents according to your needs.

### Handles Selective Extraction and Assembly

Allows extraction of documents according to selected parameters, and facilitates their reuse and assembly into new documents while keeping track of the sources.

### Handles Structured Queries

Allows queries on every element within modules of information and retrieves the relevant modules.

### Allows for Variable Granularity

Allows you to choose the level of granularity of documents that the system should handle as independent information modules.

For example, if you are a documentation publisher and your system only manages complete manuals, then each document is going to be too large and unwieldy to manipulate. You may decide that, for convenience, you want the granularity of management at the chapter or procedure level, because these correspond to a meaningful module of information worthy of separate management. This means that the basic modules authors and users will be able to manipulate will be a chapter, recipe or a procedure. Apart from being easier in terms of access time, it often makes more sense when you offer online search and retrieval access to information.

### Manages Modules and Module Collections Individually

Manages all the information modules separately and allows you to assemble completed documents from various modules. Several collections based on the same modules should be allowed to be created and stored separately, and it should be possible to control and check the edition of a module that gets used.

After authors are done producing the necessary modules, your system must allow the sequence in which they wish the modules to be read or published to be defined and keep track of how the final document must be built.

## 3.1.2.4    Formatting Engines and Applications

Formatting engines and applications are special cases of transformation engines and applications, discussed in Section 3.1.2.5. A formatting (or "composition" or "rendering") engine provides specialized technology for transforming SGML documents into files that contain presentational markup (for example, using a page-display language) which can be interpreted by a printer driver or display software. A formatting application is a customized or parameterized use of such a technology.

---

### Note

You should start building or reviewing your layout specifications and corporate identity charter as soon as you contemplate building a formatting engine. Experience shows it's often the case that unless your company specializes in publishing, any corporate layout specifications you have are probably not detailed enough to serve as the basis for the stylesheets you'll need. When trying to define the presentation of all the potential combinations of markup in documents, you're likely to discover that the initial presentation requirements for documents are very thin and require further work.

---

Mechanisms for producing formatted output are especially important in an SGML-based document production system, not just because they help produce documents that are suitable for delivery, but because they serve a "marketing" function: They are the tools that help prove the whole system works. Until authors, managers, and users see good-quality typeset output produced from an SGML instance, they may be suspicious of the ability of a system based on structured markup to output "real" documents. This is one of the reasons why, in some projects, the formatting applications are developed before any other component, although the initial improvement expected from the new system is to release electronic or online documents. The new system is expected to output at least what the old one did—that is, paper.

To build a formatting application, you need to make a transformation from SGML markup to the markup of the layout software you have chosen. You need to tell the software what the presentation must be for each element according to its attributes and its context. This mapping is usually referred to as a stylesheet.

It is relatively easy to build several stylesheets to apply to the same instances. Unfortunately, the stylesheets of most formatting products are in a proprietary form that cannot be read by other formatting engines. This lack of compatibility across software means that the presentation information for SGML documents is not nearly as portable as the source SGML documents themselves.

---

### Stylesheet Standards

An early attempt at stylesheet standardization was made within the CALS program of the U.S. Department of Defense, which resulted in the definition of a stylesheet format that is itself expressed as an SGML document. The DTD to which these stylesheets must conform is called the OS, for Output Specification, and each stylesheet document is called a FOSI, for Formatting Output Specification Instance. Two companies offer products that operate on FOSIs.

Efforts have been conducted within ISO to develop a more robust output specification that includes stylesheet capabilities, called DSSSL (Document Style Semantics and Specification Language). DSSSL has been accepted as ISO International Standard 10179, and at this writing subsets of its complete functionality are being implemented.

---

You have two main choices in formatting engines. If you buy an integrated software package and develop stylesheets for it, the package will be responsible for transforming SGML documents all the way into printable or otherwise deliverable form. Alternatively, if you acquire a programmable transformation language, you can program applications that turn your documents into markup systems of your own choosing (for example, inputting the results of the transformation into desktop publishing or word processing software for eventual output). In general, parameterizing an integrated package is easier and requires less programming skill, but for sophisticated output schemes, both approaches may require advanced programming skills.

People usually judge a formatting engine by its ability to render all the fine details of the traditional presentation of their company's documents. However, it is just as important to consider whether the engine works on the source SGML instance or on a transformed source file. The farther away from SGML the files must be for formatting, the more likely it is that any kind of late alteration during the layout process will not make it back to the original SGML instance and will be lost for the next editions. If the alterations are only presentational, there is no harm done, but often late alterations also affect the content, which is dangerous. If you choose a formatting engine that requires a proprietary data format and can't operate directly on the SGML instance, you have to either enforce strict procedures to forbid content alterations at the layout stage, or set up a mechanism whereby the content alterations can be added back to the original files.

For print, it may be useful and cost effective for you to implement a formatting engine with both a limited capability for proofing or preview and a full-blown capability for mastering or producing the final copy. The proofing engine is limited to automatically laying out and printing the document according to a set stylesheet when you click on a button. It does not offer all the fine enhancement capabilities that you may require for printing quality, and does not give anyone access to formatting functions. The fact that it prevents authors from spending time tweaking the presentation of documents at this stage can result in savings of time and money. This part of the software can be available to authors, reviewers, and all the other actors in the document production line until the content of the documents has been completed and validated.

Only then are the documents sent to compositors, who are equipped with the version of the formatting engine that gives access to the full capabilities of a professional layout tool. It allows them to do manual copyfitting until the documents reach the required printing quality.

This two-pronged approach saves time and money on the content development phases, allows a more accurate estimation of the layout resources needed, and improves the quality of the printed result because it is conceived and carried out by professionals.

### 3.1.2.5   Transformation Engines and Applications

Transformation is a much more satisfying process than conversion because the starting point, SGML document data, is unambiguous and precisely marked up. There are three main types of transformation:

- The transformation of an SGML document to any non-SGML format

- The transformation of an SGML document from one DTD to another DTD

- The transformation of an SGML document to a different instance conforming to the same DTD

As we've already discussed the transformation of SGML documents to various output formats in Section 3.1.2.4, here we'll concentrate on the other two types.

The transformation from one DTD to another DTD is necessary when one must interchange documents with business partners or subcontractors using an agreed-on or industry-specific DTD (which we'll call "DTD A" here). This DTD may not be used as is in-house because such DTDs are often considered too large, too complex, and ill-adapted to the specific needs of a specific task within a company. If a different DTD (which we'll call "DTD B") is used in-house, it means that interchanging using DTD A will require two transformations: from DTD B to DTD A when documents are exported, and from DTD A to DTD B when they are imported. The two transformations are not similar because when exporting you *must* leave out everything that is company-specific, and when importing you *can choose to leave out* the information you do not need.

Transforming from one DTD to another is also widely used when an in-house DTD has been upgraded and all the documents produced with the old DTD must be transformed to be compliant with the new one.

In both cases, the difficulty lies in the convergence or divergence of the markup models. Some divergent structures are extremely difficult to map. The rule of thumb is to build an in-house DTD that is structurally compatible with the interchange DTD to and from which you will transform. And when you upgrade your DTD, remember that you will have to upgrade all the documents already marked up. So make sure that the new DTD does not prevent the upgrade of the old instances.

The transformation process is based on the parsing of the SGML instance and the use of application languages. The parser reads the instance and transforms it into a sequence of events consisting minimally of the "Element Structure Information Set" (ESIS).[3] This sequence of events is then read by an application language that is programmed to recognize each markup event and to trigger the appropriate action.

Just as in conversion, the necessary actions depend on a number of contextual factors. If these factors occur before the spot where they are needed, it is not difficult to test for their existence. It is much harder to look ahead for them in the instance and come back to the point where the context is required. This is one of the reasons why some tools load the whole ESIS representation of the document in memory so as to be able to analyze and manipulate it at will. Although such a solution is very powerful, it is also very costly in memory and may dramatically slow down the transformation process of large documents. Depending on your ultimate transformation needs, you can choose the tool best adapted to your situation.

---

3.  The ESIS is described in ISO 13673, "Conformance Testing for SGML Systems." At the time of this writing, this standard is in the final editing stage and should be available in the near future.

### 3.1.2.6    Search and Retrieval Engines

Electronic delivery is often the major reason for moving to an SGML document production system. The underlying rationale is usually that if your data is marked up in SGML, and the search and retrieval engine you choose uses SGML markup as its own markup system, most traditional document preparation steps are obsolete. Many of the usual processing tasks—conversion of data to specific markup, consistency control, error correction, inclusion of offset addresses for nontextual objects, manual assembling of document structures, and programming of relevant fields for multicriteria search—become unnecessary, since they are solved in the following ways through the use of SGML as the native markup:

- SGML instances do not require transformation.

- SGML instances that have been validated with a parser do not need any additional validating control.

- Links to nontextual objects, if encoded with entity references, are well defined and can be used to manipulate the objects once their presence at the right location has been ensured.

- The "database fields" (the elements themselves) are already built in and do not need further processing to become accessible for searching.

As a consequence, switching to SGML for electronic delivery appears to be powerful in exploiting the potential of the data, as well as time- and cost-effective.

If you use one of the commercial SGML-aware search and retrieval engines on the market, you only need to launch an indexing process on the available documents. Most engines build the table of contents to offer a hierarchical search, build a word index to offer full-text search, and index the content by element so as to offer multicriteria search.

Once you have run the program that indexes the documents in your information system or your document repository, you can distribute the document base on line (locally or on a public network), on CD-ROM, or on any media adapted to the volume of your data and your distribution channels. It is usually necessary to attach a run-time version of the retrieval engine and a viewer to enable the users to search the base and view the documents. The viewer usually needs to apply a stylesheet that you have defined to render the documents with the adequate presentation.

This indexing process is not required when you want to put your data on the World Wide Web. You need only transform your data to HTML format and make it available on a Web server to make it instantly accessible worldwide to people who have an Internet connection and who have acquired any one of several free Web document browsers. While HTML is not very scalable to large document bases, recent advancements in browser technology and availability will soon make it possible to serve documents on the Internet in their original SGML form, conforming to any DTD.

---

> **The World Wide Web**
>
> The World Wide Web, also called "the Web" or "WWW," is a protocol on the Internet for distributing documents, most of which are marked up with a DTD called HTML (for Hypertext Markup Language). HTML is a very simple presentation-oriented DTD that also offers multimedia links. Its very simplicity, and the fact that Web browsers don't require documents to be valid before displaying them, has allowed a large number of companies and individuals to put their information on line without knowing much about SGML.

The search issue is still problematic with large documents. The Web community has not defined the granularity of documents which will travel on the net and the information which must travel with each chunk of information. So today it is the server's responsibility to divide the information into browsable chunks.

### 3.1.2.7    Other Processing Applications

Any additional applications that you require should be taken into account in your planning; typically, these applications must be programmed *ad hoc*. Such applications might include

- Enriching documents from a database of part numbers, glossary entries, and so on

- Filling a database from document content

- Computerized information analysis

- SGML-aware validation of sentence construction

For example, one French publisher has combined all its dictionaries into one huge SGML database out of which it now extracts new dictionaries according to various parameters.

### 3.1.2.8    Document Engineering Toolbox

In your planning for a document production system, it's important not to overlook the maintenance of the tools and data used in the system. We use the name "document engineering toolbox" to refer to this collection of enabling technology and data. The toolbox is a place where you organize information about any of the following items that apply to you:

- The DTDs and their variants (see Section 3.1.3), including their maintenance documentation (discussed in Section 12.2)

- The stylesheets and templates of the various word processors the system will convert from or transform to

- Editorial and writing guides

- Presentation rules and style guides for formatted documents

- The necessary entities for special characters and symbols (see Section 8.7)

- A "reference parser," if interchange parties have agreed on one

- The validating parser used in the system components

- Application languages and software tools

When you consider the toolbox as a component of the document production system in its own right, you give it the same importance, allow the appropriate resources, and apply the same procedures as with any important application. Each item in the toolbox should be fully documented, successive versions archived, and all necessary engineering information centralized and available.

The result will be to make maintenance and upgrades to any tool faster and easier and to build the proficiency of the people responsible for engineering the production line. For instance, if you have subcontracted the development and installation of your document production system, there comes a time when you need to reinstate the daily maintenance in-house, and it can be the job of the person in charge of the daily maintenance to keep the engineering toolbox in the best possible state. If this activity is seriously pursued, staff turnover becomes much less critical.

### 3.1.2.9   Dependencies Between Components

When you are faced with the problem of launching an SGML-based document system project, it is difficult to know where to start and in what order to proceed. Developing the DTD should be the starting point; how to build the DTD component is explained in this book. Then you have to choose what to do next, with the goal of concluding as quickly and efficiently as possible. One way is to run several subprojects, corresponding to each component of the production line, in parallel. In what order should you launch the production of the components of the system, and which components of the system can be produced in parallel?

The answer varies according to the priorities of each project, but there are some dependencies that cannot be avoided, whatever the project. When planning your project, you have to anticipate four main steps in the subproject for each component:

- Analysis and specification

- Development

- Test and correction

- General deployment

The first rule is that you can start specifying any subproject once the DTD has been at least specified or, better, developed. Never start any development of a subproject before the DTD has been tested, corrected, and stabilized, even if it is not in its final form.

The second rule is to have, after the second subproject, enough valid SGML instances to help specify, test, and validate all the other components. After building the DTD, the second subproject to tackle depends on your choice of architecture. If you have decided to work with traditional tools and regularly convert the documents to the DTD, the second task should be the setup of the conversion engine and applications to help test the DTD and evaluate the performance of the converter and the potential constraints on source documents that must be formalized more strictly. If you plan to use an SGML-aware editor, the second task should be to program the editing environment based on the editor of your choice so that authors will test the DTD and start producing new valid documents that can be used to test and finalize other components.

The third subproject to deal with again depends on your priorities. You may need to build one or more proof-of-concept formatting applications immediately, or you may need to build the document management system if you have many documents to handle.

In each case, you will need the reference DTD and valid instances from which to work, as well as the precise specifications for the project's results, before starting the development. Because you will also need to test the performance of the components developed in the second subproject, you will need a large number of documents and not just a few samples.

Subsequent subprojects can be in any order that meets your criteria.

A project advancement chart could look as shown in Table 3-1.

**Table 3-1**    Interdependencies in the Components of a Document Production System.

|  | Toolbox, reference DTD | Editing tools, custom work | Conversion from two WP formats | Format apps, style sheets | DBMS, custom work | Search engine, custom work | Two-way interchange, DTD transformation |
|---|---|---|---|---|---|---|---|
| Analyze and specify | Done | Done | Done | Done | In process | Done | In process |
| Develop | Done | Done | Done | In process | | In process | |
| Test and correct | Done | Done | In process | | | | |
| Deploy generally | Done | In process | | | | | |

### 3.1.3    The Reference DTD and Its Variants

When we talk about "the DTD," we are really referring to the **reference DTD** common to a group of users within a company, an industry, or an interest group. Often such a DTD isn't used as is, except as a hub format used in processing. Each activity in the production of documents may require a derivative version of the generic model. We call these derivative versions **variant DTDs**.

The reference DTD should be developed first. It encodes the "ideal" markup language for a complete document type. It is the DTD to which a whole document should conform when its content is complete, before it is processed for any particular purpose. Figure 3-3 shows the typical variant DTDs and their derivation. Variant DTDs for additional processes might also be created.

**Figure 3-3**    Derivation Pattern for Variant DTDs.

#### 3.1.3.1    Interchange DTD

The interchange DTD, unlike the authoring, conversion, and presentation DTDs, is usually imposed on a company or department, and thus is seldom derived from an in-house DTD (unless you are involved in a business deal where one of the partners has imposed its own in-house reference DTD as the interchange DTD). In most cases, the interchange

DTD is an industrywide DTD or a DTD on which a large interest group has agreed. (Section 7.2 describes how this process can be undertaken.) The interchange DTD is a kind of external reference DTD to which you must transform but that you cannot alter.

If you build your in-house DTD after having identified which interchange DTD you will have to conform to, then you need to ensure that the structure of your own DTD is compatible and transformation is possible. If the interchange DTD is imposed after you have built your own reference DTD and have produced documents with it, it is safer to compare both DTDs, find out if transformation is possible, and, if it is not, alter the necessary element types and structures so as to make transformation possible. Then transform your old instances to make them compatible with the new DTD.

The transformation of documents from a reference DTD to an interchange DTD usually consists of removing proprietary and secret information and adding control information and revision status. It often includes generated or augmented information such as the table of contents, which normally would be built as part of the formatting process but is contractually required to be delivered with the source files.

The problem becomes tricky if you find out that your company has to conform to two unrelated interchange DTDs. This usually happens in large companies that support activities for widely differing customers. For instance, a company building equipment for aeronautical and aerospace activities may have to conform to both the CALS DTDs for their military clients and the Air Transport Association DTDs for their civil clients.

There is no easy solution to this problem. Our recommendation is to analyze whether the same documents are really interchanged with both types of clients or partners. If they are, your needs analysis should favor the DTD to which you will transform documents more often, in larger volumes, and for delivery to the partners most important to your business. Refine your transformation choices for the process whose result must be of the highest quality, and don't compromise your own company's requirements for leveraging your information investment. You may nevertheless find that the choice between the two interchange DTDs is a toss-up. In this case, you may need to make your in-house DTD loose enough to accommodate as much as possible of the transformation requirements from and to both interchange DTDs.

In conclusion, we can say that the in-house reference DTD of a company in a specific trade should probably be a variant of the interchange DTD used in that industry. But the fact that transformation back and forth must be possible does not mean that no information is discarded in the process. By documenting the differences between the two DTDs, it is possible to list all the information that is lost in the transformation process in each direction. As long as this information is consciously evaluated as unnecessary to the use of the target documents, the loss of information is unimportant.

### 3.1.3.2    Authoring DTDs

Authoring DTDs are built for editing purposes. Reference DTDs are usually huge, and not every part of them is useful to authors. So the first action is to downsize the DTD so as to make it smaller and simpler where possible. In environments where authors work in small chunks (such as chapters) that are later assembled into whole documents, the authoring DTD is often a sub-DTD inside the document hierarchy of the reference DTD.

The authoring DTD may need to be looser than the reference DTD so that SGML validation does not cause a string of irrelevant errors when the work is still incomplete. For instance, if two subsections with some minimal content are required in a chapter in the reference DTD, the requirement for content can be removed from the authoring DTD so as to allow the author to write only one subsection at a time and still validate the draft.

Authoring DTDs are often optimized for use with a specific editing environment. To ease the markup process in an SGML-aware editor, it may be useful to add layers of container elements so that the list of allowed elements in a certain context does not overwhelm the author. Alternatively, the use of an unstructured editor may call for the implementation of aggressive minimization schemes and possibly the flattening of some structures.

Finally, authoring DTDs can be adapted to specific organizations. In large companies, there may be a need for several authoring DTDs adapted to each department's philosophy and needs. For instance, at Groupe Bull, one product line documentation unit wanted access only to the general text entities associated with that unit's products, another product line required a set order for some elements that the reference DTD allowed in random order, and a third product line needed a DTD that would easily transform to the interchange DTD it was required to use. All these needs can be met by devising adapted authoring DTDs.

Authoring DTDs must adhere to two rules. The first is that, whatever the needs met by the authoring DTDs, they must transform to the reference DTD without loss of information. The second is that all the differences from the reference DTD must be fully documented. Attached to each authoring DTD, one must find the date of the changes, their contents, and the reasons why they were made. This information is crucial if one is to maintain the authoring DTDs effectively a new request is made or the reference DTD is upgraded.

### 3.1.3.3    Conversion DTDs

A conversion DTD is an intermediate DTD between the source markup and the target DTD. (The target is usually the reference DTD, but it may also be the authoring DTD.) It is usually similar to but looser than the reference DTD so as to accommodate all the normal and abnormal structures found in source documents. It might also include presentation-related elements and elements that hold conversion data, which don't appear in the reference DTD.

In the abstract, there could be as many conversion DTDs as there are source markup systems because each source markup–target DTD pair is unique. But some conversion engines have their own basic intermediate conversion DTDs that they adapt and use in two-step conversions. And to save time and money, other conversion engines are beginning to rely on a single DTD, the "Rainbow DTD," for holding the intermediate results of conversion from word processor formats. Rainbow is a highly presentation-oriented DTD that records the formatting information which was present in the source markup. It allows clarification of the original markup by translating it into a simple SGML form, which is much easier to process than system-specific markup in further conversions. The Rainbow DTD is not linked to any target DTD, so once the conversion has been made to Rainbow, it is the transformation process from Rainbow to the target DTD which is unique.

The rule about conversion DTDs is that they must allow a one-way transformation to the reference DTD without losing any of the source information. And unless you plan on doing the conversion of your legacy documents once and for all, it is important to document the conversion DTD and how you use its results in the conversion process for further reuse or to understand markup errors that may appear later on.

### 3.1.3.4    Presentation DTDs

Presentation DTDs are made to hold the results of augmenting SGML documents with processing or formatting information. They are useful for storing the results of processing if there are several complex stages of document conditioning to perform before the output stage. For example, presentation DTDs may have attributes that explicitly control literal features such as typefaces, or they might add markup for hyperlinks that have been generated from content-based markup, such as tables of contents or indexes. Presentation DTDs may also organize previously random elements in a strict linear or alphabetical order so that they can be output in that order.

Some presentation DTDs, such as the Hypertext Markup Language (HTML), are becoming widely used to hold output from original-form SGML documents. These languages are typically used with software that is customized to process or display them. Transforming SGML documents to languages such as these could obviate the need for a presentation DTD that is based on the design of the reference DTD.

The rule for presentation DTDs is that they must allow a one-way transformation from the reference DTD. Documenting all the augmentations made to the reference DTD can be useful if you decide to change the formatting engine. In this case, you can reuse the underlying analysis and change only the programming.

### 3.1.3.5   Data Flow among the DTDs

Although all the variant DTDs are built from the reference DTD, the actual flow of documents follows a different pattern altogether. Documents typically go from creation (by editing or conversion) to storage and then output, as shown in Figure 3-4. Each stage of the document is reached after a conversion or a transformation process based on one of the variant DTDs. The added value of such a workflow is that each process is secured by the control of a parser, which ensures the validity of documents at all times.

## 3.2    Preparing to Launch the Project

Just as with any project, before you launch it you must assess the risks, define the goals and other project parameters, and write the project plan. This section is therefore aimed at the project manager or project leader who will be assigned these tasks.

### 3.2.1    Defining the Project Goals and Directions

When you start a project, there must be a solid rationale for doing so. The most common goals are to improve the cost-effectiveness of document production, to rationalize and control document production, and to offer a better quality of documents on a wider variety of media. These are generic goals one hears a lot about, but for *your project*, you should make sure the specific goals of your company are clearly stated with short-, middle-, and long-term objectives and results. When there are several goals, you should make sure everybody agrees on the priorities of those goals.

For instance, a company may decide that what is most important is the protection and longevity of its data. The short-term goal is to develop a DTD that accommodates all the existing documents, and the middle-term goal is to convert all the legacy data into SGML instances which will suddenly become hardware-, software-, and operating-system-independent, thus justifying the investment. The long-term goal may be to deploy a robust document management system that will help find any version or edition of a given document within seconds for viewing or updating purposes.

For another company, the priority may be to offer all its documents on paper, on CD-ROM, and on the Internet, and to create new types of documents by cleverly processing the existing ones. In that case, the priority will be to quickly put on the market new products (old documents on a new media or new documents) for a quick return on investment.

A third type of goal may be for a literature department in a university to adapt the Text Encoding Initiative (TEI) DTD to the type of documents they are studying and then mark up all the necessary documents to launch the analysis applications necessary to their study.

Beware of bizarre goals or hidden agendas. Your awareness of these may turn out to be crucial to the viability of a project where politics plays a big role. Among those one finds the following:

- We should do SGML. We don't know why, but it is fashionable.

- Our competitors are moving to SGML; we should do the same.

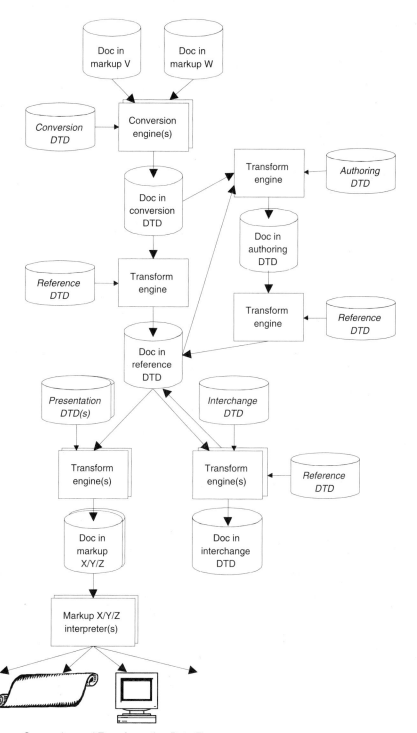

**Figure 3-4**     Conversion and Transformation Data Flow.

⟵――――――――――――――――――――――――――――――――――――――――⟶

- Morale is low in the documentation department; why not launch a motivational project?

- Our production department is overstaffed; SGML is difficult enough to help us figure out who we should keep.

- We need to upgrade the perception of our organization's technological edge; why not do SGML?

- I need a high-visibility project to boost my career; why not launch a new document system?

Clearly, some of these goals are so hollow and so far from sound business practice that they are likely to endanger the DTD development project. The only way to know if a project is viable is to be able to prove that the benefits for the company greatly outweigh the drawbacks. So let's assume that in your company, the strategic directions that make DTD development necessary are legitimate and that you just need to formalize them. The following questions will help you do so.

- What documents are concerned?

- Will the project cover existing documents, new documents, or both?

- To what uses will the documents be put?

- Will they be created and utilized internally, externally, or both, and how?

- What is the expected outcome of the project in terms of organization, quality of documents, image, cost-effectiveness, standardization, return on investment, and so on?

- What are the expected dates for the first results and for the completion of the project?

Once you have all the answers with their relative priorities, you can formalize the goals of the project, check that they match the strategic directions of your company, and have them officially approved.

Even though DTD development was mentioned as a subproject up to now in this chapter, we will now begin to concentrate on DTD development alone, and refer to it as "the project."

## 3.2.2    Controlling the Project Risks

Developing a DTD is a part of the document engineering toolbox component of the whole document production system. Because this component is seldom identified and consequently not well provided for, the main risks in launching a DTD development project are as follows:

- Not to handle it as a project at all

- Not to consider it as important as the other tools

- Not to put it in the right perspective of its future uses

- Not to include it in the bigger project for a new document production system

- To entrust incompetent people with its development

- Not to give its developers goals

Any of these mistakes will end up in burying the project and making sure it is never completed or applicable. Unless a DTD project is officially defined, included in a company strategy, properly staffed, and formally launched, it is so fragile and inconsistent that it can be subject to any resource reallocation, budget cut, or change of direction if a manager leaves. We have heard of many similar failures where the people who had invested much time and effort were terribly frustrated to see the DTD project be dropped halfway, to see that the DTD was never used, or to learn that finally a completely different DTD had been selected.

In other words, whether you are a manager, a project leader, an author, or a developer, do not invest in a DTD development project unless you have proof that it is necessary to your company or organization, that it has been officially acknowledged as necessary, that the goals of the project are clearly defined, and that the necessary means (attention, human resources, budget, and time) have been allocated through the end of the project.

## 3.2.3    Staffing the Project

One of the pitfalls to avoid is to gather all the people who are interested in SGML and start working on a voluntary basis. When the project starts having problems (people do not show up at meetings, they are busy elsewhere, no one seems to care anymore, interested people are told priorities are somewhere else), the appropriate questions are asked, but it is usually too late.

- Who makes decisions?

- Who funds the project?

- Who decides who is involved?

- Who is actually concerned?

- Who informs the managers of these people?

- Who is in charge of the project and responsible for the results?

We suggest you ask these questions before you start and that you start only when they have been answered and the appropriate organizations have been set up. As is typical for the management of most projects, we suggest you formally organize three bodies, as shown in Figure 3-5.

- The steering committee is composed of decision makers and funders of the project. It includes the project manager.

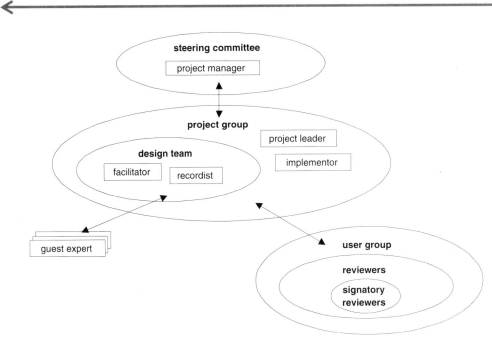

**Figure 3-5**    Project Staff.

- The project group is composed of the people who will do the work. It is led by the project leader and includes the members of the design team, some reviewers, eventually the DTD implementor, and occasionally some guest experts. The design team includes a facilitator and a recordist.

- The user group is consulted to give their opinions and to test and validate the work of the project group. Some user-group reviewers have sign-off responsibility.

If these people are clearly identified and have accepted their job, then the risk of the project failing halfway through is very small. All the individuals may not be selected yet, especially in the design team, but the project leader must be identified and must start helping to launch the project. Section 3.3.1 goes into more detail about selecting the project group members.

## 3.2.4   Listing the Project Deliverables

Before launching a DTD development project, especially if you plan on subcontracting parts of it, you have to define the document set it must cover (see Section 3.3.3), the test documents, and the validating parser. Unless you make these decisions upstream, you will not be able to validate and accept the deliverables of the project.

The minimum deliverables of a DTD development project are as follows:

- The document analysis report recording all the expressed needs, the decisions that were made, and the rationale for them

- The DTD "code" and some demonstration or documentation of the fact that the DTD is syntactically valid

- The DTD maintenance documentation and user documentation (see Chapter 12)

- The files for the test documents marked up with the DTD

## 3.2.5    Planning the Schedule and Budget

The amount of time and the budget necessary to successfully complete a DTD development project varies according to several parameters:

- The scope of documents (the wider it is, the longer and more complex the project will be)

- The complexity and variety of the structure and content of the documents

- The number of constraints there are on the project

- The competence of the project leader

- The availability of the members of the design team

- The existence of a competent DTD implementor

- The discipline of the whole project group in following a DTD design methodology, documenting all their ideas, decisions, actions, and samples and seriously reviewing all the documents and "code" delivered

We know of a computer company DTD that was developed in three staff-weeks, over a period of three months, by an expert in DTD writing helped by a few technical writers of that company. In Digital and Bull, it took several staff-months over a period of one year. The difference lies in the size of the companies (the larger the company, the longer it takes to reach consensus), the variety of documents covered by our DTDs (we had to provide for very different technical documentation backed by very different technical cultures), and the amount of documentation delivered with the DTDs. In a related effort to build an industrywide software documentation DTD, although it was specified by people who were all experts in DTDs, it took over three staff-months of meetings with 15 people over a period of two years to deliver the analysis report. (Reaching consensus was a killer in that case.)

This is why it is impossible to give recommendations about the time your specific project will take. Nevertheless, some rough generalizations can be made:

- Preparation for the project launch

  This step can take from a week to a month.

- Launching the project

  Depending on the good will of all the people involved, it can take from a month to three months to have the people available, trained, and operational.

- Document analysis, modeling, and specification done by the project group

  The minimum is 15 days of hard work (including the writing of the document analysis report), to be spread according to the frequency of meetings. The calendar time could be three weeks, but if the team plans on meeting on a weekly basis, this phase can take up to four months.

- Review and validation of the document analysis report

  This can take from 15 days to a month.

- Final design and implementation of the DTD

  This can take two weeks, with additional questions going to the design team.

- DTD test and validation

  This step can take a week to two months, depending on the number of test documents to mark up, the availability of an SGML-aware editor, and the proficiency of the people who will validate the DTD.

- Documentation

  Developing documentation can take about two months, but starts as soon as the design work is over, so it does not add much delay.

Thus, it seems unreasonable to plan on delivering a good DTD with all the necessary documents in less than three and a half months, but there seems to be no maximum if you consider all the delays bad organization can add to a non-priority project.

The same is true in terms of budget. If you subcontract the job and only count what you will pay in cash to a subcontractor, then the bill can be relatively low. But if you take into account the effort of all the people involved in the design, coding, review, validation, and documentation, the price is higher. (Apart from the time spent, do not forget the hardware and software for the tests.) It is worthwhile, though, because it guarantees the quality and instant usability of the delivered DTD.

## 3.2.6   Writing the Project Plan

At this stage, the DTD development project should be ready to start because every aspect has been thought of, discussed, and organized. But this information is scattered in the notes and heads of all the people involved in the project. So to make sure that there is a consensus on what the DTD development project is going to be, it is necessary to write all the planning information down in a project plan.

The project plan includes all the information about the goals and the constraints of the project and the way it will be carried out. It lists all the tasks to be achieved and subdivides them into more precise steps. For each task or step the schedule, the budget, the resources, and the expected results must be fully described, as must the dependencies between tasks. Simple software packages are available help you build the project plan methodically and efficiently.

The final document must be validated by the steering committee that funds the project, and must be accepted by all the people involved before the DTD work can actually begin.

We purposely do not mention a business plan here, although we know project leaders are often hard pressed to write any kind of justification for writing a DTD. Since a business plan consists of analyzing and listing all the expected expenses, then figuring out and recording what the expected revenue is and defining when and how the company will reach a return on investment, there is no sense in performing this exercise just for the task of developing DTDs. Obviously, DTD development, isolated from a whole document migration to SGML project, is only a cost center and can never have a return on investment as such. A real and viable business plan, including the quantitative and qualitative benefits, can be built only for a global project and not solely for DTD development.

## 3.3   Launching the Project

Launching the project is the responsibility of the project leader. As soon as you have identified the members of the project group, you can start working to make this phase as short and efficient as possible.

### 3.3.1   Setting Up the Project Group

The project group is composed of permanent members and part-time members. Some member roles are required, while others are optional. All members have a precisely defined role that they must understand and accept.

The project group is composed of a project leader, the document type design team, the DTD implementor, and guest experts.

### 3.3.1.1    The Project Leader

The project leader is a person from within the company or the organization who is selected for his or her skills of leadership, organization, knowledge of the document world, and ability to complete a project.

The role of the project leader is to interface with and report to the steering committee, to reach the specific goals of the DTD project while keeping in mind the goals of the global project, and to keep all the team members at work until the project is completed. The project leader is in charge of keeping the project on schedule and within budget, and is responsible for obtaining all the deliverables and ensuring their quality.

### 3.3.1.2    The Design Team, Facilitator, and Recordist

The document type design team is composed of representatives of all the actors who interact with the documents to be modeled. They must have intimate knowledge of the documents, either as producers or as users. To set up the design team, you need to select the persons who can best represent each actor community.

These people can be found among the authors; the marketing people; the editors; the librarians (or others in charge of managing and archiving the documents); the users (in-house, partners, or clients); the company quality, standards, and methods people; the publishers; and people who have a vision of what future documents will or should be like.

The role of the design team members is to analyze the existing documents and other relevant data, express the needs of their community, specify the markup model, select interesting samples and test documents, review and validate the final analysis report and all interim output, and test and accept the DTD. Part 2 of this book can guide them in achieving these tasks.

The project leader must make sure that the selected people are officially assigned to this job and that the necessary amount of time is cleared in their schedule. If people are assigned the design work on top of their usual commitments, they will not be able to do the job seriously. And if they are only made available for the meetings, they will not be able to do the necessary homework between meetings. This homework involves reading the meeting reports, doing research on controversial topics, and filling out forms and proposals. The usual estimate for the necessary time is to double the meeting time estimated by the facilitator.

For reasons of group dynamics, the design team works more efficiently if it does not have more than eight participants. The project leader should try to resist the natural impulse of each department and subdepartment to have their own representative in the design team by stressing the amount of time and work involved in design and by offering interested people an opportunity to be reviewers.

All the members of the design team will be subject matter experts, but they will need the help of a facilitator who is competent in document type modeling. The role of the facilitator is to explain the design methodology being used, to organize meetings, to lead and direct discussions, to listen to all expressed needs, to make sure that everything said is recorded, to point out inconsistencies or oversights, and to complete all the necessary documents to hand over to the implementor. The facilitator is the interface with the project leader and the implementor.

The person in the role of facilitator must

- Be credible as an unbiased leader
- Be able to lead groups of heterogeneous origin to produce effective work
- Know enough about the document set at hand and the traps and the tricks of document modeling
- Know the DTDs available for various industries and their best ideas
- Be thorough enough not to skip a step or leave anything out
- Be persistent enough to keep asking questions to the subject matter experts until all issues have been cleared
- Be sensitive to the potential variations of the meanings behind the words used by professionals
- Know enough SGML to interface with the DTD implementor and convey the messages from the design team

Ideally, this person should be picked within the company staff because he or she can coordinate all the logistics and hierarchical aspects of the work in an easier and more timely fashion. But if no one in-house has this profile, it will probably be necessary to hire a consultant to help. In this case, all the administrative aspects of the work will fall to the project leader.

The person in the role of recordist must

- Write easily and well enough to report all the decisions in a rigorous and clear fashion
- Be able to distribute interim reports on demand
- Be prepared to write the final document analysis report

If possible, find someone for this job who can follow and capture relatively complex and esoteric discussions, without injecting a bias into the notes through being too experienced or familiar with the arguments.

### 3.3.1.3    The DTD Implementor

The implementor is in charge of designing the markup model and the architecture of the DTD, writing the DTD "code," documenting it, successfully validating the DTD with a parser, and eventually participating in the DTD tests. The implementor may also occasionally participate in the design team work to offer advice and direction when choices are to be made.

The best person to serve as the implementor is an SGML specialist who knows the language thoroughly, is familiar with the industry DTDs, and has written at least one operational DTD. It is also useful if this person has some experience with programming or customizing an environment based on SGML, such as an editing or formatting application. It is rare to have such a profile in-house, so the project manager can either subcontract the development job or have a person from the company trained in DTD implementation and maintenance techniques. In the latter case, the selected person must be interested in document modeling and be comfortable with computer languages.

### 3.3.1.4    Guest Experts

Experts are called in when the design team feels there are decisions to be made and they do not have adequate information or competence. These experts fall into two main categories: Either they are subject matter experts in a very specific area, or they specialize in the building of certain kinds of applications.

Some subject matter experts only occasionally participate in the design team, although their expertise is much in demand, because they do not have the time to participate in the design activities full-time. Consequently, the facilitator must choose the moments when their presence is absolutely necessary and invite them then.

Application developers may also be requested to join the design team in the modeling phase to describe and explain the constraints of their art and suggest ways to solve problems. For instance, if the SGML-based editors which will be used to mark up the instances do not support SGML "marked sections," there are ways to achieve the same result by other means.

### 3.3.1.5    The One-Man Band Situation

In the previous sections we explained the different roles and tasks each player in the project group had to achieve. This does not mean that each role must be held by a different player. According to the size of your project and the distribution of skills, several different roles can be held by the same person: project leader, facilitator, design team member, and implementor. In this case, we suggest that it's a full-time job and recommend that the person filling these roles should work hard to keep the roles distinct.

To summarize, we described a project group that could be twelve people strong, but it could as easily be five people strong if the right skills are concentrated in one person. The only skill that cannot be collapsed under a certain threshold is the variety of viewpoints in the design team, which is the only warranty that the DTD will encompass all needs and that it will be used.

## 3.3.2    Identifying Future Users

As shown in Figure 3-5, the project cannot start unless the users' group has been set up. Since they will be asked to give their opinion, critique the design team's work, and test and validate the results, the real future users of the DTD must be selected as members of the user group. The user group should make sure to cover the profiles of all future users, especially those not represented in the design team.

Selecting the members of the user group, involving them, and training them from the very beginning of the project usually pays off in terms of motivation and availability for future work.

## 3.3.3    Defining the Scope of Documents

When the design work starts, it is necessary to set boundaries on the work at hand. One of them is defining precisely the categories of documents that the DTD(s) must model.

### Note

At this stage, defining whether one or several DTDs are necessary to account for all the documents selected is not part of the scope work.

To define the scope of documents to be taken into account in the project, the best way is to list all the types of documents available in the company or the organization, then to decide which ones must be selected according to the goals of the project. The list might include technical documentation; desktop publishing documents like letters, reports, memos, and marketing literature; catalogues and directories; dictionaries; novels and short stories; tutorials; electronic documents like database chunks and online help; articles; presentation slides; standards; procedures; and other documents. You might be taken aback at the variety of documents published in an organization, but it doesn't necessarily mean that there are as many document types.

The second task is to select from the list which documents will be covered by the DTD project. Beware of expanding the scope to include all the documents listed. It is usually a bad idea because of the wide variety of existing documents and their lack of commonality. Each choice must be explained and the reasons recorded in the rationale. It is important that these basic choices should be documented so that they are never questioned again and are very clear to the design team when they turn the choices of the scope of documents into design principles.

For instance, for a manufacturing company, it is very unlikely to use the same DTD to write commercial letters, user documentation, and the technical specifications for the company products. Similarly, it is most improbable for a publisher to use the same DTD for their dictionaries, novels, and interpersonal mail. In both cases, if there is a need to model all the documents, the document types are so far apart that it is more efficient to organize the design work in several phases, each one covering one general class of documents.

The third task is to define more precisely what each class of document includes. For instance, "dictionaries" could include basic language dictionaries, translation dictionaries, proper noun dictionaries, synonym dictionaries, pronunciation dictionaries, and so on. Although the content is different for each of them, the global structure is similar, so they are all part the same document class. For a manufacturer, all the technical product documentation, whether for internal staff or end users, whether it's generated by the research department or the documentation department, can be considered similar enough to be dealt with in the same overall class of document.

Defining the scope of documents also implies listing the nontextual objects to be accommodated. Although they are not directly processed like text by SGML tools, hooks to nontextual objects must be planned for in the DTD. Therefore, the design team must know if users will want to point to graphics, still images, sound, animation, video, and so on in order to provide the appropriate linking devices in the DTD.

Make your choices explicit and write the rationale down because the design team will need as much information as possible when casting the scope information into a "design principle" for analysis and modeling work.

## 3.3.4    Listing the Project Constraints

This phase aims at identifying and understanding the impact of all the factors that will constrain the design and implementation of the DTD. Some are major, others are trivial, and some matter only in later development stages, for instance, when building an authoring DTD. But to find out how important each constraint is, you need to list them all and then evaluate their impact on the current project.

Along with typical project constraints on schedule, budget, and staffing, the design and implementation of a DTD might be constrained by any of the tools and methods for document creation, management, and processing that have been decided on. Specific constraints might include

- A requirement to accommodate existing documents in the new system

  This requirement usually constrains the DTD to have a structure that is compatible with existing documents to a certain degree, suggesting that the design team should, for a start, take into account the existing markup systems during its needs analysis.

- An obligation to use or transform to a particular interchange DTD

  If an interchange DTD has been defined, ignoring it when building your own DTD would be a serious mistake. Including the interchange DTD as an unavoidable constraint from the start will prevent the design team from doing new work and then throwing it all away and starting over. This situation has occurred several times when an industry interchange DTD was defined and imposed after several companies in the industry had built their own and had started producing documents with it.

- Display devices that have limited capabilities

  For instance, if the documents are likely to be displayed on character-cell terminals, there is no chance to display graphics, images, or video. But if the same documents are likely to be displayed on a multimedia PC, then the graphics, images, and video are probably the most interesting parts of the documents. If both must be accommodated, the model will need to provide for alternative content for each output version.

  You might be in a similar situation if you must prepare documents for print-disabled people. In this case, the constraint would suggest that you must incorporate into your DTD the techniques published by the International Committee for Accessible Document Design (ICADD) so that you can use publicly available tools to generate Braille, large-print, and voice-synthesized texts.

## 3.3.5   Planning the Project Workflow

Just as for any project, you need to determine and document the tasks to perform, their order, and their dependencies. Figure 3-6 shows a typical progression of tasks, using the notation of the Mallet project management methodology. (Appendix E describes where to get more information on this methodology.) It can serve as a road map for people to position themselves in the project in terms of role, time to act, type of action to perform, and deliverables they are expected to release. Table 3-6 lists the task numbers in the figure and describes what is done at each stage.

Figure 3-6 uses the following notation:

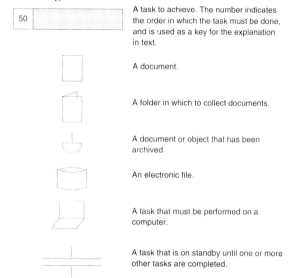

A task to achieve. The number indicates the order in which the task must be done, and is used as a key for the explanation in text.

A document.

A folder in which to collect documents.

A document or object that has been archived.

An electronic file.

A task that must be performed on a computer.

A task that is on standby until one or more other tasks are completed.

The documents and objects identified in Figure 3-6 are as follows:

| | |
|---|---|
| CF | Component form |
| CL | Component list |
| DAR | Document analysis report |
| DS | Design specification |
| DTD | Document type definition |
| LD | Launch document |
| NA | Needs analysis report |
| P | Parsing |
| RR | Review report |
| SAE | SGML-aware editor |
| TM | Training material |
| TR | Technical report |
| UD | User documentation |

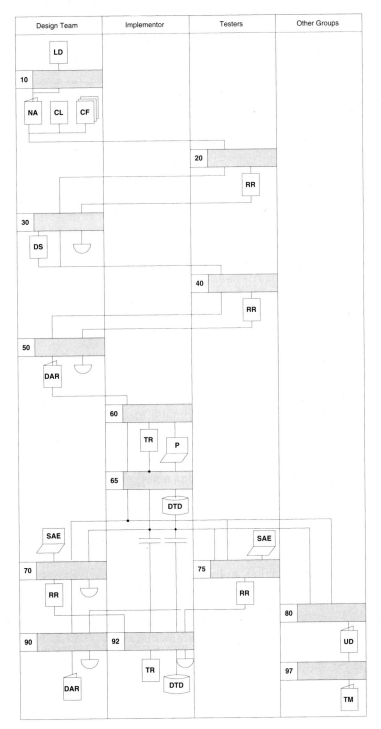

**Figure 3-6**    Typical DTD Project Workflow.

**Table 3-2**    Workflow Tasks in Figure 3-6.

| Task | Description |
|------|-------------|
| 00 | The design team meets to launch the project. The launch document records the goals, the design principles, and the constraints of the project, and describes the document samples for analysis. |
| 10 | The design team analyzes sample documents and the existing markup systems and generates a list of all the potential semantic components and a filled-in component form for each of them. All these documents are gathered in an analysis report that records the output from the needs analysis work. |
| 20 | The analysis report is sent to the reviewers who must validate the analysis work. They write a review report and send it back to the design team. |
| 30 | The design team does all the necessary corrections and starts the modeling phase. When this phase is over they hand out a design specification that records the output from the modeling work. |
| 40 | The design specification is sent for review to the user group and the reviewers, who inspect the design specifications and send a review report to the design team. |
| 50 | The design team makes the necessary alterations and produces the document analysis report, which is then sent to the implementor. |
| 60 | The implementor studies the analysis report and the design specifications and then produces an architecture report that includes all the additional technical information necessary for the implementation phase. |
| 65 | The implementor then writes the DTD, validates it, and delivers it with the architecture report to the design team, the user group, and the technical writers in charge of producing the user documentation for the DTD. |
| 70 | The design team tests and reviews the DTD, probably using an SGML-aware editor to edit documents, but also reading the DTD itself. They write a review report and send it back to the implementor. |
| 75 | The user group makes the same tests and writes a double report that describes the technical problems in the DTD itself (for the implementor) and the design errors (for the design team). |
| 80 | The technical writer in charge of the DTD user documentation starts building the various manuals. This action takes a while and can only be completed when the finalized documents are received from the design team and the implementor (after steps 90 and 92). |
| 90 | The design team makes all the necessary alterations to the design, informs the implementor, and updates all the relevant pieces of the document analysis report so that its final version is coherent with the corrected DTD. They publish the updated version of the document analysis report. |
| 92 | The implementor makes all the required alterations to the DTD and updates the architecture report, and then delivers the final architecture report and the final DTD to be distributed. |

**Table 3-2**     Workflow Tasks in Figure 3-6. (Continued)

| Task | Description |
|------|-------------|
| 97 | The people in charge of building the training material will use all the final documents produced by every group, including the user documentation, to generate the training material and training program. All the documents that are not part of the final delivery must be archived when the necessary action has been taken in the organization where the action was taken. When all the relevant documents have been delivered, tested, and accepted, the DTD development project is over, and the maintenance phase can start. |

# 3.4   Handling Project Politics

There are a number of political issues the project leader and project manager must be aware of throughout the DTD development project. In this section we will list the typical issues, to help you identify them from the very start and deal with them elegantly. If they don't all apply to the specific situation in your company, take it as a blessing! Make your own list of the problems you foresee in your project and try to deal with them as early as possible.

Section 7.2 discusses the political realities and other considerations of conducting industrywide DTD development projects.

### Share Ownership of the Project

It's usually desirable to attain standardization throughout a company by making sure a DTD is used across the board for every appropriate purpose. Unfortunately, it is difficult for some departments to accept being told how to craft their documents by another department. If you anticipate that people will refuse to use a DTD unless they design it in their organization, include eminent representatives of that organization in the design team.

If you think this participation will not be enough, you may need to let a neutral body in the company (such as the corporate standards department or the quality assurance department) take official leadership of this operation.

### Communicate Project Details Early and Often

Writing under the control of a DTD is, in most cases, a heavy burden on authors in the early stages. Not everybody is eager to change their way of thinking, to learn new tools, and to face the possibility of failure or difficulty. This is why the introduction of any novelty in a work organization is usually met with suspicion.

We've found that the earlier managers communicate with future users about the DTD and what the new information system will offer, the more time the users will have to get used to the idea. We have also found that broadly advertising the level of user participation in the design team helps the users to accept the whole process.

To further broaden the base of users involved in the analysis, design, and test activities, a wide user group should be built, trained, gathered often, regularly kept informed, and asked their opinion on all the project documents released.

All these communication actions happen while the DTD development project is underway. They must not prevent the people in charge from preparing for the pilot use of the DTD and the early days of general deployment.

## Motivate the Team to Stay Efficient

The project leader has a special role in ensuring that the work within the project group is harmonious and efficient. The problem does not always come from the design team members themselves. Since that group is often a federation of individuals coming from various organizations, with various individual objectives and goals, the reasons for trouble can often be found in their parent organizations. At the beginning of the development work, all the members are usually motivated and interested, as are their managers. After a while, people tend to be less interested and less available, and are often diverted by their management to "more important tasks."

It is the job of the project leader to keep people motivated, to ensure that tangible deliverables are released often enough for the managers to be aware of the amount and quality of work being produced, and to regularly remind the members of the group and their bosses of their assignment and engagement.

To minimize the risk of the project group being diluted, the project leader should keep a tight agenda with only the minimum time between meetings for writing the reports and working on individual assignments.

## Choose a Decision Model Carefully

Although we recommend different ways to avoid conflict in Chapter 4 and Chapter 5 (for example, by requiring proof of need and by deferring decisions until the issue is solvable), disagreements do occur. The natural tendency in any heterogeneous group like this, where everybody's voice is as important as a neighbor's, is to try to reach 100 percent consensus. Our experience shows that it never works. People come from backgrounds or have needs that are too different, or have orders from their bosses that are too prescriptive to allow consensus to be reached at all times.

Our recommendation in the matter is to allow for a set time of discussion on controversial subjects for everyone to express their point of view, to suggest that the members with the hottest opinions put them in writing before the next meeting, and to allow for a set time at the following meeting to discuss the subject again. If agreement cannot be reached then, make members vote and settle for a majority or super-majority.

This recommendation is especially valid when the project is to build an industrywide DTD (a proposition discussed in Section 7.2). In this case, the conflicts of interest can be so severe that consensus has no meaning. Each decision is based on either the majority of votes or, sometimes, negotiations based on trade-offs.

## Plan for DTD Maintenance

Usually a new technological project attracts attention, budget, and motivated dynamic people; in such conditions, good work can be achieved—up to the point when the DTD is released with all its accompanying documents. But because a DTD is used daily and needs to evolve regularly, it is the responsibility of the managers who launched the project in the first place to assign the appropriate resources in time, budget, and staff for the DTD to be properly maintained. This will not happen if a person is not officially in charge of that task and is not assessed regularly on that objective.

Our experience is that the motivated people who know the DTD inside and out have a propensity to move on to other interesting projects after the DTD development project is over, and that usually no one takes over. DTD maintenance requires that someone be in charge of collecting all the bug or enhancement requests, synthesizing them, gathering a knowledgeable change control board, and applying the decisions of that board.

DTD maintenance is discussed in more detail in Section 5.4.

# Part 2

## Document Type Design

This part addresses the work that the document type design team will perform: designing the requirements for the DTD's markup model.

The complete list of steps for analysis and modeling is as follows.

1. Identify potential needs, defining them as thoroughly as possible.

2. Classify them into logical categories, thereby taking their definition a step further.

3. Validate the needs against other analyses of similar data.

4. Select the needs that the markup model should ultimately address.

5. Build the model for the document hierarchy.

6. Build the models for the information units.

7. Build the models for the data-level elements.

8. Populate the remaining branches of the model.

9. Make connections within the model and from the model to the outside world.

10. Validate that the model is complete and that it has been informed by similar models already developed.

Steps 1 through 3 make up the analysis work, discussed in Chapter 4, and steps 4 through 10 make up the modeling work, discussed in Chapter 5.

Chapter 6 offers advice on modeling techniques that the design team can apply, and Chapter 7 describes special circumstances under which the usual steps of analysis and modeling might need to change.

The analysis and modeling phases of DTD development bear some resemblance to the phases of software and systems development. The analysis work generates functional requirements, and the modeling work generates a partial design specification, which is recorded in a "document analysis report." Later, the DTD implementor designs and documents the choices made in the final markup model and the DTD's architecture, which completes the final design specification. (The implementation process is discussed in Part 3.)

# Document Type Needs Analysis

The document type design team will go through four phases of work: preparation, needs analysis, modeling, and reporting. This chapter discusses the first two, and Chapter 5 discusses the last two. For the purposes of explaining the phases and steps, we'll assume a project where a new document type is being designed. For information about the process of customizing an existing model and how it compares to the process for a new DTD, see Section 7.1.

Analysis involves identifying potential needs, classifying them into logical categories, and validating the needs against analyses and models that have already been prepared. Here, "needs" refers to descriptions of the basic intelligence that the documents must encode rather than a specific SGML-based model for their required organization or hierarchical structure.

As a simple example of analysis work, say that the team members notice there are document constructs that are conventionally called "procedures"[1] and "steps" in the documents being examined. They first name and define these constructs clearly. Then, as they proceed, they group the constructs with other similar constructs that are discovered, such as "lists" and "items," so as to be able to consider their status and their design requirements in tandem. Finally, they compare their understanding of these constructs against the work that other people have done with procedure constructs.

The output of the analysis work lists, describes, and categorizes the distinctions potentially needed in the document type. In the modeling activity, the team will decide which distinctions should be addressed in the project and will use SGML modeling techniques to devise a cohesive markup model that takes into account each of the accepted distinctions.

The natures of the analysis and modeling phases differ in two important ways:

---

1. Here we mean documentation of how a human should perform a function rather than procedural markup that tells a computer how to format document data. A recipe instruction list is a kind of procedure.

- In analysis, team members observe specific document constructs in relatively random order, and then make generalizations about those constructs. By contrast, in modeling they go from the generalizations to specific models that approximate a final SGML form, working down from the top of the hierarchy. This approach ensures a complete analysis and a cohesive design.

- Most of the analysis work is nonjudgmental in nature. The modeling work, on the other hand, is entirely prescriptive. Both phases require open minds and creativity, but answers to modeling questions are only "forced" later in the process.

Section 4.1 discusses how to prepare for the document type design work, and Section 4.2 discusses how to perform the actual analysis.

## 4.1  Preparing for the Design Work

The team's preparation has the following parts:

- Training in SGML (discussed in Section 4.1.1) and in various concepts and techniques needed for analysis and modeling (discussed in Sections 4.1.2 and 4.1.3)

  Some of this training might be provided by an outside trainer, but the project-specific parts should be provided by the team facilitator, who will have been identified when the project was launched.

- The development of "design principles" that identify the project parameters (discussed in Section 4.1.4), and an introduction to both the deliverables that will be expected (discussed in Section 4.1.5) and the rules of teamwork behavior (discussed in Section 4.1.6)

- The gathering of sample documents and other sources of analysis input (discussed in Section 4.1.7)

The group-oriented training and preparation can take from less than one day to as much as three days, depending on the experience the team members already have with structured markup, the clarity of the project goals, and the availability of analysis input. Much of the gathering of input can be done outside the group setting.

### 4.1.1  Learning Basic SGML Concepts

The members of the design team need to receive some minimum level of SGML conceptual training covering its basic philosophy, the strengths and limits of SGML technology, and the rudiments of SGML markup.

The following technical topics are likeliest to be helpful at this stage:

- DTDs as sets of rules

- Elements, including the various content model configurations for occurrence, sequence, and exceptions

- Attributes, including ID/IDREF linking mechanisms

- Entities and the notion of non-SGML data notations (Figure A-3 shows the functional classes of entities in a way that may be helpful to nontechnical people)

- Character data

The introductory material in Chapter 1 illustrates a useful level of conceptual training, though not all the topics listed are discussed there. Advanced topics such as markup minimization won't contribute much to the kind of understanding that the team members need, and may even be confusing or overwhelming at this stage.

Following is some advice for avoiding common mistakes and making the best of the training opportunity.

### Avoid Training on SGML Syntax and DTD Implementation

Unfortunately, an emphasis on syntactic details can spoil the outlook of people who are technically minded. If everyone on the team already thinks of themselves as DTD-writing experts, some "unlearning" might even be in order, so that enthusiasm for clever content modeling can be kept to the implementation stage rather than allowed to intrude on the analysis and modeling stages.

### Don't Study Other DTDs Yet

We do not believe in having the team members study other DTDs before they start to define their own needs. Experience shows that they become so influenced by what they have read that they tend to think only in terms of what they already know, which negatively affects their contributions to the project at hand.

### Consider Using Structured Editors in the Training

It can be helpful to give the team members an awareness of the markup responsibility placed on authors by letting them play with SGML-aware editing tools and a standard DTD as part of the training—even if there are no plans to use structured editing tools in the real environment.

## 4.1.2   Recognizing Semantic Components

The team will spend a great deal of its time working with units of specification that we call **semantic components**. A semantic component corresponds to an expressed need for a distinction between one kind of data and all others. For any proposed component that has been accepted, the result will be SGML markup that reflects the difference in some way.

To illustrate, we can take an example from phonology, the science of speech sounds in natural languages. A "minimal pair" of words is used to elucidate which sounds are significant in a language. For example, in English, "pack" and "back" mean two different things, proving that the differences between the $p$ and $b$ sounds are significant, even though they are produced in a physiologically similar way (differing only in vocalization). On the other hand, "rack" with an American-sounding $r$ and "rack" with a rolled French-sounding $r$ mean the same thing in English. Thus, English has only the three "sound components" $p$, $b$, and $r$. Given appropriate sets of word pairs in another language, it might be determined that the four unique sounds ($p$, $b$, and the two kinds of $r$) represent a different set of sound components.

Likewise, in examining document information, if two pieces of information should be considered the same kind of information, they form examples of only one semantic component. But if they mean something different, or should be treated differently by applications or represented differently to readers, they form two components, a "minimal pair" of kinds of information.

The difference between sounds in natural languages and pieces of document information is that the document type design team has a choice about what to consider different or the same. The basis for making this choice is the *motivation* to do so, based on the kinds of desirable utilizations that become possible or are facilitated when a new distinction is made.

An everyday example shows how important such motivation can be in determining the richness of choices. In warm climates, people give little thought to frozen precipitation, and can usually get away with using the one word "snow" to talk about the subject. In colder climates, people who drive cars need to know more about snowy conditions, and listen avidly to radio reports that tell them how deep the snow is, whether it is slushy, windblown, icy, and so on, and whether sleet, freezing rain, or hail might also be approaching. People who ski may want to determine whether each of the layers of snow on their favorite mountain is machine-made, machine-groomed, powdery, granular, loose, packed, and so on, along with how deep it is. The point is that if you care enough about the information (or about what you plan to accomplish once the information is in your possession), you can make amazingly fine distinctions. Conversely, if you don't care about the information, the distinctions can get in your way—in other words, they can be too costly to be worth making.

The equivalent, in terms of document type needs analysis, would be to compare two kinds of information and see if they're really different. For example, you might weigh having several different kinds of procedures, for example, installation versus troubleshooting procedures, against having only a single kind. It's not right or wrong to have one versus several dozen semantic components for a particular category of information; the choice simply depends on your focus for use of that information.

It may seem to you that a semantic component corresponds directly to an SGML element type, and once a team has moved on to the modeling phase, a one-to-one mapping is often the result. However, SGML markup distinctions can be made in a number of ways: with a new element, with an existing element made available in a new context, or with an attribute value, for example. The goal of analysis is only to identify the desired distinctions. The team will have the opportunity to choose their expressions as elements and attributes in the modeling phase, even if the choice seems intuitively obvious earlier in the process.

How do team members identify potential semantic components? They must extract them from sample documents and other sources. This process requires having a certain outlook that accords with the "generalized" philosophy of SGML. The following sections discuss concepts and techniques that can be useful in teaching team members to recognize potential components.

## 4.1.2.1   Recognizing Content, Structure, and Presentation

Components can reflect differing amounts of information about "meaning" versus formatting, and can be described by reference to the following categories:

- **Content-based** components indicate what the information is (or represents) in an abstract sense, and avoid implying what its ultimate appearance will be. Content-based components most closely model things from "the real world" in SGML.

  Following are examples of relatively content-based components:

      Addresses, streets, and postal codes
      Machine part numbers, quantities, and prices
      Software command names and descriptions
      Recipes, ingredients, temperatures, and preparation times

- **Structural** components make their distinctions by relying on basic characteristics of their structure and, usually, on the presentational traditions surrounding print-based typesetting and publishing. (Some people actually prefer the term "publishing" over "structural," but here we are following common usage in the industry.) Structural components are often the workhorses of markup that authors use most when composing straight "document text," but these components don't expand many horizons of document utilization.

  Following are examples of relatively structural components:

      Paragraphs
      Lists and list items
      Chapters

- **Presentational** components describe precisely how the information should look, without implying any notion of meaning (in the real-world sense). Its entire definition can be said to consist of **processing expectations**: requirements and constraints on the formatting or other processing of the document content. Presentational components can harm a document's ability to be utilized in various creative ways and are usually antithetical to the SGML philosophy; their place is usually in the stylesheets or other applications that process SGML documents for output.

Following are examples of relatively presentational components:

> Phrases that have a specified font or point size
> Regions to keep on a line or page
> Places at which to break a line or page
> Indented regions

People looking at information can interpret it in any of the three ways (or as some combination), which can result in the identification of different components. Because of this possibility for variation, the design team members need some guidelines on which to base their interpretations. First, they must realize that any information about a component that has not been made explicit in the component's definition is *unpredictable*—not consistently available to users or applications. For each potential component, the team needs to ask "What characteristics of the information should be most predictable?"

Table 4-1 lists some examples of alternative interpretations of component collections.

**Table 4-1**    Component Interpretations.

| Content-Based | Structural | Presentational |
|---|---|---|
| Machine part description entry, machine part number, quantity of part in stock, price of part | Table row, cell in row | Three-column text aligned horizontally, with each horizontal group separated by a 1-point rule, the second column starting two inches in and the third column starting four inches in, and with a dollar sign preceding text in third column |
| Copyright statement | Paragraph | Block of text in 8-point type |
| Software command name mentioned in text | No equivalent | Bold phrase |

**Table 4-1**     Component Interpretations. (Continued)

| Content-Based | Structural | Presentational |
|---|---|---|
| No equivalent | No equivalent | Characters that should be in small capitals to match a particular trademark owner's desired appearance |
| Introductory chapter | Division and division title with the content "Introduction" | The word "Introduction" on its own line, in 24-point Helvetica type |

On what basis can a team decide among the interpretations?

The content-based components allow for prediction of what the information means, but the information's appearance may be variable. For example, command names could just as easily be rendered in Courier font as in boldface. For another example, machine part information could be presented as selective hits returned from a search rather than as static tables, or could be arranged in a nontabular way. If the project goals include multiple presentations for the data or flexibility in retrieval or processing, content-based components are best.

The structural components allow for prediction of the information's organization at a crude level, but little or nothing is known about the contents; for example, tables could contain baseball scores as well as machine part information. Also, the presentation can be somewhat variable; for example, for any one table, indent levels and horizontal and vertical ruling could be applied entirely differently. If the project goals require only a simple treatment of data, structural components can serve acceptably while protecting the data from containing unnecessary presentational markup.

The presentational components allow for prediction of the information's appearance, but its meaning and even its structure may be obscure. For example, it's easy to see that a phrase is bold, but it's impossible to tell *why* it's bold, so if you want to index command names automatically, you can't safely set up an application that finds and indexes all the bold phrases. Presentational components are best where authors absolutely need control over appearance in order to provide accurate document data (for example, providing verses of poetry in units of "lines"); otherwise, they should be relegated entirely to stylesheets and other processing applications.

Because content-based components impose relatively greater amounts of overhead on the document creation process—as the examples above demonstrate, they're typically more numerous and complex than structural components—they are most appropriate for the information that falls within the document type's specialized domain. For example, cookbooks don't usually contain complex postal addresses. If some addresses appear in a cookbook, the design team can fall back on a structural component (say, a "general-purpose display") to hold the foreign information.

In general, opportunities for content-based components shouldn't be passed over lightly because these components, when appropriately turned into markup models, can help you increase the processing potential of your document data. However, often the simplest structural components can bring benefits to documents that were once encoded with system-specific markup, and they may also be more readily accepted by users.

Before people must identify real components, they need some practice. It can be helpful to examine documents from an information domain that is far removed from the one that will be under discussion so that attitudes towards decision-making aren't frozen into place early in the project. We've had success using restaurant take-out menus and newspaper articles in training sessions. For example, examine the menu fragment shown in Figure 4-1.

**Figure 4-1**    Restaurant Menu for Component Exercise.

Some people see the menu as having a general-purpose structure, with a repeatable structural component called "menu section" and another component called "menu section title" labeling the contents: soups, steamed dishes, and so on. Other people see a content-based component for "soup" information, another for "steamed dish" information, and so on. Depending on the goals of the project, either interpretation could be valid.[2]

People who use WYSIWYG systems commonly interpret the menu as a document formatted in one column, with text appearing in various fonts and point sizes and with a graphic symbol next to certain lines. However, these aspects of the menu are all transient. The layout and fonts could be changed without making the document content unrecognizable as a menu. Therefore, such items can often be rejected out of hand as true semantic components. If there is doubt about any one of them, it can be recorded as a potential semantic component and then examined more closely. Likewise, the numbers next to the dishes and the special symbols that indicate spicy dishes are artifacts of the formatting characteristics of this printed version of the menu. Different numbering systems such as letters (or no numbering system at all) could have been chosen instead. Spicy dishes could have been indicated with red type or small chili-pepper graphics.

The goal of the exercise is to draw abstractions at least to the point of recognizing the notions of "menu entry," "dish name," "dish price," "dish spiciness," and so on, rather than those of "number," "line," and "graphic symbol." (Note that if the menu being examined had used a rating system for indicating exactly how spicy a dish is, a "level of spiciness" component would be advisable, rather than just a component for "whether the dish is spicy." This more precise component might need to be considered even in the current case if the planned utilizations suggest it.)

The following checklist can help team members uncover potential semantic components.

### Discard Purely Presentational Items

If a formatter can provide a piece of printed information automatically, and the information or its presence changes depending on the chosen layout, it is probably presentational and not necessary to consider as a semantic component.

Examples might be page numbers and regularly appearing product logos.

Typically, processing applications can automatically add presentational effects based on other markup that will be present. If you're unsure, you can retain the component until the late stages of modeling and then ask the application developers to review the situation.

---

2. We'll discuss an alternative kind of content-based interpretation in Section 6.3.

## Identify Single "Source" Components for Repeated Information

If copy editors are currently checking laboriously for consistency of information when it is printed in multiple locations, the information probably needs a *single* component that records the information once, so that a formatter can retrieve it and output it in each location.

Examples might be running text, such as headers or footers that repeat a chapter title, print the release date of a product, or display the document's security status. Examples might also include tables of contents that repeat the titles and captions of blocks of information in the main body.

## Identify Components for Retrieved Information

If a piece of information can be retrieved from an existing or planned database rather than being typed in and checked by copy editors, the information most likely needs a content-based component.

Examples might be part numbers, trademarked terms and their owner-attribution notices, and glossary entries.

### 4.1.2.2    Recognizing Nested Containment

The notion of hierarchical containment is frequently a difficult one to understand, especially if many of the team members are familiar only with WYSIWYG word-processing systems. It can be helpful to practice finding nested organizations of components by circling them directly on a printed document.

For example, people with only WYSIWYG experience might at first view the menu text pictured in Figure 4-2 as a flat series of titles, various types of dishes, and descriptions, as indicated by the circles.

For purposes of uncovering SGML requirements, a more useful way to view the same text would be to recognize the larger—and smaller—logical containers, as shown in Figure 4-3.

Often, for divisions of document content such as sections and chapters, the markup system that was used previously would call a section title a "heading" with a level number attached, often leading to the impression that a section *is* merely the section heading. It can be an eye-opener to show how the entire section can be considered a large container that associates all its content with the heading text.

Most word processors have no notion of "styles" that contain other "styles," so the concept of containers with only other containers inside them can be a major stumbling block. Many SGML-aware editing products have capabilities that can illustrate the power of this kind of containment in dramatic ways, for example, collapsing and expanding containers at arbitrary levels, or simultaneously displaying both expanded and collapsed views of

**Figure 4-2**     Restaurant Menu with Flat Structure Identified.

the same document. Making such software available as part of the team training can be extremely effective, even if the software used for training will not be used in actual document creation.

The following checklist can help team members uncover nested organizations of components.

### Identify Labeled Components

If you have found a descriptive title or label, consider whether there should be a component for the information that is described by the label.

Examples might be titles on document divisions, notes to readers, and figures, which imply the presence of components for the divisions, notes, and figures themselves.

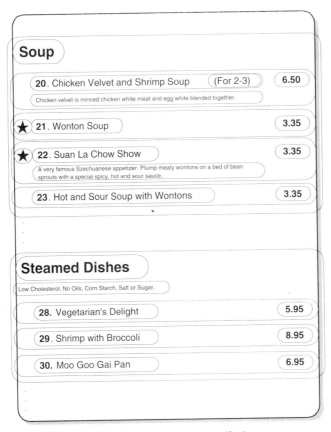

**Figure 4-3**    Restaurant Menu with Nested Structure Identified.

### Identify Container Components for Whole Series

If "one or more" components can occur, consider whether there should be a component that contains them.

Examples might be almost anything. If you tend to describe the individual pieces as a "series," "set," "collection," or "list," it is almost certain that you need a containing component with that name.

### Identify "Block" Components

If several components appear in a group and have a significant order, consider whether, taken together, they represent a higher-level component.

Examples might be pairs of glossary terms and definitions, which may imply the presence of a glossary entry component.

### 4.1.2.3　Learning about Tag Abuse Syndrome

Authors and others in charge of marking up documents are prone to a condition that we call **Tag Abuse Syndrome**, which manifests itself in using and applying markup improperly. Often the cause is time pressure or lack of training, but a poor DTD design will exacerbate the problem. Either way, the result is a poor-quality information base that can't be exploited in the ways originally intended.

The usual symptoms of Tag Abuse are as follows:

- Choosing markup solely for its formatting effect in a certain processing environment; for example, using a `publication-date` element for copyright information because the style sheet happens to output date information at the lower left corner of the title page, a location that an author might prefer for the copyright notice

- Failing to mark up information for which proper markup exists; for example, using a `paragraph` element that begins with the string "Note:" rather than using a `note` element

- Using several different kinds of markup inconsistently because they produce the same formatting in a certain processing environment; for example, switching back and forth between `emphasis` and `foreign-phrase` elements to get simple italic text, even if the word isn't foreign

- Using multiple elements indiscriminately because the author doesn't understand the distinction; for example, using `copyright` and `trademark` elements as if they were the same

The team members should understand how their work can have an effect on Tag Abuse. A DTD can encourage good markup practices by offering the right amount and depth of markup for the job, with only one way (where possible) to mark up any one kind of information. For now, the team members simply need to be aware of the need to justify the presence of all individual components that they propose in step 1, and to justify them in more depth when they select components in step 4, because excessive or duplicated markup can harm rather than help the documents.

## 4.1.3　Learning the Tree Diagram Notation

The tree diagram notation first shown in Chapter 2 will be an important part of the analysis and modeling efforts. The team should be introduced to tree diagrams at this point, though they won't yet be doing actual modeling tasks that use the notation. (They might use it to document existing DTDs that have a bearing on step 3 of the analysis work, however.)

This book contains many examples of tree diagrams, and Appendix B provides reference information on the notation.

## 4.1.4    Scoping the Work

If the design team hasn't yet been presented with the specific reasons for the SGML project, this presentation should be given now. The team needs to prepare an initial list of **design principles**, statements that will guide the team's decisions. If no recordist has been assigned yet, the team needs to choose someone to fulfill this duty. The assignment can rotate among team members.

The initial principles set the tone for the work of choosing potential components, and they also contribute to the building of derivative principles later on. Each design principle must be written down concisely and must be agreed on by the entire team. If agreement proves impossible, the team will fail in its mission to design a cohesive set of document type requirements because the goals will be ambiguous—and each team member will work towards only the set of goals with which he or she personally agrees.

The following questions can help distill the project information into a few brief answers. It's a good idea to assign each principle a short identifying label, as shown here, so it can be referred to conveniently during the analysis and modeling work and from within the document analysis report.

- What documents fall under the scope of the SGML project?

  For example:

    **Scope:** The project covers user documentation and internal specifications for the computer systems we sell.

  The scope principle often gains additional detail during the analysis process, as people suggest marginal components. In this way, the team can avoid wasting time on potential components that are clearly outside the scope. For example, questions such as the following might arise: "We said documentation was included; are training materials included? How about quick reference cards?"

  Note that the number of "document types" as such won't be determined until after the modeling phase is complete. For example, the scope principle won't state whether user guides, reference manuals, and product specifications are one document type or three.

- What are the immediate and potential uses for the documents? What is the "least common denominator" utilization that would place the most constraints on the markup model? What are the ultimate goals for our use of SGML for these documents?

For example:

> **Document utilization:** The manuals will be exchanged with business partners in draft form and will be prepared for both book (paper) and simple hypertext (CD-ROM and Internet) delivery. Eventually, we plan to generate sophisticated hypertexts from the same information.

The document utilization principle will guide the team in determining where on the "content–structure–presentation" continuum the components must generally fall.

It's important to clarify the boundaries for document utilization early on. Often, the "visionaries" on the team suggest uses of the document data that are so futuristic that they aren't yet supported by arguments for a return on the SGML investment. On the other hand, the "pragmatists" often feel uncomfortable with innovative uses for document data that they haven't yet seen with their own eyes. (A person can be a visionary about some topics and a pragmatist about others!)

- What will the method(s) for document creation be? What is the "least common denominator" creation method that would place the most constraints on the markup model?

For example:

> **Document creation:** Articles will be created and marked up with unstructured text editors such as vi. Whole journals will be assembled by the journal editor with the help of SGML-aware authoring software.

The document creation principle shouldn't unnecessarily constrain the analysis and modeling work, but can be used to let the DTD implementor know about conditions that can affect variants or adapted versions of the reference DTD, as well as markup minimization requirements.

- Who is in the audience for the DTD(s)? Who will use the DTD in document creation?

For example:

> **DTD audience:** The DTD(s) we develop will be used by people in the Documentation and Marketing departments of our company, as well as those same departments of our business partners in the Widget Consortium. Also, our data entry subcontractor will use the DTD.

The audience principle can affect the modeling decisions made later about how lax or rigid the element content models are and can help the DTD implementor determine how to prepare the DTD for customization. The extent to which Tag Abuse is expected to be a problem might shape the audience principle or might suggest the creation of another principle that demands a certain level of proof for components.

- What is the model for management of the documents?

For example:

> **Document management:** Chapter-sized chunks will be stored in the database for assembly into whole manuals. Databases for legally required notices will be used in building books so that we can meet our legal obligations.

The document management principle can contribute to the discussions about how content-based the document type design should be. It can also help the DTD implementor determine how many DTDs to build and what their architecture should be.

## 4.1.5  Planning to Prepare Deliverables

In every document type design team in which we have taken part, we have reached a point where we had to ask ourselves: "Why did we make this decision about this component?" Everyone on the team was a well-trained professional and each decision had been carefully weighed at the time it was made. However, a month later, no one could remember what the reasoning had been. We would then start the discussion all over again, and whether or not we came to the same decision, *it was usually wasted time.*

Therefore, you can imagine the situation several months or even years later, when all members of the design team have scattered and the original DTD implementor is gone. In this case, oral tradition is not very helpful. What you usually have is a pile of bug reports and enhancement requests from the current users of the DTD and nothing with which to compare them, nor any rationale for why things were done as they were originally.

This is why it's crucial, as a first step, to record all suggestions and decisions along the way so that the team can see progress through the design work and avoid revisiting topics or decisions already discussed. This requirement forces everyone to clarify their ideas, and it helps all the team members understand quickly what the problem is about. Overall it saves the team a lot of time, and since everything is already in writing, it is easy to keep track of each intervention. (Section 3.4 suggests some ways to keep the design process efficient.)

It is of no use to try to keep every document flawless before the design work is done; it would be too time-consuming and not at all cost-effective. But when it is finally over, you need to sort, clean up, and finalize the mass of documents you have accumulated by consolidating all the information into a **document analysis report**. This report will be used intensively by reviewers to validate the process and the decisions that were made, as well as by DTD maintainers and application developers.

The reviewers are not SGML experts, nor are they modeling experts. The report must therefore be understandable to them (for example, by avoiding technical SGML jargon) and practical enough to relate to their document writing experience (for example, by using familiar terminology).

Because of the importance of terminology, the design team should keep a project glossary that defines all the special terms the members use. The glossary is a useful tool for the entire project group. For example, it should define SGML technical terms used in the report to help any nontechnical reviewers, and any jargon specific to the targeted information domain to help the DTD implementor (if unfamiliar with the domain) and any reviewers who work outside that domain. It should also define any terms or phrases that the team chooses for labeling the concepts it invents during the course of the work.

For example, in work we've done on a computer documentation project, we found it appropriate to define, among others, the following terms:

- "PCDATA" to help nontechnical reviewers understand the requirements that included #PCDATA specifications

- "Volume" to help DTD implementors understand the way multiple manuals were typically grouped into sets

- "Spike" and "chip," terms we concocted to describe our complex interchange situation, to help all reviewers understand our use of these terms

Also, if you are part of an international corporation and need the requirements for the DTD to be reviewed abroad, make sure even the simplest words are well defined to avoid cross-cultural ambiguities. For instance, in the same project as the one described above, European reviewers had a hard time understanding what the American people were calling an "example." For the Europeans, an example was a fact or a thing illustrating a general rule. However, in American "computer English," it was generally accepted that an example was a piece of program code. Of course, no foreigner would have a clue if this meaning of the word were not documented.

After the report has been reviewed, there is often a pile of alterations and enhancements to be included in the requirement specifications. Make sure they are inserted in the report even if the implementor has started coding and you just intended to tell him/her orally about the necessary changes. You need to write down the team decision in each case with the rationale for it, especially if the team decides against the change. The request will probably come up again soon, and it is important to know why it was refused in the first place.

While the report is being reviewed, the reviewers often ask for more information or for explanations. If these comments are received while the design team is still holding meetings, make sure to record the questions and answer them in the final report. If the question was asked, however trivial, it means that some further explanation was needed.

DTD implementors and maintainers use the document analysis report in different ways than the reviewers do. The implementor will base all of the implementation work on this report, so what is important here is not the language or the reasons why you require something, but the completeness of the document and the precision of your requirement specifications. Make sure to include in your report all the additional information you give the implementor in response to verbal or written comments and questions, since obviously this information was missing and it is necessary for the maintenance phase.

Example 4-1 shows the typical contents of a final document analysis report with the needs analysis documents stored in an appendix as "background material."

**Example 4-1**   Contents of a Typical Document Analysis Report.

1. History of the Cookbook DTD Project
2. Design Principles
    Scope
    Document Creation

  ⋮

3. Requirements for Cookbook Hierarchy Elements
4. Requirements for Recipe Elements
5. Requirements for Low-Level Elements

  ⋮

A. Tree Diagram Quick Reference
B. Needs Analysis
    Component Forms
    Component List/Matrix
    Element Forms
    Context Population Matrices
    Element Collection Forms
    Sample Structures

  ⋮

Project Glossary

## 4.1.6    Learning About Teamwork Norms

Successful teamwork is related to both using the steps of the methodology properly and getting in the right frame of mind. Team members should heed the following advice.

### Embrace Change

In some cases it's appropriate to revisit decisions. The classification work in particular requires fluidity because as the team's understanding of a concept grows, boundaries can shift.

### Defer with Confidence

It's tempting to start doing modeling work in the analysis phase. However, the purpose of analysis is to gather data rather than decide on any structural requirements or make decisions about whether something is an element or an attribute. If the answers are obvious, it means only that the final decisions can be made quickly when the team is in the modeling phase.

By waiting, you gain a more complete understanding of similar components that should have similar treatment. In this way, you can avoid many "religious" arguments about design. In addition, it's more efficient to collect all the needs before changing over to the modeling work.

### Record As You Go

The team is wasting time and money if people can't remember exactly what was decided previously or why they decided it. The team should get into the habit of recording all decisions and rationales, even (perhaps especially!) the obvious ones.

### Remember the Power of Names

As the team develops its own unique jargon for the concepts that come up in discussion, it's important to choose names for them that are intuitive and don't have too much "baggage." For example, if you call a section a "head," team members and reviewers might tend to misunderstand and think this term applies to the title or heading of the section rather than to the section itself.

Often, people from different departments or companies use different words for the same concept. Sometimes the team may need to choose terms that are halfway between one usage and another in order to avoid superficial disagreements that prevent the process from moving ahead. For example, in computer circles, some people can nearly come to blows over whether a certain kind of computer language construct is a "parameter," an "argument," or a "qualifier." If all are agreed that the construct under discussion is the same thing, it might be best to temporarily pick a *fourth* name unrelated to the three choices, define it in the glossary, and move on.

The process of naming should always be followed by making an entry in the project glossary so that reviewers will understand the team's reports.

### Avoid Writing the DTD

In both the analysis and modeling phases, it can be tempting for people who *can* write element declarations to start doing so. However, it's crucial that work done by the team be understandable by all team members and all reviewers, not just by people qualified to be DTD implementors. Section 2.2 offered several reasons why the modeling work should be expressed in ways other than

SGML markup declarations. However, the most important reason, as far as teamwork is concerned, is that using DTD code is unfair to the nontechnical people on the project.

Furthermore, a DTD is much more than a markup model. If any prototype declarations *are* written, it should be understood that they won't be used directly in the final product, because many other factors must be taken into account in constructing the DTD.

### Respect All Contributions

Expert systems that encapsulate artificial intelligence are built in much the same way as document type design requirements—extracting the knowledge of human experts who have real-life experience. The cognitive scientists who build these systems have learned that the extraction process can become highly emotional and personal, because the experts have invested a great deal of themselves in their chosen field. So it is with document type analysis and modeling.

It's important to remember that all the team members were asked to participate on the team for the unique contributions each can make. Listen carefully to the contributions of the others and respect their right to participate, even if you disagree with what they are saying.

### Be Systematic

If the DTD project has been properly launched, the steps, processes, report deliveries, and review cycles have been planned and documented. Don't discard the project framework once you start doing the actual design work; sticking to the workflow roadmap will give you an advantage in completing high-quality work on schedule.

## 4.1.7    Gathering Analysis Input

If the information that will serve as input to the analysis hasn't already been supplied, the team members need to help gather it. After a discussion about the kinds of input that would be useful, each person should take on a "homework assignment" to locate one or more particular sources of information, become familiar with them before group-based analysis begins, and make copies of them for other team members if appropriate.

The following checklist suggests possible sources of analysis input. The team will need to determine the importance of each source to the project goals.

### Document Samples

Unless the scope of the project describes a small, closed set of documents (such as a set of ten ancient literary texts), it's impractical to analyze *all* the documents in the scope. If there are many other sources of input, the team can choose fewer sample documents, but if there are few or no other sources, the team needs to analyze as large and diverse a set as time constraints allow. If no documents exist yet, collect the plans or storyboards for their creation and design.

### Specifications and Documentation for Existing Markup Systems

This might include information on the markup systems currently in use, any DTDs on which the DTD resulting from the design work must be based, and any DTDs already available for the scope covered by the project.

For example, authors might currently use a set of Word for Windows styles or $T_EX$ macros, or even other DTDs. These sources of information shouldn't be overlooked; they often provide the most interesting insights into subtle document type requirements.

### Specifications and Documentation for Existing DTDs

If your project involves customizing or revising an existing DTD, your work will have several constraints that don't normally exist and the design process will differ from a project to develop a new DTD. Chapter 7 describes how to incorporate DTD analysis into your work.

If you don't have a requirement to use a certain DTD as a starting point, be careful not to base all the design work on an existing DTD simply because it exists. Often, real needs can be overlooked in the rush to save time and money by using an existing DTD. This is why we suggest that existing DTDs and analyses be given a thorough look only after the initial gathering of requirements. Section 4.2.3 provides more information.

### Contractual or Legal Standards for Document Delivery or Interchange

For example, U.S. Securities Exchange Commission filing statements must follow certain rules when filed electronically. These rules should have a priority in the analysis of a document type for filing statements, and may even need to be examined before the project launch to ensure that they are feasible and that different sets of requirements don't conflict with each other.

### Formatting and Editorial Style Guidelines

Formatting guidelines can be analyzed to reveal many underlying structural or content-based guidelines. For example, a style guide that specifies that the first division in a manual must be called "Preface" and must not be numbered implies that prefaces should be considered as a separate semantic component.

**Product and Document Usability Studies and Bug Reports**

These sources indicate how people actually use the documents, which can help identify where opportunities exist for more precision in markup so that customers can locate and access information in a more thorough or helpful way.

Of course, bug reports for the document production system itself are particularly useful for revisions of existing DTDs. Section 11.1 discusses the tracking of the production system in more detail.

Often, the best sources of input are more intangible than actual documents you can pick up and look at. The experience of the team members themselves, combined with an in-depth understanding of the desired ways in which the information will be put to use, is often the best source of all. First, for every document that can be examined under the constraints of an analysis session, each person working in the field has probably come across dozens or hundreds of others, whose characteristics they can introduce into the discussion. Second, any ideas for utilizations that were impossible in the existing processing environment won't easily come to light through examining existing documents.

Later in this chapter, we discuss techniques for eliciting wholly "creative" requirements, the evidence for which can't be found in a pile of existing documents.

## 4.2    Performing the Needs Analysis

Now it's time for the design team to get to work. Section 4.2.1 discusses the first step, identifying potential components. Section 4.2.2 describes how to classify them. Section 4.2.3 discusses validating the list of components against other work.

We've tried to make the steps as clear as possible and to provide simple examples, but keep in mind that the creativity and ambiguity of all but the most trivial document text can complicate analysis. You should plan on tolerating some indecision, tentativeness, and iteration in the process.

Depending on the number, complexity, and familiarity of samples and other input sources and the SGML modeling experience of the team, analysis can take from one or two days to several weeks. If the team members feel comfortable splitting up some of the analysis work among themselves and performing it individually or in pairs before or between team meetings, the work can proceed more efficiently. In fact, it can be useful to break into pairs containing one person with more experience in the documents they've been assigned and one with less, since each sees things in a different light. However, the analysis results will still have to be correlated in a group setting.

To keep track of all the information collected about semantic components, the recordist needs to keep an online or paper-based record of each component. These component forms will later be assembled into the needs analysis report and, when all their fields are complete, will provide a historical record of the analysis in the final report.

Component forms have several fields, most of which are filled during analysis. Figure 4-4 shows a blank sample of a component form.

**Component Form**

Component name: _____ Number: _____

Definition: _____
_____
_____

Classes: _____

Explanation and examples: _____
_____
_____
_____
_____

Existing markup: _____     _____
                  _____     _____
                  _____     _____

- - - - - - - - - - - - - - - - - - - - - - - - - - - - - - - - - - - - - - -

Accepted: _____

Rationale: _____
_____
_____
_____
_____
_____
_____

SGML markup/related elements: _____
_____

Creation/change history: _____
_____
_____
_____

**Figure 4-4**　　Semantic Component Form.

The explanation of the fields in Table 4-2 also serves as a map for the analysis work. In the following sections we'll show you examples of how the fields might be filled in.

**Table 4-2**    Fields in the Component Form of Figure 4-4.

| Field | When Filled In | Description |
|---|---|---|
| Component name | Step 1 | A short, descriptive name for the component. It's important that this name be intuitive and that it have as few confusing associations as possible. If you choose an unusual name, define it in the project glossary. |
| | | Avoid determining your list of potential components by working from a single existing markup language. Doing this may result in a set of components that reflects too many of the faults of the existing language. |
| Number | When the component is stable | A unique number for referring to this component during analysis and specification. If you are working on paper, keep in mind that any numbering system you supply will periodically be interrupted by new entries (or by reorganization, if you organize the forms according to their provisional classes). In this case, you may want to wait until step 4 to assign numbers. |
| Definition | Step 1 | A clear, brief definition of the meaning or role that the component serves. When a component is proposed, the team should define it before doing any further analytic work on it. Reaching agreement on the definition is crucial. Even seemingly trivial components, such as "paragraph," can provoke interesting and controversial discussions about their meaning. |
| Classes | Step 2 | One or more key phrases placing the component in appropriate logical classes and subclasses. As the definition work moves to classification work, increasingly detailed classes of components will emerge. As you feel you understand a component sufficiently, record the team's current views on its classification. If you're working on paper, keep an eraser handy! |

**Table 4-2**     Fields in the Component Form of Figure 4-4. (Continued)

| Field | When Filled In | Description |
| --- | --- | --- |
| Explanation and examples | Steps 1 and 2 | Supporting documentation that proves the component was found in the analyzed data. Provide further explanation or definition here as necessary, and reproduce or point to examples of cases where the component is used. If a proposed component is new and doesn't exist in current documents, the purpose is to explain what this new component could have been used for.<br><br>If you're able to describe examples of how the component's inner structure or outer context is typically structured, do so here with outlines or sketches. |
| Existing markup | Steps 1 and 2 | Equivalent forms of this component in any related markup languages that are under examination. For example, if the documents in the scope are currently produced with a set of word processor styles, each component should list any styles that are intended to represent or format that component's information. This information is helpful in ensuring that the analysis is complete, and it can also help in specifying the requirements for conversion and autotagging software. |
| Accepted | Modeling phase (step 4) | A Yes/No indication of whether the component has been accepted as a "need."<br><br>Why record so much information about components that may not be accepted? First, if you haven't rejected a potential component out of hand by the time you've defined it, the likelihood is high that it, or a similar or related component, will make it into the final requirements. Second, you can't accept or reject a proposed component until you understand it thoroughly enough to recognize the costs and benefits of doing one or the other. Finally, information about components that have been found to be marginally outside the scope can be fed into later, more ambitious projects. |

**Table 4-2**    Fields in the Component Form of Figure 4-4. (Continued)

| Field | When Filled In | Description |
|---|---|---|
| Rationale | Modeling phase (step 4) | All the reasons supporting the decision to accept or reject the need for the component. The rationale should refer to specific design principles and project goals in support of the decision. The process of selecting components often spurs the need to clarify existing design principles or add new ones. |
| SGML markup/related elements | Modeling phase (step 10) | A brief description of the markup with which an accepted component was ultimately distinguished, for example, the name of the element, attribute, or attribute value, and a description of the unique contexts that match this component's purpose. Filling in this field signals how the need was met and can help developers of processing applications understand how to access information correctly. When the numbers of the relevant element forms (described in Chapter 5) are known, they should be filled in here. |
| Creation/ change history | Maintenance phase | The date the form was first filled in, and the dates and brief descriptions of subsequent changes and additions. |

Throughout the following sections describing the analysis steps, we'll use, as an example, a hypothetical project to develop a cookbook DTD. The imaginary company CookThis, Inc. currently produces packets of index cards with recipes printed on them that it sells through telemarketing. It wants to expand its offerings to printed cookbooks and electronic recipe hypertexts.

For this project, the main analysis data comes from the following sources:

- Several dozen recipes marked up in a simple `troff`-like markup language used by CookThis, several of which we'll reproduce here. A processor that interprets the markup produces PostScript-formatted series of index cards.

- Editorial and internationalization guidelines for printed cookbooks, written by the CookThis editing staff in preparation for the migration.

- Usability studies on electronic recipe query sessions by users, the results of which you can see at the end of Section 1.4.

The CookThis document type design team has agreed on the following initial design principles:

- **Scope:** The scope includes individually published recipes for food dishes, along with cookbooks whose main content is organized sets of these recipes.

- **Document utilization:** The recipes will continue to be printed on individual cards and assembled into packets. The whole cookbooks will be printed and will also be made available as searchable hypertexts as part of a larger CD-ROM product to which we are contributing.

- **Document creation:** Contributing recipe authors will send us diskettes containing recipes formatted with word processors, or hardcopy recipes that must be scanned or typed in. In-house recipe authors will use the SGML-aware editor we've acquired. Each cookbook editor will contract for any necessary conversion.

- **DTD audience:** The DTD(s) will be used directly by in-house recipe authors and cookbook editors.

- **Document management:** The recipes will be stored individually in our database, and will be assembled into different cookbooks based on their characteristics. The framework text for each cookbook will also be stored individually in the database.

Furthermore, the project goals suggest using DTD fragments that are already supported in a wide variety of authoring and processing software, with the anticipation that an existing table model can already be used. Thus, with the advice of the DTD implementor, the team has added information on CALS tables to their analysis input, to be examined closely in step 3.

In this chapter and in Chapter 5, each step will be followed with a summary of the most important points to remember in performing that step.

## 4.2.1   Step 1: Identifying Potential Components

Some potential recipe components can be identified easily through simple observation; others need more imagination, and are often suggested by the project's anticipated document utilizations. Here, we'll examine several recipes and other data and identify some (though certainly not all) potential components in them, beginning to fill out the component forms in the process.

We've picked the smallest practical example that still has the richness of a typical DTD development project, and yet, as you'll see, the number of potential components can be nearly overwhelming.

The simple markup language used to produce these recipes is called `rcard`; it is documented in Table 4-3. Note that `rcard` is not a contextual language, so the markup can appear in any order and configuration according to common sense. However, the language is relatively declarative, and obviously identifies some important content-based characteristics of recipes.

**Table 4-3**    `rcard` Markup Language Documentation.

| Markup | Description |
| --- | --- |
| `.TI` *title* | Title of recipe |
| `.SO` *source* | Source of recipe |
| `.IN` | Start of ingredient list |
| Line of text inside ingredient markup | Item in ingredient list |
| `.EN` or `.TE` | End of ingredient list |
| `.NO` [*text*] | Note title (the default title text is "Notes:") |
| `^` | Typeset degree symbol (for example, `350^F` would produce "350°F") |
| [*n-*]*num*/*denom* | Fraction (for example, `1-1/2` would produce "1½") |
| Lines of text outside ingredient markup | Paragraph of text; a blank line signifies the start of a new paragraph or other construct |
| `#` | Start of comment line to be ignored in the output |

For example, the markup and content for the cookie recipe shown later in Figure 4-6 is as follows:

```
.TI Meringue Cookies
.IN
1/8 tsp salt (3 shakes)
3 egg whites
3/4 (generous) cup sugar
1 tsp vanilla
1 pkg chocolate chips, coconut, or whatever (optional)
.EN
Mix salt, egg whites; beat until stiff peaks form.
Slowly beat in sugar; you'll feel the mixture getting stiff.
Fold in vanilla (and chocolate chips).
Preheat the oven to 300^F.
Drop cookies onto greased, floured sheet.
```

```
Bake for 30 minutes.
.NO Other uses:
Cookies are good crumbled on top of ice cream.
.NO Variations:
Use rum instead of vanilla!
```

Figure 4-5 shows a recipe for chicken in its printed form.

---

### Debbie's Chicken
*Deborah Brown*

**Chicken breasts, cut up**
**Flour/salt/pepper mixture**
**Oil for browning**

**Red peppers**
**Artichoke hearts**
**Mushrooms**
**Garlic**
**Shallots**

**Caper/olive mixture**

**Chicken broth/wine mixture**

**Egg noodles**

Optionally marinate the chicken breast pieces. Shake them with flour, salt, pepper, and optional seasonings (such as basil or parsley) to coat. Cook in just enough oil to brown them—no more than 1 Tbs oil. Set the chicken aside.

Cut up the vegetables, making sure to remove stray chokes from bottled artichoke hearts. Saute— peppers first, artichoke hearts and mushrooms last. Season with finely chopped garlic and shallots.

Make a mixture of minced capers (about 1 tsp), chopped olives (a couple per person), and optionally one piece of finely chopped sun-dried tomatoes. Add it to the nearly cooked vegetables.

Add the chicken and liquids, optionally adding a bit of lemon juice and more herb seasonings. Boil the liquid and then simmer to thicken with the flour coating; add liquid as necessary to make a sauce.

Cook the pasta, drain, and top with the chicken mixture.

---

**Figure 4-5**     Sample Chicken Recipe.

Table 4-4 lists the components that might be identified so far.

**Table 4-4**    Components Identified from Figure 4-5.

| Component Name | Definition | Explanation and Examples |
| --- | --- | --- |
| Recipe | A complete description of how to prepare a dish, with food ingredients and instructions supplied | The general structure of a recipe appears to be: ingredients first, then instructions. |
| Recipe title | The official label for the recipe | Every sample recipe has a title. Titles can be fanciful (as in "Debbie's Chicken"). |
| Source of recipe | The person or institution contributing the recipe | |
| Ingredient list | A collection of information about the food substances needed for the recipe | The general structure of an ingredient list is one or more ingredients, listed in approximately the order in which they'll be needed for the preparation of the dish. Some ingredients can be further subgrouped.<br><br>Note that in this recipe, many optional ingredients are mentioned in the text that are not listed in the "official" ingredient list at the top. The way this recipe has been organized and written may later be a problem for full document utilization, even if an ideal DTD were constructed to hold ingredient information. |
| Ingredient sub-list | A subgrouping of ingredients | Not all the ingredients in this recipe need subgrouping. |
| Ingredient | A food substance required for the recipe | Each ingredient is listed on a separate line. In this recipe, ingredients don't have amounts. Sometimes a description is provided to give context to the ingredient; for example, this recipe lists oil "for browning." Also, some "ingredients" are actually a mixture of individual food substances that must be combined as part of the process. |

**Table 4-4**     Components Identified from Figure 4-5. (Continued)

| Component Name | Definition | Explanation and Examples |
|---|---|---|
| Number | A part of an ingredient's amount | This recipe doesn't mention amounts in ingredients, but the instruction text does contain some more precise amounts, with numbers. |
| Instruction list | Collection of directions for producing a dish | In this recipe, the instructions are an ordered series of blocks of text, each constituting one major step. |
| Instruction step | Single major phase in the preparation of a recipe | Each step is made of a block of text similar to a paragraph. |
| Unit of measurement | A type of amount | This recipe mentions tablespoons (Tbs) of oil. |
| Recipe type | A general category into which the dish falls, typically an indication of the course in which it is served. | This information isn't recorded in the recipe, but this dish falls into one or more categories: meat dishes, chicken dishes, main dishes, and so on. Perhaps, for our retrieval plans, we might consider recording each dish's "nationality" too. |
| Preparation time | Amount of time the recipe needs for preparation | This information isn't recorded in the recipe, but the usability studies suggested that busy cooks want to know this information. |
| Yield | The number of pieces or servings the recipe produces | As for preparation time, this may be useful information to supply. |
| Recipe cross-reference | Mechanism to help the reader find a recipe related to the current one | This recipe mentions chicken broth, and we have a recipe for homemade chicken broth, which suggests that a link between the mention and the recipe would be helpful. |

Figure 4-6 shows a recipe for cookies.

---

### Meringue Cookies

**¼ tsp salt (3 shakes)**
**3 egg whites**
**¾ (generous) cup sugar**
**1 tsp vanilla**
**1 pkg chocolate chips, coconut, or whatever (optional)**

Mix salt, egg whites; beat until stiff peaks form. Slowly beat in sugar; you'll feel the mixture getting stiff. Fold in vanilla (and chocolate chips). Preheat the oven to 300° F. Drop cookies onto greased, floured sheet. Bake for 30 minutes.

**Other uses:**
Cookies are good crumbled on top of ice cream.

**Variations:**
Use rum instead of vanilla!

---

**Figure 4-6**    Sample Cookie Recipe.

Table 4-5 lists additions and changes that might be made to the component forms.

**Table 4-5**    Possible Component Form Revisions.

| Component Name | Definition | Explanation and Examples |
|---|---|---|
| Source of recipe | | Not every recipe has a source. |
| Ingredient sub-list | | Not every ingredient list uses sublists. |
| Amount | | Amounts appear to be used in the contexts of both ingredient components (for example, "3 eggs") and instruction steps (for example, "bake for 30 minutes"). Not all ingredients have amounts listed, or at least amounts that are precise enough to be measured. One ingredient even has the notation "(generous)" in it. |
| Number | | Note that the rcard markup has a special feature for producing fractional numbers, which are common in ingredient amounts. This recipe has some fractions. |

**Table 4-5** Possible Component Form Revisions. (Continued)

| Component Name | Definition | Explanation and Examples |
|---|---|---|
| Degrees | The heat setting of an oven for baking | Note that the `rcard` markup has a special feature for producing the degree symbol for oven settings. This recipe needs this symbol. But is it an acceptable presentational component, or is it simply another unit of measurement? |
| Unit of measurement | | This recipe adds cups, packages, degrees Fahrenheit, and minutes to the kinds of units of measurement. |
| Ingredient optionality | Whether or not an ingredient is required in preparing the dish | The last ingredient line has the text "(optional)" at the end, suggesting that this ingredient doesn't need to be added. (Looking back, the instruction text in Debbie's Chicken also suggests that some ingredients not yet shown in the list are optional, so there's strong evidence that this component exists.) |
| Ingredient alternative | A suggestion for equivalent ingredients, or ingredients that achieve a different effect | This component may be related to ingredient optionality. Meringue Cookies allows chocolate chips, coconut, or a substance of the cook's choosing. Also, the recipe variation supplied in the same recipe suggests another simple ingredient substitution. |
| Instruction step | | This recipe seems to have only one major step. If it had been written differently, it could appear to have more steps, which perhaps would be more appropriate. |
| Note | A cautionary admonition or suggestion for serving the dish | The `rcard` markup suggests this component. This recipe has two notes. The general structure of a note seems to be a title followed by a block of text. (So far it's unclear whether notes are part of a recipe as a whole or part of the recipe instructions specifically.) |

**Table 4-5**      Possible Component Form Revisions.  (Continued)

| Component Name | Definition | Explanation and Examples |
|---|---|---|
| Note title | A descriptive label for a recipe note | The Meringue Cookies recipe has two different notes, neither of which uses the default note title set up by the `rcard` markup. Do these titles suggest that instead of structural notes, these should be content-based "serving suggestion" and "variation" containers? |
| Instruction optionality | Whether or not a task is required in preparing the dish | Part of an instruction in this recipe is in parentheses and corresponds to the optional ingredient, suggesting that the instructions are textually "conditionalized" for the two circumstances. |

Figure 4-7 shows a recipe for chocolate cake.

**Chocolate Cake**

6 eggs
250 grams dark chocolate (Nestlé is suggested)
190 grams sugar
3 Tbs flour
125 grams unsalted butter

Icing:
125 grams dark chocolate
3 Tbs heavy cream or crème fraîche

Preheat the oven to temperature setting 7 (210° C or 425° F).

Melt the chocolate with 3 Tbs of water on a slow fire. When it is melted, add the butter. Meanwhile, beat the whites of the eggs until they form stiff peaks.

Take off the heat and add the beaten egg yolks, the sugar, and the flour. Then fold in the egg whites very slowly, so as not to crush them.

Pour the batter into a buttered nonstick mold and bake for about 40 minutes.

Unmold as soon as it comes out of the oven and let it cool.

Icing:
Melt the chocolate with 3 Tbs of water. Add the heavy cream and stir to a smooth consistency.

After icing the cake, refrigerate it for 2 hours before serving.

**Figure 4-7**      Sample Cake Recipe.

Additions and changes listed in Table 4-6 might be made to the component forms.

**Table 4-6**     Further Revisions Based on Figure 4-7.

| Component Name | Definition | Explanation and Examples |
|---|---|---|
| Ingredient sublist | | Some sublists have titles. |
| Ingredient sublist title | Short description of a collection of some of the ingredients needed for a recipe | This recipe identifies the ingredients for the frosting separately, though the process for making the frosting is simply part of the whole cake-making process. |
| Instruction title | Label on an instruction to explain its purpose | The step for making icing is labeled in this way. It could be evidence of a "subrecipe" component, but we have chosen to interpret it this way. |
| Trade-marked term | A term "owned" by someone or some organization | One of the ingredients in this recipe mentions the trade name of a kind of chocolate. We need to track uses of trademarks so that we can give proper attribution to the owner and add trademark symbols as appropriate. |
| Degrees | | This recipe uses an absolute heat setting from 1 to 10. Perhaps this component should be broadened, so that users of the hypertext version can switch between absolute settings and Fahrenheit and Celsius measurements, depending on how their ovens are marked. |
| Unit of measurement | | This recipe adds absolute heat settings and grams to the kinds of units of measurement. |

In addition, while we don't show the analysis input for it here, some of the potential components that can be identified for the overall structure and contents of entire cookbooks are listed in Table 4-7.

**Table 4-7**    Possible Components for Cookbooks.

| Component Name | Definition | Explanation and Examples |
|---|---|---|
| Cookbook | A packaged collection of recipes and related information for sale as a unit | The general structure we expect cookbooks to have is: preface (if any), then acknowledgments section (if any), then several recipe sets, then appendices (if any). |
| Cookbook descriptive information | The major identifying information about the cookbook, usually found on the title page | All the printed cookbooks will have title pages. But will our hypertext version have them? Therefore, let's not call it a "title page." |
| Cookbook title | The official label for the cookbook | For example, "Dishes from the Far East." |
| Editor(s) | The one or more people who were responsible for compiling or writing the cookbook's contents | Every cookbook has at least one editor assigned to it. |
| Legal information | The copyright notice and other legally required notices, usually on the copyright page that backs up the title page. | All the printed cookbooks will have copyright pages. But will our hypertext version have them? |
| Cookbook copyright | Information about the holder of the copyright | We own the copyright on the entire publication. Copyright information includes the owner and the year(s) the work is copyrighted. |

**Table 4-7**　　　Possible Components for Cookbooks. (Continued)

| Component Name | Definition | Explanation and Examples |
|---|---|---|
| Individual recipe copyright | Information about the copyrights held on individual recipes and the publisher's permission to use them | We sometimes reproduce recipes from other publications, with permission. Is this information part of the cookbook or of the individual recipe? |
| Trademarked term attribution | Acknowledgment of the owner of a term or phrase used in the text | Sometimes we mention brand names of cooking implements or prepared food, which names we must credit to their owners. For example, Nestlé is a registered trademark of the Nestlé Food Company. |
| Preface | An introduction to the cookbook as a whole and how to use it effectively | We plan to supply a preface for all our cookbooks. |
| Acknowledgments section | Text thanking recipe contributors and other assistants in the creation of the cookbook | We will probably supply an acknowledgments section for most of our cookbooks. |
| Recipe set | A major division of the cookbook containing closely related recipes | We may or may not number the sets. The general structure of a set is: an introduction, then the recipes, possibly with a preceding small introduction on each. |
| Recipe set title | Descriptive label for a recipe set | For example, "Chicken Dishes." |
| Recipe set introduction | Paragraphs and other material describing the nature of a recipe set | Every recipe set will have an introduction explaining the relatedness of the recipes. |

**Table 4-7**    Possible Components for Cookbooks. (Continued)

| Component Name | Definition | Explanation and Examples |
|---|---|---|
| Individual recipe introduction | Paragraphs and other material describing the nature of a recipe | Some recipes will be introduced specially. |
| Paragraph | A block of prose text | General-purpose paragraphs are different from instruction steps and so on, in that they can contain any kind of information. |
| List | Collection of related small pieces of information | In introductions and so on, lists (for example, of cooking implements that should be on hand) might appear. These are different from ingredient lists and instruction lists in that the list can contain any kind of information. |
| List item | One small piece of information in a collection, made of a block of text | These might be, for example, the individual cooking implements. |
| Illustration | A line drawing of a concept or cooking utensil | For example, we intend to illustrate julienne technique with drawings. |
| Photograph | A real-life picture of a finished dish or ingredient | The recipe sets may show a sampling of dishes produced by the recipes in the set. |
| Caption | A brief explanation of what's going on in the illustration or photograph | For example, "Old-Fashioned Flour Sifter." We're not sure if all illustrations and photographs will be captioned. Some may be relatively "incidental" to the text. |
| Table | An arrangement of bits of information along two dimensions | For example, tables containing measurement equivalents in different systems might go in an appendix. |

**Table 4-7**　　Possible Components for Cookbooks. (Continued)

| Component Name | Definition | Explanation and Examples |
|---|---|---|
| Appendix | A collection of information supplementary to a recipe set or the cookbook as a whole | For example, a cookbook might have an appendix for measurement equivalents or information on companies where certain cooking implements and ingredients can be found. |
| Appendix title | The descriptive label for an appendix | For example, "Sources of Exotic Ingredients." |

Following is a checklist of analysis tasks that shouldn't be overlooked, with comments on how they relate to the work done to date on the CookThis DTD project.

### Set Limits

For all highly complex structures, sometimes it can be a great temptation to analyze the data to the ultimate degree, and it's hard to know where to stop. For example, ingredient measurements can probably be made as complex as the energy level of the team allows. You might want to set a time limit for such discussions in the analysis phase, and let the issue mature naturally as you move to the modeling phase.

You should also assess, before spending a great deal of time on analysis, whether the information is directly related to your information domain and how much tools support will be available for processing it. For example, it is of more value to analyze "measurement equivalence tables" than tables in general. The facilitator and DTD implementor can help team members do this assessment, and in step 3 can provide information on any standard DTD fragments (such as for tables, mathematical equations, and electronic review) that might be applicable to the information.

In the CookThis scenario, the team has determined that its focus isn't on sophisticated uses of tabular information, but it could have been otherwise. For example, if the hypertext cookbooks were supposed to offer a facility for interactive computation of measurement equivalents, it would have made sense to have special markup for equivalence tables.

### Be Open to Component Ideas

Component ideas can come from anywhere. For example, the ingredient optionality component was generated from the observation that certain text seems especially significant.

Some components may suggest other obvious components. For example, the cookbook copyright information contains "owner" and "year" information—possibly two new components. And the trademarked term component may have been what suggested the idea of a trademark attribution component.

Any respectable component idea that arises in discussion should be given its day in court. For example, if the team can imagine that it's useful to put *exact* ingredient amounts in boldface type to distinguish them from *approximate* amounts, it's worthwhile to add the measurement precision component for consideration. (Alternatively, the team may decide to cast the two components in terms of an exact amount and an approximate amount.)

### Recognize Cloned Components

Some components might be better off collapsed into a single entry early on. All components should have unique names, so the repeated components should be either collapsed or distinguished by the end of step 1. In addition, any components that overlap each other in purpose or meaning should be sorted out in step 1. For example, an earlier version of the recipe components might have had "items" instead of "steps" as the contents of the instruction list, but later distinguished them from general-purpose list items.

If you have some doubt about how much distinction exists between components, don't collapse them; they may simply be good targets for creating functional classes in step 2. The component names that have been chosen may hint in this direction. For example, a "figure caption" may seem similar to a recipe title, but the fact that it is known by a different name suggests that there may be differences in structure or usage.

### Abstract Away from Presentation

Some component ideas might appear to be quite presentational in nature. Rather than dismiss these components out of hand, when you define them be sensitive to ways to make them more abstract. The components for cookbook descriptive information and legal information would have obscured useful ways of using the data if they had been thought of as "pages." For example, although a printed cookbook's title page might display the cookbook title, other places, such as the readers' comments form in the back, might reproduce the same information. The title isn't just a "title page" phenomenon.

### Document What You Find

The component explanations and examples should be as thorough as possible, since they can provide useful information for many parts of the DTD development process. For example, the description of the ingredient component describes some of the supplementary information (the purpose of the ingredient in the recipe) that might be present in what otherwise might seem to be a simple ingredient specification. This bit of background can be helpful in further analysis and in the DTD documentation.

For components with obvious "content models," provide descriptions of how their content is likely to be structured. This information will be fed into the modeling work. For example, recipes and cookbooks both have notes on the structure of their content. Likewise, it's helpful to record questions about the context of a component, as is done for notes.

### Acknowledge Fuzzy Boundaries

Differences between writing styles can be problematic as you try to fit semantic components into neat packages. For example, the explanations of the instruction-related components show that it's hard to identify the boundaries between one step and another, and it's even hard to tell how "major" or "minor" a step is. There's plenty of opportunity to ponder these issues before an answer must be forced in the modeling phase, but if a certain direction becomes clear during the analysis discussions, it should be recorded and agreed to. For example, if you can easily agree that any two wholly sequential tasks must be marked up as separate major steps, record it in the component's definition. Often, new design principles will arise out of these discussions.

### Go Beyond Printed Samples

Once the obvious components have been identified, it is useful to have brainstorming sessions to identify potential components that can help meet the project's more sophisticated goals for document utilization. This process is sometimes called "enriching the data" because it involves considering markup for information that authors haven't yet supplied. Some of the component explanations hint at the possibilities. For example, the recipe type component might suggest to the team that knowing whether a dish is vegetarian or not is useful. Should this component be considered? What about each dish's "nationality" or origin (and how does this differ from the "source" information)? Should precise nutritional information per serving be supplied for each recipe?

In order to move to step 2, the team should feel that it has extracted all the reasonable candidate components it can think of, and it should have completed at least the following component form fields. However, component forms can still be added at any time, and field values can be modified or expanded.

- Component name

- Definition

- Explanation and examples

- Existing markup

Furthermore, any phrases coined by the design team and any specialized uses of terms should be defined in the project glossary.

---

### Step 1: Identifying Components

1. Identify and thoroughly define all the potential semantic components.

2. Record the examples that prove the existence of the components in the analysis input being examined.

### Tips

- Unless a suggested component is obviously out of place, accept it in your deliberations. Wait until later stages to cross inappropriate components off your list.

- Pay special attention to proving the existence of wholly new components.

### Formalisms

- Fill in the "Component name," "Definition," "Explanation and examples," and "Existing markup" fields in the component form for each component.

- Build a simple list of all the potential components.

- Define new terms in the glossary.

---

## 4.2.2    Step 2: Classifying Components

Step 2 involves continuing to analyze the components by sorting them into classes and subclasses.

The classes can be entirely of the team's design, reflecting whatever content-based and structural similarities the team members observe among the components. For example, a list-component class might represent variations on a theme from which authors might choose when marking up "enumerated" information. The modeling phase will superimpose a common set of superclasses on the components in order to help the modeling work proceed in an organized way, but you may find that the added classes bear a strong resemblance to some you've already constructed in this step.

Sometimes no natural home can be found for a component. However, we've found that attempting a thorough classification has several advantages.

- It clarifies any remaining misunderstandings about the components and can bring to mind missing components and new places to apply existing ones.

- It can eliminate unnecessary components. The grouping of seemingly similar components can reveal that they are actually *identical*, whereupon they can be collapsed.

- It allows similar components to be treated similarly in the modeling work (as well as allowing the resulting markup to be treated similarly by processing applications where appropriate).

- It begins the modeling process that will be conducted in earnest in the modeling phase. By the time you finish the classification work, you'll probably have strong suspicions about the nature of the markup many components will end up with (though you should wait until the actual modeling phase to determine the outcome for all components).

- It will later help the DTD implementor to structure the DTD for easy maintenance and customization.

Following is one possibility for classification of the recipe and cookbook components identified in Section 4.2.1. The components are indented to show their approximate hierarchical relationship, which begins to suggest how they might be structured when they are expressed as elements and attributes in the modeling phase. Some elements are in multiple classes. The "Classes" fields in the component forms should be filled in with the class names shown here.

**COOKBOOK STRUCTURE**
Cookbook
  Cookbook descriptive information
    Cookbook title
    Editor(s)
  Legal information
    Cookbook copyright
    Trademarked term attribution
  Preface
  Acknowledgments section
  Recipe set
    Recipe set title
    Recipe set introduction
    Recipe
  Appendix
    Appendix title
**RECIPE STRUCTURE**
Recipe
  Recipe title
  Source of recipe

Recipe type
Recipe preparation time
Recipe yield
Recipe copyright
Recipe introduction
Ingredient list
Instruction list
Note
**LISTS**
Ingredient list
 Ingredient sublist
  Ingredient sublist title
  Ingredient
  Ingredient optionality
  Ingredient alternative
Instruction list
  Instruction step
  Instruction optionality
  Instruction title
List
  List item
**TEXT-BASED BLOCKS**
Note
  Note title
Paragraph
**PICTURES**
Illustration
  Caption
Photograph
  Caption
**TABLES**
Table
**SIGNIFICANT DATA**
Number
Degrees
Unit of measurement
Recipe cross-reference
Amount
Oven setting
Trademarked term
**LABELS**
Cookbook title
Recipe title

Recipe set title
Appendix title
Note title
Ingredient sublist title
Caption

Make sure to record your chosen classes in the component forms. If you invent any terminology in naming your classes (for example, "significant data"), define them in the project glossary.

---

**Step 2: Classifying Components**

Classify the potential semantic components according to your sense of their similarities.

**Tips**

- Some components may be in multiple classes, and some classes may have subclasses.

- In this activity, intuition is better than tortured intellectual discussions. Classifications are typically obvious, and if they aren't, don't worry about making really fine distinctions.

**Formalisms**

- Fill in the "Classes" field in the component forms.

- Optionally, organize the list of potential components according to class.

- Define new terms in the glossary.

---

## 4.2.3   Step 3: Validating the Needs

Step 3 offers an opportunity for the team to examine its list of potential components in light of any DTD work that has been done for similar documents, if such work exists.

The reason this comparison is done third, rather than first, is that looking at material developed by other people can bias the results of your own work. Once the team has begun to develop a working style and has charted a course, looking at similar DTDs can remind the team members of obvious components they missed and help them resist adding components for which they honestly see no need.

Why not just start with an existing DTD and change what needs to be changed, rather than going through steps 1 and 2? In some cases, discussed in Chapter 7, the project may indeed have specified constraints and requirements that suggest customizing an existing DTD rather than starting from scratch. However, needs analysis is still required for that process. Also, the time and cost savings of starting with an existing DTD are often over-rated because the goals of the designers of the original DTD don't match those of the vari-ant-DTD designers.

Along with examining DTDs that already exist for the information domain of the project, it may be appropriate for the team to examine existing DTD fragments that might be able to be used whole, such as tables, mathematical equations, and constructs for electronic review of documents. The facilitator and DTD implementor can help with this examina-tion. In the case of the CookThis project, the DTD implementor has suggested the CALS table fragment, and has spent some time describing its characteristics and how it com-pares to other table fragments supported by specific software vendors. Ultimately, the team felt comfortable accepting the CALS model.

One task to which you should pay particular attention at this point is comparing the defi-nitions of similarly named components, elements, and word processor styles. Often the same terminology is used for radically different things, and you may want to consider aligning your terminology with accepted industry practice, if there is sufficient precedent.

At the conclusion of step 3, the team members have a pile of forms describing all the potential markup distinctions that the model needs. For convenience in the modeling and specification steps discussed in Chapter 5, the recordist should compile a list of all the component names, possibly with their existing markup equivalents next to them arranged in a matrix for quick reference.

---

### Step 3: Validating Needs

Compare your analysis so far with other similar efforts, if they exist.

### Tips

- Don't accept someone else's analysis if you don't understand it. Ultimately, any markup models you design either will be useful because they reflect your deep understanding of your information, or will represent a waste of time and money because no one knows what they're for.

### Formalisms

- Refine the component forms and list.

- Define any new terms in the glossary.

# 5

# Document Type Modeling and Specification

The goal of the modeling and specification phase is to peruse all the potential components and to turn them into a specification for an exhaustive and coherent markup model for the document type. The output of this phase is a document analysis report that records both the specifications for the model and the process undergone to reach them.

Chapter 4 explained how the design team identified potential needs and classified them into logical categories. This chapter takes the team through the design and reporting portions of the work, which include:

- The preparation for the modeling work (described in Section 5.1)

- The modeling and specification steps (described in Section 5.2)

- The production of the document analysis report (described in Section 5.3)

- The eventual updating of the model (described in Section 5.4)

We continue to assume a project where a new document type design is being created. For information about the process of customizing an existing model and how it compares to the process for a new DTD, see Section 7.1. Chapter 6 offers specific advice about modeling considerations.

## 5.1  Preparing for the Modeling Work

Unlike the analysis phase, where all ideas and suggestions are welcome and studied with interest, the modeling phase involves making choices and decisions. It can be a difficult time because it generates a number of conflicts, with each member having a personal interest in backing his or her ideas. At this point, it may be useful to reaffirm the decision model under which you operate.

Team members need to consciously keep an open mind and remember that anybody's requirements, as long as they are properly supported, are likely to become requirements at some point for the departments that the other team members represent.

At the same time, you need to avoid the effects of a design team that is too cohesive—exhilarated by their work and their power to model all future documents, so that they want everybody in the company to work the way they decided. DTDs are not perfect models to be admired in a rarefied atmosphere, but tools to be used daily by people in the field, whom the team members have a responsibility to represent.

As a consequence, purity may have to give way to efficiency and theoretical principles to be replaced by down-to-earth, practical recommendations. Team members will need to abandon their fond hopes of imposing their personal views of writing style through the DTD. (Section 6.4 discusses some ways to test whether a proposed model is too prescriptive.)

These efficiency-driven attitudes must be recorded in new principles each time a general rule is formulated for how decisions must be made. As you will find out, the number of principles will grow significantly in this phase of the work, but it will also significantly help the decision process because you will be actively ranking the various trade-offs, for example, the opportunities for consistency versus the intuitiveness of a model.

Of course, your principles must reflect the project's overall goals. At this stage, it is useful to remind the team members of what those goals are. For instance, if the company intends to switch to electronic distribution, whether on CD or on line, and a marketing survey shows that customers expect no less than state-of-the-art multimedia features, any team member claiming that "we do not need a video element because we have never produced a minute of video in this company" is wrong. The company intends to do it in the near future and will need hooks for incorporating its video clips within documents.

Similarly, the team needs to remember the constraints on the project and integrate them in their decision process. For instance, if the company has decided not to build any kind of document management system and expects each author to handle his or her own work on a workstation, then the granularity of the DTD will probably have to be the book or the manual, and cross-document cross-referencing becomes useless. Also, if the company has a very strict policy on labeling safety or security information, the team would need to ensure that automatic label generation is enabled by the chosen markup model. (Section 6.7 discusses some of the complexities of preparing for generated text.)

The role of the facilitator will become ever more challenging as the work progresses. It will be crucial for the facilitator to make sure that all members have a chance to express their opinions, that decisions are made after each discussion, and that work keeps to the schedule without constant revisiting of decisions. The role of the recordist is also more complicated because discussions are likely to be animated and complex, and this person must not only record the gist of the discussion, but also make it understandable for non-specialists and ensure that all relevant points are transcribed faithfully and completely. If possible, team members should review the interim reports between meetings and offer corrections at the next meeting.

## 5.2  Performing the Modeling Work

Up to this point, the team members have catalogued the potential semantic components by defining them, classifying them, and validating them against other analyses that have been done. Thus, the upper half of all the component forms is complete. To keep track of all the information collected during the modeling phase, the team will fill in the bottom half of the component forms, and will also use tree diagrams (described thoroughly in Appendix B) and some new forms, the main one of which is the element form. We'll introduce the others as we go along.

Element forms keep track of information on the modeling of the elements. Along with the component forms, the element forms will later be assembled into the document analysis report and, when all the fields are complete, will provide a historical record of the design in the final report and a reliable basis for the writing of the DTD's reference manual.

The element form can be thought of as a continuation of the component form, particularly in cases where an accepted semantic component is represented directly by a single whole element type in the resulting model. Each element form refers to its corresponding component forms by their numbers to avoid duplicating relevant information, and it is fully filled out only after the actual DTD is implemented, so that information such as the generic identifier (the "tag name") can be filled in.

Figure 5-1 shows a blank sample of an element form.

Table 5-1 explains the fields and also serves as a map for the modeling work. In the following sections, we will refer regularly to the element form and give examples of how it can be filled in.

**Table 5-1**      The Element Form Fields.

| Field | When Filled In | Description |
|---|---|---|
| Element name | Steps 5 through 8 | The full name of the element; a phrase that describes it uniquely. |
| Number | When the element is stable | A number given to enable cross-referencing from and to the corresponding component forms. |
| Generic identifier | After DTD implementation | The generic identifier; the short form of the element name that is actually used in tags. |
| Class(es) | Steps 5 through 8 | The one or more classes into which the element falls. Make sure to include its superclass: document hierarchy, information unit, data-level, link, or special. |

## Element Form

Element name: _____  Number: _____

Generic identifier: _____

Class(es): _____

Model:




Contains: _____
_____
_____
_____
_____
_____
_____

Rationale: _____
_____
_____
_____
_____
_____
_____

Is contained in: _____
_____

Related components: _____
_____

Creation/change history: _____
_____
_____

**Figure 5-1**    Element Form.

**Table 5-1**      The Element Form Fields. (Continued)

| Field | When Filled In | Description |
|---|---|---|
| Model/Contains | Steps 5 through 8 | A concise and clear description of the internal structure of the element, plus the corresponding tree diagram if appropriate. |
| Rationale | Steps 5 through 8 | All the reasons why the element was modeled this way, including, for example, why "wrapper" elements were created or not, and why subelements were optional or not. |
| Is contained in | Steps 5 through 8 | A description of where the element can be found elsewhere in the model. It can be expressed in words with a list of parents, with one or more tree diagrams if the number of parents is very limited, or with a table when the potential contexts are numerous. Many elements will not have an answer for this field until step 8. |
| Refers to components | Steps 5 through 8 | The numbers of the component forms where the initial semantic components that this element represents were thoroughly described. This field helps to avoid duplicating useful information. |
| Creation/change history | Maintenance phase | The date the form was first filled in, and the dates and brief descriptions of subsequent changes and additions. |

By the end of step 3, the team members have a list of semantic components to choose from and a number of tools to help them formalize their modeling work. They can now move to step 4, where they choose which semantic components should be kept.

## 5.2.1   Step 4: Selecting Semantic Components

The design team needs to select, out of the original compiled list, the components that represent markup distinctions needed for the project at hand. To do this, the team members will probably need to make a couple of passes over the list, taking care of the easy cases first. Throughout this process, the facilitator and recordist must work in tandem to ensure the results are fair, swiftly accomplished, immune to rediscussion, and recorded.

To make a first pass, examine the entire list of potential semantic components and select all the components that are obvious ones to be kept. For each component, the team must be able to formulate a rationale stating why this component should be kept in the model. If a component is just *too* obvious and the only rationale people can think of is "Because we need it," make sure an example has been given that demonstrates the necessity of the component.

During the review of the list, some components will seem obvious to some members and absolutely not to some others. If agreement cannot be reached within a time limit of five or ten minutes, just drop the subject and defer the contentious cases for the time being.

By the time the list has been gone through once, usually fewer than 20 percent of the components remain for a closer analysis. At this point, it pays to be highly methodical and disciplined. For each component on which the team does not agree, the team should consider the following factors based on the design principles.

### Fits Within Scope

Is the component within the defined project scope? If not, don't go any farther; reject the component. If a more ambitious project is undertaken later that includes the component in its scope, the analysis done to date will be a useful starting point.

### Isn't Too Presentational

Is the component too presentation-related to be kept? A component might be a holdover from a previous markup system that gave authors inappropriate control over appearance (such as "centered text"); these should be discarded. It might be a presentational interpretation of a legitimate component (such as "title page"); these should be recast to be more structural or content-based. Or, it might be a processing or formatting function that authors *must* have control over; these should be kept and their purpose explained thoroughly. They will probably end up being addressed in step 9.

### Enables Project Goals Today or Tomorrow

Can a team member show examples of where this component is necessary today? For example, do instances of information described by this component look different from all other similar kinds of information, or does it need to be uniquely searched on?

If not, can someone explain a legitimate future use of this component? The trick here is to be realistic; don't rely on fanciful imagined uses.

The component selection step often forces the realization that two or more components, which have survived so far as unique items, have differences so minute that examples can't be found to differentiate them. In these cases, the two components should be collapsed into one and then accepted as a single component.

For the few really tough cases where a decision can't be reached, try keeping the component and waiting for a further step to make a final decision when the team's process has matured. The team may decide to pose the question during testing and let the users decide for themselves.

Table 5-2 lists some results of the selection of components for the CookThis project. Most of the components are accepted because of their clear relevance to the task at hand; the few difficult cases and all the rejected cases are shown here.

**Table 5-2** CookThis Component Selection.

| Component Name | Accepted? | Rationale |
|---|---|---|
| Acknowledgments section | Yes | If individuals donated recipes, they must be thanked. This section is different from the preface in that we like to give the names of these people prominence, and being able to uniquely identify the place where they are thanked will help us do so. |
| Recipe set introduction | Yes | People browsing a set on the CD-ROM will want to see an overview of the set before they open the whole thing. We can also extract these for other uses (such as marketing material). |
| Source of recipe | Yes | Even though the acknowledgments section will informally mention all these people, each recipe has to be able to "travel" sufficiently all by itself when we produce the index cards. Thus, the source of each recipe (if known) should be provided with the recipe. |
| Recipe type | Yes | Knowing this information for each recipe will allow us to generate new sets based on different criteria. |
| Recipe preparation time | Yes | Busy people need to know this information, and it may be a search criterion. |

**Table 5-2**      CookThis Component Selection. (Continued)

| Component Name | Accepted? | Rationale |
| --- | --- | --- |
| Ingredient alternative | No | Many times, alternatives are just suggested casually in the text. Having a formal way of storing this information doesn't fit in with the way our recipes are structured or written. It would be too hard to get people to force recipes into the mold. |
| Instruction optionality | Yes | We clearly have many cases where a step can simply be left out. We hope to set off these steps somehow. |
| Instruction title | No | We debated this for a long time, but even though we have one or two clear cases of a seeming "title" on instructions, it's not appropriate according to our style. The text of each instruction should explain its special purpose, if any. |
| Number | No | It's obvious what a number is; any processor that had to operate on numbers could easily find them without their being marked up. As long as amounts are marked up, random numbers don't have to be. |
| Degrees | No | A degree setting is simply another kind of amount, so this is already taken care of. We'll remove degrees as a separate component and keep amount. |
| Unit of measurement | Yes | An amount is useless without the units it is expressed in. We need to be explicit about this information. |
| Oven setting | No | This is another kind of amount. This should be rejected because it is already covered. |

At the end of this step, the list of potential semantic components bears a "yes" or "no" decision in front of every component name, and each component form bears the same information in the "Accepted" field, along with the reasons for that decision in the "Rationale" field. The rationale can be a plain explanation, an example of use, the reminder of a principle, or a mixture of all three. It must be clear, precise, and definite enough to prevent any impulse to revisit the decision. The recordist should also build a new list containing just the accepted components, for convenience in the rest of the steps.

With the list of accepted classified components, the design team holds the raw material for its future work. The team can now begin to work top-down to build a model that accounts for all the accepted components. To do this, the team members will iterate over the list of components, extracting from it all the components related to each distinct layer of the document type model, and then actually model them as elements and attributes using tree diagrams. These distinct layers are the "standard" superclasses that overlay your unique classifications. We'll introduce them individually at each step so that you can concentrate on one layer at a time.

---

## Step 4: Selecting Semantic Components

1. Examine each component and decide whether you want to keep it.

2. Record the reasons for keeping it or discarding it.

### Tips

- Don't accept a component if you can't imagine doing anything realistic with it.

- Don't take shortcuts in writing the rationale.

- In cases of strong disagreement, favor keeping the component.

### Formalisms

- Add a "Y" or "N" next to each component in the list of classified components.

- Fill in the "Accepted" and "Rationale" fields in the component forms.

- Build a list of accepted classified components.

---

## 5.2.2   Step 5: Building the Document Hierarchy

The first layer to be modeled is the document hierarchy. The following sections describe the process of identifying and modeling the document hierarchy components and their related metainformation components.

### 5.2.2.1   Modeling the Document Hierarchy Components

The **document hierarchy** is our name for the class of components that represents the upper part of the document type. These components capture the essence of that type, and once they are modeled, they give a characteristic "shape" to every instance conforming to that model. As a consequence, authors usually have little choice about markup at the upper levels, though they may have a choice about how deeply to nest the basic divisions of content within the hierarchy.

The document hierarchy ends where "unspecified text" begins to appear—the locations where authors begin to have a great deal of freedom in how they structure and compose the content. (Unspecified text will remain unmodeled until step 8; we use "clouds" in tree diagrams to serve as unspecified text placeholders.) Some of the colloquialisms people use to describe this material are:

Stuff
Text
Prose
"Real" content

Figure 5-2 illustrates the document hierarchy concept.

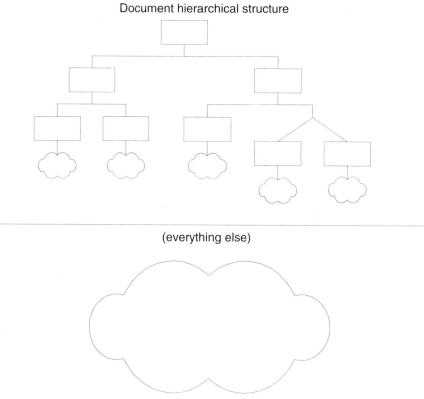

**Figure 5-2**    Identifying the Document Hierarchy Components.

The team has probably already grouped the document hierarchy components together, perhaps in a class called "structure" or "divisions." In the CookThis analysis, this class had the name "cookbook structure." If such a class hasn't already been identified, here are the criteria to find out if a component is part of the document hierarchy.

For technical manuals, academic books, novels, and any other type of document that is large enough to have a table of contents, start by seeing what's in that table. What you usually find is the way the document is subdivided. Depending on the document, the table of contents may not represent all the levels of subdivisions that the document contains. To make sure, peruse the documents' actual contents and check all the subdivisions and organizational containers of the document that you encounter against your classified component list, until you reach places where unspecified text appears.

For documents that don't have tables of contents, the process of identifying hierarchical components can be trickier, because the hierarchy may seem surprisingly flat. For instance, if you look at a restaurant menu, you have to build the table of contents in your head because it is not provided in the document. However, the mental process is the same. In all cases, check for evidence of levels of structure that are above, below, and between the levels that you can easily see.

To take the restaurant menu example a little further, here's what you might find:

- The obvious divisions might be for appetizers, entrées, desserts, and drinks.

- The obvious subdivisions of entrées might include children's dishes, vegetarian dishes, chicken dishes, and so on.

- There may be a nonobvious level of division at the top, if additional menus exist for desserts and wines and if they can sometimes be included together with the regular menu content.

Note that in this example, the components actually identified may have been structural (for example, "high-level division" and "low-level division"), or they may have been content-based (for example, "appetizer division" and so on). The discussion of levels can take place regardless of the component choices made. (Section 6.5 discusses some of the issues in modeling divisions and their nesting.)

There are some documents whose hierarchy is basically flat because they present a collection of similar information that is grouped, for clarity's sake, in only one or two levels of hierarchy. For example, dictionaries, catalogues, indexes, reference manuals, and cookbooks usually fall into this pattern. According to the CookThis analysis done in Chapter 4, a cookbook's overall document hierarchy would include little more than large sets of recipes. The number of division levels would reach a maximum of two: recipe sets and the recipes themselves.

The act of identifying document hierarchy components will have started the modeling process. To formalize it, visualize the components as elements and attributes, working top down, using the tree diagram notation to help you. This is where a large whiteboard comes in handy, so people can easily propose alternatives to a suggested model.

You will have finished the modeling work for the main part of the document hierarchy when all the branches of your tree end up with clouds representing unspecified text. You then need to record both the trees and the corresponding prose in the "Model" and "Contains" fields of a series of element forms, one for each element you have modeled.

In the CookThis cookbook model, the bulk of the document hierarchy might ultimately be described by the tree diagram shown in Figure 5-3. This diagram shows nearly the entire structure except for recipes themselves and the "metainformation" element, which we'll defer to Section 5.2.2.2. Note that where an element appears multiple times, its potential model is shown in only one place; in all its other locations, an ellipsis serves as a placeholder for its model.

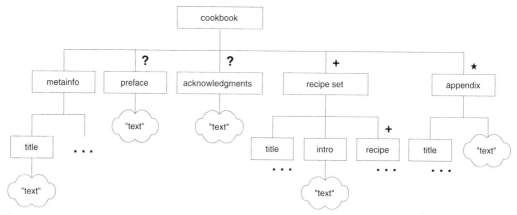

**Figure 5-3**    Initial Cookbook Document Hierarchy.

Figure 5-4 shows the detail for the recipe element's model (minus its "metainformation"). Also note that the main contents of recipes are deferred for now because they appear in other classes, and will benefit from the general treatment given those components in a future step.

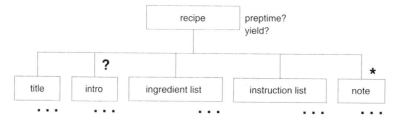

**Figure 5-4**    Initial Recipe Document Hierarchy.

This recipe structure may seem obvious, but it's worth pointing out that the results might have been very different if the recipes had used a different style. For example, one common recipe style is as follows:

> **Boil** 1 cup of rice in 2 cups water. **Season** with salt...

In general, you don't have to worry about all the structures your information *could have* used, just the ones it *does* use, so in the case of CookThis, this new style doesn't have to be accounted for. If your project requires that you account for the widely diverging organizations of content, you may want to create a separate model for each one in order to maximize the information's usefulness for various purposes.

Table 5-3 shows the filled-in "Element name," "Contains," and "Rationale" fields for the elements shown in Figure 5-3. The following fields also need to be filled in:

- In the component forms associated with the document hierarchy, fill in the SGML markup/related elements field with a precise description of the markup that resulted from each accepted component, and list the numbers of the relevant element forms.

- In the element forms, also fill in:

  Number
  Class(es)
  Is contained in
  Related components

**Table 5-3**       Filled-In Fields of Figure 5-3.

| Element | Contains | Rationale |
|---|---|---|
| Cookbook | A cookbook contains a required metainformation block, followed by a single optional preface and a single optional acknowledgments section, followed by one or more recipe sets, followed by zero or more appendices. | The metainformation is needed to identify the cookbook. <br><br> The prefatory material and acknowledgments may not appear in any one cookbook. <br><br> Our children's cookbook will have only a single recipe set, so we only need to require one. If there were zero, the cookbook would be empty of main content. Any one cookbook might have no appendices, one, or several. |

**Table 5-3**    Filled-In Fields of Figure 5-3.  (Continued)

| Element | Contains | Rationale |
|---|---|---|
| Metainformation | The metainformation contains at least the recipe title. | The metainformation is at the beginning for convenience of processing. (More on metainformation in Section 5.2.2.2.) It was decided that a container is needed to group both the descriptive information and the legal information, so that all this material will be stored in a single, easily accessible place, and we can build markup templates for authoring convenience. |
| Title | A title contains unspecified text for now. | The same title element is used to label several different elements: recipes, recipe sets, appendices, recipes, and ingredient sublists. The reason is that the context (the immediate parent) can easily distinguish them all. |
| Preface | A preface contains unspecified text for now. It is expected to have a generated label. | Since there can be only one preface, and its label ("Preface") is dictated by the corporate standards department, this element needs no title element; we have the ability to generate a label for the preface automatically, which will allow it to be absolutely consistent across cookbooks. |
| Acknowledgments | An acknowledgments section contains unspecified text for now. It is expected to have a generated label. | Since there can be only one acknowledgments section, and its label ("Acknowledgments") is dictated by the corporate standards department, this element needs no title element; we have the ability to generate a label for this section automatically, which will allow it to be absolutely consistent across cookbooks and spelled correctly every time. |

**Table 5-3**      Filled-In Fields of Figure 5-3. (Continued)

| Element | Contains | Rationale |
|---|---|---|
| Recipe set | A recipe set contains a required title, followed by a required introduction, followed by one or more recipes. Recipe sets aren't expected to be numbered. | The title is required to label the sets, since there can be more than one.<br><br>The introduction is required, so that the reason for this particular grouping of recipes will be explained to the reader.<br><br>In rare cases, such as in the Elephant Meat set in the planned Exotic Cookbook, only one recipe may currently exist in a set. At least one is required, though, or else there's no point in having a set. |
| Appendix | An appendix contains a required title, followed by unspecified text for now. Each appendix is expected to be numbered. | The title is required to label the appendices, since there can be more than one.<br><br>There are no cases of appendices that have a complex internal structure; they all just contain their main content straightaway. |
| Introduction | An introduction contains unspecified text for now. | No label is needed on an introduction, since by definition it introduces the content of the element it's in (recipe set or recipe). The same introduction element is used to label several different elements; the context (the immediate parent) can easily distinguish them all. |

**Table 5-3**    Filled-In Fields of Figure 5-3. (Continued)

| Element | Contains | Rationale |
|---------|----------|-----------|
| Recipe | A recipe contains a required title, followed by optional source information, followed by an optional introduction, followed by a required ingredient list and a required instruction list, followed by zero or more notes. | The title is required in order to distinguish recipes.<br><br>The introduction is optional because sometimes there simply isn't anything to say.<br><br>Even the simplest recipe has at least one ingredient, so a formal list should be present to help the reader know what to assemble.<br><br>Likewise, even the simplest recipe has at least one instruction, so a formal instruction list is required. |

Some components that were identified as being in the document hierarchy haven't yet been accounted for in the CookThis model: the ones that describe characteristics of a cookbook or recipe itself. These are covered in Section 5.2.2.2.

## 5.2.2.2  Modeling the Metainformation Components

**Metainformation** is information about information. For example, the metainformation for the book you are reading now might include its title, its price, its authors, its publication date, and so on—everything except its actual content about developing DTDs. Likewise, in a cookbook, everything related to cooking techniques, utensils, and recipes is content. The information about the cookbook *as a publication* or *as a body of information* is metainformation. This includes the information that appears on the cover and title page, as well as navigational devices such as the table of contents.

Metainformation isn't simply "everything at the beginning of a book"; it can include all sorts of information that might appear at the end or in other places, such as summaries, certain kinds of back matter, bibliographical references, and an index.

Also, metainformation isn't just "everything about the book as a whole." Smaller pieces of information can have their own narrowly scoped metainformation, too. For instance, a top-secret security status might apply to a whole technical manual, but it might also apply to only a single paragraph or section. Similarly, a manual can have a global abstract, but it might also contain an abstract for each chapter. Thus, each time the design team models information content, they must make sure to model the related metainformation and to keep this approach even when modeling the subdivisions of a document type and other elements.

In the CookThis example, metainformation can potentially be found at the following levels (some of which have already been modeled):

- Cookbook metainformation

  ○ Title

    Not everyone considers titles to be metainformation; because they are always output in each presentation instance, they act like real subject matter content themselves. But in the sense that they *describe* content, they can be considered metainformation.

  ○ Cookbook descriptive information with the cookbook title and the editor

  ○ Legal information with the cookbook copyright and trademarked term attributions

  ○ Preface

    Some people consider a preface to be metainformation because it introduces the rest of the document and thus serves a "meta" function. However, it also often contains real subject matter content. Like titles, prefaces have one foot on each side.

  ○ Acknowledgment section

    Like titles and prefaces, acknowledgment information can be seen both ways.

- Recipe metainformation

  ○ Title

  ○ Source of recipe

  ○ Recipe type

  ○ Recipe copyright

Once the team has identified all the metainformation components, it must model them as elements and attributes and fit them into the rest of the document hierarchy, considering whether each component makes sense at multiple levels of the structure.

It often seems, on first reflection, that metainformation components should always be represented by attributes, since a piece of metainformation "qualifies" or further describes the document element or a lower-level element. However, if the information is likely to be output along with regular document content (as titles usually are), representing the component with an element is usually the better choice, and if the information must itself contain markup, an element is the only choice. Any metainformation that records one of a set of finite states, such as a draft status of "in review" versus "complete," is a natural candidate for an attribute.

Often, the DTD implementor is the person best suited to choose, for each metainformation component, the best expression in SGML markup, based on your description of what the metainformation will be used for. Thus, it's especially important that you record, along with your modeling recommendations, the processing expectations for the metainformation. For example, if you expect part numbers to be checked by the document management system to ensure that certain fields in them have valid values, say so; the implementor may decide to use attributes to hold the different fields, with "data types" (declared values) that constrain the values so that they can be validated by parsers without development of additional software.

Because metainformation is by its nature outside the flow of document content, usually the position of its output is variable; that is, it can change according to the media. For example, in paper form, legal notices might appear on a copyright page that appears behind the title page, but in a hypertext document, a special menu item might exist for legal notices, and there might be links from every occurrence of a trademark to its related legal notice for the trademark attribution. Because of this fact, the order in which metainformation is supplied in the SGML document instance is less relevant than for the document subject matter, over which authors typically have at least some control. Therefore, the best way to model metainformation is to choose a single location where it will reside in each level of division.

To ensure that metainformation is always identifiable in instances and can be used efficiently by processing applications, it's best to put metainformation before the information to which it applies, so that the document can "tell a processing application what it's going to tell it" before it actually "tells it" what the content is. This scheme allows even the simplest applications to prepare in advance for manipulating the coming content. For interchange, it is especially useful to model metainformation elements in a fixed order, so that a wide variety of interchange partners can build different applications that reliably find all the metainformation they need and output it (or transform it to a reference DTD) in their own unique order and style.

Figure 5-5 shows a complete tree diagram for the document hierarchy of the cookbook document type, including recipes and metainformation.

The rationales for the modeling choices are as follows. Most of the cookbook metainformation has been put into elements because it is highly textual in nature and may need to be further marked up. A container element has been added to hold all the names of the editors so that the information can easily be retrieved all at once. The trademark and copyright information has also been grouped into a container element for the same reason. Some of the recipe metainformation is in attributes, and some in elements. The attributes can be used to ensure that the values supplied are acceptable to the retrieval and formatting systems. (Step 9 may give rise to additional metainformation, such as ID attributes, that may appear on multiple elements.)

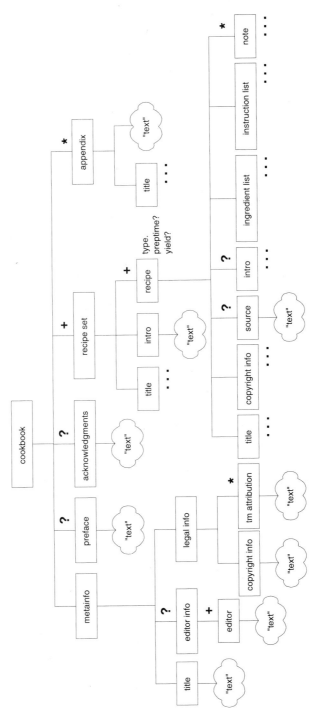

**Figure 5-5**    Complete Cookbook Document Hierarchy.

---

### Note to DTD Implementors

If you implement metainformation as attributes, put the attributes directly on the elements to which they apply (for example, the top-level cookbook element), not on any special metainformation containers (such as the metainformation element in this example). Processing applications generally make it easier for lower-level elements to "inherit" attribute values from a parent element than from an unrelated element that appears before them in the linear flow.

---

### Step 5: Building the Document Hierarchy and Metainformation

1. Extract from the classified component list the components related to the document hierarchy and global metainformation.

2. Organize them top to bottom as elements and attributes using tree diagrams, stopping when you reach unspecified text.

3. Record the results in tree diagrams and in prose.

**Tips**

- Unspecified text might be recognized by team members as the material they think of as "stuff," "running text," "content," and so on. You'll know it when you see it!

- The Contains text should paraphrase the tree diagrams and add detail on whatever can't be drawn.

**Formalisms**

- Fill in the "SGML markup/related elements" field of the component forms for the document hierarchy components.

- Fill in the "Model" fields of the element forms with tree diagrams.

- Fill in the "Contains" fields of the element forms with the "what" information, and fill in the "Rationale" fields with the "why" information.

## 5.2.3   Step 6: Building the Information Units

When the design team starts step 6, the members know what the overall hierarchical structure of the document type is like, and they have a sorted list of all the rest of the components. Most of these remaining components are related to the **information pool**, the collection of elements from which authors choose, largely at their own discretion, in marking up, organizing, and composing the "main content" of documents. In identifying the components in the information pool, you will gradually turn the large cloud in Figure 5-2 into organized classes and subclasses of elements, as shown in Figure 5-6.

Document hierarchical structure

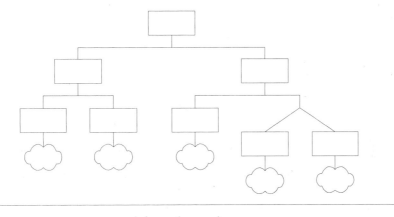

Information pool

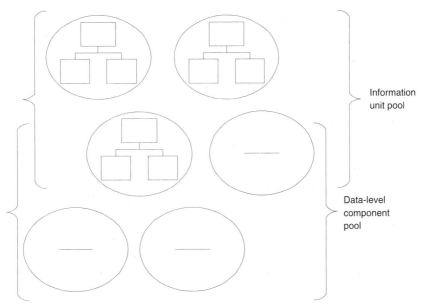

**Figure 5-6**    Identifying the Information Units in the Information Pool.

As the figure shows, the information pool tends to break down into two layers: the components associated with **information units (IUs)**,[1] and the **data-level components**. This step deals with IUs and step 7 deals exclusively with data-level components, but we'll define them both here.

An IU is a high-level component that can, to some degree, "stand alone" in order to be understood by a reader, such that its content must "travel together" during information processing and assembly. IUs also typically have a complex internal structure (represented in Figure 5-6 by a small tree diagram), and thus need to be modeled with their associated subcomponents in mind; for instance, all subcomponents related to a list would be modeled together. Even when the internal structure of an IU is more complex, like a procedure including several steps that each lists several instructions, you still know that the procedure must be considered as a whole to be correctly interpreted.

By contrast, data-level components are small, important bits of information that need to be processed or handled differently from the surrounding character data for some reason. These bits of information, all by themselves would be meaningless without their context, which almost always consists of prose. They rarely have any complex internal structure.

IUs are sometimes called "displayed" or "block" information, and data-level components are often called "in-line" information. However, these presentation-based descriptions may be confusing and inconsistent rather than helpful; it's possible, though relatively infrequent, for some components to be part of both the IU class and the data-level class.

The design team needs to peruse the list of components and extract those it considers unique IUs, along with all the components that are obviously subparts of those IUs. Then the team can build a classified list of all the identified IUs and rebuild a list of the rest of the components to work from in the next step. Then the team needs to model the IUs in each class in turn, deciding how many elements will represent all the IUs and determining what the models for those elements are, using tree diagrams. If any metainformation was discovered in the previous step that might apply to pieces of information are smaller than the whole document, now is the time to apply them to the resulting IU markup.

Particularly in the areas that are specific to your information domain, IU modeling work is highly creative. Content-based IUs are the most interesting, but even the relatively structural components may surprise you with their controversies, and we hesitate to recommend a single paragraph, list, or quotation model to you because your situation may have special needs and constraints. Chapter 6 covers many common modeling problems and possible solutions.

The CookThis example is a simple case; the design team has determined that the following classified IUs should each be represented with its own element:

---

1. We've been asked why IUs were favored with an abbreviation and data-level components were not. It's purely historical. When modeling, we tend to call the latter simply "data" for short, which will be recognized by SGML experts as a misnomer because real data (as defined in the standard) is devoid of markup.

- In the list class:
  - Ingredient list (with ingredient sublist, title, ingredient, and ingredient optionality)
  - Instruction list (with step and instruction optionality)
  - List (with list item)
- In the text-based class:
  - Note (with note title)
  - Paragraph
- In the picture class:
  - Illustration (with caption)
  - Photograph (with caption)
- In the table class:
  - Table (with the CALS table model)

Describing the internal structure of a few common IUs can be quite easy because their structure is essentially flat. For instance, a paragraph usually immediately contains unspecified text. Most IUs are more complex and require some thought and careful recording, because there are several possible ways to structure them.

In our CookThis example, it turns out that the ingredient list IU has a relatively deep structure: An ingredient list can contain a mixture of ingredients and ingredient sublists, and the sublists can optionally contain a title and must have a minimum of two ingredients. Each sublist has an optional title and is composed of at least one ingredient. Ingredients contain unspecified text and have an "include" attribute, whose default is that the ingredient is required to be included in the recipe. The tree diagram for an ingredient list is shown in Figure 5-7.

Note that some IU components might ultimately be represented by the same element, only in different contexts or with an attribute to distinguish them. For example, it might be decided that illustrations and photographs are functionally the same kind of document information. If you want to collapse some IUs completely, remember that you have already justified keeping the distinction between them; look at your step 4 rationale for keeping the two components to remind you of why it was so important to have two instead of one. If you do collapse them, make sure to update your component forms. (Section 6.1 discusses some strategies for representing multiple related components.)

When all the IUs have been tackled, the design team needs to record, in words and with tree diagrams, the internal structure of the IUs and the reasons why such a model was designed. If the model is based on specific processing expectations, such as "There is no title on our examples because the title is always the same and will be generated," these expectations should be recorded too so that application developers will know what to do

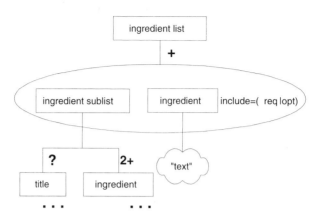

**Figure 5-7**     Tree Diagram for Ingredient List.

and interchange partners will know how to interpret delivered SGML documents. Along with filling in the "Contains" and "Rationale" fields of the element forms for each element created, the recordist should cross-reference the element forms with the component forms.

---

## Step 6: Building the Information Units

1. From the list of remaining components, identify the information units and refine their classifications as necessary.

2. Model their internal structure and content according to your design principles and the similarities of components within classes.

3. Describe the model both in words and with tree diagrams, and write the rationales for your modeling choices.

### Tips

- Unspecified text here is running text at a lower level than in step 5, but you will know it when you see it anyway (even if the text chunks are physically smaller).

### Formalisms

- Build the classified list of IUs.

- Build the tree diagrams for each IU.

- Fill in the element forms and cross-reference against the relevant component forms.

## 5.2.4   Step 7: Building the Data-Level Elements

The starting point of step 7 is the list of remaining components, out of which the design team must extract, refine the classifications of, and model the components at the data level.

To reiterate the criteria for data-level components, they need surrounding character-data context (usually a sentence) to make any sense, and they must be associated with some intended processing or special handling.

Some potential processings of data-level components include:

- Simply formatting a word or phrase in text differently, in order to set it off (for example, general-purpose emphasis or "verbatim" text)

- Giving a certain presentation to phrases according to their meaning (for example, file names, product names, and trademarked terms, which must be distinguished from the surrounding material and from each other) or according to custom (for example, dates, measures, addresses, and honorific titles, which may need special treatment in translation to other languages)

- Automatically linking words or phrases with associated information (for instance, linking all the command names in a computer user's guide with the corresponding modules in the reference manual, or linking glossary terms in text with their definitions)

- Building or assembling parts of documents based on the words or phrases found elsewhere in the document (for example, building the glossary based on the presence of glossary terms actually used in the document, or building a paper or online-retrieval index based on special technical phrases identified in the document)

For now, the team should defer components that are exclusively related to "linking," as well as any stubborn components that are highly presentational in nature. Both of these kinds of components will be addressed in step 9.

Often, more data-level components will have been accepted in step 4 than are practical for authors to use, a situation that is a major contributor to Tag Abuse problems. Now that the data-level components have been through a few rounds of analysis and classification, and the modeling process is well understood, an additional "elimination round" may be necessary.

To identify only those components that have a purpose, whether immediate or planned for the future, make sure as you model each component that it has unique processing expectations, that is, that the distinction made in the markup has a legitimate use. If some components fail this test, they can still be rejected or collapsed with others at this stage—and, of course, their component forms should record the decision and the rationale.

There are usually two subclasses of data-level components:

- The relatively "structural" components that can be found in most document types

  For example, brief quotations and emphasized phrases typically fall into this class. (Since their internal structure is usually minimal, it might be better to call them "publishing-oriented" in this instance.)

- The relatively content-based components, which have an intrinsic meaning and are usually specific to the domain of activity described by the document type

  For example, for a series of books on gardening, there might be components for soil depth measurements and the names of insect and plant species. We call this class the **key data** components. Describing the processing expectations for these components is especially critical, since much of what makes a document type uniquely useful for processing is its body of key data components.

There may also be outright presentational components at the data level, such as "font control" or "bold," which have made it to this stage of the proceedings. If you have a good rationale for keeping them, defer dealing with them until step 9.

In the CookThis example the list of accepted data-level components ("significant data") might now be subclassified as follows:

- General data

    Trademarked term
    Recipe cross-reference (which we'll defer for now)

- Key data

    Unit of measurement
    Amount

As was done for the IUs, the team must determine how the data-level components correspond to elements and attributes, and design their internal structure. Most data-level components actually don't have any complex internal structure; they can be designated as containing "unspecified text" directly. A few may have structure, though. For example, if the team is considering how to model a data-level mailing address, it may construct an address element that directly contains a series of subelements for addressee name, street number, street name, city or town, postal code, and so on, which may all finally contain unspecified text.

The CookThis team has modeled the data-level components as shown in Figure 5-8.

The trademark component has been realized as an element, and some optional attributes describing the type of trademarked term have been added so that the term can be properly attributed with a generated symbol (for example, for unregistered trademarks). The

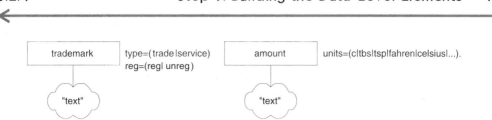

**Figure 5-8**   Tree Diagrams for Recipe Data-Level Components.

type and registration status were not originally components, but discussion has brought out a need for them, and new component forms should be added to ensure that they are sufficiently defined and justified.

The amount component has also been realized as an element. The component for unit of measurement has been realized as a required attribute on the amount element, with the processing expectation that the chosen unit will result in the appropriate generated text before or after the amount (for example, "Tbs" for tablespoons). The reasoning was that this approach will result in editorial consistency.

---

## Note to DTD Implementors

The list of attribute values for the "amount" element is incomplete. This is a common situation with the modeling of attributes, and it will require you to investigate the boundaries of the list. See Section 8.3, and particularly Section 8.3.1, for advice on handling such attribute specifications.

---

All of these discussions, expectations, models, and rationales must be carefully documented, and the appropriate element and component forms filled in.

In a few cases, a single logical component may seem to live a double life as both an IU and a data-level component. For example, often there is a need for both large graphics that appear as stand-alone units and small graphics that appear inside sentences. If you determine that they have the same markup model and should logically be represented with the same element, it may be the case that differing contexts will enable processing applications to tell them apart; a graphic inside a paragraph, for example, might be interpreted as an "in-line" graphic. If context *isn't* sufficient—for example, if you have "complex" paragraphs that are allowed to contain graphic IUs as well as data-level graphics—you will need to create two elements in order to give authors control over distinguishing one from the other.

It's even trickier to handle the case of single elements that have characteristics of both IUs and data-level components. The content of a footnote clearly counts as an information unit, but a reference to a footnote is a data-level component because it must be attached to a particular place in the prose. If the design team chooses to handle both the call for a footnote and the content of the footnote in the same element, it becomes difficult to figure out whether the footnote structure is an IU or a data-level component. For purposes of proceeding with the modeling work, luckily the difference doesn't matter too much until step 8, where we'll make specific suggestions for solving this problem. (Note that linking components are covered in step 9.)

---

### Step 7: Building the Data-Level Elements

1. From the list of remaining semantic components, identify and refine the classification of the data-level components.

2. Map them to elements and attributes, describe the content model of any elements that actually have a model other than "unspecified text," and record why it is important to differentiate their contained information from the surrounding text.

#### Tips

- Do not try to define too many data-level elements. As long as the project's needs are met, the fewer there are, the more properly they will be used.

- Data-level information is the dreariest kind of information for authors to mark up, so keep these elements simple if you can.

#### Formalisms

- Build the list of data-level components.

- Build the tree diagrams for those elements that have an internal structure.

- Fill in the element forms and cross-reference to the relevant component forms.

---

## 5.2.5    Step 8: Populating the Branches

The design team will have done a tremendous amount of work at this point. The conclusion of step 7 might be a good time to take a break and reconvene later with renewed energy, because step 8 will require the team members to change mental gears.

If you look at all your tree diagrams, there should be "unspecified text" clouds all over the place. The goal of this step is to replace each text cloud with a model: the collection of elements and/or character data allowed freely in this context (represented by an oval with either an asterisk or a plus sign on it). Each tree branch can be thought of as a unique context, and for each context the content model must be defined. We call this matching of contexts and contents "populating the branches."

This step is particularly important because it allows the team to build an interface between the major layers of the markup model for the document type. It is a long and tedious task that benefits from a matrix approach, which ensures that no context or content model will be left out. The general structure of the matrix you will be filling in looks like Figure 5-9.

The form that records more detailed information about each element collection is shown in Figure 5-10.

Following is the procedure for populating branches:

1. Gather the classified lists of IU elements and data-level elements.

2. Build two context population matrices, one intended for contexts that have IU contents and one for contexts that have data-level contents. Start building the first matrix by listing the classified IUs along the vertical axis. Start building the second by listing the classified data-level elements along the vertical axis, along with "character data." In the matrices, list each class as a major row, with minor rows beneath it showing the individual elements.

3. Go through the branches of all the trees you have built and find out what general content is possible in each context. There will be three possibilities:

   ○ A high-level collection containing IUs

   ○ A low-level collection containing character data and (potentially) data-level elements

   ○ A mixed collection containing both

   For example, the data-level matrix at this stage might look like Table 5-4.

**Table 5-4**     Data-Level Matrix at the Beginning of Step 8.

| Contexts | | | | | |
|---|---|---|---|---|---|
| Contents | | | | | |
| General Data: <br><br> trademarked term <br><br> recipe cross-ref | | | | | |
| Key Data: <br><br> amount | | | | | |
| Character Data | | | | | |

## Context Population Form

Level: _____     Page _____ of _____

| Contents | Contexts | | | | | | | | |
|---|---|---|---|---|---|---|---|---|---|
| | | | | | | | | | |
| | | | | | | | | | |
| | | | | | | | | | |
| | | | | | | | | | |
| | | | | | | | | | |
| | | | | | | | | | |
| | | | | | | | | | |
| | | | | | | | | | |
| | | | | | | | | | |
| | | | | | | | | | |
| | | | | | | | | | |
| | | | | | | | | | |
| | | | | | | | | | |
| | | | | | | | | | |
| | | | | | | | | | |
| | | | | | | | | | |
| | | | | | | | | | |
| | | | | | | | | | |

Creation/change history: _____

_____

_____

**Figure 5-9**     Context Population Matrix.

**Element Collection Form**

Element collection name: _____ Number: _____

Contexts: _____

Contents:

Rationale: _____
_____
_____
_____
_____
_____
_____

Creation/change history: _____
_____
_____

**Figure 5-10**    Element Collection Form.

Create a column entry in one or both of the two tables per branch considered, labeling it with the element name or simply numbering it. For each context, go through the list of contents on the left and check which classes or individual elements are allowed in that context, making sure to record the reasons why you chose the way you did. Link the tree diagram location and the matrix column by replacing the cloud at the end of each tree branch by an oval representing an element collection, and numbering or labeling the oval according to its corresponding column in the relevant table.

4.  Look for recurrent patterns as you work through the tree diagrams. You will probably start noticing that the same contents are appearing in several different contexts represented by different numbers in column headings. If the various contexts with the same contents have the same rationale, group them under a column with a single descriptive name, which can either reflect the common denominator of the contexts where the contents are allowed (for example, "basic division mixture" or "title contents") or, if the contexts are too diverse, the nature of the collection (for example, "just paragraphs").

    Wherever the rationales differ, even if the content model is the same, do not collapse the collections into one by giving them the same context name. Your team or other designers may later decide to alter a content model in a specific set of contexts independently of the others.

5.  Go back to the tree branches and name the relevant portions of the content model with the name of the collection. Decide whether some content is required to appear in that context or not. If content is required, mark the collection oval with a plus sign (+); if not, mark it with an asterisk (*).

---

### Note

Collections that contain character data can't be guaranteed to have content in them; parsers allow elements to contain *zero or more* characters in order to satisfy the content model. You can use a plus sign on such collections, but be aware that extra-SGML validators would be needed to actually check that there is content.

---

6.  Complete an element collection form for each unique collection, filling in the contents, the contexts where it is referenced, and the rationale for the choice of contents.

Filling in the branches becomes faster and faster as more and more contexts accept already defined collections. This fact does not preclude some contexts from being unique, in which case you can give them a name descriptive of their uniqueness, if feasible, or you can simply keep the context number written in the column headings of the context tables.

Table 5-5 shows an example of how the CookThis project's context population matrix for data-level elements might look halfway through the process of identifying and filling in "unspecified text" branches. This is a very simple markup model, but some patterns are starting to emerge. (See Section C.2.3 for an example of a complete set of context population matrices, constructed from an existing DTD.)

**Table 5-5**       Data-Level Matrix Halfway through Step 8.

| Contexts / Contents | title | editor | para | trademark | amount |
|---|---|---|---|---|---|
| **General Data:** trademarked term recipe cross-ref | X | | X | X (minus self) | |
| **Key Data:** amount | X | | X | | |
| **Character Data** | X | X | X | X | X |

When each context has been considered, its content model described, and the rationale for the design written, it is necessary to review the element forms to complete the tree diagrams (replace all the little clouds with collection names) and the rationales, and to fill in the "Is contained in" field. For some elements, filling in this field will require so many items that it saves time just to list the names collections in which they appear.

Following are a few words of advice.

### Don't Forget Processing Expectations

You usually can't explicitly control the amount of content supplied where collections are allowed. For example, it isn't practical to use markup models to require that abstracts contain "some number of paragraphs and lists, but no more than five elements total." And, of course, it's impossible to use SGML to specify that the abstract "should fit on a single page." However, if you have a specific amount of material in mind for each context, you should describe it, so that application developers can take it into account and possibly even develop additional validating software.

A typical expectation for data-level elements is that they contain "word"-sized, "phrase"-sized, or "paragraph"-sized data; usually the word-sized elements have tightly restricted contents. You could make use of this distinction in naming your data-level element collections.

### Beware of Self-Containing Elements

Some IU-related elements might themselves contain IU elements directly or indirectly (for example, list items containing nested lists), and some data-level elements might contain data-level elements directly (for example, a quotation that can contain trademarked terms). As a result, you might end up with the same element on both axes, one being the context, the other the content. This amounts to asking whether this element should be allowed to appear inside itself. If the answer is "no," but otherwise the collection (including the rejected element) is used in several other contexts, then the rejected element should be excluded from the collection as a special case.

---

## Note to DTD Implementors

Special exclusions such as these usually translate to an SGML exclusion from the content model, as described in Section 9.3.

---

### Keep "Content" and "Context" Issues Distinct

In some cases, a single element can *contain* IU elements but *appear in* data-level contexts. For example, you may have modeled a single *footnote* element as both a container for the footnote content and the placeholder for the footnote reference at the end of the word or phrase of interest. In this case, the footnote might contain IUs, which means it will have its own column in the IU context population matrix but also be available as one of the data-level elements, which means it will have its own row in the data-level context population matrix.

### Create Relatively Generous Collections

Use whole element classes as building blocks as much as is practical. Authoring, processing, and DTD maintenance will be simplified all around if you can check off whole element classes rather than individual elements, and the nature of classes will tend to support such decisions.

Also, don't be too miserly with the contents of each collection. Authors find it annoying to discover that common elements have been disallowed in certain rare contexts. Typically, the simpler contexts will contain most of the structural elements but will leave out most content-based ones. Don't exclude too many structural elements without good cause.

Of course, you will need to balance these suggestions against the benefits of having a content model tight enough to provide proper validation and good support in SGML-aware authoring environments.

---

### Step 8: Populating the Branches

1. Build two tables, one with classified IUs on the vertical axis and the other with classified data-level elements and "character data" on the vertical axis.

2. Go through each context (represented by each terminal branch of the tree diagrams where clouds appear), and identify whether IUs and/or data-level elements can appear there. Make each context the head of a column in one or both of the tables, and check off the elements or whole classes of elements that should be allowed in each context, recording the rationale for each column.

3. Number these contexts, or name them when a recurrent pattern emerges, and fill in the tree branches with ovals containing the relevant name or number, choosing the occurrence rules for each collection.

### Tips

- Don't hesitate to work back and forth between tree diagrams and context tables.

- Give the contexts meaningful names.

- Favor populating contexts with entire element classes and keeping the number of distinct collections relatively low.

- Don't give up! There is only one modeling step left.

### Formalisms

- Build and fill in the context population matrices and the corresponding collection forms.

- Complete all the branches of the tree diagrams.

- Complete the element forms.

---

## 5.2.6    Step 9: Making Connections

By now, your list of remaining components should be much smaller. What should remain are the components that are exclusively related to making connections, that is, revealing or recording relationships between pieces of information and between an SGML document and the "outside world."

### 5.2.6.1    Links

**Link** components are components that record the relationship of two or more pieces of information. Figure 5-11 represents the addition of links to the model.

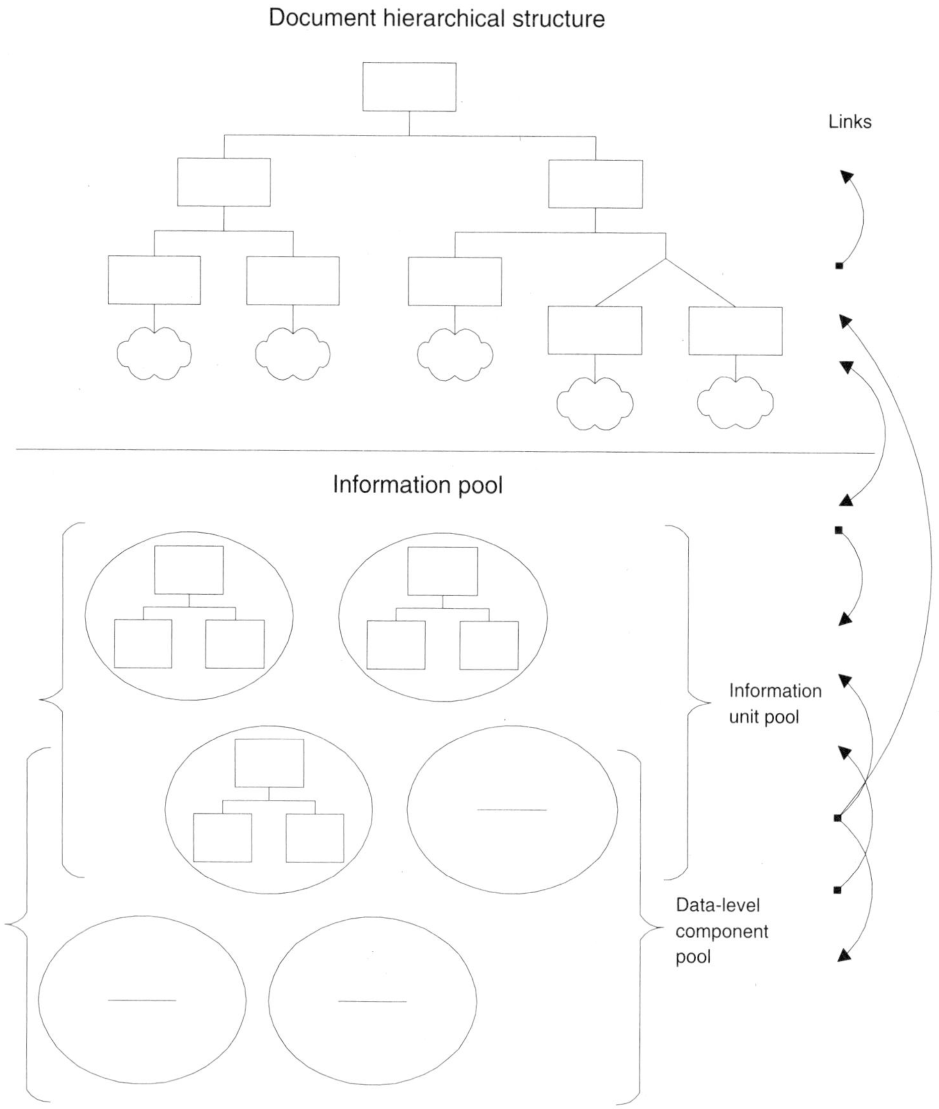

Document hierarchical structure

Links

Information pool

Information
unit pool

Data-level
component
pool

**Figure 5-11**    Identifying Links.

There are different types of links, and the recent swell of interest in hypertext and hyper-
linking has produced a variety of typologies. For argument's sake we present a simple
link classification scheme here, but you do not have to adhere to this particular scheme as
long as your own classification process is sufficient for your purposes.

There are two main types of links that the design team will need to address:

- Links that serve as instructions for content to be pulled into the document at a certain location when the document is assembled or delivered, even though the content resides elsewhere. These "include-by-reference" links are often referred to as anchor points, and they are used for pulling in, for example, illustrations and multimedia sequences; entity references of all kinds also fall into this class of links. Links such as these can be said to be relatively presentational or procedural.

- Links that connect two or more pieces of information, whether inside the same document or not, because of the inherent relatedness of their subject matter. Their purpose is to draw the attention of the readers and to suggest that they follow the link by some means (turning pages, clicking on an icon, or whatever) to browse through further related information. Textual cross-references fall into this class of links. Links such as these can be said to be relatively structural or content-based.

Some content-based links can be automated simply because of the presence of the source and target(s), like links between commands appearing in a technical manual and their corresponding reference modules, or links between terms used in a document and their corresponding glossary entries. It is possible to automate links when some sort of directory exists (or can be generated) that maps all the possible source and target points, or when either of them is generated from the other one (like tables of contents and indexes).

Other links have to be handcrafted, which means that the author has to define the source, the target(s), and possibly the type or nature of the link.

In both cases, the design team seldom knows how to design the precise markup for the links, because of the sophistication needed to architect them correctly and the changing state of the art. Consequently, the choice of markup for the linking devices is the sole responsibility of the DTD implementor. But to help this person in the task, the design team must provide a sufficient description of each relationship they want the markup to encode by doing the following:

- List all the necessary link components with all their potential source points (contexts where the source point can occur) and their potential targets. For example, for anchor-point links, the targets might include graphics, sound or video clips, footnotes, and so on. For cross-reference links, the targets might include specific points in the prose, sections, illustrations, other documents, content within those documents, and so on.

- Note the direction(s) of each link and its type, and list the possible values.

- Define which elements need to be systematically identified so as to become potential link targets. For example, each element that can be linked to probably needs an ID attribute. In fact, it's common to put optional ID attributes on most or all elements in the entire markup model so that arbitrary elements can become link targets for management and/or presentation purposes.

- Describe how the links will be used and for what purpose. For example, a link might be used to help paper navigation through the generation of page number cross-references, or to help online navigation through the creation of a hotspot that can be clicked on, or to launch the appropriate multimedia viewer to run a video clip.

- Fully describe the processing expectations. Must the links be handcrafted, or will they be automatically generated? What text should be generated in place for cross-references? What new pieces of the document might be generated for the presentation instances? For example, you may want to explain that the table of contents will be generated from the headings in the document, and that each item of the table must be linked to the relevant section. Also, specify what character strings or icons the application must generate according to each type of cross-reference, the language, and the media.

- Describe any constraints. For example, if your documents will be delivered on the World Wide Web, you should list this as a constraint, and require the links to be compatible with or transformable to the HTML linking technique and the URL identification technique.

With all the relevant information on links available from the design team, the implementor will be able to build a link architecture that is adapted to the project needs and constraints. The implementor may want to use a simple ID/IDREF method (discussed in Section 8.3.2), HyTime constructs and techniques such as architectural forms and linking indirection, or other methods. As long as the linking techniques can be implemented on an existing computer system and are sufficiently supported in the chosen authoring environment, the actual implementations of the links in the markup model will be irrelevant to the authors and users of the documents.

There is one obvious opportunity for linking in the CookThis project: recipe cross-references. The team has specified that this component must link to a recipe, with the expectations that the name of the target recipe will be generated in place and that, in a hypertext environment, the name will be a hotspot that can lead the reader to the actual recipe. This requires that all recipes be uniquely identifiable with ID attributes so that they can serve as link targets.

There are also other linking opportunities in CookThis. For example, trademarked terms might serve as anchor points for trademark attributions, so that the attributions can be assembled automatically into documents that mention the terms and can be made available to hypertext users who come across the terms. (The motivation for this link may be more for legal protection than for publishing quality!) Also, if cookbooks are expected to have paper indexes, there may need to be markup for the construction of "index hits" that can be extracted and sorted, forming links back to their original locations.

The task of building links is over when all the accepted linking components have been fully specified and their rationales and constraints documented.

## 5.2.6.2  Special Features

The motley list of remaining components are the ones that present tricky modeling issues; they constitute the "special features." Each special feature must be described thoroughly, and should be accompanied by a rationale for its usage and a list of circumstances in which it is to be used. The task of the design team is only to define the special features as best they can, because the ways to implement special features are numerous and complex and should be left under the responsibility of the DTD implementor.

One kind of special feature is related to presentational issues and other downstream processing needs, and thus usually runs counter to the SGML philosophy of purity in declarative markup. These might include presentational controls that were part of the existing stylesheet or available on the previous word processor, without which the authors and production specialists cannot achieve the proper quality of publishing. For example, there might be a component for controlling the depth to which hypertext documents will be split into individually accessible topics, or a component for controlling page breaks when the printed version is going through a copyfitting process.

Another kind of special feature is not presentational at base, though the obvious modeling solutions may seem to be presentational. For example, components for revision bars in margins, redlining, the switching of character sets for multiple-language publishing, effectivity control, and so on can be interpreted as presentational, but they can also be interpreted more abstractly—as revised regions, regions written in a certain language, or regions that apply only to one product configuration. The team should make its best attempt to interpret these features as content-based and to describe the processing expectations.

---

### Note to DTD Implementors

Depending on the circumstances, any of the following might be appropriate for special features, and the answers might be different for reference DTDs and authoring DTDs:

- Attributes on existing elements

  For example, elements could have language and locale attributes that indicate to processing applications that special character sets, spell checking, and so on are necessary. Or, there could be global effectivity attributes to indicate the "flavor" of presentation instance in which the element content should appear.

---

## Note to DTD Implementors  (Continued)

- Pairs of "asynchronous" elements that are empty but associated by their mutual processing expectations

  For example, simple redlining and revision bars can be achieved with appropriate "beginning of region" and "end of region" elements. Note, however, that sophisticated information management can be hindered by this approach, and it can even defeat some of the advantages of using an SGML-aware editor.

- SGML marked sections

  For example, information that applies exclusively to one product variant can be stored in marked sections that are controlled by IGNORE and INCLUDE status keywords stored in parameter entities.

- SGML processing instructions

  For example, copyfitting instructions are appropriately stored in processing instructions, which can be ignored by the processing applications of interchange partners.

---

### 5.2.6.3   Entities

Finally, the design team needs to let the DTD implementor know what reusable strings and special characters need to be available to authors.

If some names, phrases, or acronyms are regularly used by authors and are likely to change globally, it will be cost and time effective to replace them with an entity whose equivalent can be modified at will and at little cost. Also, authors probably won't be able to use a keyboard alone to enter all the desired symbols and characters needed. For example, to get certain accented characters and symbols such as arrows ($\Rightarrow$), authors may need to use a reference to an entity instead of just typing some sequence of keyboard keys.

Appendix D describes the character entity sets defined by the ISO 8879 standard, and Section 8.7.2 explains to DTD implementors how to use them.

---

**Step 9: Making Connections**

1. Identify and explain the characteristics of all the link components. Describe where they can be initiated, where and what they can lead to, for what use and with which type, what the processing expectations are, and what the result should be.

2. Describe each special feature and its processing expectations.

3. List all the reusable character strings and all the special characters that will be needed in the authors' daily work.

**Tips**

- Don't be discouraged by the feeling that the specifications are an unfixable mess, which is common at this stage. If you work methodically, you will end up with a complete model.

- Confusion arises easily over linking and special feature components. Do not hesitate to state the obvious in specifying your needs.

**Formalisms**

- Elaborate on the component forms for the linking and special feature components, and create element forms where necessary.

- Build a list of reusable character strings.

- Build a list of the necessary special characters.

---

## 5.2.7   Step 10: Validating the Design

Before disbanding, the design team needs to go through a final effort to review the specifications and make them as faultless as possible. This inspection includes going through the body of work that has been produced and doing the following:

- Tying up loose ends

  In the final stage of such an intense effort, it's not uncommon to find many small errors: forgotten components, unfilled fields in forms, tree branches with clouds instead of element collection names, and so on. All the overlooked details must be fixed at this stage.

- Checking the component lists against the component forms

  Not only should the "yes" and "no" decisions match, but a rationale should exist for every decision, particularly rejection decisions.

- Checking the consistency of the explanatory text

Often, terms and concepts are refined over time; the terms are not used for the same underlying concept at the beginning and end of the work, and the text should be made consistent. The graphics should also be compared against the text.

- Checking that the glossary is complete

  The glossary should include all the necessary terms (including terms that will be unfamiliar to readers of the specifications, terms used with a special meaning, and names created by the team), and the terms' definitions should be understandable by nonspecialists.

Before the document analysis report summarizing the specifications can be written, the specifications must be validated by external reviewers. Although the team members may feel that they are running out of time, it is crucially important to have potential users give their opinions on the design of the future model.

If reviewers are unhappy with the design specifications, they must respond with comments saying why, offering convincing arguments and/or examples, and indicating what, in their opinion, would constitute a more appropriate design.

If future users are not very motivated to carry out this task, the facilitator must help them review the design by presenting its conclusion in one or more live sessions with the reviewers. The recordist can write down all the remarks and critiques that are made, and summarize them in a review report.

Once the review report or the individual comments are delivered, the design team needs to meet to study them and change the model in response as they see fit. For each change, the rationale should be recorded and an entry made in the "Creation/change history" field.

The design team work is now over for a while. The facilitator and the recordist are then in charge of producing the document analysis report.

---

### Step 10: Validating and Reviewing the Design

- Check the coherence of all the documents produced.

- Tie up loose ends and add all missing information.

- Check that all the lists, forms, tree diagrams and tables are present and sorted.

- Send the specifications out for review, possibly making a presentation to reviewers.

- Integrate all the remarks and finalize the specification documents.

> **Step 10: Validating and Reviewing the Design** (Continued)
>
> **Tips**
>
> • Do not skip the design work review. If you do, you will have to integrate remarks much later, and it will represent more work and time. Also, you may not have the proper people handy later.
>
> • Check that *all* necessary documents are available. It will save time on writing the document analysis report.
>
> • Aren't you glad you wrote down all the reasons for your decisions?
>
> **Formalisms**
>
> • Make an inventory of all the documents produced.

## 5.3    Producing the Document Analysis Report

Once the team has finished specifying the document type design and gotten its interim work reviewed, the final document analysis report must also be written and reviewed. We've already described the contents of a typical document analysis report in Example 4-1.

You shouldn't plan just to assemble the component and element forms and be done with it; the need for a single document presents an opportunity to synthesize the results properly. Also, if review comments result in design changes, make sure to record the rationales for the changes just as you've done all along.

## 5.4    Updating the Model

Once the DTD has been implemented, tested, and corrected (as described in Chapter 11), it is ready for use. However, as soon as it starts being used, it faces its true test: being used in a real environment by people who must get their work done, *or else*. You will almost certainly hear many new complaints about DTD problems at this point. Therefore, you should be prepared with a DTD maintenance program and the proper resources to carry it out.

Most problems directly related to the DTD will require analysis and design efforts similar to those performed in steps 1 through 10. Thus, you'll need to assemble a change control board that functions a little bit like the original design team. The board will need to review DTD-related bug reports and enhancement requests on a regular basis and request appropriate DTD changes. Keeping a change control board active and having a DTD implementor ready to do the requested work helps to guarantee the longevity, coherence, and quality of the DTD.

Ideally, a change control board should be composed of some of the members of the project team, who know the DTD inside and out and remember parts of the rationales for decisions, plus a few newcomers. In reality, though, this composition is unrealistic. Members of the initial project team often scatter once the DTD has been validated. Also, as it is less exciting to maintain an existing system than to build a new one, few people clamor for the opportunity to run a maintenance program or be on a change control board. As a compromise, the members of the board should at least have the same profile as the original team members and should be current active users of the DTD. The board can be smaller than the original team; three or four people will suffice.

The maintenance work consists of the following:

- Receiving and filing the bug reports and enhancement requests

- Compiling them for presentation to the change control board and communicating with the senders to let them know what is happening

- Gathering the board and presenting the issues

- Answering each sender of a report to tell them what the board's decision was

- Updating the DTD according to the board's requests

- Documenting the changes and the reasons for them

- Updating the document analysis report, technical report, and maintenance documentation

- Updating the user documentation

- Distributing the new DTD with an accompanying release bulletin that explains the changes and their reasons

- Organizing additional training if the updates are significant

These tasks are usually a prelude to the tasks of updating all the variant DTDs, modifying the processing applications and aspects of the work environment that are based on the DTD, and possibly transforming existing SGML documents to make them conform to the updated DTD.

The following practices will help to make your DTD a long-term success.

### Define and Apply a Rigorous Reporting Procedure

Section 11.1 describes how to define a problem reporting procedure that can help you keep track of all comments efficiently.

### Encourage Feedback

Make sure all users know that you will respond to all complaints and suggestions as long as the users follow the reporting procedure, and make sure they
know what that procedure is. This message has three positive effects:

- It makes users formalize what they are unhappy about, so groundless
  complaints can be avoided and the rest are easier to understand.

- It greatly decreases the anxiety level of users.

- It makes users actually follow the reporting procedure.

### Follow a Stable and Sane Update Policy

If at all possible, keep the DTD stable for long periods of time so that users
don't have to keep retraining and you don't have to keep updating all the associated applications and documents. Backwards-incompatible changes (changes
that require some transformation of existing documents) are more rare than
changes that merely add optional extras to the model, so these major updates
may be able to be done only once a year, once any major bugs have been
shaken out.

### Take Maintenance Seriously

Often, the proper resources for DTD maintenance are never assigned. But even
in cases where they are, sometimes the people assigned to do the work are
given subtle messages that the "important work" lies elsewhere. The best way
to address this problem is to ensure that the job performance of the assigned
people is actually measured based on criteria such as these:

- Are reports being filed and numbered? Are actions being taken and
  report senders being informed? Is the bug list (a sample of which is
  shown in Figure 11-2) kept up to date?

- Is the number of problems decreasing regularly over time?

- Have all the problems dealt with during the most recent change control
  board meeting been fixed in the DTD and documented in the appropriate
  places?

If you send the message that maintenance is important, the quality of your DTD will
improve rapidly.

# Modeling Considerations

Every DTD development project is unique. However, many of the modeling problems you face will probably have much in common with the problems of other projects, particularly if the main goal of the project is to publish and deliver documents. This chapter presents some general advice about common modeling issues. (Chapter 8 discusses complex modeling problems that usually need the help of a DTD implementor to uncover and resolve.)

## 6.1   Distinctions Between Components

The primary question in SGML modeling is, "How should we use elements and attributes to distinguish among kinds of information?" There is no single right answer. The following sections use the example of bulleted lists and numbered lists to explore the major possible choices and their likely effects on modeling and processing application implementation.

It is a common misconception that restricting the number of elements in a DTD means the DTD is less complex. For authors and application developers to understand and use a DTD properly, not only every element but every attribute value and every novel context for an element must be documented; in other words, what DTD users need to understand is the *components* rather than just the elements. Therefore, if all the components represented in the model are necessary (which you should have established sufficiently by the time you performed step 4), then the markup is necessary too, and keeping the number of elements to a minimum by using contexts and attributes creatively won't help. If the presence of many elements threatens to make authoring more difficult, the team can consider creating an alternate model for an authoring DTD (see Section 3.1.3.2), or using methods of markup assistance such as forms interfaces, markup templates, or the customization of an SGML-aware editor, in order to help simplify the process.

## 6.1.1　Multiple Elements

The simplest and most common way to model components is to map each component to a unique element type (see Figure 6-1). For example, numbered lists and bulleted lists might each have their own element types: number-list and bullet-list.

**Figure 6-1**　Modeling Choice with Multiple Elements.

The basic currency of an SGML document is the element. All SGML processing applications can locate unique elements and process their content, so designing a model that relies on unique elements is a simple way to help ensure that the data can be processed in the desired ways. Also, every element type can have its own unique content model, attribute list, and allowable contexts, which is a level of flexibility you might want in your modeling efforts. However, if you feel that the number of elements has become overwhelming for users of the DTD, or that not enough distinction exists among the components to justify separate elements, you can use one of the other choices.

## 6.1.2　One Element in Different Contexts

Another way to model components is to map multiple components to a single element type that occurs in various contexts (see Figure 6-2). For example, numbered lists might be identified by a list element when it is inside a procedure element, and bulleted lists might be identified by a list element in all other contexts.

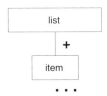

**Figure 6-2**　Modeling Choice with Context-Dependent Element.

A common way to use this modeling choice is to create a single title element, and use its occurrence inside various division elements, such as chapter, appendix, and section, to identify each unique titling component. This is a good modeling choice as long as the markup characteristics of the single element type are suitable for all contexts in which the element will be used, and as long as the various kinds of information can be considered as logically "the same." If they seem fundamentally different, separate elements may be more appropriate, even if the elements are otherwise identical. For example, a division title and a bibliographic citation to the title of a different document are not logically the same thing, even though you might want to call them both "titles" and might design the same content model for them. Thus, two different elements would be appropriate.

If the context requirements result in processing applications having to perform an especially complex query on the SGML documents (for example, "if element X is the third from the last child inside element Y, *and* Y is anywhere inside Z but not directly inside W"), it is likely that there are multiple logical distinctions that can be made, which may result in multiple elements rather than just one. At the least, the DTD implementor or application developers may request model changes or suggest simplifications.

## 6.1.3    One Element with Partitioned Models

A somewhat complex way of modeling components is to map multiple components to a single element type, relying on the use of a different portion of the available content model in each instance, as shown in Figure 6-3. For example, numbered and bulleted lists might both be represented by a `list` element, but instances of one would contain a series of `number-item` elements, and instances of the other would contain a series of `bullet-item` elements. The content model would make the item choices mutually exclusive.

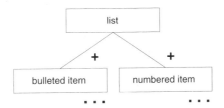

**Figure 6-3**    Modeling Choice with Single Element and Partitioned Content.

The most common case in which this modeling choice is used is to allow an optional title inside another element (such as a figure). If the title is present, the figure is formatted in one way, and if the title is absent, the figure is formatted in another way. This choice usually does not have a very strong rationale because the content-model alternative can't be controlled by the DTD, and authors could choose the "wrong" alternative in inappropriate circumstances. Furthermore, many applications find it difficult to apply processing to elements based on characteristics of their internal contents (as opposed to characteristics of the outer context in which they appear).

## 6.1.4   One Element with Attribute Values

You might choose to model components by mapping multiple components to attribute values on an element type (see Figure 6-4). For example, numbered and bulleted lists might both be represented by a `list` element that contains a series of `item` elements, but a `type` attribute value of `"number"` would identify numbered lists, and a value of `"bullet"` would identify bulleted lists.

**Figure 6-4**    Modeling Choice with Single Element and Multiple Attribute Values.

It was once the case that many processing applications couldn't handle attribute values very well, but tools now generally support attributes. Therefore, this is a legitimate modeling choice, particularly if the attribute value represents a "flavor" of the entire element rather than corresponding to some fragment of its content model (as described in Section 6.1.3). For instance, a `trademark` element for trademarked terms might have an attribute value indicating whether the term is a registered or unregistered mark. However, if the attribute value chosen has a dramatic effect on the meaning of the element or on its anticipated processing, you should consider whether the components would be better represented with multiple elements, even if their markup characteristics are identical.

---

### Note

You cannot constrain a content model through attributes, nor by means of another attribute. If you want to apply different attributes to different configurations of content and you want validating parsers to be able to enforce the constraints to the highest level possible, you need a separate element type for each configuration.

---

If presentation or other processing information must be supplied in an SGML document, try to store the information in attributes if possible.

## 6.2 Container Elements versus Flat Structures

When is it a good idea to realize a "grouping" component as an element? There are two main considerations: the complexity of the group's contents and the sophistication of the desired processing. These factors are somewhat related because highly complex models are usually the result of a strong motivation to process the data creatively.

For example, the complexity of the group shown in Figure 6-4, indicated by the arrow, suggests that a container element for the whole group would be a logical addition.

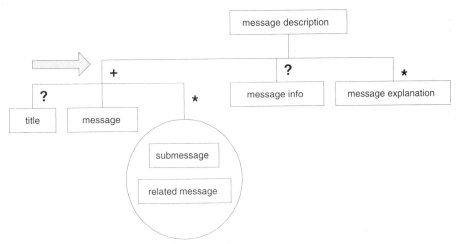

**Figure 6-5**    A Complex Group of Elements.

Many people consider container elements to be nuisances because such elements can easily swell the overall number of elements in a DTD. If the presence of such elements is justifiable but they are found to get in the way of authoring, various solutions are possible. First, in non-SGML-aware authoring environments, omitted-tag minimization can obviate the need to provide most container elements. Second, authoring DTDs can remove the container elements entirely, and transformation engines can add them back when they are needed.

However, container elements can be an asset rather than a liability. Typically their presence is required, so SGML-aware authoring tools can insert them automatically and make it easy to manipulate and display whole blocks of information. Also, as already mentioned, processing applications can use container elements to their advantage in associating various kinds of processing with the beginnings and ends of the blocks.

For example, a definition list model usually has one of the two basic structures shown in Figure 6-6.

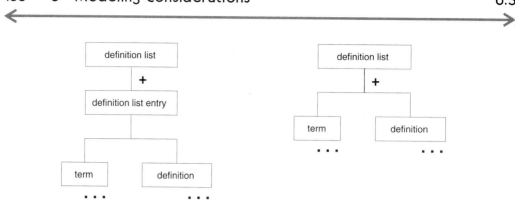

**Figure 6-6**    Basic Structures of Definition Lists.

Even if all you want to do is format the definition list information in a simple way that doesn't require the container element, its presence can make it easy to count how many entries have been written and to rearrange the order of the entries.

Finally, consider whether a group of elements might need to have an ID or any other attribute values attached to it. If so, it may be necessary to add a wrapper element on which to put the attributes.

## 6.3    Documents as Databases

For information that lends itself to management in a database or to database-like treatment, you can open up many possibilities for sophisticated processing by designing relatively flat models representing "records."

For example, in Chapter 4 we used the example of restaurant take-out menus to demonstrate the process of uncovering and interpreting structure. We mentioned two possibilities for organizing groups of related dishes on a menu: structural section elements somehow labeled with the type of dish versus content-based elements specifically to gather the soups, the steamed dishes, and so on. A third possibility would be the interpretation of each dish as a "record," one characteristics of which is its type. No explicit grouping is done in the SGML document at all; rather, a database of dishes is built up, and the relevant dishes can be extracted based on their types as needed. The goals for the Cook-This project described in Chapter 4 suggest exactly this kind of handling.

If the processing required for such a model was not planned to be developed or acquired, the motivation for the extra processing must be weighed against the cost. Following are examples of the consequences of choosing one type of model over another.

A traditional glossary entry model might look like Figure 6-7.

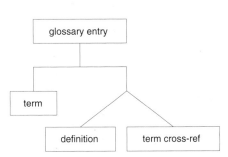

**Figure 6-7**      Glossary Entry Model.

This structure allows for providing both a definition and a cross-reference to a definition, for example, in cases where an acronym is listed in the glossary solely in order to help readers find the expanded version of the term. Both kinds of entries need to be put in alphabetical order for traditional paper-based publishing, by either an author or an application that does assembly and sorting.

```
<gloss-entry id="tas-def">
<gloss-term>Tag Abuse Syndrome</gloss-term>
<gloss-def>
A condition that afflicts authors who choose
inappropriate markup to get a certain formatting
effect or choose markup that isn't as precise
or accurate as possible. A poor DTD design often
exacerbates the problem.
</gloss-def>
</gloss-entry>
    .
    .
    .
<gloss-entry>
<gloss-term>TAS</gloss-term>
<gloss-see gref="tas-def">
</gloss-entry>
```

**Tag Abuse Syndrome**

A condition that afflicts authors who choose inappropriate markup to get a certain formatting effect or choose markup that isn't as precise or accurate as possible. A poor DTD design often exacerbates the problem.

    .
    .
    .

**TAS**

See: Tag Abuse Syndrome

The drawback to the traditional model is that it requires the phantom entries and their links to the real entries to be maintained by authors, as if the phantoms were real entries themselves. Its benefit is that an application that creates and sorts the phantom entries doesn't have to be developed.

A more sophisticated database-like model might look like Figure 6-8 instead.

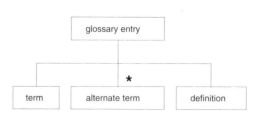

**Figure 6-8**    Database-Like Glossary Entry Model.

In this case, every entry in the original SGML document represents a single glossary entry "record," and an application must generate "phantom" entries for the alternate terms and alphabetize as necessary.

```
<gloss-entry id="tas-def">
<gloss-term>Tag Abuse Syndrome</gloss-term>
<gloss-term-alt>TAS</gloss-term-alt>
<gloss-def>
A condition that afflicts authors who choose
inappropriate markup to get a certain formatting
effect or choose markup that isn't as precise
or accurate as possible. A poor DTD design often
exacerbates the problem.
</gloss-def>
</gloss-entry>
```

### Tag Abuse Syndrome
A condition that afflicts authors who choose inappropriate markup to get a certain formatting effect or choose markup that isn't as precise or accurate as possible. A poor DTD design often exacerbates the problem.

⋮

### TAS
See: Tag Abuse Syndrome

The database-like model does require that an extra application be developed, but such an application can help greatly with consistency and ease of document maintenance.

Intuitively, it seems ideal to store only as many entries as there are term/definition sets, which would suggest a choice of the database-like model. However, constraints on application development or conversion processes may suggest that a nearer-term solution using the traditional model is best for the moment. In the absence of application issues, however, the more sophisticated model is usually better, *if* there is enough motivation to actually implement the clever utilization ideas that the team and the developers come up with.

Make sure you explicitly state all your processing expectations for complex models. If the database-like model had elements for a term and its "abbreviation," rather than a "primary term" and "alternative lookup terms," and if the processing expectation held that the primary term is always the preferred lookup term, authors couldn't choose to list an abbreviation as the preferred term (for example, with the definition under TAS instead of Tag Abuse Syndrome).

Let's look at a second example: bibliography entries. A very simple example of a traditional model might look like Figure 6-9.

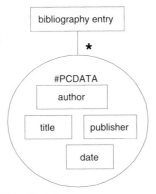

**Figure 6-9** Simple Bibliography Entry Model.

A database-like model might instead look like Figure 6-10.

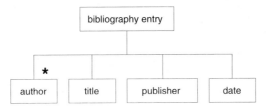

**Figure 6-10** Database-Like Bibliography Entry Model.

The traditional model makes it easy for authors to get their desired bibliographic format by providing their own punctuation, and it avoids having an application insert the necessary symbols.

```
<biblio-entry>
<author>Digregorio, Charlotte</author>,
<title>Your Original Personal Ad</title>:
<publisher>Civetta Press</publisher>;
<date>1995</date>.
</biblio-entry>
```

Digregorio, Charlotte, *Your Original Personal Ad*: Civetta Press; 1995.

However, what if the approved bibliographic format used by the organization were to change? The old bibliographic format has been "locked in" to the files, and typographical errors and missing fields can't easily be caught.

The database-like model can make all the entries consistent and change the bibliographic format through application wizardry. Furthermore, with the database-like model, entries are much more likely to have all the pieces of information identified properly and consistently so that the entries can be searched on as if they were records in a simple relational database.

```
<biblio-entry>
<author>Digregorio, Charlotte</author>
<title>Your Original Personal Ad</title>
<publisher>Civetta Press</publisher>
<date>1995</date>
</biblio-entry>
```

> Digregorio, Charlotte, *Your Original Personal Ad*, Civetta Press, 1995.

Note that if your model requires every field to be marked up but leaves the element order variable, the advantages of the database-like approach will be undermined.

## 6.4   Strictness of Models

It's a good strategy to start with a model that is relatively tightly circumscribed and expand it as necessary during testing. This way, the later changes will be compatible with any converted or newly written documents, and authors won't have a chance to use dubious markup features before testing has determined whether the features are appropriate. However, DTDs don't have the ability to *deprecate* or *recommend* models, only to allow or disallow them. Therefore, if a particular configuration of markup is needed, even if it is appropriate only rarely, the model must allow it.

Of course, even the most prescriptive DTD isn't able to enforce every single rule to which you may want your documents to adhere. For example, a DTD can't ensure that an element that's supposed to contain a string of data characters actually contains any, because the various keywords that represent data characters (such as #PCDATA) stand for "zero or more characters." And you can't write a content model that ensures that all your "cautions" start with imperative verbs. In these cases, you will need to rely on additional validation applications or human checking to make sure the documents meet all requirements.

DTDs are often used to encode editorial and stylistic guidelines so that companies can keep authors from violating the guidelines simply by requiring that documents be validated before they are accepted for publication. This is often one of the main motivations for migration to SGML in the first place. The question you will need to ask in your modeling effort is: When should a guideline be a DTD rule? For example, you might need to consider whether your sections should be required to contain at least one paragraph or other information unit.

If, by allowing a looser model, the DTD could produce nonsensical document content or document content that causes problems for processing, the model should be restricted. If a restriction would not cause actual problems, there are other factors you can examine to help you make the decision.

### Realism of the Restriction

If the documents in the project's scope have a problematic structure but must remain that way, the reference DTD needs to accommodate them. For example, your company might be planning to convert legacy documents that were written before the time when editorial rules had been established (or at least before the time that sufficient validation was being done). However, if you are able to upgrade the quality of documents being newly written, the authoring DTD can encode the desired restrictions in order to help authors conform to the rules.

Beware of prescribing strict content models for a whole company or industry just because a small group of people—the design team—thinks the existing documents are "flawed." Often you must ignore real legacy and sample documents in making such restrictions. For example, if some documents really do have divisions that split immediately into subdivisions without containing any explanatory paragraphs, a rule that requires divisions to have paragraph content is unrealistic.

### Enforceability of the Restriction

If authors can subvert the intention of the rule by committing Tag Abuse (for example, inserting empty paragraph elements in order to avoid validation errors), you'll need to use additional applications or human checking anyway, despite the fact that the DTD "enforces" the rule. Once the additional validation is in place, you may want to remove the enforcement of the rule from the DTD to reduce the annoyance factor for authors.

Some rules impose restrictions that authors would tend not to violate anyway, except through making an honest mistake. For example, where a title is required, authors will tend not to insert an empty `title` element to get around the rule. In these cases, the DTD will probably enforce the rule sufficiently, and any usual editorial reviews will catch the remaining problems.

### Benefits of the Restriction

Authors usually feel that restrictive markup rules are an imposition on the creative process. However, particularly in SGML-aware environments that offer a palette of markup choices to the user in each context, restrictions can be a real benefit. It does the author no good to be presented with a dozen choices of element when only two or three are really appropriate; in fact, such inefficiencies in the authoring process can also raise the costs of training, support, and copy editing. Even if the reference DTD must be relatively loose for some reason, it may be helpful to create a tighter authoring DTD.

## 6.5   Divisions

In modeling the document hierarchy, you will probably need to deal with divisions. Most large documents use division elements to collect their information into topical bundles. For example, novels have chapters, and technical reference manuals often have "reference modules." Your choices for division structure and nesting must be sensitive to both your processing expectations and the authors' writing methodology, each of which exerts an influence on the other.

Chapters provide a good example of the importance of expectations on writing style. Chapters in a technical manual might very well be read out of sequence, and perhaps even accessed in a hypertext environment independently of the rest of the manual. By contrast, chapters in the average novel would be very unlikely to make sense if read out of order. Technical writers will tend to make the content of individual chapters relatively independent of information residing elsewhere (except in cases where an explicit cross-reference can be added), while novelists will be free to use transitional prose at the beginnings and ends of chapters. In these two cases, even though the chapter structures are similar, there is no guarantee that the information's functional roles in the documents are similar.

Technical information tends to be organized into multiple levels of division because of its complexity. Chapters or their equivalents might allow for subdivision several levels deep, or in some cases might even "skip" levels. Multiple levels of division pose additional modeling challenges.

Following is a checklist of issues to consider when modeling divisions.

### Navigation by Table of Contents

The natural hierarchy present in a document is usually an effective place to start when readers begin to navigate a document. Most document-browsing software presents a hypertext table of contents that shows the division titles at the various levels, and they might also allow for other presentations based on the hierarchy, such as dynamic collapsing and expanding of the divisions. Many other SGML-aware processing applications also expect to find a coherent hierarchy from which to work.

If your model allows some levels of division to be skipped or to be used in inside-out order, you may not be able to take advantage of the hierarchy present in your documents when you use these applications.

## Relationships with Upper, Lower, and Sibling Divisions

Even though successive levels of containment are useful in organizing content, a hierarchical organization can obscure other useful relationships between divisions. The relationships mainly have to do with the type and degree of dependency that a division has on other divisions above, below, and beside it.

Does a lower-level division need the information provided at higher levels to make sense? The expectations for the management and retrieval of dependent and independent divisions will most likely be different; in fact, it's most likely that dependent divisions will always be stored along with their ancestral independent container.

If the reader accesses a dependent subdivision separately, what will be missing? How will the reader be informed of what the missing pieces are? Most browsing applications can automatically offer readers a way to move "up in the tree" to fill in gaps in their knowledge, a useful feature for dependent divisions. For independent divisions, authors may need to handcraft cross-references to related subjects.

Do the divisions at any one level need to be read in order? It's usually easy to tell whether content-based division markup has a significant order, but hard to tell about structural markup; the safest assumption is that the author's supplied order is significant. For example, content-based encyclopedia entries are in alphabetical order merely for convenient lookup, but the sections in a technical manual may or may not be organized in random order. If you plan to take an especially sophisticated approach to information management and navigation, you may want your markup model to reflect different kinds of division that are "randomly ordered" versus "sequentially ordered," or even to reflect divisions that are "optional" versus "required" for understanding of the subject.

## Division Depth

The maximum depth of nested divisions is a contentious topic. The guardians of editorial guidelines usually prefer a relatively flat structure for ease of reading and navigation, but in the new world of shared content and automatically assembled documents, authors often prefer an arbitrary number of levels so that they can freely promote and demote information in the hierarchy when they reuse it in new locations. The markup model will have to reflect the needs for reuse and transplanting of marked-up information.

Many DTDs have a structural division model that uses explicitly numbered divisions to limit the depth of nesting: `section1`, `section2`, and so on. Since this markup model would impede efforts to reuse or transplant a section at one level to a different level, a different model might be in order. Often, the simplest solution seems to be to allow divisions to contain nested versions of themselves down to an arbitrary depth—that is, recursive divisions. This would allow any "subtree" of information to be transplanted anywhere in any document's hierarchy. As already mentioned, however, even if the markup model is suitable for transplanting, the prose may not be. The lower the level of division used when the information was first written, the more likely that the division has a highly dependent role and can't be reused in other divisions at the *same* level, much less at a *different* level.

(Note that some SGML-aware authoring environments handle automatic promotion and demotion of divisions by actually changing the markup as necessary. Thus, it may not be necessary to cater to "transplantation" concerns with an authoring DTD, but rather can be done with software customization.)

If shared content and heavy reuse are goals for your project, instead consider identifying islands of reusable content—content-based modules that are designed to be highly independent. You can allow them anywhere in your document hierarchy that you wish, and give them their own internal hierarchy that will always be required to travel with their main division. The internal hierarchy can be allowed to nest as deeply as needed, though usually it is kept relatively flat (no more than two to three internal divisions) for editorial reasons. Recipes, encyclopedia entries, and UNIX™ man pages are perfectly suited for this treatment.

If content-based markup doesn't make sense for your divisions, it may still be helpful to identify a structural module element that can serve the same function. In fact, several popular writing methodologies, such as Information Mapping™, define such modular units.

## 6.6   Paragraphs

In the traditional word processing world, a paragraph is well understood: It is a freely wrapped block of characters, usually arranged into sentences, that uses vertical space and indenting for separation from other paragraphs. This meaning is enshrined in the notion of "paragraph styles," which are collections of procedural instructions relating to the vertical space, indenting, and margins of such blocks. We can call these "simple paragraphs." An abstraction of their model would be something like Figure 6-11.

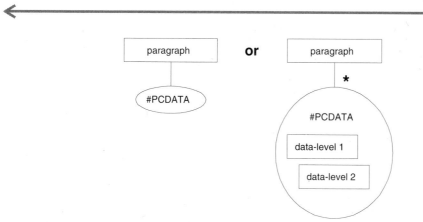

**Figure 6-11**      Simple Paragraph Model.

In the world of hierarchical containment, however, a less presentational and more structural definition of a paragraph might apply, perhaps something like the following: It is a very small (perhaps "atomic") subdivision of a document that addresses a single topic and is presented to readers in such a way as to indicate its unity. Of course, there is still no question that paragraphs must somehow be formatted with vertical space, line breaks, or some equivalent. However, this definition would encompass the entirety of the following prose:

> Before disassembling the motor, gather the following equipment:
>
> • A socket wrench (part number 1750–A)
>
> • A piece of string (part number 1750–B)
>
> These parts will be essential to the disassembly and reassembly processes.

It is clear that without the list, the first sentence is incomplete, and that without the second sentence, the point introduced by the first sentence remains unfinished. A container element for both the character data and the list might be called a "complex paragraph," and an abstraction of its model might look like Figure 6-12.

It is useful to store the entire unit in a single paragraph container for reasons of authoring and formatting convenience.

First, the container allows the content to travel together without leaving stragglers behind when being reorganized. It is quite common for authors to write a set of paragraphs in a section and then change the order several times to get the "flow" just right. Having the list travel automatically with the two sentences can be immensely useful in an SGML-aware authoring environment.

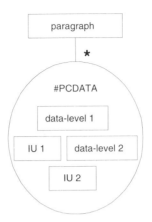

**Figure 6-12**    Complex Paragraph Model.

Second, the container can help the formatting process, precisely because it represents a logical grouping rather than a presentation-based one. For example, if you plan to use paragraph formatting with an indent on the first line, the container element can also do away with the need to have a "continued paragraph" element or an attribute on paragraphs to indicate when they shouldn't indent: Any block of characters after the first one is obviously a continuation of the same paragraph, and can be formatted as such with no other intervention by an author.

Many existing DTDs use complex paragraphs, with some even making "one or more paragraphs" the entire main content of divisions. Even if the concept seems odd at first, it may be worth your consideration.

At this point, you might object that perhaps this new container is not a paragraph at all, but rather a larger "chunk" or "nugget" of some kind—or perhaps a multiple-paragraph container is needed in addition to hold entire "topics" or "threads" within a division. This idea raises interesting questions. What is the size of granule that users need to retrieve from documents? Below which size is it impractical to retrieve information without also providing its surrounding context? How can the benefits and costs of authoring with multiple "paragraph levels" be balanced? (Section 6.5 discusses some of these issues.)

Often, simple paragraphs, complex paragraphs, and threads don't make ideal retrieval objects; they are all too dependent on the context provided by the rest of the division (or other significant container) in which they reside. In these cases, the value of making such fine distinctions may be minimal.

## 6.7   Generated Text

Generated text (that is, strings of characters interwoven through the output of a document by a formatting application) plays a large role in most stylesheets developed for the formatting of SGML documents. For example, list items might need to have bullets or consecutive numbers inserted, and page numbers might need to be output somewhere on each page. Generated text can help achieve stylistic and editorial consistency, but it can also pose some modeling challenges.

If certain text strings will be required in the output (for example, because of corporate style policy), it's usually best to generate them and not to have an element that represents the generated text. For example, if all `note` elements must have the title of "NOTE," there is no point allowing or requiring a `title` element on notes. A stylesheet will do a much better job of inserting the right title text than authors will, and the stylesheet can ensure that the title is always spelled and capitalized correctly (and that the correct language is used, if the document is translated or maintained in different languages).

For the application developers to know they are expected to build this behavior into their formatting applications, you need to document your processing expectations; in this case, part of the basic "meaning" of the `note` element would be that it has a title, and the title always reads "NOTE."

If, instead of requiring a "NOTE" title, the corporate policy allows individual authors to override a default value, you have the following basic modeling options:

- Require a `title` element on notes and use other means, such as providing markup templates or customizing the text editor, to instruct authors to prefer the text "NOTE" in the title content.

  This option removes any special title-processing expectations from the `note` element; it just has a regular title, similar to many other elements.

- Make the `title` element on notes optional; when it is not supplied use "NOTE," but when it is supplied, use its content as the title.

  This option has processing expectations that are more complex than they might seem. When the title is absent, the note is nonetheless still a "titled" element because a title will be supplied on output; it's just that the SGML document instance doesn't explicitly represent this fact about the note. Any processing actions on titled elements will need to be applied to notes without `title` elements, too.

  (Note that if the formatting of the entire note happens to depend on the presence or absence of the `title` element, some processing applications may need to operate in more complex ways, because they will already have encountered the note's start-tag by the time they can determine whether the title was supplied.)

- Always represent the title in the markup somehow, whether or not the default title is used.

This modeling option may require some advice from the DTD implementor. For example, it might be appropriate to design a special kind of attribute for the `title` element (an attribute with a #CONREF default value) that, when filled in, represents the generated title and prevents element content from being supplied, and, when left blank, allows element content to be supplied. While this is a tricky solution, it actually makes the document instances seem more "whole" and makes the processing expectations plain.

---

### Note

If you design a markup model that allows authors to override generated text, you are building some Tag Abuse potential into the model. For example, if authors can change the title of a note, they may be able to simulate information of a different kind, such as warnings, by manipulating the title text accordingly. You will need to balance the desired flexibility against the cost of ensuring markup precision.

---

The most difficult problem in dealing with generated text is planning how it will fit into its surroundings, such as in the middle of a sentence. Your DTD implementor and the application developers might need to help you sort out the various processing expectations. By the time the DTD is implemented, it's essential that the expectations be precisely determined and documented.

To illustrate the importance of processing expectations, let's assume you have designed a model where an empty `figure-cross-ref` element links to a figure. The plan is that a stylesheet will generate some text that represents the figure in place of the empty element. If the cross-reference is to the third figure in the first chapter, the generated text might be any one of the following (assuming a scheme where figures are numbered in a way that is subordinate to chapter numbers):

1. "1–3"

2. "Figure 1–3"

3. "See Figure 1–3"

4. "(see Figure 1–3)"

5. "(See Figure 1–3.)"

Each of these choices would require a different sentence structure to surround it. Some choices, such as the full parenthetical sentence, are more independent of their surroundings than others, which may be a useful quality. However, no matter which choice has been implemented in a stylesheet, if an author expects a *different* choice, the formatted result could be nonsensical. For example, if the stylesheet produces the effect of choice 5 but an author assumes that 1 is being used, sentences in the document might read:

> For an illustration of the julienne technique, see Figure (See Figure 1–3.).

Similar problems might arise if glossary terms were stored in a database in the singular form (for example, "file name") and referred to with links in the document that stylesheets will replace with the term names. All references would need to be worded to support singular rather than plural constructions.

These problems are due to the variety inherent in written and spoken natural language. One way to overcome them is to expect that generated text will always be wholly independent of their surroundings, and to make this expectation clear to all authors. Another is to build presentational markup into the model that allows authors to have control over the form of the generated text. For example, the glossary term database mentioned above could store variant forms of each term (see Table 6-1).

**Table 6-1**    Variant Forms in the Glossary Entry Database.

| Lowercase | First initial capital | All initial capitals | Plural lowercase | etc. |
|-----------|----------------------|----------------------|------------------|------|
| file name | File name | File Name | file names | |
| system | System | System | systems | |

Then each cross-reference to a glossary term could supply an attribute value indicating which form would be appropriate to generate in the current context.

## Note

If your documents will be translated, the difficulties of fitting generated text into its surroundings will become even more complex. If you do add any presentational attributes, it's likely that they won't have precise analogs in any of the other languages. Word ordering may be an additional problem.

## 6.8   Augmented Text

Large blocks of generated text are often called "augmented text" because they add to the content of a presentation instance in a fundamental way, and may even be "fed back" into the original SGML instance. Tables of contents are an example of augmented text. Following are suggestions for choosing how to model augmented text. The DTD implementor and application developers should have a hand in the discussion if possible.

### No Markup

In many cases, it isn't necessary to represent augmented text in the markup model; processing applications can just build the appropriate output along the way. This is usually the ideal choice because different presentation instances may have widely differing requirements on how the augmented text will appear and where it will be output.

### Metainformation Placeholder

You could allow a placeholder element (usually an empty element) for the construct to appear somewhere in the metainformation container, regardless of where it will appear in the final processed document. For example, you might have an optional empty "TOC" element somewhere in the metainformation element. This solution allows authors to control the presence or absence of the generated construct in the types of presentation instances that have tables of contents.

### Location-Specifying Placeholder

You could allow a placeholder element to appear in the linear order wherever it should appear in the output. For example, you might allow the "TOC" element to appear optionally before the preface, after the preface, and after the appendices. This solution allows authors to control the position of the table of contents in some types of presentation instances.

### Full Markup Model

You could design an element for the construct that has a real content model, and allow it in either the metainformation or the linear order (as described above). For example, you might have a "TOC" element in the metainformation that contains one or more "TOC entries," each of which contains a title and either a page number or a link to the relevant division.

This solution allows authors to provide some default information or to correct generated information that has been fed back into the document instance after processing. This solution is also useful if the final delivered form will be the SGML documents themselves, in which case it may be useful to recipients to take delivery with this metainformation already generated. However, keep in mind that the accuracy of the generated information is guaranteed only just after it has been generated.

Glossaries are similar to metainformation in that they help readers with their understanding of the content, but they usually also provide subject matter content, and their placement in the output might be controllable by an author. Some companies generate glossaries from databases of defined words based on the presence of those words in the content, which makes the glossaries act somewhat like tables of contents. However, sometimes authors must still "craft" a definition or provide a definition that isn't in the database, so a structure must usually be provided for glossary elements.

## 6.9   Graphics

Most document information containing "characters" can be modeled in SGML, whether or not the characters are arranged as sentences. The decision in these cases often involves choosing how "content-based" or "structural" to make each semantic component.

However, sometimes the information being modeled seems so presentational that an SGML representation is pointlessly inefficient. For example, a graphical bitmap needs to look exactly the way it was created, with every pixel controlled. You could model the color of each pixel using elements and attributes, but storing the bitmap in a non-SGML form, such as a TIFF format, makes more sense. In these cases, the markup model needs to provide a way to point to or include the non-SGML data, such as a graphic element with an attribute that references an entity. Often, presentational markup is needed so that authors can gain the appropriate control over the appearance of the graphic. The DTD implementor can help with the technical aspects of this modeling task, and the project plan should indicate the non-SGML formats needed.

Just as with all components, though, you shouldn't overlook opportunities to interpret the graphics as being content-based. For example, if you are modeling a set of books on card games, each graphic showing how to deal a hand can be interpreted as mere graphical data—or it can be interpreted as *cards*. If the contents of the graphics can be modeled as "spreads" showing "hands" and "stocks" of "cards," with each card having a "suit" and a "rank," the necessary graphics might ultimately be generated from such markup. Given that card-game books are your business, the cost of developing the software to generate the graphics might easily pay you back in

- A lower budget for original artwork

- Graphics that are consistently laid out

- The flexibility to change the designs on the backs of the cards to reflect the new logo of the publisher in subsequent editions

- The ability to publish for print-disabled audiences with "graphic equivalents" explaining the spreads

- Error-checking to catch mistakes where the same card is mentioned twice in the same spread

If your processing gets really sophisticated, it could even create a multimedia environment in which card deals and draws are shown in animated fashion.

# 7 Design Under Special Constraints

If you're designing a document type from scratch for your own organization, Chapters 4 and 5 describe what you need to know. However, if your project has one of the following unusual characteristics, this chapter explains how the document type design process might differ:

- Customizing an existing DTD (for example, an industrywide standard) for use in your own organization (discussed in Section 7.1)

- Designing one of these industrywide standard document types themselves (discussed in Section 7.2)

## 7.1 Customizing an Existing DTD

It can be advantageous to use an existing DTD or DTD fragment as the basis for a new document type, because the similarity to the existing model may allow you to use processing applications that are already developed, and you may be able to benefit from the availability of existing expertise, documentation, and training courses. If you must interchange documents with business partners, basing your reference DTD on an industry-standard DTD will almost certainly make sense if such a standard DTD exists for your industry segment. (The relationship between these DTDs is described in Section 3.1.3.) The document type design process will need to change to reflect this reality.

One obvious difference is that the supporting documentation for the existing DTD will play a major part in both analysis and specification. Therefore, it is essential to assess the available documentation and ensure that it is complete and understandable before you begin. In a customization project, usually the DTD implementor or another person fluent in SGML or in that particular DTD, must be available to give a "running interpretation" of the DTD. In fact, it's not uncommon for SGML consultants to be hired to reorganize and redocument a standard DTD so that its assumptions about scope, constraints, usage, and processing can be made clear (or reconstructed, if they were documented insufficiently in the first place). An extremely effective technique for starting to read and understand a DTD is to sketch out its tree diagrams; the effect of recreating the model by hand is very powerful.

Another difference is that the design team will need to become familiar with the different types of variation between markup models: subsetting, extension, and renaming (discussed in Section 10.1). The team members may need some help from the DTD implementor for this relatively technical topic, but it's important to know the costs and benefits of each type of variation so that they can be factored into design decisions. If certain constraints along these lines are known at the outset, the project documents will make this clear. For example, it may already be dictated that some parts of the original markup model must be subsetted out, or that the model must be extended to account for proprietary information.

Often, it will be stated as a goal that the reference DTD must be a proper subset of the interchange DTD, meaning that all instances of the former should conform to the latter. However, be aware that this is often an unrealistic goal. What usually happens is that authors will be instructed to use the standard DTD in ways that are unique to that organization, in effect creating semantic extensions (a notion discussed in Section 8.4.1) while conforming to the "letter of the law." Thus, document instances might still require transformation of some sort when they are exchanged with business partners.

Table 7-1 compares the design steps in projects for new document types versus customized document types.

**Table 7-1**    Comparison of Design Steps for New and Customized Document Types.

| Step | New DTD | Customized DTD |
| --- | --- | --- |
| 1 | Identify potential semantic components. | You should place a heavy priority on identifying component ideas from the original DTD, while taking note of your unique requirements. |
| 2 | Classify components. | If the documentation for the original DTD already mentions some classifications, consider whether they make sense for the current analysis. Using them allows you to stay within the terminology and "mindset" of the interchange DTD, while leaving you free to recognize additional patterns. |
| 3 | Validate components. | Check carefully to make sure the original DTD is well represented. |
| 4 | Select components. | Your project may already hold the assumption that certain types of components are "in" or "out," but you should ensure that your own legitimate needs aren't rejected. Make sure to state the rationale for each rejection of a standard component. |

Table 7-1 Comparison of Design Steps for New and Customized Document Types. (Continued)

| Step | New DTD | Customized DTD |
|------|---------|----------------|
| 5-7 | Build document hierarchy, information units, and data-level elements. | For each component that has a representative element in the original DTD, instead of starting with a blank slate, use its model as a proposed starting point and modify it as necessary. For components with no representation in the original DTD, model them the usual way. Document the rationale for every extension of the original model, in addition to documenting the "absolute" rationale for your modeling choices. |
| 8 | Populate the branches. | Pay close attention to the element collections used in the original DTD, and try to subset rather than extend them, except where you have added your own unique elements that must be included. Extensions in this area can make it very difficult to transform documents into compliance with the interchange DTD. If the original DTD doesn't already use a building-block approach for managing its element collections, you may want to model them in a matrix just to clarify the existing choices. |
| 9 | Connect the model to the outside world. | Except for linking mechanisms, such connections tend to be idiosyncratic to each variant DTD. |
| 10 | Validate and complete the design. | Same. |

Doing a proper job of customizing will demand just as much skill and expertise as a ground-up effort or maybe even more, and the results will be unsatisfying unless you do a real analysis—not just one that assumes the standard DTD describes the entire universe of potential semantic components. If may even be best to perform an analysis and only then choose a DTD to serve as a base, if you have this flexibility.

It usually takes less time to customize an existing DTD than to design one from scratch because the modeling phase can be completed more quickly. However, because of the time and skills needed for analysis, customizing an existing DTD should be done primarily for reasons of interchange and application availability, not for reasons of cutting the DTD development schedule in half.

## 7.2 Designing Industry Document Types

Quite a few efforts have already been conducted for the creation of DTDs that can be used across an entire industry, for example, for aircraft maintenance, semiconductor manufacturing, and computers. Many more such efforts will be undertaken as the use of SGML grows. If you participate in an effort to design a document type for a whole industry, be prepared for the process to be more complex, more costly, and more lengthy than any single-company project. It's not uncommon for the project to take 18 to 24 months.

Because the participants usually represent competitors, they tend to have strongly conflicting perspectives and may be reluctant to share analysis data that they feel is proprietary or sensitive. This situation can result in an air of suspicion over the proceedings, as well as temporary political alliances to serve business agendas unrelated to DTD development. On the other hand, the participants are usually counterparts in their respective organizations and may have more in common with each other than with their colleagues back at the home office, which can make the work a pleasurable meeting of the minds and a chance to stay current in the field.

Following are specific suggestions to help an industrywide effort be successful. (Section 3.4 discusses handling the politics of DTD projects in general.)

### Keep Participation Stable and of a Controllable Size

For every company added as a participant, the potential for complexity increases. To make the work as efficient as possible, it's ideal to have only one representative from each company on the design team, and some limited number of additional representatives from each company on the steering committee (which is likely to be larger than for a single-company project). If the enormous effort required of participants is made clear from the start, you have a better chance of keeping the participant population to a reasonable number and having the same people participate throughout the project.

### Clarify and Document the Process Beforehand

The design team should have a clear decision model, and may even need to go as far as signing a written description of the processes for offering suggestions, making decisions, and handling deadlocks. Each design team representative should be officially empowered by his or her company to participate in the decision-making so that the discussions and results will have validity.

The design team's facilitator and recordist can be picked from among the participants, *if* it is generally agreed that they can be impartial. If such people can't be found, the consortium of companies may need to resort to hiring consultants.

### Be Organized and Disciplined

It probably seems like dull advice, but you won't regret any of your efforts in planning the work, resources, and schedule; stick to the plan; document every single decision you make; and insist on thorough reviews and explicit signoffs. Because of the toll that cultural conflicts can take on the effort, be sure to define and check your understanding of all terms, even the seemingly most obvious. You may need to resort to using neutral terms that no company uses in real life so as not to favor any particular culture.

### Consider Building Some Flexibility into the Result

Depending on the project's goals, the markup model might appropriately be either prescriptive or descriptive. Regardless of its general approach, though, the model for an industry DTD often must be relatively forgiving in order to accommodate divergent cultural and structural styles. If some of the participating companies already use SGML, some parts of the modeling work can resemble a massive DTD customization effort, where all the existing models are unified into a new model that accommodates their essential characteristics.

Usually, the main goal of an industrywide DTD project is to ease interchange between business partners. A subsidiary goal may be to encourage software vendors to support the resulting DTD, which will be widely used in a robust way. There is potential for conflict in these goals because the perfect interchange DTD will probably not be a perfect authoring or presentation DTD, even though some participants may expect to use off-the-shelf software directly with the DTD sanctioned by the industry group.

Even for DTDs whose only ostensible purpose is interchange, often a segment of the user population will plan to author and process documents using the interchange DTD. It's essential to be realistic and accurate in your goal-setting. Particularly for very large models and user populations, you may want to consider casting your effort as the modeling of a "library" of elements, of which a subset can be chosen for actual use, an approach that is particularly useful for elements in the information pool. The DTD implementor can then structure the DTD with appropriate kinds of customization in mind. (Techniques for DTD reuse and customization are discussed in Chapter 10.)

### Recognize Special Interchange Needs

Industry interchange situations may require that information about the original presentation or delivery of the document travel with it. For example, it may be necessary to ship augmented information (as discussed in Section 6.8) that has been folded back into the instance. This requirement makes the interchange DTD act somewhat like a presentation DTD.

### Don't Give Up Until All Decisions Have Been Made

Because the effort is so expensive and can drag on for such a long time, often the participants run out of steam and some work is left undone. Before you start, recognize that this failure to finish can seriously jeopardize the whole effort, and commit to finishing the job properly. Not only will the project have a greater chance of success, but all the participants will have a sense of personal satisfaction.

# Part 3

## DTD
## Development

This part of the book is intended for DTD implementors. With the completed document analysis report and other project documents in hand, you implement the DTD and the SGML declaration by doing the following:

- Designing the markup model for the document type and implementing it in SGML form. This work mainly involves designing and creating the element and attribute declarations. Chapter 8 describes some of these design considerations.

- Using good technique for maintenance and readability. This work mainly involves the artful use of parameter entities and comments. Chapter 9 describes some useful techniques.

- Constructing the DTD to allow parts of it to be reused and customized. This work involves breaking up the DTD into modular files and using parameter entities and marked sections. Chapter 10 shows how to do this work and describes considerations for customizing an existing DTD.

- Validating and testing the DTD. This work involves checking your DTD implementation with a validating parser and testing the markup model for effectiveness on real documents. Chapter 11 describes some common DTD validation problems and solutions, and discusses testing strategies.

These topics aren't separate sequential stages of DTD implementation; they're just different techniques that solve different problems. You're likely to move back and forth among them, especially as you gain experience. Careful planning in each area helps you avoid making "design at the keyboard" implementation decisions that are based on expediency rather than on project needs.

To use these chapters effectively, you need to understand basic SGML terminology from the ISO 8879 standard, and how to read and write SGML markup declarations. (Appendix A provides reference information on markup declaration syntax.) No matter what your level of expertise, you should have one of the several available SGML reference books handy (see Appendix E for suggestions). Remember also that existing DTDs make an excellent teaching tool.

# 8

# Markup Model Design and Implementation

While the document analysis report might seem very specific about element and attribute specifications, the correspondence between the specifications and the SGML implementation is not always obvious or complete; a set of tree diagrams or English descriptions is not tantamount to a finished markup model.

You need to transform the specifications into real element and attribute declarations—a task that requires interpretation skills, good two-way communication with the document type design team, knowledge of the syntax and constraints of SGML markup declarations, and an understanding of the environment in which the SGML documents will be created, managed, and processed.

The following sections cover some basic issues to address in interpreting the document analysis report and designing and implementing the specifics of the markup model:

- The number of DTDs to build (Section 8.1)

- Approaches to interpreting element specifications (Section 8.2)

- Approaches to handling attribute specifications (Section 8.3)

- Useful elements and attributes to consider adding (Section 8.4)

- Design of markup names (Section 8.5)

- Design of minimization schemes (Section 8.6)

- Other considerations in building an SGML markup model (Section 8.7)

We'll largely ignore the topic of using parameter entities and other SGML "programming" constructs to achieve customizability and maintainability goals. Rather, where we do mention them here it will be in the context of using them to control the overall characteristics of the markup model created by the DTD. Chapters 9 and 10 provide details on how to take advantage of these constructs.

## 8.1   Determining the Number of DTDs

The document analysis report already identifies each of the one or more document classes, in the general sense, required to model the documents in the project's scope. However, *you* must decide where to draw the lines between related document types in creating individual DTDs.

In general, if multiple document classes are closely related and have even a small chance of being used in combination in a single document, you should build one DTD for them. For example, user manuals, tutorials, and reference manuals might share many features and might be combined into single delivered documents.

However, the more distantly related the document classes are, the less appropriate it is to combine them into a single DTD. In these cases, it's better to separate out the similar portions and modularize the DTDs so that they can take advantage of a single core set of markup declarations. For example, customer letters and manuals bear almost no structural resemblance to each other, but share the same information pool. (Section 10.2.1 discusses how to modularize DTDs.)

You must also take into consideration the practical nature of the document creation, management, and processing environments, which may argue for creating variant DTDs, such as separate authoring, conversion, and presentation DTDs, based on the reference DTD for each document type. (Variant DTDs are discussed in Section 3.1.3.)

If you need to implement even a few variant features, you should seriously consider creating multiple DTDs instead of just one. It can be tempting to put all the features into a single DTD, especially if your resources for developing processing applications are limited or you must compile the DTD for your SGML-aware software systems. However, along with the efficiencies you gain, you are also likely to incur some costs, especially if your documents are written by humans rather than generated entirely by autotagging software. For example:

- If you choose to provide lax content models and attribute specifications to help the document creation process, you have no way to check whether the documents meet all your completeness criteria when they are finished.

- If you provide markup for controlling layout and formatting in the DTD that is used for document creation, authors can undermine the presentation-independent quality of the markup by using these features.

- If you include markup that authors are not responsible for using, you steepen their learning curve for the DTD, particularly if the editing environment cannot hide unnecessary markup choices from authors. Furthermore, including unnecessary markup can contribute to any tendencies in the editing software to have performance and memory problems.

If you decide to create variant DTDs for specialized functions, avoid simply copying the reference DTD and making changes to the copied files because maintaining them will rapidly become impossible. You can use a number of techniques to create variant DTDs whose features automatically track those of the reference DTD. Typically, a variant feature has one of two effects:

- Reducing the scope of the document type to a lower level, in effect creating "nested" document types

- Modifying a content model or attribute list to loosen or tighten its specifications

The following sections describe how to choose techniques to achieve each of these effects. (Chapters 9 and 10 describe in much greater detail how to apply SGML "programming" techniques.)

## 8.1.1    Creating DTDs for Nested Document Types

You can use three different techniques to create nested document types for specialized purposes:

- Treating a single DTD as if it were multiple DTDs during parsing

- Modularizing a DTD

- Using the SGML SUBDOC feature

If you want to keep all your nested document types together in a single stored DTD, simply make sure that the DOCTYPE declaration in each document instance supplies the document type name that matches its document element.

For example, a single DTD for computer software documentation might encompass nested document types for manual chapters, whole manuals, volumes containing multiple manuals, and document sets containing multiple volumes. Figure 8-1 shows how the general structure might look.

A single DTD might appear to cover only the top-level document set, as follows:

```
<!ELEMENT set           - - (title, volume+)>
<!ELEMENT volume        - - (title, manual+)>
<!ELEMENT manual        - - (title, chapter+)>
<!ELEMENT chapter       - - (title, ...)>
<!ELEMENT chapter       - - (title)>
<!ELEMENT title         - - (#PCDATA)>
```

However, you could use the following declaration in an instance consisting of a single chapter in order to parse and process it. The declarations for elements at higher levels than chapter are ignored. (Formal public identifiers are used here and throughout this chapter for references to DTDs in DOCTYPE declarations. For more information about formal public identifiers, see Section A.10.)

```
<!DOCTYPE chapter PUBLIC "-//Ept Associates//DTD Set of Books//EN">
```

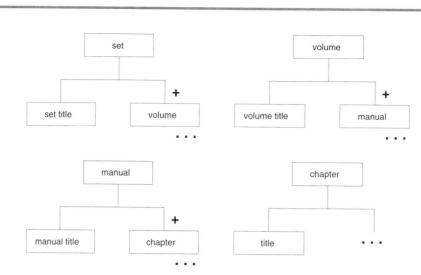

**Figure 8-1**    Tree Diagrams for Nested Document Types.

If this solution doesn't meet your needs, you could instead use a modular DTD structure, which would allow you to target DTDs more precisely to the document instances. To modularize the DTD, put all the declarations related to chapters and their contents in one file, those related only to the manual level in another, and so on. In the files for the upper levels, incorporate the declarations in the lower levels by means of parameter entity references. The declaration for the `title` element would go in the lowest-level module, since it is needed at all the levels.

For example, the contents of `chapter.dtd` might be as follows:

```
<!ELEMENT chapter      - - (title, para*, sect*)>
<!ELEMENT title        - - (#PCDATA)>
<!ELEMENT para         - - (#PCDATA)>
<!ELEMENT sect         - - (title, para*, subsect*)>
<!ELEMENT subsect      - - (#PCDATA)>
  :
```

The file for the manual DTD would contain the following:

```
<!ENTITY % chapter-module PUBLIC "-//Ept Associates//DTD Chapter//EN">
%chapter-module;
<!ELEMENT manual       - - (title, chapter+)>
  :
```

The volume-level and set-level files would each similarly point to the next lower module. The document instances at each level would point to one of the four files in order to "activate" the appropriate subset of the markup model, and you could compile and develop processing applications for each nested document type separately.

Note that if you want to use the same file in multiple documents which start at different levels, you need to store the bulk of the file's content separately from its document type declaration. For example, to use a file containing a chapter at multiple levels, the chapter entity file must look like this:

```
<chapter>
<title>Fruitbats in Their Natural Habitat</title>
 .
 .
 .
</chapter>
```

A complete chapter document might look like this:

```
<!DOCTYPE chapter PUBLIC "-//Ept Associates//DTD Chapter//EN"[
<!ENTITY chap SYSTEM "chapter.sgm">
]>
&chap;
```

A complete manual document might look like this:

```
<!DOCTYPE manual PUBLIC "-//Ept Associates//DTD Manual//EN"[
<!ENTITY chap SYSTEM "chapter.sgm">
]>
<manual>
<title>Biology and You</title>
 .
 .
 .
&chap;
 .
 .
 .
</manual>
```

Even if you modularize your DTD files for other reasons, you might not be able to manage an environment that has multiple processing applications targeted to each level. If you want to keep all the compiled DTD information together, you need to add a container element at the top level, as follows:

```
<!ELEMENT computerdoc    - - (set|volume|manual|chapter)>
```

Then, all your document instances, no matter at which logical level they start, would all have the following DOCTYPE declaration and top-level markup.

```
<!DOCTYPE computerdoc PUBLIC
          "-//Ept Associates//DTD Computer Documentation//EN">
<computerdoc>
 .              chapter, manual, volume, or set markup
 .
</computerdoc>
```

Finally, you could use the SUBDOC feature to manage nested document types if your SGML-aware software supports this feature.

To use SUBDOC, first make sure the feature is set to YES in the SGML declaration for your document instances. Second, use a DTD like the following for the upper-level document types; here, the DTD for manuals is shown.

```
<!ELEMENT manual        - - (title)>
<!ATTLIST manual
        chapfiles       ENTITIES                #REQUIRED
>
<!ELEMENT title         - - (#PCDATA)>
```

The DTD for chapters can remain as shown earlier. With the SUBDOC feature in use, chapter instances must have their own document type declaration, as follows:

```
<!DOCTYPE chapter PUBLIC "-//Ept Associates//DTD Chapter//EN">
<chapter>
  ⋮
</chapter>
```

The manual document must declare subdocument entities for the chapter files and make references to them, as follows:

```
<!DOCTYPE manual PUBLIC "-//Ept Associates//DTD Manual//EN" [
<!ENTITY chap1 SYSTEM "chap1.sgm" SUBDOC>
<!ENTITY chap2 SYSTEM "chap2.sgm" SUBDOC>
]>
<manual chapfiles="chap1 chap2">
<manual-title>...</manual-title>
</manual>
```

There are a number of drawbacks to using SUBDOC.

- The processing of an attribute that references an SGML text entity is left completely unspecified by the SGML standard. For example, if you use SUBDOC in the manner shown above, there is no guarantee that the chapter entities will be parsed, validated, incorporated into the document data stream where they are referenced, or whatever other behavior you expect. This fact, and the fact that few product vendors support SUBDOC in any way at all, argue against using it.

- Using SUBDOC requires that lower portions be stored in separate entities from upper portions.

- Because SUBDOC relies on attributes with an ENTITY declared value rather than on entity references that appear in the normal flow of markup, you can't enforce that the lower portions conform to the same DTD used in the upper portions.

- Subdocuments have a different ID name space from that of the containing document, so you cannot use the ID/IDREF mechanism to cross-refer between levels or between subdocuments.

## 8.1.2    Variant Element and Attribute Declarations

If you want to create variants of your DTD that loosen, tighten, or change content models and attribute lists, parameter entities and parameterized marked sections can help you make the changes while letting the variant track the original DTD in all other respects.

For example, a reference DTD for a technical journal might require content inside submitted papers, because it would be inappropriate to have empty papers when the journal is published. On the other hand, the authoring DTD might allow papers to be entirely empty except for a title so that all the material (introductions and so on) other than the actual papers can be written without generating "content missing" errors when a journal is parsed. Following are the two different forms of the element declaration for paper.

*reference form:*
```
<!ELEMENT paper          - - (title, abstract, intro?, section+)>
```
*editing form:*
```
<!ELEMENT paper          - - (title, abstract?, intro?, section*)>
```

You can use marked sections to conditionally include or ignore each of the two declarations as follows, changing the definitions of the marked sections to suit yourself for DTD compilation or document validation. Using marked sections directly allows you to keep the two versions close to each other so that you can compare and correct them as necessary.

```
<!ENTITY % reference  "INCLUDE">
<!ENTITY % editing    "IGNORE">
<![ %reference; [
<!ELEMENT paper          - - (title, abstract, intro?, section+)>
]]>
<![ %editing; [
<!ELEMENT paper          - - (title, abstract?, intro?, section*)>
]]>
```

Alternatively, you can use a small-scale parameter entity for the portion of the content model that must change, and use either marked sections or differing sets of entity declaration modules to "activate" the correct version of the content model for compilation or validation. In this case, storing a fraction of a content model far away from the declaration in which it's used can make it difficult for you to read and maintain the DTD.

```
<!ENTITY % paper-content "abstract, intro?, section+">
<!ENTITY % paper-content "abstract?, intro?, section*">
<!ELEMENT paper          - - (title, %paper-content;)>
```

Chapter 10 describes how to use marked sections and parameter entities in much greater detail.

## 8.2   Handling Element Specifications

SGML offers a great deal of power in constructing content models. Because of the nature of teamwork and the distribution of SGML expertise in the project, you can't necessarily rely on design teams to come up with subtle programmatic solutions to difficult modeling problems. As a result, if you take the document analysis report at face value in designing content models, your resulting element declarations might incorrectly reflect the design team's intent or, worse, be syntactically invalid.

The following checklist summarizes areas where you can uncover potential element-related problems in the document analysis report. Some of these areas are discussed in greater detail in the following sections.

### Suspiciously Similar Elements

For example, for divisions at three levels, `div1`, `div2`, and `div3`, the team may have specified the creation of three different division title elements, `divtitle1`, `divtitle2`, and `divtitle3`.

The team may have intended to collapse these elements into one element, or may not have considered using the context to distinguish the different roles for a single element. It's best to check with the team members.

### Single Elements Acting Like Multiple Elements

For example, within a single `list` element, the team may have specified content of *either* normal list items *or* description blocks for equipment error messages.

This is often a case of trying to do the work of multiple elements with one. The element should probably be broken down, in this case to a `list` element and a `message-list` element.

### Recursive Elements

This often happens with data-level elements, which are often specified to contain a collection of `#PCDATA` plus "all the data-level elements" without the realization that this includes the parent element itself. For example, the team may have inadvertently allowed cross-reference citations to contain nested citations. The most practical way to deal with undesirable recursion of this kind is often to use a content model exclusion.

For elements that contain themselves deliberately, first make sure the element isn't *required* in the content model. If it is, naturally it will be impossible for any instance of this element to satisfy the content model.

In any case, you need to look into whether very deep nesting (for example, generic document divisions like `div` that can be nested to dozens of levels within themselves) is a legitimate way to structure the information. You may want to keep the recursive content model, but use some means other than the DTD to catch too-deep nesting (such as having human copy editors check the documents, or writing additional validation software). An alternative to recursive content models is to create a different element for each allowed nesting level, making the level part of the element name (for example, `div1` for a top-level section, `div2` for the next level of section, and so on).

### Elements that Act Like Entity References

In general, it's inappropriate to have an empty element such as `include-chapter` with an `ENTITY` attribute for pulling SGML-encoded chapters into a document, since parsers won't validate the external SGML material as part of the document. Regular entity references should be used for this purpose.

### Inappropriately Complex Content Models

Make sure that highly complex content models will have a return on the investment. If the burden of applying correct markup is likely to overwhelm authors, and the task cannot be made easier through templates, forms, or autotagging software, some data will probably escape being marked up or will be marked up incorrectly. These areas in the document analysis report should at least be watched closely in the DTD testing period. An authoring DTD may be necessary.

### Ambiguous Content Models

Just as it's possible to write a content model in SGML that you later discover through parsing has an ambiguity problem, it's possible for design teams to hand you specifications that have an ambiguous nature. In these cases, you must work with the design team to decide how to modify the specifications to make an acceptable content model. Section 8.2.1 describes how to solve ambiguity problems.

### Elements that Could Mistakenly Be Empty

Sometimes, working on individual components, design teams can overlook the broader consequences of their choices. This situation occasionally happens with specifications for content models containing ordered sequences or any-order groupings of elements, all of which are optional. If leaving them *all* out is unacceptable, you need to come up with a content model that's quite a bit more complicated than the one suggested by the specifications. Section 8.2.2 describes how to construct the alternate content models.

### Collections Containing Elements that Should Have Limited Occurrence

Often a specification will come up for a model that contains a collection of some elements, among which there are one or more elements that *can't* appear multiple times; these must appear once or not at all. This specification is much easier to express in English than in tree diagram form (or in SGML form, for that matter). In such a case, the team might even supply an inaccurate diagram and supplement it with further English description. Section 8.2.3 describes how to construct the necessary content models.

### Problematic Mixed Content

Often, the most difficult modeling choices are those for elements that contain #PCDATA, because such elements often need to contain other elements as well. The ISO 8879 standard makes specific recommendations about mixed content models in order to avoid confusion over SGML's handling of white space in document text. Section 8.2.4 discusses ways to handle mixed content.

## 8.2.1   Removing Ambiguous Content Models

If the document analysis report contains a specification that specifies an ambiguous content model, you must choose an appropriate way to change the model because parsers will report an error in cases of ambiguity.

---

### Ambiguity in SGML Content Models

SGML doesn't allow content models where the same element can satisfy multiple potential branches of markup, because parsers can't look ahead in the document content to determine adherence to the DTD. In other words, as they examine each element in turn, parsers must be able to pinpoint their precise "location" in the content model at all times.

For example, parsers will report an error for the following content model:

```
<!ELEMENT a    - - ((b, c)|(b, d))>
```

The following state diagram representation of this model shows how the precise branch can't be chosen.

## Ambiguity in SGML Content Models (Continued)

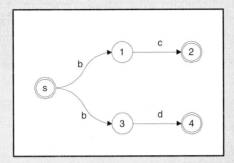

Once a parser recognizes that an instance of element a has been opened, it is in starting state "s." When it comes across an instance of element b, it has no way of determining whether to change its internal state to 1 or 3 except to look ahead to see whether c or d occurs next, but lookahead isn't allowed. Therefore, the parser must report an error.

To solve this case of ambiguity, you would collapse the two references to the b element into one and put it before the OR group at the same level. Changing the model in this way means the parser doesn't need to "know" what the next element should be, since either c or d would be acceptable:

```
<!ELEMENT a     - - (b, (c|d))>
```

The new state diagram shows how the ambiguity has been removed. A parser can change to state 1 on occurrence of b.

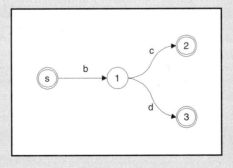

Certain common kinds of specifications suggest ambiguous content models. For example, the specification shown in Figure 8-2 specifies that the part-info element can contain part-number twice, the first time optionally.

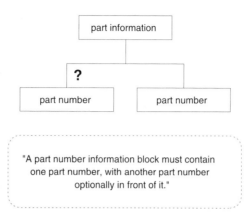

**Figure 8-2**    Specification for Part Numbers Resulting in Content Model Ambiguity.

The part number example may seem farfetched, but it's adapted from a real-life specification. The reasoning of the team was, "An internal inventory number is always supplied, but we know that if an external number is supplied, it always goes first." This specification shows that the design team was trying to do two specialized jobs with different occurrences of the same general-purpose element.

Without further analysis, this specification would suggest the following content model:

```
<!--                        one           two         -->
<!ELEMENT part-info   - -  (part-number?, part-number)>
```

However, this declaration is ambiguous because when a parser comes across the first part number in a document, it won't know without looking past it whether it's supposed to represent the "part number one" or the "part number two" of the element declaration.

Two kinds of solutions are possible: keeping the model general or making new, more specific elements. Both require feedback from your design team before you can proceed.

***stay general:***
```
<!ELEMENT part-info   - -  (part-number, part-number?)>
```

***or get specific:***
```
<!ELEMENT part-info   - -  (ext-part-number?, int-part-number)>
```

If you and the team conclude that you honestly won't need to query on, format, or otherwise process internal part numbers separately from external ones, you might as well use the first solution, which solves the ambiguity problem. However, it's more likely that you've flushed out a need for more precision in your markup. In this case, you should replace the original general-purpose element with two specialized ones.

Figure 8-3 shows another common configuration where ambiguity is a problem. Again, it involves trying to do too much work with a single element. The following shows a specification for two document divisions, both of which allow a special-purpose joke element in their introductory mixtures of information unit elements. However, the container for a joke collection also expects to contain joke as its primary content.

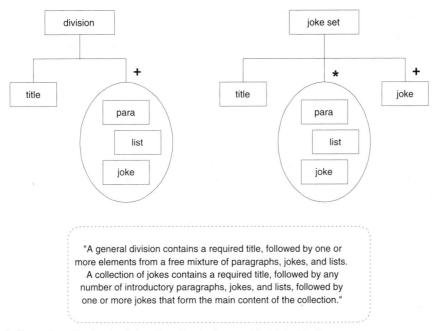

"A general division contains a required title, followed by one or more elements from a free mixture of paragraphs, jokes, and lists. A collection of jokes contains a required title, followed by any number of introductory paragraphs, jokes, and lists, followed by one or more jokes that form the main content of the collection."

**Figure 8-3**     Specification for Jokes Resulting in Content Model Ambiguity.

This kind of specification suggests the following pattern of declarations:

```
<!ELEMENT division   - - (title, (para|joke|list)+)>
<!ELEMENT joke-set    - - (title, (para|joke|list)*, joke+)>
```

However, the second declaration is ambiguous because, on occurrence of a joke element in your document, the parser won't know whether it's meant to be an introductory joke or the start of the main joke content of your specialized joke-set container. Three kinds of solutions are possible (assuming you can't entirely do away with introductory material).

- Add a wrapper element in one of two places.

  **add a wrapper element in one place:**
  ```
  <!ELEMENT joke-set   - - (title, joke-intro?, joke+)>
  <!ELEMENT joke-intro - - ((para|list|joke)*)>
  ```
  **or the other:**
  ```
  <!ELEMENT joke-set   - - (title, (para|list|joke)*, joke-group)>
  <!ELEMENT joke-group - - (joke+)>
  ```

  This solution adds a bit of markup complexity. However, the extra container can be useful in processing and SGML-aware processing.

- Rename jokes in one context or the other.

  **change the joke element name in one place:**
  ```
  <!ELEMENT joke-set   - - (title, (para|list|intro-joke)*, joke+)>
  <!ELEMENT (intro-joke|joke) - - (#PCDATA)>
  ```
  **or the other:**
  ```
  <!ELEMENT joke-set   - - (title, (para|list|joke)*, main-joke+)>
  <!ELEMENT (main-joke|joke) - - (#PCDATA)>
  ```

  This solution is problematic because it doesn't allow jokes to be reused easily (for example, stored as an entity and referenced) in all the contexts where jokes are allowed, and it increases the difficulty of retrieving all the jokes in a document database.

- Restrict the collection to exclude jokes.

  **leave out the general-purpose joke:**
  ```
  <!ELEMENT joke-set   - - (title, (para|list)*, joke+)>
  ```

  This solution contradicts the letter of the design team's specification, but may be an option they want to consider. (This solution can get tricky if you use parameter entities to manage your collections, which is usually the case; Section 9.3 describes how you can handle this.)

The decision requires feedback from your team before you can proceed.

## 8.2.2   Forcing Element Occurrence

In some circumstances, allowing a container element to be entirely empty may be a strategic decision; for example, you may want to have a reference DTD that disallows empty elements of a certain type, and an authoring DTD that allows them. However, in cases where an empty container element would be an absurdity, you may need to construct a somewhat complex content model to prevent it from being empty.

For example, the specification shown in Figure 8-4 is for an optional back matter element containing any number of appendices, a glossary, and an index, all of which are optional.

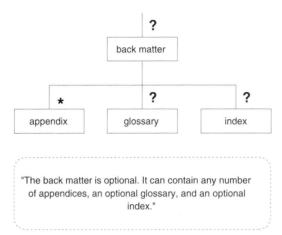

**Figure 8-4**    Specification for Back Matter That Can Be Empty.

Without further analysis, the specification would suggest something like the following declaration:

```
<!ELEMENT back-matter  - - (appendix*, glossary?, index?)>
```

The back-matter element is optional, but even if it is present, it may not have any content. Assuming the design team agrees that an empty back-matter element is wrong, you need to ensure that the DTD requires enough information to be supplied.

The following solution might come to mind:

```
<!ELEMENT back-matter  - - (appendix|glossary|index)+>
```

However, while this content model ensures that the element won't be entirely empty of content, it removes the requirement for element order and allows multiple glossaries and indexes, while a maximum of one each was desired.

Another solution might suggest itself.

```
<!ELEMENT back-matter  - - ((appendix+, glossary?, index?)
                            |(appendix*, glossary, index?)
                            |(appendix*, glossary?, index))>
```

Unfortunately, this content model is ambiguous because parsers can't know, on occurrence of an appendix element, which line of the declaration, as shown here, is the correct one to follow. (Section 8.2.1 discusses ambiguity in more detail.) The same problem would occur with glossary, if parsers were able to get that far.

The solution is close at hand, however, and is similar to this content model. Use a "water-fall" approach: Assume for each optional element, in turn, that its occurrence is required and the previous ones are not present at all, and build a model group for it inside a larger OR group.

```
<!ELEMENT back-matter  - - ((appendix+, glossary?, index?)
                           |(glossary, index?)
                           |(index))>
```

Figure 8-5 shows the final tree diagram for this content model.

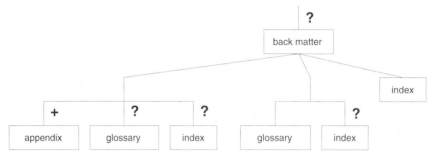

**Figure 8-5**     Final Tree Diagram for Back Matter that Always Has Content.

You can apply similar logic to any-order groups of elements. For example, if the original specification suggests the following content model, a could be entirely empty.

```
<!ELEMENT a - - (b? & c? & d?)>
```

If having an empty a element is wrong, you would need to apply "waterfall" thinking to uncover the following solution. In this case, the inner groups must be made sequential instead of any-order, so that your assumption about which element appeared first can be tested for each of the three cases.

```
<!ELEMENT a - - ((b, (c? & d?))
               |(c, (b? & d?))
               |(d, (b? & c?)))>
```

---

## Note

#PCDATA in an element's content model can be satisfied with *zero* data characters—the null string. Thus, for elements that allow #PCDATA anywhere in the content, you cannot use a validating parser to ensure that the element has content. If you want greater control of your SGML documents in this respect, you must build other applications to do the checking.

---

## 8.2.3    Limiting Element Occurrence

If you are faced with a specification to limit the occurrence of an element that appears among collections of other elements, don't give up: It *is* possible to construct a content model that doesn't result in a free-for-all.

For example, the somewhat fanciful specification shown in Figure 8-6 is for song lists for rock 'n' roll music CDs. Any one CD can have any collection of bombastic rock songs and danceable rock songs, but a maximum of *one* ballad. The tree diagram inaccurately represents the specification.

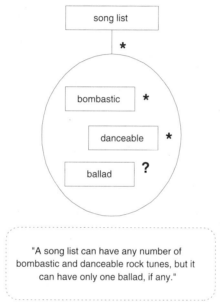

**Figure 8-6**      Specification for Song Collection Including Ballads.

If you allow all the song elements in a collection, as follows, you can't control the occurrence of ballads.

```
<!ELEMENT songlist  - -  (bombastic|danceable|ballad)*>
```

Another attempt at the declaration might look like the following.

```
<!ELEMENT songlist  - -  ((bombastic|danceable)*, ballad?,
                          (bombastic|danceable)*)>
```

However, this content model is ambiguous because, before a ballad occurs in the song list, it's not clear whether any instance of a bombastic or danceable rock song should satisfy either the first or second collection block. (Ambiguity is discussed in Section 8.2.1.)

For the desired effect, move the optionality from the ballad to a group containing the ballad and the final collection.

```
<!ELEMENT songlist - - ((bombastic|danceable)*,
                        (ballad, (bombastic|danceable)*)?)>
```

An accurate tree diagram for this solution would look like Figure 8-7.[1]

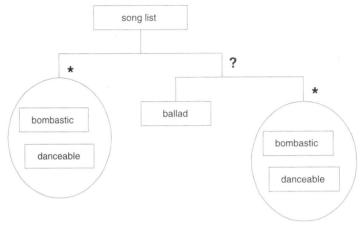

**Figure 8-7**     Final Tree Diagram for Song Collection Including Ballads.

A more complicated situation would arise if you had more than one element that needed to be restricted. For example, you might need to model dictionary entries, some of which contain any-order blocks of information about word origin (`origin`), usage notes (`usage`), and famous quotations containing the word (`quote`), along with other general-purpose descriptive elements (`block`). In any one entry, the specification is for a maximum of one of each of the specialized elements to occur, but for multiple general-purpose elements to be allowed (because each is about a different subject that can't yet be identified).[2] The tree diagram might look like Figure 8-8, which doesn't quite correspond to what is wanted.

---

1.  Note that if you want to ensure that the CD isn't entirely empty, as discussed in Section 8.2.2, you need to use the following waterfall model:

    ```
    <!ELEMENT songlist - - (((bombastic|danceable)+,
                            (ballad, (bombastic|danceable)*)?)
                           |(ballad, (bombastic|danceable)*))>
    ```

    Here, either a ballad or one of the other two types *must* appear in the song list.
2.  In this case, the general-purpose element works like an "escape hatch" to account for needs not anticipated or quantified during DTD development. We call this concept semantic extension; we discuss it further in Section 8.4.1.

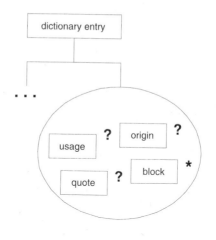

**Figure 8-8**     Specification for Dictionary Entry Collection.

A first attempt at the corresponding element declaration might look like the following:

```
<!ELEMENT dictentry - - (..., (origin|usage|quote|block)*)>
```

However, this content model allows multiple occurrences of the specialized elements. Instead, you might try one of the following models:

```
<!ELEMENT dictentry - - (..., (origin? & usage? & quote?), block*)>

<!ELEMENT dictentry - - (..., (origin? & usage? & quote? & block*))>
```

However, the first declaration won't allow you to capture general-purpose information before or between the special elements, and the second forces all general-purpose information to be either before *or* after the other elements, or in *one* single location between any two of them.

Another option might be to allow block as an inclusion to the content model of dictentry.

```
<!ELEMENT dictentry - - (..., (origin? & usage? & quote?) +(block))>
```

However, this model allows `block` to appear anywhere in the *main* part of the entry (represented by the ellipsis), as well as anywhere between or *inside* the special-purpose elements.

If you want the DTD to be highly prescriptive about the desired configuration (that is, if you want a validating parser and not some other mechanism to be in charge of enforcement), you need to resort to the following content model:

```
<!ELEMENT dictentry - - (..., block*,
                        ((origin, block*)?
                        &(usage, block*)?
                        &(quote, block*)?))>
```

This model allows any number of general-purpose elements before, between, and after the special elements, allows the special elements in any order, keeps each occurrence of a special element to a maximum of one, and ensures that the content model is unambiguous. This kind of construction gets very unwieldy as more specialized elements are added, and large AND groups make high demands on parsers and DTD compilers because they are shorthand for a choice among many SEQ groups. However, if your project has a strong requirement to do this validation work with the parser, it can be done.

## 8.2.4   Handling Mixed Content

The "leaf" elements of a DTD usually contain #PCDATA. However, many of them must also contain other data-level elements, a situation that must be handled delicately in content models because of potential problems related to lines, or records, of stored document data.

For example, a specification for lists might specify that the list items should contain character data, followed optionally by some paragraphs that further explain the first short phrase. Figure 8-9 shows the specification.

This specification suggests something like the following declarations:

```
<!ELEMENT listitem  - - (#PCDATA, para*)>
<!ELEMENT para      - - (#PCDATA)>
```

In the following example, REs are indicated by the symbol **RE**. Validating parsers will report an error on occurrence of line 6.

```
1:  <listitem> RE
2:  Oranges RE
3:  <para> RE
4:  Oranges are a lovely RE
5:  orange-colored fruit. RE
6:  </para> RE                                    ERROR
7:  <para> RE
8:  They are grown in warm climates. RE
9:  </para> RE
10: </listitem> RE
```

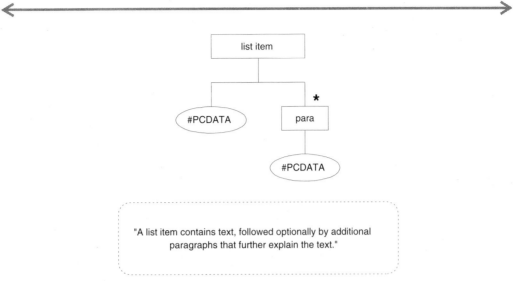

"A list item contains text, followed optionally by additional paragraphs that further explain the text."

**Figure 8-9**     Specification for List Items with Problematic Mixed Content.

The error is reported because once the first para element in a list item is opened, the content model of listitem prevents it from directly containing any more character data, and the RE at the end of line 6 counts as data.[3]

It's best to follow the recommendation of the ISO 8879 standard to use #PCDATA either alone or in repeatable OR groups, so that you can avoid the possibility of this kind of error. In fact, trying to limit the occurrence of character data is usually a sign that more analysis is needed. You can see the likely need for more analysis from the appearance of the tree diagram in Figure 8-9, where the position of the first block of #PCDATA in the diagram looks like an obvious candidate for an element.

There are two ways to reorganize the model: a collection solution or an isolation solution.

First, you can turn the content model into a collection containing #PCDATA and the other element.

```
<!ELEMENT listitem  - -  (#PCDATA|para)*>
<!ELEMENT para      - -  (#PCDATA)>
```

---

3. If the parser can get as far as line 9, another error will be reported for its RE. Normally, REs just after start-tags and just before end-tags are ignored because they can unfailingly be interpreted as being separator characters, and the RE on line 9 appears just before the listitem end-tag on line 10. In this case, however, because SGML parsers can't look ahead to determine conformance, the RE on line 9 will be flagged as misplaced #PCDATA before line 10 is ever reached.

This model eliminates the risk of parser errors for mixed content problems. However, since list items tend to have their own internal structure, this solution should be avoided if you have another acceptable alternative, because it would allow the out-of-place nonparagraph text on line 7.

```
1:  <listitem>
2:  Oranges
3:  <para>
4:  Oranges are a lovely
5:  orange-colored fruit.
6:  </para>
7:  They are grown in warm climates.
8:  </listitem>
```

The collection solution is more appropriate inside elements for which the bulk of the content is likely to be character data, such as full sentences or paragraphs of text.

The alternative solution, and in the case of list items the better one, would be to isolate the character-data portion of the list item's content model in a subelement of its own, either in another para element or in a new, specialized element.

***interpret first paragraph as the list intro:***
```
<!ELEMENT listitem  - - (para+)>
<!ELEMENT para      - - (#PCDATA)>
```

***or create a new specialized element:***
```
<!ELEMENT listitem  - - (listintro, para*)>
<!ELEMENT listintro - - (#PCDATA)>
<!ELEMENT para      - - (#PCDATA)>
```

---

## The Mixed Content Problem

In a document instance, each record ends with a nonprinting character known as a **record end**, or RE. An RE is typically produced when document authors press the Return or Enter key on their keyboards, or inserted automatically by word processors or SGML-aware authoring tools as the authors' typed words wrap to the next line. Both REs and spaces are in a special category of characters called "separators" (which you may know as "white space"). In elements with element-only content, separator characters directly inside the parent element are "ignored"; that is, they're not passed from the parser to any further applications. The notion of separator characters allows document authors to put markup on separate lines and otherwise create tidy-looking document source files.

---

**The Mixed Content Problem (Continued)**

In elements with mixed content, however, most separator characters can't be ignored because they might be part of the actual data content of the element. #PCDATA encompasses both regular data characters and those that can be considered separators. In a content model where #PCDATA is relegated to specific sequential regions of the content, as in a section that contains data (representing a title) followed by some number of paragraphs, separators must be prohibited from the other regions in the content so that parsers can check for the incorrect presence of nonseparator data in those regions. Thus, separator characters meant innocently to make markup easier to read might be interpreted by parsers as out-of-place data characters, which will produce an error.

Because of the possibility of such errors, which can be troublesome to authors who type in their own markup (as opposed to using SGML-aware authoring tools, most of which position the separator characters correctly so as to avoid any problem), the ISO 8879 standard recommends using #PCDATA only by itself or in content models consisting solely of a repeatable OR group. The result of such an arrangement is that #PCDATA—including both normal data characters and separator characters—is allowable anywhere inside the element.

Note that REs passed along by the parser as data to a processing application may still be discarded by that application. For example, REs in a paragraph will probably be discarded so that the text can be wrapped and filled, whereas REs in a poetry element might be interpreted as signals to break the line in the formatted output.

---

## 8.3   Handling Attribute Specifications

Often, document analysis reports are vague or incomplete regarding attributes and their acceptable values. Because attributes are often used to control specific functions in the processing environment, design teams often defer some of these matters to later stages when processing software will be developed. You may need to do some research to fill in the blanks.

The following checklist summarizes areas where you can uncover attribute-related problems or insufficient specifications in the document analysis report. Some of these areas are discussed in greater detail in the following sections.

### Subclass Attributes

In certain circumstances, it may be appropriate to further describe an instance of an element by providing an attribute value (for example, indicating whether a trademarked term is "registered" or "unregistered"). However, you may want to consider breaking up the element into separate elements in the following cases:

- The attribute value is required.

  For example, if the content in a `productname` element *must* be marked up as being a product for either resellers or the consumer market, it suggests that the two kinds of product may be sufficiently different to warrant two elements, even if they have the same content model and are allowed in the same contexts.

  Reducing the number of elements only to replace them with attributes can be false economy. An element with a required attribute that has one of ten possible values will need all the documentation and training resources that ten separate elements would have had. Also, depending on the authoring tool chosen, the single-element solution might even be more difficult to apply to document content.

- Each attribute value is associated with different sets of other attributes.

  For example, if you have a single `list` element with an attribute to indicate whether it is bulleted or numbered, and there are other attributes to refine the choice of either bullet or number, it's more sensible to have two list elements. Attributes can't control whether authors provide other attributes, so authors could specify an incorrect combination of attribute values if you put all the attributes on the same element.

- Each attribute value is associated with different choices of content from the same content model.

  For example, if you have a single `list` element with an attribute to indicate whether it is for regular text or for computer message descriptions and the model allows for *either* one or more list items *or* one or more message description blocks, you have a clear case of two elements masquerading as one. Attributes can't affect content models, so authors could specify an incorrect combination of attributes and content if you don't separate out the models.

### Attributes Containing Free Text

Sometimes the flexibility to provide an attribute value of arbitrary length and contents is needed; in this case, the CDATA declared value is appropriate. However, the parser has no control over CDATA text, thus inviting consistency problems in specifying attribute values and leaving the job of handling the attribute value entirely in the hands of processing applications. You should consider whether NAME or one of the other declared values might be a better choice.

If the attribute value is intended to be output as document content (for example, a `title` attribute), the attribute should almost certainly be made into an element instead. If the markup model has many cases of CDATA attributes in it, they should at least all be used consistently (treated as keywords, invisible author comments, document content, or whatever).

### Presentational Attributes

Formatting information can adversely affect the data's portability and longevity, whether it's in an element or an attribute. You should find ways to abstract away from presentation-related information where possible (though it's better to capture this information in attributes, if it must be supplied).

### "Current" Default Values

Beware of default values that are supposed to pick up the most recently assigned value for an instance of that element. Such attributes would need a default value of `#CURRENT`. These attributes are problematic because they effectively tie down the element to one static location in the document, making the element entirely dependent on its linear context. For any dynamic document-building scheme or for document types that do not depend on the linear order in which elements are provided, such attributes are inappropriate.

### Correspondence of Common Attributes

If possible, attributes with the same name on different elements should have the same purpose, and attributes with different purposes should have distinct names. Otherwise, you'll have a problem documenting the proper use of the attributes.

### Attributes with Enumerated Values

Section 8.3.1 discusses strategies for handling attributes for which you want to create a list of values.

### ID and ID Reference Attributes

Attributes with a declared value of `IDREF` place an extra documentation burden on the DTD implementor. Section 8.3.2 discusses strategies for handling attributes that use this SGML mechanism for symbolic identification.

### Attributes with Implied Values

Attributes with a default value of `#IMPLIED` place an extra documentation burden on the DTD implementor. Section 8.3.3 discusses the considerations in designing attributes with implied values.

See Section 10.2.4 for information on using attributes in a special way for variant DTDs.

←————————————————————————————————————————————→

## 8.3.1   Enumerated-Type Attributes

Sometimes it's appropriate to provide a finite list of choices as the declared value of an attribute. For example, the following declaration creates a status attribute with two possible values: "draft" and "final":

```
<!ATTLIST doc
       status  (draft|final)   #IMPLIED
>
```

In these cases, you may find that it's a good idea to leave the way open for values you haven't yet thought of. For example, for the doc element, you might want to do the following to allow for different levels of draft status that might be designated in the future. Unfortunately, it isn't valid SGML.

```
<!ATTLIST doc
       status  (draft|final|NAME)      #IMPLIED
>
```

What this declaration tries to accomplish is a kind of semantic extension (a concept discussed further in Section 8.4.1), since the DTD is, in some cases, leaving it up to the document instance to supply some of the semantics of the content. Following are the ways you can accomplish this goal for attributes.

- Use a NAME or NMTOKEN declared value instead of enumerating the valid literal token values.

```
<!ATTLIST doc
       status  NAME            #IMPLIED
>
```

This solution leaves you no way to control, through the parser, what attribute values are supplied. Authors and conversion programs must adhere to conventions for supplying values (or must use other software to check for adherence) if consistency is desirable.

- Enumerate the token values, add an "other" value, and add an additional attribute to hold the new values.

```
<!ATTLIST doc
       status          (draft|final|other)     #IMPLIED
       otheratt        NAME                    #IMPLIED
>
```

When "other" is supplied in the status attribute, only then should the processing application notice the value of otheratt, if it has any. This is an excellent system for controlling values while allowing an escape hatch, its main drawback being that you can't force a value for otheratt to be supplied if the status value was "other". (Section 8.4.1 describes additional ideas for semantic extension along these lines.)

Note that if you don't have an `"other"` keyword and simply use the impliability of the `status` attribute to indicate that `otheratt` should be examined, you prevent the possibility of implying a value for `status` besides `"other"`; for example, you won't be able to assume the value is `"final"` based on whether the document was set to be read-only in the database.

- Use parameter entities to allow the list of enumerated token values to be extended in an internal declaration subset of the DTD.

   ***newvals can be extended by being redefined as "|newvalue"***
   ```
   <!ENTITY % newvals "">
   <!ENTITY % statusvals "draft|final %newvals;">
   <!ATTLIST doc
           status    (%statusvals;) #IMPLIED
   >
   ```

   This solution works almost as well as the previous one, but has some of the dangers of allowing markup model extension. (The technique and the risks are discussed in detail in Chapter 10.)

A typical enumerated list of attribute values serves as a Boolean (two-state) toggle: yes/no, on/off, or true/false. Boolean attributes are the kind most often affected by SGML's requirement that the set of declared token values for all attributes on a single element type be unique.

This requirement exists because of the SHORTTAG minimization feature (controlled by the SGML declaration), which, among other things, allows authors to omit those attribute names and specify only their values in element start-tags, as follows.

```
<doc final>content...</doc>
```

So what's the problem? Say you want to put these two attributes on your document element:

- An attribute to record whether the document is orderable through the online sales catalog

- An attribute to record whether comments on the document are solicited from readers

Parsers will report an error for an attribute list declaration like the following:

⊘
```
<!ATTLIST doc
        orderable      (yes|no)        yes
        comments       (yes|no)        yes
>
```

This declaration sets up the possibility that an author could supply the following ambiguous markup:

```
<doc no>content...</doc>
```

Two approaches are common in avoiding this problem. One is to pack more information into each token, as follows:

```
<!ATTLIST doc
        orderable       (orderable|notorderable)  orderable
        comments        (sendcomments|nocomments) sendcomments
   >
```

The other is to use NUMBER declared values, where "0" is understood to be "no", "off", or "false", and any other number is understood to be "yes", "on", or "true" (the number-value approach can work for more than two distinct values, of course).

```
<!ATTLIST doc
        orderable       NUMBER          1
        comments        NUMBER          1
   >
```

Several industry-standard DTDs use the NUMBER declared value in this fashion to good effect. However, in situations where authors must directly choose values (as opposed to, for example, table-editing environments that manage attribute values away from the authors' view), you might want to use meaningful keywords instead. Keywords will be easier to document and may avoid the confusion that results from mistaking the logical sense of the attribute ("Is 1 supposed to mean it's orderable or it's not?").

## 8.3.2   ID and ID Reference Attributes

It's common to use the ID declared value for attributes that contain an element's symbolic identifier, because validation by an SGML parser will ensure that all IDs within any one document are unique and that any attributes containing IDREF references to these IDs are valid. In addition, most SGML-aware applications are prepared to perform special processing on ID and IDREF values. Thus, the choice of ID for element identifiers is appropriate for most DTDs.

However, you might find the length or character requirements on SGML names (on which the ID declared value is based) to be too restrictive. If you're able to make your processing applications perform any of the validation and other work that would have come for free with ID/IDREF, you could use CDATA instead. In this case, attributes containing references to IDs should also have a declared value of CDATA.

No matter how you declare your ID attributes, you may find that it's useful to allow IDs on every element type so you can manage, process, and store elements by their identifiers.

For each attribute that serves as a reference to a unique identifier (of whatever declared value), make sure to determine the element types whose identifiers should be able to be referenced from the attribute, and document the results in DTD comments or documentation. For example:

```
<!ELEMENT glossref - - (#PCDATA)>
<!ATTLIST glossref
        link    IDREF    #REQUIRED --to glossentry--
>
```

## 8.3.3  Attributes with Implied Values

From the perspective of document creators, an attribute with a default value of #IMPLIED simply means an attribute value that is "optional to supply," just as if an actual default value were available. But developers of processing applications need to know more:

- Can the application proceed without any value at all for the attribute?

- If not, how should the application derive the correct value?

When you implement attributes with #IMPLIED default values in a DTD, you should be able to answer these questions in DTD comments or documentation.

Following are some common answers.

- An attribute might be truly optional, not needing to be supplied for the application to proceed.

```
<!ATTLIST para
        id     ID      #IMPLIED --OK not to have value--
>
```

- It might need to be inherited from the nearest ancestor with a specified value.

```
<!ELEMENT example           - - (title, computer-listing)>
<!ATTLIST example
        audience            (novice|expert) novice
>
<!ELEMENT title             - - (#PCDATA)>
<!ELEMENT computer-listing - - (#PCDATA)>
<!ATTLIST computer-listing
        audience            (novice|expert) #IMPLIED
                                    --get from parent--
>
```

- The attribute value might depend on the element's context in the instance.

```
<!ATTLIST numlist
        numstyle            (arabic|alpha)  #IMPLIED
                                    --occurs inside self?--
>
```

- The value might depend on characteristics of the environment in which the information was assembled, formatted, or retrieved.

```
<!ATTLIST procedure
         audience        (novice|expert) #IMPLIED
                                         --value of USERTYPE
                                         environment variable?--
      >
```

## 8.4   Useful Markup to Consider

Certain kinds of elements and attributes may be useful to add to any DTD. This section describes markup for "semantic extension" to extend the life of the DTD and markup to help in conversion of data.

### 8.4.1   Semantic Extension Markup

It's unlikely that a DTD development project can anticipate every semantic component needed in the data format. Unusual document samples can come to light after the environment has been developed and tested, and new needs can always arise. Furthermore, the more precise and complex the markup model, the more likely that it will be unsuitable for data that is only slightly different. Therefore, it's a good idea to add markup to a DTD that can serve as "escape hatches" to capture data that would not have been marked up otherwise, as long as conventionally agreed-on uses of the escape hatches are well documented.

We call this notion **semantic extension**. You can use semantic extension markup to help you extend your markup model indefinitely, but more likely you will want to use it to inform the design of future versions of your DTD and help manage conversion of your documents to the new versions.

For example, you might have defined a highly structured model for light bulb jokes. It might have elements or attributes for the kind of person changing the light bulb, the number of people required to do the job, and so on. The more you make your element the embodiment of the *light bulb* joke model (as opposed to, say, the elephant joke model, or the model of jokes in general), the less possible it will be to use the element for encoding other jokes.

In this case, you may want to provide a corresponding general-purpose element for encoding the (possibly as yet unknown) other kinds of jokes that may not fit the existing molds, and allow data and markup in it that can be free-form to the degree necessary. For example, along with the `lightbulb-joke` element, you might create a `general-joke` element that simply contains one or more paragraphs. If it later becomes clear that the general element is being used frequently for a class of jokes (for example, knock-knock jokes) for which more SGML structure would be beneficial, a new element for that structure could be created, and instances of the general element could be converted to instances of the new element.

General-purpose elements such as this are, in effect, abdicating some of the responsibility for identifying the element's type. Since you can't know beforehand what the precise type is, it's helpful to provide an attribute to allow (or even require) the author to fill it in for each instance of the element. This attribute is sometimes called `role`. For example:

```
<general-joke role="knockknock">
<para><quote>Knock knock.</quote></para>
<para><quote>Who's there?</quote></para>
  .
  .
  .
</general-joke>
```

Especially if your DTD will be an industry standard or otherwise widely used by many different audiences, you might want to consider putting the `role` attribute on every element, even the specialized ones. In this capacity, it provides a powerful semantic extension mechanism that guarantees compliance to the original element structure, attribute list, and general intention, while adding information about the element's "flavor" that individual organizations can use in their own environments. Using this attribute can even help decrease the pressure on organizations to extend the standard markup model materially for their own use.

For example, suppose a DTD for software documentation offers an element for general random-order lists, but not for specialized lists of restrictions on software functionality. If a department using the DTD wants to be more specific in marking up some of its lists, it can "borrow" all the characteristics of the original list but add one detail:

```
<!DOCTYPE randlist [
<!ELEMENT randlist   - - (item+)>
<!ATTLIST randlist
        role            NAME            #IMPLIED
>
<!ELEMENT item       - - (#PCDATA)>
]>
<randlist role="restrictions">    now functions as a restrictions list
<item>
Command line output redirection doesn't work.
</item>
<item>
File names cannot have more than three characters.
</item>
</randlist>
```

Armed with this extra knowledge about its lists, the department can format restriction lists differently from regular lists, keep a statistical database on software restrictions, and so on. At the least, it will be prepared for an expected future version of the DTD that will incorporate a new element for this purpose.

Note that the `role` attribute here was defined to have a declared value of `NAME` so that its value would be forced to be a "keyword." However, if you want to allow document creators to supply longer descriptions of the role, `CDATA` is more appropriate.

Authors often request a set of one or more elements for font control (`bold` and so on). These elements are usually inappropriate to add to the DTD. Supplying a `role` attribute value on existing elements can actually diminish the need for these elements, since sometimes authors merely want to mark up a new "flavor" of an existing data-level element. If the content of such elements needs to be formatted differently from the default, authors must negotiate with the application developer to make their new `role` attribute values be recognized by the formatting software. This requirement for negotiation helps you control the misuse of elements a little more closely.

If your DTD puts a set of common attributes on all its elements (for example, for revision status and security access), you may want to consider adding a general-purpose data-level element that can serve as an "attribute hanger" for otherwise unremarkable regions of text that are smaller than a paragraph. Such an element is sometimes called `phrase`.

If your markup model has both specific elements and general-purpose elements for semantic extension, you run the risk of Tag Abuse by authors, who might use the general-purpose versions where the specific version is warranted. Author training, markup review, and markup assistance (through structured editors, templates, forms interfaces, or generation of data and markup from other sources) can help lower this risk.

## 8.4.2   Conversion Markup

In converting legacy documents to SGML or transforming SGML documents to conform to a different DTD (or to the same DTD but with different or augmented contents), you might have a series of conversion DTDs that get the data closer and closer to the ultimate desired form. It may make sense to add special markup to hold the results of conversion.

If the target DTD is less specialized than the source form, you may want to retain information about the source markup as you convert so that you can later transform in the other direction. To hold this information, you could put an attribute on every element in the DTD. Such an attribute is sometimes called `remap`.

```
<!ATTLIST elem
      remap    NAME    #IMPLIED
  >
```

For example, suppose the source form has a specialized element for lists of software restrictions (this is the reverse of the situation described in Section 8.4.1). If you convert an instance of this element to a DTD that has no such specialized list but has a general-purpose list with the same structure, you can record the original semantic information in `remap`.

```
<!DOCTYPE randlist [
<!ELEMENT randlist   - -  (item+)>
<!ATTLIST randlist
          remap              CDATA                #IMPLIED
>
<!ELEMENT item        - -  (#PCDATA)>
]>
<randlist remap="restrictions">    used to be a restrictions list
<item>
Command line output redirection doesn't work.
</item>
<item>
File names cannot have more than three characters.
</item>
</randlist>
```

If the source and target forms are so different that no such simple one-to-one mapping is possible, or if you anticipate a conversion whose results will not be 100 percent correct, other markup may be more helpful. The conversion software might have occasion to make notes on the ongoing process, for example, noting that the results in one case or another are merely a guess at the correct element. It could output these notes as SGML comments.

```
<!-- *** CHECK: probably the wrong element choice -->
<specialterm>...</specialterm>
```

However, comments are discarded by SGML parsers and therefore can't be used in further processing. It would be more helpful for later processing stages or for the manual cleanup process to use a conversion-specific element and attributes that can store important conversion information.

```
<!DOCTYPE document [
<!ELEMENT document - - (...) +(conversion-note)>
<!ELEMENT conversion-note - - RCDATA>
<!ATTLIST conversion-note
          date             CDATA              #IMPLIED
          source           CDATA              #IMPLIED
          remap            CDATA              #IMPLIED
          problem          CDATA              #IMPLIED
          notes            CDATA              #IMPLIED
>
 .
 .
 .
]>
 .
 .
 .
<conversion-note
   date="11 Sep 1995 14:23.00"
   source="troff"
   problem="wrongelem"
   notes="Might be a commandname">
```

```
******************************************
WRITER: The following specialterm may be
a commandname instead. You should check
the intent and change the markup as
necessary.
******************************************
</conversion-note>
<specialterm>...</specialterm>
  .
  .
  .
```

If special elements are used to mark up data during conversion but are not actually added to your DTD, conversion personnel can use a validating parser to help them find and fix conversion problems.


## 8.5    Designing Markup Names

Application developers and authors know an element by its **generic identifier**—its name.[4] If your documents will be generated by a conversion or assembly process and won't ever need to be seen by human eyes as they are processed, you could probably get away with giving the markup unintuitive names; a paragraph element could be called x23 and no one would care. A similar situation might hold for structured editors with aliasing schemes and displays that completely hide the real element names from users.

However, the more likely case is that at some point authors, application developers, or other people will actually have to see and understand the element names and other markup names as they are declared in the DTD. Therefore, they should be as easy to read and understand as possible, given length constraints.

---

### Note

This section makes suggestions about English markup names, although some advice may apply to other languages as well, particularly Western languages.

---

In naming elements, you need to respect the technical jargon that has been used by the design team. Especially if you're not a subject-matter expert yourself, it's important that you check with the team before choosing names that stray from the terminology used in the document analysis report.

---

4. They might also know an element by the attribute that identifies the architectural form to which it conforms. See Section 10.2.4 for more information.

For most environments, it's useful to give elements relatively long names so that similar elements are easily distinguished and people don't need to keep looking things up in the DTD documentation. However, there are some factors that will encourage you to keep names short. The project planning documents should help you determine your situation.

### Markup Is Keyed Directly into Files

If SGML documents will primarily be created through the use of unstructured editors to enter data and markup, limit the length of markup names to cut down on keyboarding (along with setting up the environment to offer shortcuts, templates, and forms for help with markup insertion). You'll see even bigger benefits from using a markup minimization strategy if your environment supports minimization (discussed in Section 8.6).

One way to increase readability while keeping typing to a minimum is to use longer names for infrequently used high-level elements and shorter names for data-level elements that occur frequently in text.

### Names Must Adhere to the Default NAMELEN Quantity

Must you adhere to the reference NAMELEN quantity in the SGML declaration because of parser or other application constraints? The reference value for NAMELEN is 8, but few SGML-aware applications force you to adhere to this limit, and some widely used applications, including those for CALS, use a NAMELEN value of 32. By contrast, in environments where authors are accustomed to short, cryptic markup or when compatibility with all environments is a goal, they may insist on very short SGML markup names of, say, eight, four, or even fewer characters.

### Storage Space Is Limited

If storage space for SGML document files is a concern, short markup names may be necessary. However, you could achieve greater savings with an aggressive markup minimization strategy if your environment supports minimization (discussed in Section 8.6).

### Conversion Services Are Based on Character Counts

If you are paying "by the byte" for data conversion services, you may want to keep your costs low by choosing the shortest markup names possible. If you then want to lengthen the names for editing purposes, you can perform a simple one-to-one mapping.

If it's necessary to abbreviate words in the markup names, take a moment to plan when and how to abbreviate. For example, will you eliminate vowels to get spscr for your superscript element (which doesn't help much and is cryptic), or will you simply shorten the word to super or even sup? It's sometimes difficult to identify consistent patterns of abbreviation, partly because languages themselves aren't consistent. Try to choose "natural" abbreviations that authors themselves might use if they were, say, taking notes during a meeting.

For long markup names that are hard to read, you might want to use certain characters to break them up. The basic SGML declaration allows hyphens (-) and periods (.) in the second and subsequent character positions of markup names. These characters allow you to break up an element name such as `emailaddress` into `email-address` or `email.address`.

You might find that you want to add a prefix to subelements of a highly structured element to serve a self-documentation function, indicating which element they belong in and helping authors find them in the alphabetized reference documentation for the DTD. Naturally, it's a good idea to keep the prefix consistent. For example, in your glossary elements, don't name the "term" subelement `glterm` while naming the "definition" subelement `glosdefn`.

By default, markup names other than entity names are case-insensitive. You can change this setting in the `NAMING` section of the SGML declaration (described in Section A.9) and add to the set of characters allowed to be used in markup names, though in general it's not a good idea to do so. In certain circumstances where legacy documents already contain markup that uses a larger set of characters, it may be necessary to extend the set of name characters, typically to add the underscore (_) character. Note that not all SGML-aware software supports changing `NAMING` settings.

One final suggestion: The SGML standard recommends that all attributes in a DTD with the declared value `ID` have the same name. By convention in the industry, that name is usually `id`, and attributes with the declared value `IDREF` are *not* named `id`. If you use a different convention, you should have a very good reason for it and document these attributes carefully.

## 8.6   Designing Markup Minimization

Markup minimization allows markup in a document to be represented by fewer characters than it would need in a fully normalized document. It can be thought of as a kind of markup compression. You might want to design a minimization strategy to help authors who must type in their own markup or to save on disk space. Because most SGML-aware editors manage the insertion of markup without requiring authors to type it in, these editors don't make use of minimization when they write out SGML document files.

Here we'll briefly discuss the most commonly used types of minimization and the effect they can have on markup model design:

- Short reference minimization
- Short tag minimization
- Omitted tag minimization

Short references allow regular data characters to be interpreted as markup, for example, using keyboarded quotation marks (") to stand for `quote` element start- and end-tags. This mechanism is very powerful in certain circumstances and can dramatically decrease the character count of markup in SGML document files, but can be tricky and time-consuming to implement. Short reference minimization is available to all SGML documents, but it may be meaningless to use short references in SGML-aware software environments that hide the actual markup from authors.

Short tag minimization allows selected pieces of individual tags to be left out. You enable it by setting the SGML declaration's SHORTTAG feature to YES. Once this feature is enabled, you have no control over the extent to which it is used in the document files, and some kinds of short tag minimization can make the files extremely hard to read.

Following are the ways in which tags can be shortened, in order from most useful (and least distracting) to least useful (and most distracting).

1. Attribute values in start-tags can do away with quotation marks if their content conforms to the rules for SGML NAME tokens.

```
<document status=final>
```

2. Some attribute values can be supplied without their corresponding attribute names and equal signs (=).

```
<document final>
```

3. An empty pair of end-tag delimiters (</>) can be used to represent an end-tag for the most recently opened element.

```
The <command>grep</> command...
```

4. The start- and end-tags for an element can be modified in form as follows:

```
The <command/grep/ command...
```

5. In certain circumstances, an empty pair of start-tag delimiters (<>) can be interpreted as the top-level document element, a start-tag repeating the previously opened element, or an end-tag.

6. When two tags are next to each other, the ending delimiter (>) of the first one can be left out.

```
<section<title>Title Text
</para></section>
```

←—————————————————————————————————————————————→

Omitted tag minimization allows certain start-tags and end-tags to be left out of document instances based on specifications provided in element type declarations. It is a less efficient but more easily managed method of minimization than either short references or short tags.

---

## Omitted Tag Minimization

You enable omitted tag minimization by setting the SGML declaration's OMITTAG feature to YES. If OMITTAG is enabled, your DTD must supply an omitted tag minimization scheme in every element declaration. A hyphen (-) means the tag is required to be present, and the uppercase or lowercase letter "O" (*not* a zero) means the tag can be omitted if it is contextually required to exist anyway. For example:

```
<!ELEMENT section - O (title, para*, section*)>
<!ELEMENT title   O O (#PCDATA)>
<!ELEMENT para    - O (#PCDATA)>
```

Here, although section is given a minimization scheme that allows its end-tag to be omitted, in practice the end-tag must always be present because the element can appear recursively inside itself. Since it is valid for another section start-tag to appear *inside* a currently open section, </section> end-tags are needed to close previously opened sections explicitly. On the other hand, title need not have any of its tags present in the section context, since the opening of a section demands that a title appear next, and since the appearance of a para start-tag will be interpreted as closing the title.

```
<section>This Is the Title of This Section
<para>This is the text of the first paragraph
of this section.
<section>This Is the Title of a Subsection
<para>This is the text of another paragraph.
</section>
</section>
```

However, if the minimization scheme of title had specified that one or both tags must be present, the tags could never be omitted.

The ISO 8879 standard recommends that certain elements should be given an omitted tag minimization scheme of "- O" to remind readers of the DTD that, under certain circumstances, the elements aren't *allowed* to have an end-tag. Elements with a declared content of EMPTY are in this category, as they can never have an end-tag. Elements with an attribute that has a default value of #CONREF also should have this minimization scheme because, if the attribute value is supplied, the element can't have an end-tag.

If it makes sense for your project to use omitted tag minimization, you should plan the pattern of omission you will assign to the elements. Often, it is confusing to read SGML document source files that have been heavily minimized; consistency can alleviate this problem. Following are some suggestions:

- In general, avoid allowing start-tags to be minimized. The absence of clues as to the current element can be disconcerting to readers of the document files. Also, if attribute values must sometimes be specified for such an element, the pattern of markup for that element will inconsistently go back and forth because a start-tag must be present in order for attribute values to be supplied.

- The document hierarchy elements can often have their end-tags omitted because they have distinct components that are incompatible with each other. For example, a new chapter start-tag implicitly closes the previous chapter, preface, or other similar division. For example:

```
<!DOCTYPE doc [
  .
  .
  .
<!ELEMENT chapter - O (title, ...)>
  .
  .
  .
]>
<chapter><title>Chapter Title</title>
chapter content
<chapter><title>Another Chapter Title</title>
chapter content
```

This pattern of omission doesn't save many tags, but for some reason it is common in environments where omitted-tag minimization is heavily used.

- The elements for many information units tend to need an end-tag under all circumstances so that they can be closed unambiguously. For example, if a note element can contain paragraphs and can also appear at the same level as paragraphs, a </note> end-tag will always be required. However, paragraphs and information unit subelements, such as items inside lists, can often have their end-tags omitted. For example:

```
<!DOCTYPE doc [
  .
  .
  .
<!ELEMENT section  - - (title, (para|note)+)>
<!ELEMENT title    - - (#PCDATA)>
<!ELEMENT note     - O (title, para+)>
<!ELEMENT para     - O (#PCDATA)>
  .
  .
  .
]>
<section><title>Section Title</title>
```

```
<para>
This is a paragraph. When the note comes along,
this paragraph will be implicitly closed
because paragraphs can't contain notes.
<note><title>Note</title>
<para>
This is a paragraph inside the note. The
only way to tell that the note is done is
to use a note end-tag; another para start-tag
would be interpreted as being inside the note.
</note>
```

- For data-level elements in the free flow of text, it can be convenient to allow end-tags to be omitted if you expect them to appear relatively often just before the end of a higher-level element. Typically, however, the presence of the data-level end-tag will be required.

## 8.7    Addressing Other Design Factors

In addition to the basic markup model expressed in the DTD, you may be responsible for other related features of the DTD and markup-related pieces of the "documentation engineering toolbox."

- Characters usually used as markup delimiters that are needed in document content

- Entities for special symbols and characters

- Text databases and templates

- Default entity declaration

The following sections discuss these issues.

### 8.7.1    Markup Characters as Content

As with all markup systems, SGML has the problem of how to allow document instances to contain, as data content, characters that are normally interpreted as markup. The two main examples are the left angle bracket (<), which normally begins a tag, and the ampersand (&), which normally begins an entity reference. If a document contains one of these characters followed by a valid NAME character, validating parsers will report an error if the string turns out not to be a legitimate piece of markup.

For instance, this example produces an error because <b looks like the beginning of a start-tag that is improperly closed.

```
If a<b then fill in the total amount here.
```

The following example, however, produces no error because <4 can't possibly be the beginning of a start-tag—a digit is not allowed to be the first character in an element name (unless you've changed the NAMING settings in the SGML declaration).

```
This game uses only the cards <4 in the deck, including aces.
```

If you don't provide any mechanisms for allowing these characters to appear as content, authors do have one method at their disposal for inserting the character: a CDATA marked section, which surrounds a region that should not be parsed for element or entity reference markup. For example:

```
If a<![ CDATA [<]]>b then fill in the total amount here.
```

CDATA marked sections can't contain a series of two right square brackets (]]) as content, since this string is treated as the markup that closes the marked section.

The easiest general way to enable left angle brackets and ampersands as data content is to provide SDATA ("specific" character data) text entities corresponding to the characters so that when the documents are processed after being parsed, the appropriate characters will be inserted in place of the entity references. For example:

**for ampersand:**
```
<!ENTITY amp SDATA "INSERT-AMPERSAND">
```
**for left angle bracket ("less-than" symbol):**
```
<!ENTITY lt SDATA "INSERT-LESSTHAN">
```

These entities might be used as follows:

```
The Mother&amp;Daughter Moving Company is having a sale!
We guarantee that your moving expenses will be &lt;five
hundred dollars.
```

SDATA entities, by definition, contain instructions that are specific to one system or processing application, and so they can present portability problems. However, the standard ISO entity set for numeric and special graphic symbols, discussed in Section 8.7.2, comes with ready-made entities for left angle brackets and ampersands that should work with most SGML systems. Thus, if you include this entity set in your DTD, the entities will be available to authors.

---

### Note

If you use an SGML declaration that makes changes to the reference concrete syntax (the default assignments of characters to markup delimiter "roles"), for example, substituting a left square bracket ([) for a left angle bracket, make sure that SDATA entities are available for your choices of markup characters.

---

For any DTDs that will be used for the actual documentation of how to use an SGML system, it is a common problem to need to "escape" examples of tags and document instance fragments. You may want to add element types to the markup model that take the self-referential nature of the information into account. For example, you might have a data-level element called `start-tag` that, when processed, outputs the necessary tag delimiters.

```
<!DOCTYPE dtd-manual [
 ⋮
<!ELEMENT start-tag  - - (#PCDATA)>
 ⋮
]>
<dtd-manual>
 ⋮
At the beginning of a trademarked term,
use <start-tag>trademk</start-tag>.
 ⋮
</dtd-manual>
```

## 8.7.2    Entities for Symbols and Characters

If your documents need to contain symbols and characters that can't be entered directly into document files with keyboard key presses, the DTD needs to define SDATA ("specific" character data) text entities that represent the symbols so that applications can add the appropriate symbol during processing.

The informational part of the ISO 8879 standard defines several sets of SDATA entities that can be used to produce many common symbols and characters. For example, the "ISOlat1" entity set defines the following symbol, among others:

```
<!ENTITY eacute SDATA "[eacute]"--=small e, acute accent-->
```

If this entity declaration is included as part of the DTD, document instances can refer to the entity. For example:

```
<para> This dish makes a perfect entr&eacute;e on a
cold winter's night.
</para>
```

Commercial SGML-aware products capable of handling the ISO entities can output the correct symbol in place, with the correct point size, weight, and so on.

> This dish makes a perfect entrée on a cold winter's night.

Many SGML formatting applications support the standard SDATA instructions for the ISO entities "out of the box," and even include the entity sets and various predefined formal public identifiers with their products in order to simplify the use of the entities in any DTD. For example, the file containing the ISO entity set for publishing characters has probably been set up to map to the following public identifier:

```
ISO 8879:1986//ENTITIES Publishing//EN
```

If so, you can include the following parameter entity declaration and reference in your DTD to make these entities available to authors:

```
<!ENTITY % ISOpub PUBLIC "ISO 8879:1986//ENTITIES Publishing//EN">
%ISOpub;
```

Appendix D summarizes the available ISO entity sets and shows one possible formatted representation of the symbols and characters. The entity sets for Latin 1 characters, diacritical symbols, numeric and special graphic characters, and publishing characters are probably the most frequently needed for general publishing. If you want to use smaller portions of any of the sets, you can assemble only the entity declarations you need, as long as you include the copyright statement found in the original files. Remember to ensure that all your processing applications support the characters and symbols you make available in the DTD.

If you have an application that needs the instructions in these entity sets to be in a different form, copy the entity sets to new files, change the values for the entities, and make sure that the application is directed to the changed files instead of the original ones.

If the ISO entity sets or other available entity sets don't meet your needs, you may need to define your own SDATA entities. For example, if your documents need a character that looks like a happy face, you can define something like the following entity:

```
<!ENTITY happyface SDATA "INSERT-HAPPYFACE">
```

Your applications must then be made to operate appropriately on the SDATA value passed to them during parsing, such as inserting the symbol and ensuring it is of the appropriate point size. For example:

```
<para>
If the command returns a status of 0,
the outcome was successful.&happyface;
```

This reference to the entity might result in the following output.

> If the command returns a status of 0, the outcome was successful. ☺

For each application or system that needs a different system-specific SDATA instruction, you will need to provide a different definition for &happyface;. For example, if you need to prepare your documents for a simple character-cell display with no graphics capabilities, the processing for that system might use an alternate set of entity declarations that includes the following:

```
<!ENTITY happyface SDATA ":-)">
```

The use of this declaration in processing might result in the following appearance; in this case, the SDATA value is simply passed on to the output.

```
If the command returns a status of 0, the outcome
was successful.:-)
```

If the character set being used for your documents happens to have a character position that corresponds to a happy face, you can make the SDATA instructions contain a special kind of entity reference called a "character reference," which explicitly calls for the character that resides in a certain numbered position. Character references look like regular entity references, except that their opening delimiter consists of an ampersand followed by a number sign (#), and the entity "name" that is referenced must be a number. (Documents can also contain character references directly, without needing an SDATA entity to be defined.) For example, if the happy face is in position 99:

```
<!ENTITY happyface SDATA "&#99;">
```

Using character references makes your document files less portable because they depend on a particular character set rather than on processing that can change according to the circumstances.

Section A.9.1 describes how an SGML declaration sets up the interpretation of numeric codes as characters.

## 8.7.3    Text Databases and Templates

Many content-based markup models are meant to facilitate the creation of a text fragment database for assembling document content. For example, glossary entries are often treated this way, as are legal publication statements such as copyright notices and trademark attributions. If the project's utilization goals include this sort of text reuse and it is to be accomplished using SGML entities, you, the DTD implementor, will probably be responsible for creating and maintaining the entity declarations and ensuring they are included in the DTDs used by all documents that need them.

The project may also need templates containing data and markup, so that authors can work from a common base when writing new documents. This is especially true in cases where some editorial guidelines aren't able to be enforced through validation with a parser. You are likely to be responsible for developing and maintaining the templates and ensuring that they incorporate valid use of the DTD.

## 8.7.4    Default Entity Declarations

If a document refers to an entity that has not been defined, validating parsers will report an error. To avoid this error during validation and help authors find the problem in formatted text or to attach special processing to these occurrences, you can provide a declaration in your DTD that will be used for any entity references whose entities haven't been declared explicitly. Supply #DEFAULT as the entity name.

```
<!ENTITY #DEFAULT "ENTITY NOT DEFINED!">
```

# Techniques for DTD Maintenance and Readability

This chapter provides suggestions on how to structure DTDs to make them easier to read and maintain. Your main tools for this work are comments in the DTD, the organization of the markup declarations, and the use of parameter entities in various creative capacities.

---

### Note

If you are using a computer-aided DTD development or viewing tool, some of the techniques described here may not be relevant to you. However, in areas where you have a choice about organizing and structuring your DTD through these tools, you should put some thought into making the DTD readable and maintainable by people who don't have software to help them.

---

Various commercial software products and public-domain tools are available to help make DTDs readable in printed and viewed form.

---

### Note

Some of the techniques suggested in this chapter can affect and be affected by your decisions about modularizing your DTD and preparing it for reuse and customization. Chapter 10 describes these additional techniques.

---

The following checklist summarizes ways to make your DTD more readable and maintainable. Some of these areas are discussed in greater detail in the following sections.

### Use Comments and White Space

Use comments and white space effectively and consistently in the DTD. Section 9.1 describes some common styles and offers advice.

### Use a Source Code Control System

We strongly recommend that you store the DTD files under a source code control system that records descriptions of changes. If this is not done, comments in each file should include a detailed change history.

### Organize Declarations According to Their Appearance in Content Models

Put element/attribute declaration pairs in visual top-down, left-right order, grouped by relative level in the DTD. Section 9.2 describes how to organize your DTD along these lines and the reasons for doing so.

### Keep Pairs of Element/Attribute Declarations Together

You can think of an attribute declaration as "local" to its related element declaration because it applies only to that element. Some DTDs contain *all* the element declarations followed by *all* the attribute declarations. However, storing the two far away from each other is inconvenient; readers must hunt through the DTD to find all the relevant information for an element. Also, keeping the declarations together helps if you later decide to put some declarations into a separate module.

### Generally Collect Parameter Entity Declarations at the Top

Entity declarations, unlike other declarations, are position-sensitive. In the linear flow of your DTD, you must declare parameter entities before you can reference them. Therefore, you'll need to collect global parameter entity declarations somewhere near the top of each DTD module.

However, if you have a parameter entity that is referenced only in one portion of the DTD, keep the entity declaration close to the places where it is used for ease of editing. For example, if you use a single list of attribute value choices three times for the attributes of three related elements, store the list in a parameter entity near all the attribute declarations. Again, this helps you if you later decide to put some of the declarations into a separate module.

### Use Parameter Entities for Element Collections

Use parameter entities to manage element collections that are commonly used and, when you must manage several such collections, control the dependencies and complexity of the entities. Section 9.3 describes why and how.

### Synchronize the Declarations of Similar Elements

Use parameter entities or name groups to synchronize the content models or attribute lists of multiple elements. Section 9.4 describes how.

### Document the DTD through Parameter Entities

Use parameter entities to "document" attribute declared and default values. Section 9.5 describes how.

(See Appendix C for a sample of many of the techniques described in this chapter.)

## 9.1   Using Good "Coding" Style

DTD style is highly subject to personal taste. If you are new to DTD development, you may want to play around with different styles and look at various published DTDs before you settle on a style of your own to use, and if several people will be contributing to a single DTD or a series of element sets, choosing a DTD style policy and putting it in writing can be helpful. Changing from one style to another in midstream can be time-consuming and frustrating.

Style issues fall into two broad categories: comments and white space.

### 9.1.1   Comment Style

When you put comments in a DTD, you need to strike a balance between stuffing the whole DTD user documentation set into the DTD on the one hand, and leaving DTD readers mystified on the other. It's reasonable to include a brief comment to explain the purpose of each element type, attribute value, and major parameter entity, along with comments explaining any subtle or tricky content models. DTD maintenance documentation that you've written separately should explain how the DTD is structured and the right and wrong ways to customize it, and user documentation should explain to authors how to choose the right markup for each kind of document content. (Chapter 12 suggests the necessary components of full DTD documentation.)

Comments at the beginning of each file making up the DTD should do the following:

- Identify the file's creator and provide contact information for problems
- Provide the file's name, version, and change history (through the use of source code control system variables, if possible)
- Give a brief purpose statement
- Indicate any dependencies of this module on other modules
- List the formal public identifier, if this file has a preferred form by which to be identified (formal public identifiers are explained in Section A.10)

For example:

```
<!-- .................................................... -->
<!-- Self-Help Book DTD, Version 1.3, 9 November 1995 -->
<!-- File selfhelp.dtd -->

<!-- This DTD is maintained by Vanity Press, Ltd.  Send comments
     or corrections to the acquisitions editor:
     editor@vanitypr.com or +1 800 555 1212.
-->

<!-- This DTD is for the markup of self-help books and tutorials.
     It is not intended for general publishing.  It depends on
     two lower-level modules, selfhier.mod and selfpool.mod.
     Please refer to this DTD with the following public
      identifier:

       "-//Vanity Press//DTD Self-Help Book V1.3//EN"

     This DTD is accompanied by an SGML declaration.
-->
<!-- Change history ....................................... -->
<!-- 09 Nov 95 exi: Updated formal public identifier. -->
<!-- 21 May 95 emi: Allowed titles to contain graphics. -->
<!-- 18 Mar 95 jea: Added more ISO entity sets. -->
<!-- 06 Mar 95 alb: Changed chap to allow sections directly. -->
   .
   .
   .
```

## 9.1.2   White Space Style

The physical organization of each markup declaration is allowed to vary widely, as long as the parameters of the declaration appear in the proper order. You can use white space (tabs, spaces, and blank lines) to make your declarations more readable.

Most people consider it good form to align markup declaration parameters in some fashion. Some implementors prefer a strict alignment such as the following:

```
<!ELEMENT  elemname      - -   (content-model)   -(exceptions)   >

<!ATTLIST  elemname            attname   NUMBER    #IMPLIED    >

<!ELEMENT  otherelem    - O   (#PCDATA)                        >
```

This style has a clean appearance, but during active editing of the DTD, it can be tiresome to make each field align properly, particularly the closing angle bracket. Also, if the DTD tends to have long element and attribute names or complex content models, the wrapping of lines can undermine any advantages of the appearance.

One alternative, and the style used in this book, is to align parameters approximately and to indent wrapped lines to the relevant place below the previous line, but to add no extra white space around the "constant-width" parameters:

```
<!ELEMENT elemname      - - (content-model) -(exceptions)>

<!ATTLIST elemname
        attname1        NUMBER          #IMPLIED
        attname2        (yes|no)        yes
        attname3        (dosetvalue
                        |dontsetvalue)  #REQUIRED
>

<!ELEMENT (otherelem1
        |otherelem2) - O (title, (complex-model1
                                 |complex-model2
                                 |complex-model3))>
```

The attribute fields are simply separated by tabs to allow for easy reading; other ATTLIST declarations might align the fields differently. Note that the closing angle bracket for the ATTLIST declaration is on a separate line, which allows for convenient switching of the order of the attribute definitions.

## 9.2   Organizing Declarations

To match the expectations of most DTD readers, put the declaration pairs for elements and attributes in visual top-down, left-right order as they occur in content models, grouped by relative level in the DTD. For collections of elements that are allowed in any order, organize these elements' pairs of declarations alphabetically by class.

For example, if the content model for a list element contains the specialized subelements listtitle and listitem, in that order, provide declarations for first list, then listtitle and its contained elements, then listitem and its contained elements. Be as consistent as you can in this organization.

```
<!ELEMENT list            - - (listtitle?, listitem+)>
<!ELEMENT listtitle       - - (longlisttitle, shortlisttitle?)>
<!ELEMENT longlisttitle   - - (#PCDATA)>
<!ELEMENT shortlisttitle  - - (#PCDATA)>
<!ELEMENT listitem        - - (%list-para-mix;)+>
```

Some DTDs strictly alphabetize all the declaration pairs by element name, which arguably makes it just as easy to find element declarations as any other scheme, but it can be annoying to have to look up shortlisttitle in the S section, even though it's related exclusively to lists. Also, if you later want to move all the list-related declarations to a separate module, this scheme will hinder your efforts.

A question often arises for elements used in multiple contexts: Where should their declarations be stored? For example, in a software documentation DTD, you might allow a command element at the data level for command names mentioned in text, as well as inside specialized diagrams for command line syntax. The declaration for command could logically be put either near the other data-level elements or with the syntax diagram elements. You should determine, before you put the whole DTD together, a pattern of where you'll put multiple-purpose elements so that readers of the DTD can get to know the pattern. It's usually best to keep the declarations together in a general-purpose section of the DTD, and then just refer to those elements with a comment in the special-purpose sections. This way, the section containing general-purpose element declarations can serve as a multipurpose "element library."

You may find it useful to provide comments in the "holes" where the declaration would have been if you had been going by strict top-down left-right declaration order. For example:

```
   :
<!-- ==== Command Syntax Diagrams ================ -->
<!ELEMENT command-syntax - - (command, argument*)>
```
**the following comment looks similar to an element declaration:**
```
<!--ELEMENT command          (see Inlines section) -->
<!ELEMENT argument       - - (#PCDATA)>
   :

<!-- ==== Inlines ================================ -->
<!ELEMENT command        - - (#PCDATA)>
   :
```

---

## Note

Some SGML processing applications expect to identify the document element (the top-level element) by finding the first element type declared in the DTD. If this is the case with applications you plan to use, either make sure this element declaration appears first, which is generally a good idea anyway, or parameterize the application to choose the document element by other means.

---

# 9.3   Parameter Entities for Element Collections

Most DTDs have elements that contain collections—groups of elements and possibly character data that offer a "palette" from which a document creator can choose without restriction.

Collections correspond to optional-repeatable or required-repeatable OR groups, such as the following:

```
<!ELEMENT trademark   - - (#PCDATA|emphasis)*>
<!ELEMENT chemname    - - (#PCDATA|emphasis)*>
   :
```

```
<!ELEMENT para        - - (#PCDATA|trademark|chemname|emphasis)*>
<!ELEMENT legalnote   - - (#PCDATA|trademark|chemname|emphasis)*>
  ⋮
<!ELEMENT abstract    - - (para|quotation)+>
<!ELEMENT copyright   - - (para|quotation)+>
  ⋮
<!ELEMENT division    - - (title, (para|quotation
                                  |numbered-list|unnumbered-list
                                  |chemical-formula
                                  |figure|table)*, subdivision*)>
<!ELEMENT subdivision - - (title, (para|quotation
                                  |numbered-list|unnumbered-list
                                  |chemical-formula
                                  |figure|table)*)>
```

Because the contents of such collections are susceptible to adjustment during testing and maintenance of the DTD, you should use parameter entities to store collections that should stay in synchronization across many element content models. This way, you can avoid needing to edit dozens or hundreds of element declarations when you want to add or subtract an element. Following is how the same element declarations might look if parameter entities are used:

```
<!ELEMENT trademark   - - (%simple-data-mix;)*>
<!ELEMENT chemname    - - (%simple-data-mix;)*>
  ⋮
<!ELEMENT para        - - (%full-data-mix;)*>
<!ELEMENT legalnote   - - (%full-data-mix;)*>
  ⋮
<!ELEMENT abstract    - - (%simple-para-mix;)+>
<!ELEMENT copyright   - - (%simple-para-mix;)+>
  ⋮
<!ELEMENT division    - - (title, (%div-para-mix;)*, subdivision*)>
<!ELEMENT subdivision - - (title, (%div-para-mix;)*)>
```

While readers of the DTD must now go through a level of indirection to see exactly what the content model is for one of these elements, if the number of different collections is kept reasonable and is managed and documented well, the benefits outweigh the costs.

Chapter 5 discussed how the document type design team can determine the right collection for each context using the notion of element classes. Where a common collection appears in several elements, as happens repeatedly in the above example, it can be helpful to treat the collection as a construct standing on its own—something like a "phantom element," with a name, child elements, and parent elements.

For example, if authors come to know the collection of para and quotation as the "simple paragraph collection," this shorthand name can be used effectively in the DTD documentation to explain the contents of all the parent elements that use it—abstract, copyright, and others. The same might be done for the more diverse "division collection" that appears in the two levels of division and the two different data-level collections. Since the design team will have named each collection it designed, ready-made labels should already exist for these phantom elements.

What constitutes good management of parameter entities for element collections?

### Name Entities Distinctively

Make sure to give a distinctive name to all parameter entities for collections that contain #PCDATA. For example, you could include the word "data" in the entity names. DTD readers should be able to tell at a glance which content models have mixed content and which don't, because of the special nature of these content models and because of the potential problems with them (discussed in Section 8.2.4).

Alternatively, you can leave the #PCDATA keyword out of the collection entity and put it directly in the content model group.

### Don't Nest Entities Unnecessarily

Keep the levels of parameter entity indirection to a minimum so that readers of the DTD won't have to work backwards repeatedly just to figure out the content model of an element. There are few things more frustrating than conducting a parameter entity "treasure hunt."

### Control Entity Dependencies

Don't make collection entities depend on each other if they don't have to. For example, if you define the larger "division collection" entity partly in terms of the "simple collection," as follows, you can't change them independently of each other.

```
<!ENTITY % simple-para-mix "para|quotation">
<!ENTITY % div-para-mix    "%simple-para-mix;
                           |numbered-list|unnumbered-list
                           |chemical-formula
                           |figure|table">
```

In a small or simple DTD, you can address the nesting and dependency issues together by using only a single level of parameter entity that directly contains the appropriate element collection. If your DTD has several large collections, however, the best way to attack the problem is to make use of the element classes that the document type design team built. The following simple example shows how to fix the problems inherent in a "traditional" approach to creating collection parameter entities.

The document analysis report might contain the IU context matrix in Table 9-1 for a pharmaceuticals-related document type.

**Table 9-1**          IU Context Matrix for Pharmaceutical Document.

| | simple mixture | general-purpose nontechnical mixture | technical mixture | full division contents mixture |
|---|---|---|---|---|
| **text blocks** paragraph quotation | X | X | X | X |
| **lists** numbered list unnumbered list | | X | X | X |
| **chemical related displays** chemical formula | | | X | X |
| **illustrations** figure table | | | | X |

To work with this matrix, the first thing you need to do is reverse the axes, as shown in Table 9-2. (This matrix has been simplified by the removal of the individual elements, since in these collections they happen never to be used apart from their element class.)

**Table 9-2**          Working Version of Table 9-1.

| | text blocks | lists | chemical related displays | illustrations |
|---|---|---|---|---|
| **simple mixture** | X | | | |
| **general-purpose nontechnical mixture** | X | X | | |
| **technical mixture** | X | X | X | |
| **full division mixture** | X | X | X | X |

Using a traditional approach to constructing parameter entities that we call the "onion" approach, you would make successively larger collection entities that wrap around smaller ones, as shown in Figure 9-1. However, this approach creates unnecessary dependencies between entities and makes it difficult for DTD readers to follow what's going on.

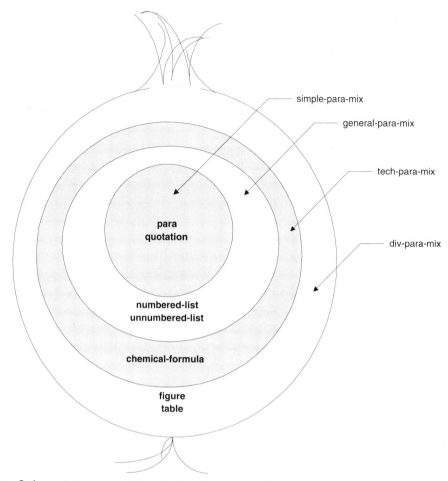

**Figure 9-1**     Onion Approach to Collection Parameter Entities.

Using the onion approach, you might or might not store the element classes in their own entities for convenience. The structure in Figure 9-1 would correspond to entity declarations along the following lines, if you haven't used entities to hold each element class:

```
<!ENTITY % simple-para-mix   "para
                             |quotation">
<!ENTITY % general-para-mix  "%simple-para-mix;
                             |numbered-list
                             |unnumbered-list">
<!ENTITY % tech-para-mix     "%general-para-mix;
                             |chemical-formula">
<!ENTITY % div-para-mix      "%tech-para-mix;
                             |figure
                             |table">
```

Alternatively, the declarations would look more like the following if you did use parameter entities for element classes:

*element class entities:*
```
<!ENTITY % textblocks     "para|quotation">
<!ENTITY % lists          "numlist|unnumlist">
<!ENTITY % chemical       "chemdiagram">
<!ENTITY % illustrations  "figure|table">
```
*collection entities:*
```
<!ENTITY % simple-para-mix  "%textblocks;">
<!ENTITY % general-para-mix "%simple-para-mix;|%lists;">
<!ENTITY % tech-para-mix    "%general-para-mix;|%chemical;">
<!ENTITY % div-para-mix     "%tech-para-mix;|%illustrations;">
```

Either way, you can't adjust the contents of any of the lower collections without affecting higher ones, and you force DTD readers to search through as many as four levels of complex entity contents to figure out what a division contains.

A "building block" approach, as illustrated by Figure 9-2, is preferable. With this approach, you make entities for the element classes and use those entities as the basic raw material for the collection entities.

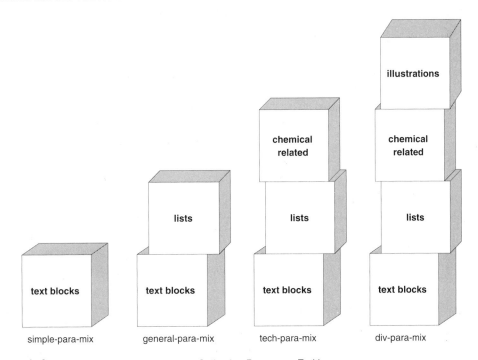

**Figure 9-2**    Building Block Approach to Collection Parameter Entities.

This scheme would look as follows.

```
element class entities:
<!ENTITY % textblocks      "para|quotation">
<!ENTITY % lists           "numlist|unnumlist">
<!ENTITY % chemical        "chemdiagram">
<!ENTITY % illustrations   "figure|table">
collection entities:
<!ENTITY % simple-para-mix  "%textblocks;">
<!ENTITY % general-para-mix "%textblocks;|%lists;">
<!ENTITY % tech-para-mix    "%textblocks;|%lists;|%chemical;">
<!ENTITY % div-para-mix     "%textblocks;|%lists;|%chemical;|%illustrations;">
```

This scheme keeps the nesting of entities to two levels at a maximum. Also, even though four element class entities are mentioned in the largest collection entity, they are the *only* entities to which DTD readers will ever need to refer when looking up element contents, and the element class entities are largely self-documenting.

With this scheme, when you need to make adjustments to collections, you have pinpoint control: If a new text-block element such as `note` is added, you can simply edit the `%textblocks;` element class entity. If, as a result of testing the conversion of legacy documents, you discover that the contents of "simple" elements need to be broadened to include lists, you can simply edit `%simple-para-mix;` to add `%lists;`. Note that even though the `%simple-para-mix;` and `%general-para-mix;` might now have the same contents, the elements that refer to each one retain their autonomy; you can still modify one group independently of the other.

Furthermore, the building block scheme facilitates the creation of collections that pick and choose more discriminatingly from the element classes at hand, rather than building solely on smaller collections. For example, what if, in addition to the four desired collections, you needed to add a new one such as that in Table 9-3, which "skips" an element class?[1]

**Table 9-3**     IU Collection that Skips an Element Class.

|  | text blocks | lists | chemical related displays | illustrations |
|---|---|---|---|---|
| nontechnical division mixture | X | X |  | X |

The onion approach, even with element-class entities, would be at a disadvantage because the relationships of the different collections become more and more obscure. You need to branch out to two different "onions" after the innermost layer, `%simple-para-mix;`.

---

1.  Needing to customize collections by removing one element class from them is actually a fairly common occurrence that results from ambiguity problems such as those discussed in Section 8.2.1.

```
<!ENTITY % simple-para-mix       "%textblocks;">
<!ENTITY % general-para-mix      "%simple-para-mix;|%lists;">
<!ENTITY % tech-para-mix         "%general-para-mix;|%chemical;">
<!ENTITY % div-para-mix          "%tech-para-mix;|%illustrations;">
<!ENTITY % nontech-div-para-mix  "%general-para-mix;|%illustrations;">
```

On the other hand, you could make everything clear (and continue mimicking the matrix in the document analysis report, even to the point of leaving a "hole" in the declaration) with the building block approach.

```
<!ENTITY % simple-para-mix       "%textblocks;">
<!ENTITY % general-para-mix      "%textblocks;|%lists;">
<!ENTITY % tech-para-mix         "%textblocks;|%lists;|%chemical;">
<!ENTITY % div-para-mix          "%textblocks;|%lists;|%chemical;|%illustrations;">
<!ENTITY % nontech-div-para-mix  "%textblocks;|%lists;          |%illustrations;">
```

Note that this "skipping" technique only disallows the chemical-related elements from appearing *directly* inside elements where the %nontech-div-para-mix; collection has been used. For collections at the data level, it's common to need to customize collections so that a particular element (or a whole class) is disallowed from appearing *anywhere* within itself. Creating a huge set of slightly differing collections will be ineffective for this purpose, and will cause a maintenance headache as well. A better solution is to use "regular" collection entities, but to put SGML exceptions on the individual element declarations involved. For example:

```
<!ENTITY % basic               "emphasis|partnumber|...">
  .
  .
  .
<!ENTITY % general-data-mix    "%basic;|...">
  .
  .
  .
<!ELEMENT emphasis - - (%general-data-mix;)* -(emphasis)>
```

---

## Note

Be careful of interactions between SGML exclusions and the granules in which your information will be created, stored, and reused. If the document hierarchy imposes global restrictions through SGML exclusions, but the information is created in nested "document" units at lower levels where there is no explicit restriction, assembly, and validation of whole documents will reveal invalid uses of restricted elements. It's safest to use exceptions only at low levels, preferably the data level, and just for the purpose discussed above.

---

## 9.4   Synchronizing Elements

The document analysis report may have indicated which elements should have the same content model or attribute characteristics, or you may find that you're repeatedly running across the same whole or fragmentary content model or attribute declaration. In cases where the model should stay in synchronization across the DTD, use parameter entities or declaration name groups to stand for the repeated parts.

If multiple elements should, by design, have identical content (including all inclusion and exclusion exceptions), you might want to use a name group in place of a single generic identifier in the element declaration, as shown, to ensure that the content models will stay in lockstep.

```
<!ELEMENT (numbered-list|unnumbered-list)  - - (item+)>
```

Likewise, if multiple elements' attribute declarations should, by design, be identical, you might want to use a name group in the attribute declaration.

```
<!ATTLIST (note|caution)
        security        (open|confidential)       open
>
```

Often, the elements that need this treatment are members of the same class. If all members of an element class have identical content or attributes, and you have a parameter entity that records the class members, you can refer to the entity in the declaration.

```
<!ATTLIST (%admonitions;)
        security        (open|confidential)       open
>
```

However, don't join declarations that aren't designed specifically to stay in synchronization with each other, because using name groups (whether through parameter entities or not) for unrelated elements can make it harder to find the declaration you want when reading the DTD.

If you think you might be breaking up the joined declaration in the future, or if the declarations can be joined for either the elements or the attribute lists but not both, instead use parameter entities to stand for the specifics of the content model or attributes, and keep the declarations separate.

```
<!ENTITY % list.content   "item+">
<!ELEMENT numbered-list     - - (%list.content;)>
<!ELEMENT unnumbered-list   - - (%list.content;)>

<!ENTITY % secur.att
        "security       (open|confidential)       open">
<!ATTLIST note              %secur.att;>
<!ATTLIST caution           %secur.att;>
```

For parameter entities that provide some fraction of a content model, you'll need to decide where to put the group delimiters (parentheses) and occurrence indicators—outside or inside the entity definition. In general, leaving them off gives you flexibility in changing the entity's characteristics at the point of reference, and putting them in ensures that the entity contents are used consistently. For example, look at the following three options:

*option 1:*
```
<!ENTITY % list.content    "item">
```

*option 2:*
```
<!ENTITY % list.content    "item+">
```

*option 3:*
```
<!ENTITY % list.content    "(item+)">
```

Option 1 is best for class and collection entities. It ensures that item is the element used but lets you decide at each point of reference how many must be supplied.

Option 2 ensures that at least one item must be present wherever this entity is used, but allows you to specify other elements as part of the model group in a natural way.

Option 3 is usually the best choice for general content model fragments. It lets you use the entity as the entire content model for each list with no additional parentheses supplied, which can indicate your intent to disallow additions to the content model. However, you still have the ability to use the entity in building larger models, just as with option 2.

## 9.5   Creating New Attribute Keywords

For every attribute definition, you need to supply a declared value, which serves as a kind of "data type" declaration, and a default value. However, the keywords for declared and default values are far from self-documenting, and, unfortunately, even though attributes usually need more explanation than elements, attribute documentation usually gets short shrift.

You can use parameter entities to make customized "SGML keywords" that help communicate your design intent to readers of the DTD. Using parameter entities also gives you an easy way to update your DTD if you decide to change the underlying keyword. Following are some examples of user-defined keywords that you may find helpful.

Especially if you have chosen to use a declared value other than ID for your symbolic ID attributes (as discussed in Section 8.3.2), you might want to make your own keyword for ID values.

```
<!ENTITY % id        "CDATA">
   ⋮
<!ATTLIST document
        id      %id;     #REQUIRED
>
```

For attributes that have a yes-or-no (Boolean) value, you might have chosen to use the NUMBER declared value (as described in Section 8.3.1) and interpret zero values as "no", "false", or "off", and nonzero values as "yes", "true", or "on". In this case, you could make your own keywords for both declared and default values.

```
<!ENTITY % yesorno    "NUMBER">
<!ENTITY % yes        "1">
<!ENTITY % no         "0">
  .
  .
  .
<!ATTLIST document
        incatalog        %yesorno;        %yes;
>
```

In cases where you must use attributes to contain physical measurement information related to formatting the document, such as graphic heights and table cell widths, make keywords for the unit of measurement to be assumed by processing applications.

```
<!ENTITY % picas  "NUTOKEN">
  .
  .
<!ATTLIST figure
        figdepth        %picas;        #REQUIRED
>
```

Where you have specified a default value of #IMPLIED, the action that must be taken by processing applications isn't explicit. (This situation is discussed in Section 8.3.3.) Using special keywords for the different requirements can help make your processing expectations clear.

```
<!ENTITY % get-from-parent "#IMPLIED">
  .
  .
<!ELEMENT section          - - (title, para+)>
<!ATTLIST section
        approach          (leftbrain|rightbrain)    leftbrain
>
<!ELEMENT title            - - (#PCDATA)>
<!ELEMENT para             - - (#PCDATA)>
<!ATTLIST para
        approach          (leftbrain|rightbrain)    %get-from-parent;
>
```

# 10

# Techniques for DTD Reuse and Customization

You could construct your DTD to be contained in a single file, with all relevant declarations provided "in the flesh" (that is, with no portions pulled in by reference to external parameter entities) and with no expectation that you or anyone else will customize it. However, if your project goals include creating a family of similar DTDs or making your DTD available to a broad secondary audience that will need to customize its markup model, you will want to build mechanisms into your DTD that support reuse and customization.

In this chapter we concentrate on two related ways to generate multiple markup models using the same DTD "code":

- Setting up collections of markup declarations in DTD modules, files that can be used in multiple DTDs by means of an external parameter entity

- Facilitating the addition, removal, and change of various features of markup declarations in a DTD, primarily by using parameter entities that are specifically intended to be redefined

If you've had to answer the question of how many DTDs to build (discussed in Section 8.1) because you're dealing with an interrelated set of document types, you can probably already understand the motivations for using modularity: It allows you to maintain a single copy of certain declarations rather than typing, validating, and tracking several copies of the same thing, and it lets you ensure that the definitions for similar document types are synchronized. Modularity makes sense for most large DTDs as preparation for future expansion, even if the immediate needs don't seem to call for it.

Building customization placeholders into a DTD needs a stronger rationale. The project documents should help you determine whether this is appropriate for your DTD.

If you need your DTD to be used precisely as it was originally written, you may not want to encourage its customization. However, it's possible you can increase the value of your own data by encouraging others to use the DTD, and it's likely that other organizations will need to customize the DTD before they can use it. Your goals in making the DTD widely used may be compromised if other users customize it in inappropriate ways or ways that are incompatible with each other, or if they feel compelled to write new DTDs that do essentially the same job as yours. Therefore, you have an incentive to encourage the kinds of customization and reuse that *you* prefer by building in features that facilitate them.

Section 10.1 summarizes the three fundamental ways a DTD markup model can be modified (subsetting, extension, and renaming) and their effects on document processing and interchange. Section 10.2 describes how to use techniques for facilitating customization of your DTD and reuse of portions of it. Section 10.3 contains advice on customizing and reusing portions of existing DTDs.

(Chapter 12 discusses documenting the methods you've supplied for DTD customization and the constraints you want to place on variant-DTD implementors, and Appendix C contains a sample of many of the techniques described in this chapter.)

# 10.1  Categories of Customization

In terms of conformance to the markup model of an original DTD, there are three basic kinds of changes that can be made: subsets, extensions, and renamings. An entire variant DTD can fall into one or more of these categories, and individual changes to the markup model can be categorized along these lines as well.

Think of a DTD as describing a set of document instances. All document instances that conform to the rules of this DTD are in this set, but instances that would cause a validating parser to return one or more error messages fall outside it, as do instances that conform to radically different DTDs. The sets of instances produced by variant DTDs have different relations to the original instance set.

- Subsetted DTDs produce a smaller set of instances that fits wholly within the original set.

- Extended DTDs produce a set containing at least some instances that are outside the original set (though it may not contain all the instances in the original set).

- Renamed DTDs produce a "shadow" set that's identical to the original except for the actual element names.

Figure 10-1 shows these relationships.

Any variation can be described in these terms, whether or not any special features for customization were built into the original DTD. Each type of variation from an original markup model has advantages and drawbacks; you can combine them to achieve the effect you want. This section discusses each type of variant and the consequences of using it or encouraging it to be used by others.

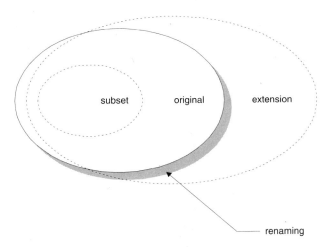

**Figure 10-1**    Relationship of Subsetted, Extended, and Renamed Markup Models to the Original.

---

### Note

It's possible to change a DTD without changing the markup model. In fact, the same markup model could be expressed in two entirely different DTDs with different amounts of modularity, parameter entities, comments, and so on, implemented by different people—as long as the element and attribute markup amounts to the same set of markup rules. What we're discussing in this chapter is the customization of *markup model* characteristics, though they're facilitated by *architectural* mechanisms such as parameter entities.

---

## 10.1.1   Subsetted Markup Models

If all valid instances of the variant DTD are guaranteed to fit inside the set of original valid instances, the variant is a **subset** of the original.

The markup model changes in this category might not intuitively seem to be acts of "subsetting." The following pairs of DTD fragments each demonstrate a subsetting. In each case, the result is a subset because the variant fragment places tighter restrictions on the markup than the original does and still produces instances that conform to the original fragment.

```
original:
<!ELEMENT div  - - (title, subtitle?, para*)>
variant (subset):
<!ELEMENT div  - - (title, subtitle, para+)>
```

*original:*
```
<!ATTLIST document
        status          CDATA           #IMPLIED
>
```
*variant (subset):*
```
<!ATTLIST document
        status          (draft|final)   #IMPLIED
>
```

Subsetting is usually desirable when the markup model being considered has many elements (typically in its information pool), of which only a fraction are needed in any one document-processing environment. Removing unwanted elements becomes especially important for authoring tools that show authors all the defined elements before allowing them to choose one for insertion. Subsetting is also common when the DTD being considered has content models that are less prescriptive in enforcing stylistic standards than the project's needs dictate.

Often, large industry- or government-standard DTDs used by a wide audience are subsetted for actual use. Of course, the larger the DTD, the more likely it is that incompatible subsets will be developed, which may defeat the purpose of developing a standard DTD for interchange. Identifying "packages" of subsets (for example, modularizing the DTD so that it's easy to use each relevant portion in its entirety) in effect creates several easily categorized types of conformance to the standard so that document interchange negotiations can pinpoint the modules used.

If you plan to facilitate subsetting of your own DTD or to subset a standard DTD, consider the following factors. If an organization uses a subsetted DTD and anticipates importing documents that use the original DTD (or a subset that is incompatible with its own), it may want to try to persuade its interchange partners to use its own subsetted version. If the organization has developed processing applications for only its own subset of features, it may need to develop processing for additional features, filters that convert imported documents into the subsetted form, or some mix of the two. At the least, the maintenance documentation for the subsetted DTD should identify the conversions that would provide the best semantic fit of original-form documents into or out of the subsetted form.

## 10.1.2   Extended Markup Models

If some or all instances of the variant DTD are guaranteed not to be valid according to the original, the variant is an **extension** of the original.

While it takes some care to ensure that a change to a markup model is a subset, almost anything else you do to change the original is likely to be an extension. Thus, facilitating *any* customizations to your original DTD can be risky if you're trying to avoid extensions.

The following example shows a typical situation where extension is performed and has a profound effect on the markup model. If the parameter entity containing the basic collection of paragraph-level elements is extended through redefinition of `%local.para.mix;` (a technique discussed in Section 10.2.2), every element containing that collection becomes extended as well.

```
<!ENTITY % local.para.mix "">
<!ENTITY % para.mix     "p|list|note|figure %local.para.mix;">
<!ELEMENT div          - - (title, (%para.mix;)*)>
<!ELEMENT listitem     - - (%para.mix;)*>
<!ELEMENT note         - - (title, (%para.mix;)*)>
```

The following is another typical DTD variation that results in an extension. By removing layers of containment, this model makes variant instances nonconforming to the original.[1]

*original:*
```
<!ELEMENT deflist      - - (defentry+)>
<!ELEMENT defentry     - - (terms, defs)>
<!ELEMENT terms        - - (term+)>
<!ELEMENT defs         - - (def+)>
```

*variant (extension):*
```
<!ELEMENT deflist - - ((term+, def+)+)>
```

Extending a DTD might be appropriate if the original DTD being considered is suitable for general needs, but doesn't take into account the specialized needs of one company or department. Also, as demonstrated by this example, extension might be useful if an authoring DTD needs to be "flatter" than the reference DTD. Any area of a DTD might be in need of extension, but it's common to customize the metainformation while standardizing on the rest of the document hierarchy, and to extend collections of elements in the information pool, as shown in the first example above.

---

1. Note that in cases like this, if OMITTAG minimization is used, it's possible to partially simulate the lack of nestedness by making the start-tags of the container elements omissible, as follows:

*original:*
```
<!ELEMENT deflist      - - (defentry+)>
<!ELEMENT defentry     O O (terms, defs)>
<!ELEMENT terms        O O (term+)>
<!ELEMENT defs         O O (def+)>
```
*variant (extension):*
```
<!ELEMENT deflist - - ((term+, def+)+)>
```
*valid instance of both:*
```
<deflist>                              def and terms start-tags omitted
<term>apple</term>                     defs start-tag omitted
<def>A bright red fruit.</def>         all end-tags omitted
</deflist>
```
Of course, if you must specify attributes on the missing start-tags or if instances of the original must be normalized, this trick wouldn't help.

It's also common to extend a DTD to include the results of an automatic conversion into SGML, to include editorial information in order to assemble documents from fragments that have been imported from many sources (such as articles being assembled into a journal), and to augment a document with format or layout information as part of a series of processing passes.

If you plan to facilitate extension of your own DTD or to extend a standard DTD, consider the following factors. If an organization uses an extended DTD and anticipates exporting documents to recipients that use the original DTD (or a subset of it), it may want to try to persuade its interchange partners to accept deviations from the standard. The organization may need to develop filters to transform its documents to the original form. At the least, the maintenance documentation for the extended DTD should identify the conversions that would provide the best semantic fit back into the original form.

## 10.1.3    Renamed Markup Models

If all the instances of the variant DTD are structurally valid according to the original and apply the markup in the intended manner, but some or all of the element names used are different from those in the original, the variant is a **renamed** version of the original.

There are two common situations in which renaming is needed: specific renaming and general renaming.

In the first case, an existing DTD otherwise suits an organization's needs, but the technical or cultural jargon used in naming some of the markup differs. (You might also need to change a few names in a standard DTD fragment in order to avoid naming clashes with your DTD.) Each name is considered separately for possible renaming.

In the second case, the organization needs two or more versions of an entire DTD in different languages, so that authors can use markup in the native language in which the text is being written. The renaming is thus a result of a top-down decision affecting all markup. (Often, translated documents simply retain the markup of the original language and so don't need this treatment.)

The following is an example of renaming from one language to another.

*original:*
```
<!ELEMENT numlist  - - (item+)>
<!ATTLIST numlist
        type            (arabic|alpha)            #IMPLIED
>
<!ELEMENT item    - - (para+)>
```

*variant (French renaming):*
```
<!ELEMENT listord - - (item+)>
<!ATTLIST listord
        type            (numérique|alphabétique)        #IMPLIED
>
<!ELEMENT item      - - (p+)>
```

Keep in mind that it may be possible to change your processing applications, rather than your DTD, to accommodate the desires of authors. For example, some editors and word processors have the ability to "alias" the name of an element within the editing environment, but to write out SGML document files that use the real generic identifier.

If you plan to facilitate renaming of markup in your own DTD or to rename the markup in a standard DTD, consider the following factors. An organization that uses a renamed DTD might need to export documents to or import documents from interchange partners that use the original DTD, or to use processing applications that work only with the original DTD. If the organization has developed processing applications that work only with the variant names, it needs to develop filters that map markup names to and from original and variant forms, add to its applications the ability to handle multiple name alternatives (such as by using "architectural forms" to identify functionally similar elements), or a mixture of the two. At the least, the maintenance documentation for the renamed DTD should identify the mappings from one set of names to the other.

Section 10.2.4 discusses the DTD techniques that facilitate renaming.

## 10.2 Facilitating Customization

The following sections discuss various techniques for allowing controlled customization of a DTD's markup model.

- Section 10.2.1 discusses how to modularize DTDs.

- Section 10.2.2 describes ways to put placeholders into element declarations and attribute definition list declarations to make them customizable.

- Section 10.2.3 discusses how to use marked sections to conditionalize the inclusion of markup declarations.

- Section 10.2.4 describes techniques for allowing customization of element names and other markup names.

### 10.2.1 Making DTDs Modular

Just as for programs written in procedural languages such as C, it's often valuable—particularly for very large markup models—to build DTDs made up of standalone modules. Modular DTD fragments allow for mixing and matching along well-defined seams in the structure of the document type, greatly increasing the similarities of document sets that use the markup between those seams and facilitating the creation of modular processing applications.

A DTD module is a file containing a collection of related markup declarations, which is included in a larger DTD by means of an external parameter entity. You might have modules containing element and attribute declarations, notation declarations, entity declarations, and so on.

Creating modules and reading modular DTDs might seem complicated, but the benefits nearly always outweigh the costs. Following are typical scenarios where modularity makes sense. They are illustrated with stacked boxes representing the modular structure, where the horizontal boundaries between boxes show the amount of dependency of upper modules on lower ones.

### The Same Markup Is Used in Several Related Document Types

For example, many of the elements in the information pool for pharmaceutical information may be appropriate for use in new-drug applications, medical product literature, internal plans, and other widely differing high-level document hierarchies. By storing the declarations for these elements and attributes in a module, you can call them into several DTDs while maintaining them centrally. Figure 10-2 represents the resulting modular structure.

| DTD 1 | DTD 2 | DTD 3 |
|---|---|---|
| new drug application | brochure | marketing plan |
| information pool | | |

**Figure 10-2**    Modular DTD Structure for Sharing One Information Pool among Several Document Hierarchies.

### The Document Types Are Nested

If, for example, documents will be created and validated in fragmentary form and then assembled for processing, your environment might call for a nested DTD within a full-blown document DTD (as discussed in Section 8.1). Rather than duplicating the identical portions of the two DTDs, you'd construct appropriate modules that can stand on their own or be pulled into larger DTDs. Figure 10-3 represents the resulting modular structure.

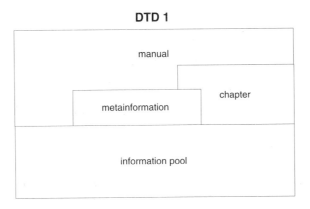

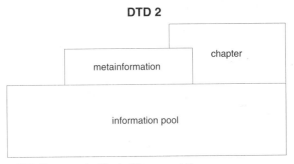

**Figure 10-3**    Modular DTD Structure for Nested Document Types.

 ### Existing DTD Fragments Are Used

You may be planning to use a standard DTD fragment to leverage already-developed processing capabilities or meet interchange requirements. If you are going to use a standard fragment in your DTD, or for that matter any fragment whose design you have no control over, you should include it by reference using an external parameter entity (rather than retyping it for your own use) and customize the fragment only in documented ways, in order to maximize the validity of your documents according to the standard.

The common examples of this case are standard table and equation DTD modules, which involve sophisticated formatting that you're unlikely to want to develop from scratch. However, other specialized fragments might also exist in your information domain. Figure 10-4 shows the resulting modular structure.

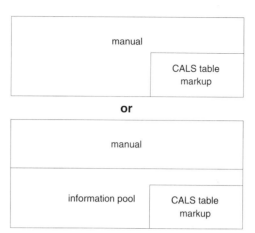

**Figure 10-4**    Modular DTD Structure for Incorporating Standard Fragments.

The following example shows a DTD made up of two modules, one containing the document hierarchy and one containing the information pool. (This example and all the examples in this chapter use formal public identifiers for referencing DTDs. For more information on formal public identifiers, see Section A.10.)

```
<!DOCTYPE modulardoc [
<!ENTITY % infopool PUBLIC
        "-//Ept Associates//ELEMENTS Information Pool//EN">
%infopool;
<!ENTITY % dochier  PUBLIC
        "-//Ept Associates//ELEMENTS Document Hierarchy//EN">
%dochier;
]>
```

For this setup to work, certain relationships need to hold between the two modules. For example, if one module defines any parameter entities that the other uses, the module containing the definitions must be referenced first because SGML doesn't allow "forward references" to entities that haven't yet been defined in the linear flow of declarations. In the example above, and in most modular DTDs, low-level modules precede high-level modules because the latter make use of parameter entities defined in the former. Beyond this inflexible rule, here are other good practices to follow when constructing modules.

### Use Native SGML Mechanisms

Use SGML mechanisms such as external parameter entities and marked sections, rather than non-SGML ones such as makefiles or scripts, to piece together the modules. This way, anyone with any SGML parser can get the benefit of the DTD's modularity.

### Use Public Identifiers

Rather than using system identifiers (for example, file names) to reference modules from within DTDs, use public identifiers so the locations of the modules can be stored outside the actual DTD. This indirection helps the DTD be more portable across computer systems and more useful when interchanged.

With public identifiers, the actual locations are stored in a separate file that maps the public identifier to information on how to locate or retrieve the desired module. The SGML Open organization has issued Technical Resolution 9401, which specifies a syntax for this mapping file, called a **catalog**, that most SGML software vendors support. Using a catalog in this form allows entities to be more portable across not only computer platforms, but across SGML software applications.

For information on the syntax of formal public identifiers and on catalogs, see Section A.10.

### Control Dependencies Between Modules

Where possible, make the dependencies between modules go in only one direction. As mentioned above, higher levels generally have dependencies on the lower levels, so make sure your low-level element set doesn't rely on any characteristics of the document hierarchy elements. If it does, what you'll have instead is DTD *fragments* that can't be reused except with their related fragments.

A special case of controlling module dependencies is to use element name indirection between them. For example, say you have a document hierarchy module whose content models mention information pool elements. If you want to be able to reuse the upper module with different lower-level modules, or you anticipate some fluctuation in the element naming scheme, use parameter entities to represent the element names wherever you mention them.

In addition to helping you reuse collections of declarations at a broad level, modules are also important for building customization features into your DTD, and parameter entities are essential for accomplishing all of these tasks. Two characteristics of parameter entities have a strong effect on how DTDs must be structured for reusability and customizability. First, as already mentioned, you cannot use a parameter entity reference unless a declaration for that entity has been provided previously in the flow of the DTD code. For example, the following is invalid:

```
<!ELEMENT list  - -    (%list.content;)>
<!ENTITY % list.content "item+">
```

Second, entities can have multiple declarations in a DTD, with the first declaration taking precedence. In the following, the first parameter entity declaration is the one used.

```
<!ENTITY % list.content "title?, item+">  active
<!ENTITY % list.content "item+">          inactive
<!ELEMENT list   - -     (%list.content;)>
```

Note that you can use the internal subset of a document type declaration (the part between the square brackets of the DOCTYPE declaration) to redeclare parameter entities, since the internal subset is read *before* any parts of the DTD pulled in by reference to a system or public identifier. For example:

**remote DTD containing article-content parameter entity declaration**
```
<!DOCTYPE journal PUBLIC "-//Ept Associates//DTD Journal//EN" [
```
**redefined parameter entity**
```
<!ENTITY % article-content "para">
]>
```

Even though the internal subset appears to occur after the remote portion, it is actually read first, and any entity declarations here take precedence over those in the remote portion.

If you plan to use a software product that compiles DTDs, you may not be able to use internal subsets to change the markup model. In this case, you can use a DTD-nesting technique. Assume that the following is a customization of the journal DTD.

**redefine article-content:**
```
<!ENTITY % article-content "para">
<!ENTITY % main-journal PUBLIC "-//Ept Associates//DTD Journal//EN">
```
**pull in the original DTD:**
```
%main-journal;
```

A document could then reference the entire changed DTD, which itself contains the original DTD:

```
<!DOCTYPE mod-journal PUBLIC
          "-//Ept Associates//DTD Modified Journal for Authoring//EN">
```

Some DTD implementors choose to store declarations for individual element types (particularly those in the information pool) in separate modules, building up a so-called "element library" that can be recombined in different ways for different DTDs. However, in our experience the complex interdependencies between information pool elements are easier to understand and maintain if the entire information pool is stored in a single module, with marked sections (discussed in Section 10.2.3) used to "modularize" individual element types.

Appendix C contains a sample modularization of a monolithic DTD structure.

## 10.2.2  Making Content Models Customizable

You can use parameter entities to facilitate both subsetting and extension of content models and attribute lists. If you create such entities, your DTD documentation needs to explain how to use them properly. It's a good idea to use a consistent prefix, such as `local.`, for entities that are intended for direct customization.

> ### Note
>
> Remember that SGML allows variant-DTD implementors to redefine all entities in a DTD, whether or not this was your intent. Your documentation will need to make clear which entities are not for use in customization.

To make a content model directly customizable, identify logical parts of the model and make some parts replaceable where you know flexibility is needed—for example, where different departments in the company have expressed strong but opposite views on the content of a certain element.

Typical examples of customizable constructs are blocks of titles and other labeling information on divisions. The following example allows variant DTDs to add or subtract labeling information associated with divisions by redefining the `%local.title;` parameter entity. Note that this setup implies that all levels of division should have the same set of labeling information, even if that set is customizable.

```
<!ENTITY % local.title "title, subtitle?, shorttitle?">
 .
 .
 .
<!ELEMENT div       - - (%local.title;, para*, subdiv+)>
<!ELEMENT subdiv    - - (%local.title;, para*, subsubdiv*)>
<!ELEMENT subsubdiv - - (%local.title;, para*)>
```

Alternatively, you could use different parameter entities to indicate where the set of labeling information is allowed to differ.

```
<!ENTITY % local.hightitle "title, subtitle?, shorttitle?">
<!ENTITY % local.lowtitle  "title, subtitle?, shorttitle?">
 .
 .
 .
<!ELEMENT div       - - (%local.hightitle;, para*, subdiv+)>
<!ELEMENT subdiv    - - (%local.lowtitle;, para*, subsubdiv*)>
<!ELEMENT subsubdiv - - (%local.lowtitle;, para*)>
```

To redefine such a placeholder, a variant-DTD implementor would place a parameter entity declaration before the original one and supply the element and attribute declarations for any newly introduced elements, in this case creating subsetted content models.

```
<!DOCTYPE document PUBLIC "-//Ept Associates//DTD Document//EN" [
<!ENTITY % local.hightitle "title, subtitle, shorttitle?">
<!ENTITY % local.lowtitle  "title, subtitle">
]>
```

If the two separate entities were not available (that is, if the first solution had been implemented), this set of customizations would have required a much more "invasive" procedure performed on the original DTD code, requiring either editing of the original declaration for each element involved or substitution of a whole new declaration.

Once you start adding placeholder parameter entities, you may be tempted to put entities between every element in a content model, "just in case." Remember that these entities are meant to encourage appropriate kinds of customization. If you don't want to compromise the integrity of your markup model, use content model placeholders only where different environments need flexibility or where variations won't affect interchange or processing.

If you use parameter entities to manage element classes and collections as discussed in Section 9.3, you can offer a great deal of flexibility for customization, since you can make the classes and collections independently customizable.

To allow for extension of both element classes and collections, add a placeholder parameter entity to each entity's definition and define it as containing an empty string, as follows:

```
<!ENTITY % local.blocks    "">
<!ENTITY % local.para.mix  "">
<!ENTITY % blocks          "para|quotation %local.blocks;">
<!ENTITY % para.mix        "%blocks; %local.para.mix;">
```

Variant-DTD implementors can then extend the list of elements considered text blocks and, by doing so, implicitly extend any construct containing %blocks;.

```
<!DOCTYPE document PUBLIC "-//Ept Associates//DTD Document//EN" [
<!ENTITY % local.blocks    "|mytextblock">
<!ELEMENT mytextblock  - - (#PCDATA)>
]>
```

Note the vertical bar OR sequence indicator at the beginning of the entity, which is required to integrate the local portion with the already-defined %blocks; entity.

Implementors could also simply extend the list of elements allowed directly in the paragraph-level collection, %para.mix;, without affecting any other collections.

```
<!DOCTYPE document PUBLIC "-//Ept Associates//DTD Document//EN" [
<!ENTITY % local.para.mix "|mytextblock">
<!ELEMENT mytextblock  - - (#PCDATA)>
]>
```

Because the entity defined first is the one used in a DTD, sometimes variant-DTD developers can end up in a catch-22 situation: If you want to refer to other entities inside an entity you're redefining, you must define it *after* those other entities, but *before* the original definition of the entity. You might need to solve this problem, for example, if you want to

⟵━━━━━━━━━━━━━━━━━━━━━━━━━━━━━━━━━━━━━━━━━━━━━━━━⟶

redefine a collection entity to remove some of its contents, while still using most of the element class entities that were in it originally, for easier maintenance. For example, how could you redefine %mix2; in the following DTD to remove %class2;, while retaining the reference to %class1;?

```
<!ENTITY % class1    "elem-a|elem-b|elem-c %local.class1;">
<!ENTITY % class2    "elem-d|elem-e|elem-f %local.class2;">

<!--..............................................-->

<!ENTITY % mix1      "%class1;           %local.mix1;">
<!ENTITY % mix2      "%class1;|%class2; %local.mix2;">
```

The only place you could put the necessary redefinition would be in the middle:

```
<!ENTITY % class1    "elem-a|elem-b|elem-c %local.class1;">
<!ENTITY % class2    "elem-d|elem-e|elem-f %local.class2;">

<!--..............................................-->
<!ENTITY % mix2      "%class1;           %local.mix2;">
<!--..............................................-->

<!ENTITY % mix1      "%class1;           %local.mix1;">
<!ENTITY % mix2      "%class1;|%class2; %local.mix2;">
```

Because of this state of affairs, to facilitate customization in your DTDs you might want to put a "placeholder" entity between all your element class entities and collection entities, so that variant-DTD developers can make the necessary redefinitions without having to edit your original file. By default, the placeholder would contain, for example, just an SGML comment explaining how to customize the value.

```
<!ENTITY % class1    "elem-a|elem-b|elem-c %local.class1;">
<!ENTITY % class2    "elem-d|elem-e|elem-f %local.class2;">

<!--..............................................-->
<!ENTITY % redefine PUBLIC
         "-//Ept Associates//DTD Redefinition Block//EN">
%redefine;
<!--..............................................-->

<!ENTITY % mix1      "%class1;           %local.mix1;">
<!ENTITY % mix2      "%class1;|%class2; %local.mix2;">
```

To make attribute lists easily customizable, you can use the same basic placeholder techniques as for content models. To make them extensible, use empty placeholder entities. The following example allows variant-DTD implementors to add common attributes by redefining the %local.common.atts; entity.

```
<!ENTITY % local.common.atts  "">
<!ENTITY % common.atts "
        id              ID              #IMPLIED
        security        (none|high)     none
        status          (draft|final)   draft
        %local.common.atts;
">
    .
    .
    .
<!ATTLIST document
        %common.atts;
        partnumber      NMTOKEN         #REQUIRED
>
    .
    .
    .
<!ATTLIST paragraph
        %common.atts;
>
    .
    .
    .
```

To add attributes, variant-DTD developers would redefine `%local.common.atts;` as follows.

```
<!DOCTYPE document PUBLIC "-//Ept Associates//DTD Document//EN" [
<!ENTITY % local.common.atts "
        tracenum        NUMBER          #REQUIRED
">
]>
```

## 10.2.3    Including Declarations Conditionally

Marked sections around declarations, in combination with parameter entities that store the marked section's IGNORE/INCLUDE status keyword, can make it easy to customize a DTD to get just the declarations you want and eliminate the others. You can almost think of marked sections as miniature modules, since you can easily "pull them into" your DTD by using the INCLUDE keyword; the difference is that both included and ignored blocks of material are still physically present in the same file, meaning you can easily maintain them together.

Following is an example of setting up a marked section for an element that isn't wanted in all variants of a DTD:

```
<!ENTITY % big.DTD    "IGNORE">
<!ENTITY % small.DTD "INCLUDE">
    .
    .
    .
```

```
<![ %big.DTD; [
<!ENTITY % blocks "para|excerpt|epigraph">
]]>
<![ %small.DTD; [
<!ENTITY % blocks "para|excerpt">
]]>
   .
   .
   .
<![ %big.DTD; [
<!ELEMENT epigraph  - - (#PCDATA)>
]]>
```

Two kinds of marked section are set up by the declarations of the %big.DTD; and %small.DTD; entities; these keywords control whether or not epigraphs are part of the markup model. If the "small" DTD is desired (the default because %small.DTD; is defined as INCLUDE), epigraphs will be left out. If the "big" DTD is desired, %big.DTD; can be redefined as INCLUDE instead of IGNORE, which will activate the larger %blocks; entity and the epigraph element declaration.

In this example, there's no need to redefine %small.DTD; as IGNORE when you redefine %big.DTD; as INCLUDE, since the first definition of %blocks; will take precedence anyway. But there might be some circumstances in which you'd have to switch the values of both keyword entities. Following is an easy way to allow the switching of both values by redefining only a single entity.

```
<!ENTITY % big.DTD    "IGNORE">
   <!--........................-->
   <![ %big.DTD; [
   <!ENTITY % small.DTD    "IGNORE">
   ]]>
   <!--........................-->
<!ENTITY % small.DTD "INCLUDE">
   .
   .
   .
```

These entity declarations set up the ignored-region keyword first and the included-region keyword last. By redefining the first keyword as INCLUDE, you can simultaneously redefine the last keyword as IGNORE. This system works because the declaration in the middle (where %small.DTD; is set to IGNORE) is itself ignored, as long as %big.DTD; is ignored. If %big.DTD; is changed to INCLUDE, the middle declaration is "activated."[2]

A more targeted way to use marked sections is to surround a set of declarations for an individual element type with its own marked section. For example, if you have an information pool module in which some of the element types are known to be undesirable in some variants, you might want to make them removable.

---

2. We first saw this trick in Dan Connolly's work on the HTML DTD.

```
<!ENTITY % weird-elem.module "INCLUDE">
 .
 .
 .
<!ELEMENT normal-elem   - - (...)>
<!ATTLIST normal-elem
        %common.attribs;
>

<![ %weird-elem.module; [
<!ELEMENT weird-elem    - - (...)>
<!ATTLIST weird-elem
        %common.attribs;
        special          NAME             #IMPLIED
>
]]>
```

Redefining the `%weird-elem.module;` entity as IGNORE, along with redefining other elements and entities containing `weird-elem`, would allow it to disappear from the variant DTD.

This technique is very powerful because it allows both the *removal* of declarations and the *replacement* of declarations. Normally, SGML does not allow the wholesale redefinition of elements and attribute lists, but using marked sections in this way makes such redefinition possible. For this reason, if you don't want to allow radical redefinition of content models or attribute lists, you may not want to use this technique.

## 10.2.4  Making Markup Names Customizable

To facilitate changing any markup name in a DTD, you would define a parameter entity that stands for the desired name and use that parameter entity in *every* location where the name is mentioned, including in other modules. Changing the name then becomes a simple matter of redefining the entity. For example:

```
<!ENTITY % title "title">
<!ELEMENT %title; - - (#PCDATA)>
<!ATTLIST %title;
        id                ID               #IMPLIED
>
 .
 .
 .
<!ELEMENT div     - - ((%title;), para+, subdiv*)>
```

Usually, attribute names and token values are not considered for renaming. Even if you are only renaming the elements, the work involved can be immense (and the readability of the DTD will probably suffer). However, it may be worth the effort if you need to provide several different natural-language versions of the DTD for authoring purposes. Note that if you need to store and manage SGML documents from sources that use different markup-naming versions of the DTD, it may be more appropriate to customize your editing environment to present "aliased" markup names to authors rather than actually change the markup names in the DTD. Otherwise, your processing and retrieval applications may need to be much more generic than they would normally have to be.

If you need to dictate the use of a particular markup model to users of the DTD, but want to use broad strokes rather than specify the element names that must be used, you may want to consider defining **architectural forms** to guide the creation of conforming elements in other DTDs. An element-type architectural form is essentially a named set of rules for and constraints on an element's declaration; any element declaration claiming to conform to the architectural form must reference its name as the value of a special attribute. The attribute value functions almost as an additional "generic identifier." By treating your own element declarations as the set of rules for variant-DTD creation and by documenting how the special attribute values are to be added to variant DTDs, you facilitate the use of your DTD as a "meta-DTD."

For example, let's say your original DTD is an industry standard for mathematics textbooks. It has a model for lists of student exercises, but you want to allow variant-DTD developers to call an "exercise list" and an "exercise" whatever they want. You can describe to those developers that the presence of a `MathText` attribute with a value of `"exercise-list"` on their version of the `exercise-list` element will indicate to users and applications that their element should be treated like a "mathematics textbook exercise list" in every respect. Likewise, you can do the same for the other elements in your DTD.

An easy way to specify this mapping is to put the attribute in your original DTD. This way, anyone who customizes the original DTD directly will get the architectural forms for free.

*original DTD:*

```
<!ELEMENT exercise-list    - - (exercise+)>
<!ATTLIST exercise-list
        MathText           (exercise-list) exercise-list
>
<!ELEMENT exercise         - - (#PCDATA)>
<!ATTLIST exercise
        MathText           (exercise)      exercise
>
```

In the following variant DTD, the correspondence to the original model is made through an attribute that has only one choice of attribute token value, which is also the default. Thus, the attribute is effectively fixed in the DTD, with no possibility to change it in instances.

**variant DTD 1:**

```
<!ELEMENT exlist   - - (ex+)>
<!ATTLIST exlist
        MathText           (exercise-list) exercise-list
>
<!ELEMENT ex       - - (#PCDATA)>
<!ATTLIST ex
        MathText           (exercise)      exercise
>
```

Another way to achieve the same thing is the following, which uses the #FIXED keyword:

**variant DTD 2:**

```
<!ELEMENT exerlist   - - (exer+)>
<!ATTLIST exerlist
        MathText           CDATA           #FIXED exercise-list
>
<!ELEMENT exer   - - (#PCDATA)>
<!ATTLIST exer
        MathText           CDATA           #FIXED exercise
>
```

Finally, the variant-DTD developer may decide that it's valuable for individual instances to indicate that they do or do not correspond to a standard model, and allow the attribute value to change:

**variant DTD 3:**

```
<!ELEMENT ex-series - - (ex+)>
<!ATTLIST ex-series
        MathText           CDATA           exercise-list
>
<!ELEMENT ex       - - (#PCDATA)>
<!ATTLIST ex
        MathText           CDATA           exercise
>
```

Notice that if any of the variant DTDs changed the content model of the exercise-list equivalent to, say, allow zero exercises, the element would be an extension of the original—it would allow instances that do not conform to the original rules. For a variant element to conform correctly to an architectural form, it must allow either the identical content model or a subset of it.

If elements have an extra "generic identifier," applications can search for attribute values and apply processing regardless of the actual element names used. However, some systems don't allow this fine level of access to the SGML structure, a restriction that can give architectural forms some of the same problems as other mechanisms of renaming DTDs (for example, needing to filter the document instances into a form that uses generic identifiers the applications can handle). Furthermore, there is no way to validate that a variant

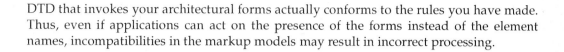

DTD that invokes your architectural forms actually conforms to the rules you have made. Thus, even if applications can act on the presence of the forms instead of the element names, incompatibilities in the markup models may result in incorrect processing.

## 10.3  Customizing Existing DTDs

For a project where the goal is to customize an existing DTD, as discussed in Chapter 7, you should make the changes carefully. Armed with the document analysis report, the project documents, and knowledge of the risks of changing the original DTD, you're ready to make the necessary changes. If the original has one or more built-in customization methods, you may find that you've already been given most of the tools you need to accomplish the changes. Even in that case, and especially in the case where the original DTD implementor gave you no help in customizing, you should change the original in ways that are as backward compatible as possible and help you maintain your variant over time, as the original DTD changes. Here are some ways you can accomplish this goal.

### Plan and Document

Most important, *plan* and *document* how the two markup models differ, and carefully specify the behavior of any transformation filters and additional applications that will need to be developed. In order to interchange and process your documents successfully, it's essential to have a clear idea of any differences and how you'll handle them.

### Emphasize Subsetting

Change only what you must, particularly if you plan to use already-developed applications, and try to subset rather than extend the original DTD.

### Avoid Editing the Original DTD Files

Avoid simply copying over the DTD files and changing them indiscriminately; try to make all the necessary changes by supplying alternate declarations for elements, attribute definition lists, and parameter entities—preferably the latter, if they're available—and by using only the modules you need.

### Use Marked Sections for Wholesale Changes

If it's necessary to edit the original files, use marked sections around your changes and around the portions you have replaced so that you can switch back and forth between the original version and the variant, or at least see clearly what was done.

# Validation and Testing

You need to perform several kinds of testing to determine whether your DTD design goals were met in the actual implementation. As a result of your testing, you may need to improve on the markup model of the reference DTD, or you may need to adapt the model of one or more variant DTDs to a particular processing application or environment. For example, usability testing might result in simplification of the authoring DTD so that authors can better choose and apply markup.

This chapter describes the steps in testing and reviewing the DTD and what to look for. Testing and review involve the following steps:

1. Reviewing the document analysis report

   The user group and other reviewers should make sure to put their comments in writing and to back up their suggestions with examples. It's best if they actually fill out a bug report (described in Section 11.1) to record problems.

2. Validating and reviewing the DTD "code"

   The DTD implementor is responsible for ensuring that the DTD is valid at each stage of testing and revision. Section  discusses how to do this.

   Technical experts should have the opportunity to read the draft DTD, with the document analysis report and the DTD maintenance documentation (discussed in Section 12.2) in hand. Again, written comments in the form of bug reports are best. Often, the comments gathered at this stage reflect the experts' desire to have a "pure" DTD; if there are reasons the DTD has compromised on some desirable features (such as mixed content models in the form approved by the ISO 8879 standard), the implementor should have recorded them in the maintenance documentation.

3. Testing the markup model provided by the DTD

   It's essential that you test the DTD by marking up sample documents. For this task, you need a conversion application or people willing to mark up documents manually in an editor (which can be SGML-aware or not, depending on the expertise and training resources available). Problems should be recorded in bug reports. Section 11.3 describes factors to be aware of during the testing.

Anyone marking up documents to test the DTD will need documentation. Usually, the DTD user documentation is far from being finalized at this point, but at a minimum the draft of the reference manual, a list of all the available elements with their definitions, and a set of tree diagrams should be provided. (Chapter 12 discusses the components of user documentation.)

4.  Testing the SGML application (DTD and SGML declaration) with processing applications

When you use the DTD and its related material with authoring, processing, and information management applications and introduce it to authors, you may find problems with the ideal model specified in the reference DTD. Alternatively, you may find problems that are due solely to the interaction between the DTD or SGML declaration and the tools. As a result, if you haven't yet branched out into variant DTDs to adapt the model to targeted purposes, you might do so at this stage. Again, the bug-reporting system should be used to record problems and suggestions.

Section 11.4 discusses what to look for in testing the DTD with applications.

5.  Testing updates to the DTD

For this job, the reviewers and testers will need not only the document analysis report and DTD maintenance documentation, but also a summary of the bugs attended to and the action taken, so they can specifically test the changes that have just been made.

## 11.1   Setting Up a Bug-Reporting System

Once the DTD has been finalized, the document type design team usually disbands, leaving behind the document analysis report as documentation for the maintenance work to come. This first generation of documentation is often adequate, because the team has had the time to do it correctly and has felt the need for that documentation. But two or three generations of DTD later, when the DTD has been altered and updated several times in a hurry or under pressure, it's easy to lose track of changes: what the changes were, why, when, and how they were made, who asked for them, and who made them. This problem is particularly critical when the history of changes to the reference DTD has been lost and its variants must be updated as well.

The best way to avoid such a problem is to implement a change control process compliant with the ISO 9000 quality assurance standard. It will assure the quality assurance certification of your department, and it will help tremendously in keeping track of the history of your DTDs.

The process and its documentation are tightly interwoven; the process cannot be completed without being documented. The change control process consists of:

1. Defining a change request form for collecting bug reports and enhancement requests.

2. Writing a procedure on how to fill out the form, to whom to send it, and how it should be processed.

3. Having someone receive all the forms, and number and process each form before giving feedback to each claimant.

4. Producing, updating, and circulating a compiled bug and enhancement list.

5. Having a change control board gather regularly to decide what must and what needn't be done. The action column of the bug and enhancement list is then completed and a rationale of the decisions documented.

6. Incrementing the revision number of the updated bug and enhancement list (corresponding to the DTD and documentation generations), sending copies to everybody involved, and archiving all the documents listed above.

With such processes and documents there is no chance of losing track of what happened during the history of the DTD. Even if the people involved have changed, continuity is assured.

Figure 11-1 shows a blank sample of a change request form.

The bug and enhancement list is a summary of the requested actions and the actions taken. It must indicate how to refer to the corresponding forms for more information. It is useful to formalize it as a table, where each bug is described in one row. The list as a whole must be identified with its list revision number and the date of issue. Each row of the table should show a selection of extracted information about a problem, as shown in Figure 11-2.

It is useful to indicate visually which problems have been fixed, for example, by shading those rows or putting a mark in front of them. It saves time in DTD change control meetings when the attendees need to review only the marked rows, either to find out why the decision has not been implemented yet or to make a decision about what should be done.

## 11.2  Validating the DTD

The most superficial kind of DTD testing you must perform is the validation of the DTD markup declarations themselves. "Validation" means different things for DTDs and document instances. Validating a DTD ensures that its markup rules are well formed, making it possible for instances to follow them, whereas validating a document instance involves checking to see that the rules were followed in that particular document. Before you can create realistic instances, you must validate the DTD.

## Change Request Form

Name of requestor: _____ Date reported: _____ Number: _____

How to contact requestor: _____

Summary: _____ Severity (high, med, low): _____

Description: _____
_____
_____
_____
_____
_____

Hardware/software configuration: _____
_____

Suspected system component and nature of problem: _____
_____

Action or workaround taken: _____
_____

Change desired: _____
_____

- - - - - - - - - - - - - - - - - - - - - - - - - - - - - - - - - - - - - - - - - - - -

Number: _____ Response date: _____

Response (or attach): _____
_____
_____
_____

Action taken: _____
_____
_____ Action date: _____

**Figure 11-1**    Change Request Form.

| # | Date | Class | Sev. | Reported by | Correction date | Problem | Action |
|---|------|-------|------|-------------|-----------------|---------|--------|
| 1 | 6 Oct 1993 | DTD | L | Nina Haagen | | I want to have more than two structural levels in the preface. | To be considered by the change control board. |
| 2 | 6 Oct 1993 | Structured editor | M | Jack Flash | February release | The backslash character cannot be inserted with keyboard keys. | &bsol; entity glyph added to the mapping file. |
| 3 | 18 Oct 1993 | Database | H | Carly Simon | | Entities corresponding to product names disappear when documents integrated in DB. | To be fixed by subcontractor. |
| 4 | 2 Nov 1993 | Formatting engine | H | Edith Ann Lazaroff | | When there are several notes, examples, and procedures in a row, they should be numbered. | To be investigated and fixed by subcontractor. |
| 5 | 2 Nov 1993 | DTD | M | Joel Painter | March release | The structure of the <INSTR> element is incorrect. | Decided on by the change control board and fixed in DTD. |

**Figure 11-2**    Bug List for SGML Project.

In general, the implementor can do this validation alone and can resolve problems without input from the design team. A few problems may need design team communication, as described below.

To perform the main part of this validation, you need a validating parser. There are several public-domain parsers available, and most commercial SGML software products contain a validating parser as well. You may also need a rudimentary document instance containing a minimal amount of content and markup, because the parser may not expect to receive just a DTD as input. If you have implemented your DTD using computer-aided DTD development software, it is probably already syntactically valid because the software ensured that only valid DTD constructs were created.

---

### Note

Subtle differences exist in the error-reporting behavior of various commercial and public-domain parsers, and at the time of writing no single test suite exists yet for assessing the conformance of validating parsers to the ISO 8879 standard. It is a good idea to validate any DTD with multiple parsers to ensure that it contains no errors and will be usable across SGML systems.

The following checklist identifies errors commonly made in typing and constructing DTD code that will be found by validating parsers.

## Unbalanced or Mismatched Pairs

Check for unbalanced or mismatched pairs of angle bracket (<>) markup declaration delimiters, parenthesis [()] group delimiters, single (') or double (") quotation mark literal delimiters, or double-hyphen (--) comment delimiters.

```
<!-- The following is used in several lists--but you
     can change it if you need to.->
<!ENTITY % listcontent "item>
   .
   .
   .
<!ELEMENT  list      - - ((%listcontent;)+ >
<!ATTLIST  list
           type              NAME           #IMPLIED
           security          (open|confid)  open
```

The comment starting on the first line has two problems: The final delimiter has only one hyphen, and the comment text contains a "dash" made of two hyphens, which will be interpreted as a comment delimiter. The entity declaration is missing a closing quotation mark. The element declaration is missing a closing parenthesis. The attribute definition list declaration is missing a closing angle bracket.

## Missing Exclamation Point

An exclamation point (!) from the opening markup declaration delimiter may be missing.

```
<!ELEMENT model-number - - (#PCDATA)>
<ATTLIST  model-number
          id              ID              #IMPLIED
     >
```

### No Omitted-Tag Specifications

The omitted-tag specifications may be missing from an element declaration when the OMITTAG feature has been set to YES, or may be present on an attribute declaration.

```
<!ELEMENT address      (street, city, country, postcode?)>
<!ATTLIST address - -
        district       NUMBER        #REQUIRED
>
```

### Zero Instead of "O"

The use of a zero (0) instead of a lowercase or uppercase letter O in an omitted-tag specification will cause an error.

```
<!ELEMENT joke - 0 (para+)>
```

Some people use lowercase 'o's exclusively because they are easier to distinguish from zeros.

### Parameter and General Entity Confusion

You may discover a missing percent sign (%) or the absence of a space after the percent sign in parameter entity declarations, and conversely, the presence of the percent sign in general entity declarations.

```
<!ENTITY %listcontent  "item">

<!ENTITY commonattribs "id  ID  #REQUIRED">
```

**if fruitbat-article contains a fragment of a document instance:**
```
<!ENTITY % fruitbat-article SYSTEM "fruitbat.sgml">
```

### Multiple Declarations

Only one attribute definition list declaration is allowed for each element.

```
<!ELEMENT glossentry (term, def)>
<!ATTLIST glossentry
        id              ID              #IMPLIED
>
   .
   .
<!ATTLIST (dictentry|glossentry)
        id              ID              #IMPLIED
>
```

Some SGML-aware products allow multiple declarations for attribute definition lists by concatenating them into one "master" list, but this is nonstandard behavior.

## Problems with Content Model Parentheses

Beware of parenthesis content model delimiters used with declared-content keywords or absent when #PCDATA is specified.

```
<!ELEMENT trademark - - #PCDATA>
<!ELEMENT indexterm - - (RCDATA)>
```

## Forward References to Entities

Entities must be declared before they are referenced.

```
<!ELEMENT docinfo  - - (%metainfo.mix;)+>
    ⋮
<!ENTITY % metainfo.mix  "title|ISBN|partnumber|author">
```

This error can indicate problems with the organization of the DTD's modules. Modularizing and parameterizing a DTD are discussed in Chapter 10.

## Ambiguous Content Model

Parsers will report an error for ambiguous content models.

```
<!ELEMENT division - - (title, para?, para+, subdiv*)>
```

In this case, the same logical model could have been achieved with the following declaration:

```
<!ELEMENT division - - (title, para+, subdiv*)>
```

However, ambiguity errors can indicate problems with the markup model that need the attention of the document type design team. Handling content model ambiguity is discussed in Section 8.2.1.

If your validating parser indicates that an error appears on a certain line of your DTD, work backwards from that point to see what might be wrong. Sometimes the problem can be far removed from the apparent error.

Many parsers return warnings for DTD constructs that are deprecated, if not actually prohibited. For example, you might see warnings for the following:

- Mixed content models that don't allow #PCDATA to appear everywhere in the model

  You might have intended the model to be constructed this way. If not, Section 8.2.4 suggests alternative design solutions.

- Elements that are defined but do not appear in any content models

  You might have intended the elements not to be used. If so, Section 10.2.3 suggests ways to eliminate the offending declarations in order to avoid the warning. If not, examine the markup model to see where the elements should appear.

Not all DTD problems are purely "syntactic" in origin. For example, it is perfectly legal to specify the following element declaration, which creates a content model that is impossible to satisfy in an instance.

```
<!ELEMENT division  - - (title, para*, division+)>
```

Because every division *must* contain a lower-level instance of itself, no document can ever contain a valid division element. The only way to discover this situation is to test the DTD with a document instance that actually contains a division element, which will result in an error. Therefore, an important part of validating a DTD, especially if you are inexperienced at implementing DTDs, is validating one or more simple documents that contain all of the configurations of markup that the DTD allows.

## 11.3   Validating the Markup Model

To test the validity of the markup model represented by a DTD, start by marking up the sample documents that were used in the analysis and design work. This provides an overall sanity check that nothing was forgotten. In addition, mark up both typical and unusual sample documents that *weren't* used in the analysis, as a second-level check. As the use of the DTD is rolled out in your organization, problems will likely continue to arise.

Two basic types of problems can be found. The markup model might not accommodate a document that falls within the scope (that is, it is wrong or overly constrained), or it might accommodate documents that fall outside the scope (that is, it is overly broad). The consequences are different for each.

There are two main ways you can use marked-up documents to validate the markup model:

- Conduct a "code review" of marked-up documents to see if they meet your expectations and to determine which markup never gets used (useful with both automatically and manually marked-up documents)

- Conduct a "contextual inquiry" with people who are manually marking up documents

  This is a technique that involves observing the authors and asking questions as they work. It can be a highly effective way to determine where markup is missing. (It is also useful for usability testing of the DTD, for example, where there are many poorly distinguished choices. Usability testing is discussed in Section 11.4.2.)

Later testing with real-world applications often highlights additional subtle problems in the markup model. For example, say you haven't allowed for marking up model numbers, but you soon find that without being able to locate model numbers easily, you can't generate cross-reference lists of machine parts that contain other parts. A thorough design process will have helped avoid this. However, if you find you must make additions to the markup model at this late date, it's possible to do so. (Of course, you may need to put your SGML documents through an additional transformation process in order to take advantage of the added markup.)

## 11.3.1   Wrong or Overly Constrained Model

If your markup model is wrong or restricts markup options too severely, you may not have enough markup in your document files to support the kinds of utilization you want. Furthermore, if authors will commit Tag Abuse just to make the data fit or to get the kind of formatted output they expect, the documents may have an inconsistent and idiosyncratic use of markup that can damage your ability to process them in any useful way.

If testing reveals that the markup model doesn't account for all the documents' needs, the model may need to be broadened or changed, or existing documents may need to be rewritten or restructured.

For example, if the model allows for chapters to be grouped into parts, but a document is then found that also groups its appendices into parts, the model may need to change to accommodate such documents. On the other hand, you may discover that the document with the grouped appendices was written poorly or violates a corporate style guideline, in which case it needs to be determined whether legacy documents with this problem can be rewritten to conform to the new, more "correct" model.

## 11.3.2   Overly Broad Model

The detection of an overly broad model is harder than that of an overly constrained model, since legacy documents don't need to be "forced into the mold," and the drawbacks of leaving it too broad are harder to quantify. Following are some possible scenarios.

If certain portions of your markup model are overly broad, validating parsers may not catch documents that violate style guidelines or structural requirements. For example, if every product description should have a part number supplied, but there is no requirement for the part number element to appear, documents may make it all the way to the delivery stage without a part number. Often, markup model standards such as this are relaxed in order to ease authoring and the conversion of legacy documents. If possible, it's better to make variant authoring or conversion DTDs for these stages of document processing, so that the proper validation can be done in the later stages.

If the model provides multiple ways to mark up the same data, authors may be confused and are likely to mark up documents inconsistently, possibly harming your ability to process the documents in the desired ways. This situation tends to occur in DTDs with a broad audience. For example, if the model offers two different locations where the document title can be stored, some authors (and applications) will use one, some the other. If possible, eliminate all cases of duplicated markup functions. If this can't be done, try to

---

> ### Note
>
> Some structural requirements are not able to be checked by validating parsers. For example, if your paragraph element allows #PCDATA, it's possible to have paragraph start- and end-tags with nothing between them. If it's important to perform this kind of validation, applications outside of the validating parser must perform them.

---

construct the model so that if one is present, the other can't be supplied. At the least, clearly document the precedence of usage and the processing expectations if both are used.

If the model offers many more elements than will be used on a regular basis, your authors may have an unrealistically steep learning curve, which can discourage the use of proper markup. You may find that the model has a variation of the problem of multiple markup methods—forms of markup that are so similar, or have such a fuzzy boundary between them, that there's no consistent way to use each one appropriately. It's often the case that DTDs offer many more data-level elements than can be used distinctively; for example, software documentation DTDs might offer several elements for command-level computer instructions, command argument keywords, environment variables, and so on.

If it *is* possible to make a case for distinguishing the elements clearly, the documentation and training must provide the means for authors to test their subject matter knowledge against the model and choose appropriately. If it turns out to be impossible, the overall number of choices may need to be reduced, which should be done with the design team's help. Using software to collect statistical data on markup usage, as mentioned in Section 13.6 in connection with quality inspection of documents, could be useful in identifying markup that never gets used.

## 11.4  Testing the DTD in the Real World

Once you're satisfied that the DTD is powerful enough to represent the documents in its scope without being too broad, the markup model can be said to be valid. However, this is not the same as saying that the whole SGML application, including both the DTD and the SGML declaration, is usable by processing applications or people. You need to test them with the intended users and applications to discover any inefficiencies or processing-related problems in the SGML application itself or in its interaction with your chosen tools, which might occasion the need to create variants for different purposes.

## 11.4.1   Usability with Applications

To test the usability of your SGML application with processing applications, you need to do two things:

- Make sure the application developers review the document analysis report and draft DTDs to catch potential problems early.

- Test the DTD with the applications.

Following are some of the problems you might encounter:

- The DTD may depend on optional SGML features, such as SUBDOC, that aren't supported by your tools. This is a problem with the tool rather than the DTD, but the latter may need to be changed to accommodate the former.

- Your tools may have resource problems related to the complexity of the documents; for example, an average document may need to nest elements to a depth of 100 levels (a fact that will need to be represented by the TAGLVL quantity in the SGML declaration, described in Section A.9.4), but your tools might not handle this depth of nesting. Again, you may need to create a variant DTD that can be handled by your tools if the tools' processing ability can't be changed.

- Your tools may have difficulty querying on your document database to find relevant information because there is too little markup. This might be a problem in the DTD (or a problem relating to authoring).

- Your stylesheets may not have the ability to do all the kinds of formatting you want without additional presentation-specific markup in the DTD to help them. This situation might call for a presentation DTD so that the reference DTD doesn't contain this markup.

## 11.4.2   Usability with People

Assuming that the testing discussed in Section 11.3.2 has found the markup model not too broad, the DTD may still be difficult to use or that it make the process of choosing markup too difficult. Either of these conditions will probably result in Tag Abuse by authors, and therefore, documents that are not marked up fully, accurately, or consistently. These results may be due to the DTD itself, to the interaction between the DTD and a particular authoring tool or environment, or to problems with the amount or quality of the DTD documentation (discussed in Chapter 12) and training (discussed in Chapter 13).

The testing methods discussed in Section 11.3, code review and contextual inquiry, work equally well here.

Following are some of the problems you might encounter. In each case, you might respond either with changes to the authoring DTD or with changes or customizations to the authoring tools and environment, depending on your resources and preferences.

- The DTD may be very large, with too many choices of elements in various contexts for authors to handle well.

  Even in an SGML-aware authoring tool, the number of element choices in some contexts might be overwhelming. For example, a typical context that contains information units might allow 30 elements, with eight of them being different types of list. One solution might be to subset the DTD to just the portions that authors actually need. If subsetting doesn't help, ensuring that elements in the same class are grouped together when presented to an author can be useful. You might accomplish this in one of several ways:

  - Actually changing the generic identifiers in the authoring DTD so that elements will be presented alphabetically in the appropriate classes (`list-bulleted` and `list-numbered` instead of `bulleted-list` and `numbered-list`)
  - "Aliasing" the elements in the authoring tool
  - Customizing the tool to produce a special dialog box that presents often-used elements first or presents the elements by class
  - Creating wrapper elements in the authoring DTD to present fewer choices to the author until a class is selected (adding a `list` element that contains one of the eight kinds of list)
  - Mapping special key presses or commands to actions that insert templates containing commonly used elements

- The tags may be too long, or the element names too hard to type or read.

  Obviously, one solution is to change the element names. If there are reasons to keep the original names, however, there are other solutions. It may be possible to "alias" the names to better ones in the authoring environment, or minimization techniques can be used to reduce the amount of typing.

- Some content models, which may be suitable for finished documents, may be too restrictive for use during the authoring process.

  If authors are continually frustrated by validation errors in their partial or draft documents, and the errors add nothing to their ability to produce high-quality documents, then the authoring DTD may need relaxed versions of the relevant content models.

# Part 4

Documentation,
Training, and
Support

This part of the book discusses how to develop the supporting framework that will give users of your SGML-based document production system the skills they need to use the DTD correctly.

Documentation and training are often given short shrift in technological projects. In DTD development, even if heavy investment has been made in the design, development, and testing of the DTD, there is usually little budget and time left over for documentation and training.

No matter how high the investment made in the early stages of a DTD development project, if documentation and training are not addressed properly, chances are that the whole project will fail because authors are not putting consistent and correct markup in documents, and therefore the investment in SGML and processing applications is wasted. Lack of training or insufficient training is the second most frequent cause of failure of SGML project implementation, after lack of managerial support.

There is another reason why you should provide documentation, training, and support to users of the system. Migrating to a new document production system, particularly one based on SGML, has many challenges. Even if you've successfully communicated the rationale for the switch and gotten agreement from all the parties concerned, the people who must use the new system will tend to be resistant to change. To help them manage the effects of the migration, you need not only arm them with the skills they will need, but also give them a secure feeling about their ability to get help when they need it.

Chapter 12 discusses creating documentation for DTD users and implementors. Chapter 13 describes how to prepare training and support and deliver them to users.

312

# 12 Documentation

It's not enough to have developed the perfect markup model for your document type. DTD documentation is essential for explaining the logic behind the model and for helping authors and application developers use the DTD properly. In fact, because markup declarations consist only of the syntax rules for markup and cannot convey the markup's "semantic" intent, the ISO 8879 standard actually *requires* documentation to be provided for the markup declarations, and technically defines a DTD to comprise both the declarations *and* their documentation. Here, we describe the kinds of documentation that are useful to supply.

Chapter 4 discussed how to prepare a document analysis report, which can be thought of as the documentation of the document type design process. Here, we concentrate on how to develop documentation for an actual DTD in the various stages of its development and use. To prepare this material, you need to take into account the following factors:

- The actual information content that must be provided

- The activity it is intended to support; for example, DTD maintenance, DTD testing, background information for use in application development, or the authoring and markup process

- The audience; for example, the DTD implementor, document type design reviewers, authors, artists, and release engineers

In this chapter, we'll focus on the documentation needed by document authors and DTD maintainers.

- Section 12.1 discusses the user documentation meant for DTD testers and reviewers, authors, and others who must apply markup or read marked-up files.

- Section 12.2 discusses the documentation meant for maintainers, application developers, and others who must read the actual DTD.

## 12.1  Documentation for Users of the Markup

DTD user documentation is essential for two reasons.

First, authors must have access to a thorough description of every distinction that the DTD makes between kinds of document data (that is, every component represented in the markup) so that they can apply the markup correctly and consistently. If they don't make these distinctions in the documents, it will be impossible to take advantage of all the uses planned for the information.

Second, computer software users from all backgrounds have come to expect easy-to-use software and readily available documentation and online help. Technical writers of product documentation, who make up a large segment of the SGML-authoring population, have even higher expectations because producing such material is their business. Providing complete and accurate user documentation helps ease the transition of authors to an SGML document production environment.

Although good documentation is always labor-intensive to produce, over time the documentation pays for itself by reducing the need for user support. Even in the short term it will be a good investment, because it can serve as the basis for some of the training materials needed immediately, and because it can be used in the testing of the draft DTD. If the document analysis report has been properly completed and reviewed, much of the material in it can be used as the basis for the documentation, which can save significantly on time and money.

Following are the minimum components of a complete set of DTD user documentation:

- Reference manual

- Task-oriented user's guide

- Quick reference and online help

- Guide to using tools specifically with this DTD

### 12.1.1  Reference Manual

A reference manual for a DTD is similar to a software reference manual. It consists of a series of stand-alone modules or "man pages," each describing a single markup construct, with the modules in each logical grouping being arranged alphabetically. Following are the typical topics of the modules, in priority order:

1.  Each element type and its attributes

    Don't document end-tags separately from start-tags, even if omitted-tag minimization will be used heavily in your environment, because it will make the documentation unnecessarily large and may be a barrier to authors' understanding of the hierarchical nature of SGML.

2. Each "common attribute"

   Any attribute that appears on multiple elements in substantially similar form should be documented on its own.

3. Each available entity set for boilerplate text, special symbols, and so on

   You don't need to create a reference module for each individual entity.

4. Each element collection that is allowed in multiple contexts

   These reference modules are necessary if the collections are identified by name in the rest of the reference modules.

The reference module for each element type should contain at least the information listed in Table 12-1.

**Table 12-1**    Minimum Information for Element Reference Modules.

| Field | Description |
|-------|-------------|
| Short name | The actual generic identifier, such as `olist`. |
| Full name | A descriptive phrase of arbitrary length that explicates the short name. |
| | For example: |
| | `olist`: An ordered list of related items. |
| Synopsis | A brief presentation of the rules for using the element. For elements in the document hierarchy, it's useful to provide one or more tree diagram fragments that show the direct parents and children of the element being described. For elements at the top level of information units, a tree diagram for the whole information unit is best. Alternatively, you can use a text-based synopsis like the following: |

```
<olist>
<item>
text, e.g., paragraphs
</item>
  .
  .
  .
</olist>
```

If the element allows minimization, this section can explain how to use it. In SGML-aware editing environments, usually minimization is not used.

**Table 12-1**    Minimum Information for Element Reference Modules.  (Continued)

| Field | Description |
|---|---|
| Description | A complete description of the element's purpose, how and where it should be used, and rules for distinguishing this element from other elements that might be used for similar purposes. The description should also include information on choosing attribute values properly.<br><br>For example, the description of `olist` might include the ways in which it is different from `ulist` ("unordered list"), which is for lists of items that are in an insignificant order. |
| Attributes | A reference description of each attribute allowed on the element with its purpose, its allowed values, its default value (if any), and whether a value is required to be supplied. |
| Contents/Contexts | It may be useful to list explicitly the elements allowed inside the current element and the elements in which the current element is allowed, if this information is not regularly part of the Description section or has not been clearly conveyed by the Synopsis section. In environments where SGML-aware editors will be used, however, this information is not as useful as it may seem.<br><br>In the case of elements that are members of collections that appear in many contexts, you may want to name the collections in which they appear, and provide a separate reference module for the whole collection, explaining where its members can appear. |
| Examples | Practical examples convey information about proper markup usage more effectively than any other kind of documentation. Show all the major configurations of the element, with various contents, attribute values, and so on. If its usage changes substantially in different contexts, demonstrate each one. Also, if minimization is allowed, you can demonstrate it here. |

**Table 12-1**      Minimum Information for Element Reference Modules.  (Continued)

| Field | Description |
| --- | --- |
| | For each example of marked-up content, show a corresponding example of formatted or otherwise processed output, if possible. While it may seem inappropriate to show processed output, since this approach does not focus on information potential and longevity, usually authors have many other goals—for example, ensuring information accuracy and meeting deadlines. The most efficient way to help authors mark up information thoroughly and consistently is to demonstrate the effects of markup and thereby provide a solid rationale for that markup. |
| | If your document production environment has not yet attached processing to some markup in your DTD, documenting the use of the markup will be difficult, not only because the effect of the markup can't be demonstrated in the DTD documentation, but also because the actual processing environment won't provide natural constraints on what the authors do. For example, if your DTD has a data-level element that produces no typographical change or other processing behavior, the motivation of authors to use that element will be extremely low. |
| Processing notes | This section can discuss the practical use of the element in a particular editing or processing environment. This is the place to explain how to work around problems in the tools. Segregating the information in this fashion makes it easier to maintain the documentation and update it when the tools or conventional markup practices change. |

In general, the entire reference DTD should be documented in the reference manual, though if an authoring sub-DTD is being used, it may be sufficient to document for this audience only the portions of the model that the authors will see. In any case, the reference manual can document the whole model without any confusion because users will look up only the markup that interests them rather than read the whole document cover to cover. If you manage the reference documentation modularly, you can combine just the reference descriptions needed by each DTD in the family.

Software tools are available that can help you produce some DTD reference information directly from a DTD. This generated information can be useful, particularly for authors who do not have an SGML-aware editing environment available. However, keep in mind that high-quality examples and descriptions must still be provided by a human. Following are some types of information that can be generated:

- Graphical diagrams or outline representations of the DTD rules

- Alphabetical lists of elements with their short and full names (if the full names have been provided in structured comments in the DTD or in some other file)

- Hypertext representations of a DTD that allow users to travel, for example, from the mention of an element in a content model to the declaration for that element

  This form of reference documentation is useful for authors who choose to read the actual DTD, as well as for DTD maintainers.

## 12.1.2    User's Guide

Providing a conceptual and task-oriented user's guide gives you the opportunity to explain the DTD from the authors' perspective rather than from the perspective of elements and attributes. The following basic topics should be covered in the user's guide:

- General SGML and DTD concepts

- How to insert elements, attribute values, comments, entity declarations, and entity references

- The job of applying markup as both a power and a responsibility, and the consequences of Tag Abuse Syndrome

In addition, the user's guide should describe all the tasks that authors most need to know about. The best way to discover what specific task-oriented topics must be addressed is to ask authors what their problems and concerns are. The periods of DTD and software testing provide a perfect opportunity to make these inquiries and discover all the problematic tasks that authors face. These topics, in order to be effective, may need to refer explicitly to the tools and environment that authors will use.

The problems typically fall into one of the following areas:

- I have some information; how do I put it in a document?

  For example, an author might need to document a procedure. If the DTD uses highly content-based markup, the user's guide could explain how to apply the elements meant specifically for procedures and provide real-life examples. Otherwise, it should explain the proper conventional usage of less precise markup, such as using a numbered list in a certain way or with certain attribute values.

A useful adjunct to descriptions of markup choices is a set of "markup cookbooks," whole documents (mock or real) demonstrating the proper use of all the available markup and the resulting processing, provided along with a task-oriented index into the documents.

- How do I achieve a certain formatting or processing effect?

  The topics arising from this question might compare sets of markup that result in similar formatting, and discuss how to choose among them. For example, an author may want to make a phrase appear in italic type, providing the opportunity to explain that the reason for the typographical distinction (for example, because the phrase is in a foreign language) is as important as the appearance for the purposes of information processing.

- Why must I use so much markup? How I can reduce the amount and do my job efficiently?

  For example, an author might be struggling with information that requires several nested layers of markup. This problem provides an opportunity to explain minimization techniques or the use of the available markup templates.

Don't neglect to build an index and a glossary. An index of tasks, employing terminology used by authors rather than that suggested by SGML or the DTD's generic identifiers, is especially helpful. Likewise, it is useful to provide a glossary that defines SGML terms in relation to terms already used in the authors' culture.

Your inquiries will identify not only tasks that need explanation, but probably also any sequences of elements that authors commonly use. You can then turn these sequences into markup templates that help authors insert consistent and correct markup.

## 12.1.3  Tool Guides

In addition to documentation that has the DTD as its focus, you also need tool guides—not the documentation provided with the editors and other software that authors will use, but rather a set of guides that are shorter and more focused on the creation of documents with a specific DTD. They contain the basic information authors need in order to do real work. Popular components of such documentation are:

- A guided tour of standard procedures

- Troubleshooting questions and answers

- Tips on becoming a "power user" of the tools

In some environments, authors are responsible only for the creation of textual document content. In others, they may be responsible for many more facets of document production. When a company switches to SGML, authors may be asked to:

- Key in markup as well as document content

- Get pieces of information (such as IDs, file names, trademarks, bibliographical references, and so on) from a database

- Produce and include nontextual objects, such as graphics

- Keep track of the workflow, validate partial and whole documents against a particular DTD, and store the results in an SGML database

- Format their documents for paper printing and prepare them for other kinds of distribution

According to the sophistication of the SGML documentation production system and the tasks assigned to the authors, they may have to learn how to use the following tools:

- The editor

- The workflow, storage, and archiving system and any additional databases

- The formatting engines

- The indexing engine for electronically distributed documents

This type of documentation will keep evolving and growing as you gather the needs of new users, and will have to be rewritten each time you change tools.

## 12.1.4   Quick Reference and Online Help

Although high-quality user documentation is crucial to any SGML project, most people hate using it. The usual complaints are that it is too bulky to handle and store, and too slow to use when you are looking for short, basic information. For this reason, users should also be provided with a quick reference card or sheet, as well as online help available from within the tools they use.

Unfortunately, most DTD quick reference cards we've seen are quite dull and not very helpful, for obvious reasons. For DTDs of over 100 elements, all that will fit on a single sheet of paper is an alphabetical list of the short and full names of the elements. For the sake of efficiency, some quick reference cards organize elements by category so that users can look in different places according to their problem: document hierarchy, information units, data-level elements, and so on. The result is still not very useful.

However, there are ways to be more creative about the format and content of a DTD reference card, with positive effects on its efficiency. Figure 12-1 shows a reference card designed for the troubleshooting DTD used in a nuclear plant, with the "help frame" side of the card being presented.

This reference card is made up of two parts: a plastic envelope composing the front and back of the reference card, and a plastic card that slides inside the envelope.

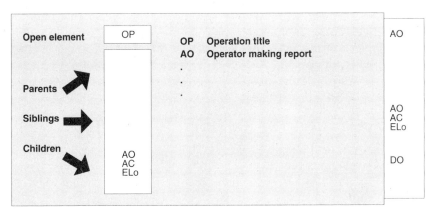

**Figure 12-1**     Quick Reference Card for Troubleshooting DTD.

On the front of the card is a diagram of the upper levels of the hierarchical structure of the DTD, a brief user's guide, and two lists of element collections, referred to by the names ELo and ELi. These names are referred to elsewhere on the card wherever the elements within the collections can be chosen from at the author's discretion.

The back of the card has two parts. On the right, there is the list of the most important elements, each with its name and occurrence rule, and on the left, the help frame. The help frame has a transparent window behind which slides the printed plastic card. By sliding the card behind the open window, you display the last element you typed and can read what the valid parent, sibling, and child elements are.

Of course, not all DTDs are small enough to be able to be represented on a small plastic reference card, but this one was very popular with users because it is simple and they can carry it on-site in the plant for manually tagging their reports. One alternative for a larger DTD is to provide a package consisting of an outline of the major choices of document hierarchy, reduced copies of the tree diagrams representing the information units, and synopses of the usage of all the data-level elements. Usually, authors need more help with the lower levels of a document type than with the document hierarchy, where there is much less choice about markup.

Other useful reference materials might be a set of two tables that relate the short element names to their descriptive names, possibly also providing the page number of the reference module where the element is described. Also, an equivalence table mapping the elements to the markup previously used is usually popular with authors, although such a table can easily be misused because the equivalences are often just rough approximations. If you provide this information, make sure to combine it with sufficient training.

If your word processor or SGML-aware editor allows for the possibility of online help, it can be very effective to provide reference information in this form so authors can look up individual elements and other markup constructs as they work. The modules written for the reference manual (discussed in Section 12.1.1) make natural starting points for online help that can be made available in an editing environment.

## 12.2  Documentation for Readers of the DTD

In addition to the user documentation, every DTD needs to be accompanied by documentation meant for reviewers of the draft DTD, DTD maintainers and customizers, developers of processing applications, interchange partners, and other readers of the DTD. This information constitutes the DTD's maintenance documentation. Usually, the starting point is the reference manual (discussed in Section 12.1.1). The following checklist shows the additional items that are essential for maintenance documentation.

### Design Specification

The implementor should explain any complex or tricky content models and descriptions of all choices made by the implementor after the initial work by the document type design team was done. If there are any significant contexts on which applications need to query, these should be described (if they haven't been covered sufficiently in the user documentation). This information can be thought of as a supplement to the document analysis report; it completes the design specification of the DTD.

### SGML Declaration Documentation

Any SGML declaration characteristics on which the DTD relies (especially if it is not accompanied by a declaration) should be documented.

### Architecture Report

This report should include an explanation of the organization of the markup declarations, the architecture of its modules and parameter entities, and how to customize the DTD. The module-dependency notation used in Chapter 10 is useful here for conveying information about the number of modules, their organization, and their overall levels of dependency on each other.

### Differences Report

The implementor should document the particulars of any variant DTDs and the differences between the reference DTD and the interchange DTD, and the expectations for transforming from one to another.

### Interchange Report

All information needed for other organizations to duplicate the intended processing should be documented. For example:

- The expected defaults for #IMPLIED attribute values

- How CDATA attribute values should be handled

- Expected processing for empty elements, ENTITY attribute values, and non-SGML notations

- Places where an application is required to generate and output text

- Markup that is intended to control the behavior of formatting applications directly (for example, presentational attributes for font choice)

- The precedence of processing for document content, where conflicting markup has been supplied

### Administrative Information and Change Reports

The contact information for the current maintainer and information on how to submit bug reports and enhancement requests should be recorded. Also, for each update, a report should be provided listing the changes made, their rationales, and the number of the bug report or enhancement request to which each change responds.

### Tool-Specific Information

The implementor should document how to use or compile the DTD with particular software tools available in the environment, where the handling differs between tools. Often this information includes an entity catalog file that specifies the system locations of various pieces of the DTD and SGML declaration.

# 13

# Training
# and
# Support

Teaching people how to mark up documents using a DTD is a fundamental part of the successful launch of an SGML project, and it should be given just as much attention and care as the previous phases of development. However, it poses a challenge not found in the other phases: The people involved often resist new concepts and tools because they perceive them as threats to their jobs. As a result, there are two aspects to DTD training, the intellectual and the psychological. In this chapter we address both aspects of the problem, to help you ensure that your trainees get into "success mode."

This chapter is meant for the person in charge of organizing the DTD training. It describes how to plan and deliver a training program for people who must use a DTD to mark up the documents they write. We explain how to organize DTD training sessions by:

- Defining the audiences for the training (discussed in Section 13.1)

- Planning for and providing support to users (discussed in Section 13.2)

- Defining the contents of the training program

    The program we suggest has five phases:

    1.  Initial training (discussed in Section 13.3)

    2.  Training follow-up (discussed in Section 13.4)

    3.  Refresher course (discussed in Section 13.5)

    4.  Quality inspection of documents (discussed in Section 13.6)

    5.  Training on updates to the DTD (discussed in Section 13.7)

- Setting up the training framework and building the training material (discussed in Section 13.8)

In Section 13.9 we provide some figures, drawn from real-life experience, that show what to expect in terms of productivity loss, learning, and assimilation time span. Section 13.10 concludes by presenting suggestions for overcoming the common difficulties of DTD training.

Organizing a training program requires you to adapt the training sessions to your situation according to several factors:

- The stage of advancement of the project

- The architecture of the information system

- The subject matter

- The profile of the people who will attend the sessions

- The tasks for which they are responsible after training

Because the variety of possible training curricula is very wide, we have chosen to limit our suggestions to the most common cases and to provide practical information that you can either use directly or extrapolate from.

For example, we assume that the trainees have already mastered the content of the documents they are likely to model and mark up. We also assume that the trainees will ultimately be using SGML-aware editing tools that provide markup assistance and validation, and that they are in charge of producing new material rather than converting existing documents or "post-tagging" existing contents that they do not fully understand. (Note that training for this last situation is a completely different problem that needs to be handled separately.)

In addition, for simplicity we assume that only one DTD is being taught. In some cases, the users need to learn several DTDs for different document types, but usually each DTD is introduced at a different time, in which case we suggest starting from the commonalities between the known DTD and the new DTD and then teaching what the differences are.

This chapter does not cover training on SGML concepts. The material in Chapter 1 provides an example of the kind of conceptual training that might be helpful for authors.

Following are basic strategies for effective DTD training.

### Teach One Thing at a Time

It's a common mistake to mix up the training on the DTD with training on basic SGML concepts and training on the editing software. Even if the different types of training are necessary, they must be carried out sequentially, in good time, so as not to generate confusion or rejection in the users' minds.

### Keep the Objective Focused

Make sure your goals for training aren't unfocused or overly broad. "Teaching a DTD" is too wide a goal. You must make sure that the trainees ultimately know enough to be able to mark up their documents, that they have good markup strategies when they encounter complex problems, and that they are self-confident and self-sufficient when facing new difficulties.

### Provide a Rationale for SGML

In DTD training, knowledge of the documents is a prerequisite, but the knowledge of DTD syntax is unnecessary, even a hindrance. To motivate the trainees, first you need to present the underlying rationale for the migration to SGML in light of the benefits that it will bring directly to the final users.

### Move from Tasks to Markup

When training on the DTD itself, take a task-oriented approach to the writing job. For instance, to reuse the recipe DTD example introduced in Chapter 1, you can ask the trainees what they do when they explain the "action" part of a recipe, then make the parallel with the step containers described in the DTD, and then finally explain what the actual markup is (the step element) and how to use it.

The other useful approach is to give the trainees strategic clues about how to find the solution if they do not remember the element names or the element hierarchy. Always go back to the logic of actions. For instance, an exchange about problem-solving in marking up recipes might go like this: "Ingredients are always before steps in a recipe; if you cannot insert steps where you are, then there must be some component required before; what is likely to be required before? Look for it or for a container which might group all the steps." If you manage to teach effective strategies to your trainees, chances are they will feel much more confident in their abilities to solve markup problems once they are on their own. That is when you have really reached the target of your training.

### Balance Concepts and Applications

Some people like to understand underlying concepts before they start acting on a piece of software. Others jump on the keyboard or the mouse and try to discover from experience how the software is built and how it works. Especially with DTDs, we believe conceptual work must always precede playing with software applications. But the training cannot be complete if people are not acquainted with the editing tool and environment they will use and do not have perspective on how the global system works. It may seem like a waste of time to teach about the overall processing system, but people enjoy knowing a little more than what their job requires. This way you demonstrate to them how they are contributing to the success of the new system and its benefits.

### Provide an Accurate Training Environment

When reaching the computer-lab stage of the training, make sure that the training environment is identical to the one trainees will be using later. This necessity often militates for in-house training. Using an accurate training environment also gives you the opportunity to explain any constraints that the environment places on the markup model so that trainees will accept more readily any previously unexplainable deficits of the model, the editor, the environment, or the whole production system.

### Use the Documentation as Training Material

Make use of the user documentation as much as possible during the training. This has a double benefit: First, it teaches the trainees to use it and find what they want in it, so it contributes to the effort to render trainees more self-reliant. Second, it will drastically reduce the amount of support you will have to provide after the training is over and people are back to their desks battling problems on their own.

### Teach and Practice Two-Way Communication

We have seen how crucial it is to the project that people feel involved in and responsible for it. Before they leave the course, trainees must know what the processes for bug reporting and enhancement requests are. They must learn to fill in the appropriate forms and know how requests are taken into account, how they will get feedback, and how often the DTD and the software are likely to change.

## 13.1  Audiences for the Training

The primary audience for DTD training includes the people who create the content (authors, writers, contributors), those who review and modify it (reviewers, editors, production specialists, possibly layout artists), and translate it into other languages. However, a secondary audience, including the system administrator, any database administrators, and the managing editor or project manager, may also need training.

The goal for the primary audience is to make them proficient in marking up texts using the DTD, and confident in their ability to find a solution when they encounter markup or technical problems. The difficulty of this goal largely depends on the cultures, motivations, and abilities of these people.

The secondary audience doesn't need the same level of proficiency in the use of the DTD. However, solid knowledge of the DTD is useful to the administrators when they are asked to diagnose and solve a problem on the files or on their content, as well as to document project managers who must mediate disputes when there are DTD or tool problems.

The people who will test and review the draft DTD are usually members of the primary audience, and they may need a slightly different kind of training, which has effective DTD review as its main goal. It is difficult to organize training for testers because they are supposedly already very familiar with what they are supposed to review. If you need to teach the DTD to reviewers in order for them to review it, chances are they will not be knowledgeable enough to carry out the task. However, during conversion or markup of test documents, you can simply conduct normal DTD training for those testers who were not part of the design process. This may result in building a draft training program based on the draft DTD and draft documentation. The organization can be similar to the users' training described in the rest of this chapter, though it is likely to be less fleshed out. Fortunately, testers are usually highly motivated and quick to grasp all the new concepts.

## 13.2  User Support

Support is invaluable to the SGML project, and to the training effort specifically. DTD user support must start to be provided as soon as the initial training is over and goes on indefinitely, with a significant decrease after two to three months.

The amount of support you will have to make available is strongly related to the quality of the training and the level of autonomy the trainees have gained during the lab sessions. It is therefore useful to have the people in charge of the support participate in the definition and evaluation of the training sessions.

Just as for the training, there are usually two levels of support that need to be given: psychological and technical.

Users will need direct help in marking up documents. This help should be provided in close coordination with the DTD training, and it must be nearly instantaneous. We have found that the psychological dimension here is crucial. When faced with markup problems, users often lose their self-confidence and start deprecating their ability to choose and insert markup. By contrast, when faced with technical problems they usually feel able to ask for help and don't blame themselves for their difficulties.

Consequently, it is important to choose support people not only for their theoretical competence but also for their communication abilities and their ease at psychologically supporting the users. This kind of support is the kind most requested in the early days or weeks of deploying your SGML editing environment, unless the system has other technical problems.

The second level of support involves technical expertise. Because of the level of validation usually supplied by an SGML editing environment (whether it offers real-time markup checking or batch checking after documents are written), the "parser" expert and the system administrator are crucial figures. The technical support people will also take over all the problems associated with the use of the editing tool, which is why it is useful to have these people involved in the lab sessions during training.

With these two types of support available, you are prepared to face the difficulties of the learning curve. After a short period of exhilaration, the real work of producing real documents takes a toll on the authors; often, after three or four weeks, everything suddenly blurs in their heads. The temptation is great for them to just give up, which is why support must be readily available during these periods.

After this crisis stage, if the authors haven't successfully overcome their apprehensions, the support team will bear all the weight of convincing these people to keep trying, and bringing them to an acceptable level of proficiency. Unfortunately, this is a long process that can take several months.

Once training has been completed, the support team may also help the authors review their markup as part of the post-training quality inspection of documents.

## 13.3  Phase 1: Initial Training

The first phase of the program is what people usually think of as "the training." It takes place in a room with a teacher and the usual training equipment, such as an overhead projector, plus computers for lab work. The initial training usually involves three types of activities: an introduction, lectures and paper exercises to teach the DTD, and computer labs to learn how to use the DTD with the available tools.

### 13.3.1  Introduction

This period may last from one hour to half a day, depending on the amount of convincing you need to do. It usually includes:

- A presentation on the project to migrate to SGML

- An introduction to the underlying principles of SGML: why SGML, who uses it, what its strengths are, a bibliography for good reference information, and so on

- A presentation on the expected gains for the company or the organization, and the benefits people in the room will individually get mid- or long-term

- A description of the foreseen difficulties, why they exist, how long they usually last, the best way to overcome them, and how much effort people will have to put in

- The training program's specific goals, outline, and schedule, and what will be expected of the trainees

Now is the perfect time to introduce the notion of Tag Abuse Syndrome to the trainees and to encourage them to take responsibility for the markup in their documents. The following "dos and don'ts" list can serve as a reminder.

 **Do:**

- Become familiar with the DTD you will be using and learn the distinctions it offers.

- Use the most precise and accurate available construct in the DTD.

- Choose an appropriate existing construct and extend its semantic role if the DTD's markup isn't powerful or precise enough.

- Use comments to explain your markup choices.

- Use standard entities and element templates or templates where they are available.

**Don't:**

- Use an element to get its formatting effect.

- Use elements with the same formatting effect interchangeably.

- Fail to mark up information just because you're unsure what markup to choose or because the markup seems difficult; ask for help instead.

At the end of this part, the trainees should know that what awaits them in the training may not necessarily be easy, but feel confident in their ability, with the trainers' help, to overcome the difficulties and become more qualified in their jobs, and that, in the long run, the effort should be worthwhile.

## 13.3.2  Lectures and Paper Exercises

Each section of initiation to the DTD ideally includes both a lecture and one or more exercises to perform with a pencil and paper. The best method is to alternate short sessions of theoretical presentation of content with the immediate application of this knowledge in an exercise.

The usual progression of topics roughly follows the layers of the actual markup model:

- Global presentation of the DTD

- The document hierarchy, with special attention given to the metainformation

- The information units, by class

- The data-level elements, by class

- Linking processes

- Miscellaneous topics

### 13.3.2.1  Global Presentation of the DTD

Each step of the training should always be presented in reference to the documents the trainees know well from their current practice. This may generate questions like "What about handling photographs?" and "How do I make sure the table and the explanation face each other on the page?" These questions are often unrelated to the DTD itself, but they are always related to the authoring and production of documents. It's a good idea to defer answering these questions until the trainees have more of a base of knowledge, writing down the questions as you go and crossing them off the list once they are addressed.

To make a global presentation of the DTD, present the following topics using existing documents as examples:

- The types of documents covered by the DTD

- The overall hierarchical structure of the documents and the main similarities to and differences from the structure of the documents to which they have been accustomed

- The vertical organization of the documents: the hierarchical structure, the information units, the data-level elements, and the linking structures

- The differences between the reference DTD and the authoring DTD and their reasons, if any differences exist

### 13.3.2.2  The Document Hierarchical Structure

Now you're ready to begin teaching specific features of the markup model. Along with real-life examples, the best way to convey the document hierarchy's organization and constraints is to use the tree diagram notation. Here is one way to proceed:

1. Ask the trainees to state in English their guesses for the hierarchical structure rules, to demonstrate how easy it is to describe them clearly, thoroughly, and concisely.

2. Teach them the basics of the elm tree diagram notation.

3. Show them the tree diagrams for the document hierarchy (by referring to the DTD user's guide, if possible), and have them interpret the trees out loud. If the trees don't show the actual generic identifiers along with the descriptive names of the elements, you'll need to provide the short-form names.

4. Immediately provide a few samples of varied document parts on paper, and ask the trainees to mark up the hierarchical structure with pencils, remembering to open and close each element and to use the correct element name. There are two ways to go about this, each with advantages and drawbacks:

   - You can use reproductions of whole documents, as shown in the training exercises in Section 4.1.2.2. These have the advantage of realism, but may confuse trainees because they will likely contain more than just "hierarchy" elements, such as paragraphs and lists. You will have to either cover these elements now too, or explain how to skip them.

   - You can use reproductions of tables of contents. These have the advantage of neatly distilling most of the important document hierarchy without involving other elements. However, because the only evidence of a division in a table of contents is the title of that division, this exercise could contribute to confusion about whether a division is a *container* or just a *heading*.

Whichever approach you choose, plan to use the same documents throughout the paper and computer exercises.

To teach the whole document hierarchy, you'll need to explain how to supply metainformation. The nature of metainformation is usually very different from that of hierarchical structure. For example, it usually relies heavily on attributes and must be explained by reference to the processing that the documents will undergo. Thus, you'll need to switch mental gears between the two topics.

### 13.3.2.3  The Information Units and Data-Level Elements

Within the document hierarchy, usually there isn't much markup choice available. Once you begin to cover elements in the information pool, however, choosing the right markup and choosing *to apply* markup become major themes, particularly if your documents have been automatically converted to SGML and either have lost important structure or never had it in the first place.

First, you need to explain the differences between the IU and data levels, and define your usages of these names. Usually the difference is intuitive to trainees, though people with only WYSIWYG experience may try to reduce the meanings to "paragraph styles" and "character styles," which isn't quite appropriate.

Then, you need to present each level in turn: first IUs, then data-level elements. As before, have trainees interpret the tree diagram for each element. As much as possible, try to move from the most frequently used elements to the rarest ones, and from the simplest to the most complex. Typically, the paragraph is both the most frequently used and simplest IU, and lists are a close second. In some DTDs, lists can be quite complex; in this case, it makes sense to teach, for example, "notes" and "cautions" or other simpler IUs before lists.

Try to introduce whole classes of elements at one time so the elements can be understood partially in terms of each other, and teach strategies for choosing among them. For each element class, use paper exercises with sample document fragments to reinforce what has been learned and to show how the markup gradually gains in completeness and quality. Any IUs that involve complex authoring interfaces, such as tables, now or can be introduced during the computer labs.

At the end of the section on IUs, make sure the trainees' "hand-tagging" on paper is accurate. If the paper exercises have gotten tedious, you can switch to the computer lab sessions (discussed in Section 13.3.3) before beginning the data-level elements, because the trainees now know enough to start marking up text using editing software.

Presenting the data-level elements is a bit different from presenting the IUs. Because the data-level elements tend to have little internal structure, you can spend your time more profitably on discussing the differences among elements in a class and describing the processing expectations for each element. Whichever elements you concentrate on most will be the most correctly used. Unless you teach this part in a lively manner with discussions, expression of disagreement, and so on, it can quickly become boring.

Have the trainees apply this new knowledge to marking up data-level components in the sample documents with which they now are quite familiar. Correct or suggest alternative markup along the way.

### 13.3.2.4  The Linking Processes

The topic of "linking," or putting two or more pieces of information in association with each other, crosses the structural organization of the DTD. It is difficult to give specific advice about teaching this topic because it very much depends on the implementation choices you made for your DTD and the types of formatting and printing applications or online viewing applications you intend to have.

---

## Note

The word "linking" is overloaded with specific technical meanings, for example, online navigation hyperlinks. But at this stage we are talking about teaching authors, often nonexperts in these specific fields, the general process of putting two things in relationship when they need to do so. The particular mechanism for making the association needs to be taught, but does not change the essential nature of the action.

---

Often, some linking can be done automatically by the system, and in this case authors need to facilitate the automatic linking process by marking up data-level information thoroughly. For example, if terms in the text can automatically be linked to a company-wide dictionary database that defines the terms, authors must only mark up the terms in text. But for associations that cannot be made automatically for whatever reason, authors must know when and how to make the link.

As we've suggested elsewhere, one way to organize links is into the following types:

- Anchors that bind an element, nontextual object, or annotation to one or more particular places within the document

- Cross-references that link to other parts of the current document or external documents, and suggest that the reader seek out the target of the link

The ease of making such links will vary according to the sophistication of your production system. In all cases, make sure the trainees understand the underlying philosophy of each linking process before they learn the mechanism with which to implement it. If they do not learn the basic concept, after a month they won't be able to remember the syntax and will be unable to find it again. If you skip this part of the training, your documents may contain few links, particularly if the basic writing methodology used is not optimized for hypertext presentation. Your DTD most likely will not prevent this situation from happening, and if you want to build a hypertext application on top of your documents, you may find the markup too poor to support it.

Again, make sure each new conceptual input is immediately followed by a paper example where various linking processes must be applied, and check the trainees' work for proper matching of IDs and references, correct location of IDs, and so on. If you have naming conventions for IDs, graphic file names, and so on, make sure to cover them here.

### 13.3.2.5  Miscellaneous Topics

In this part of the training program you address all the features of the DTD or of your specific applications that may still need some explaining.

You may want to teach how to include special characters within the text by presenting the character entities the DTD makes available and how they can be referenced.

Similarly, you should cover the use of any general entities and their text string equivalents that you have defined specifically for the line of work of your authors. As using the entities imposes additional work on the authors, it is important they understand the rationale for using the entities. Often such entities contain volatile information that might change at any time, especially at the last minute when there is no time to update documents. A typical example would be a product name changed by the marketing department of a company during the final days of manufacturing.

Once the basic concept of presentation independence has been assimilated, you can cover how trainees should properly control the look of the output by inserting processing instructions or using style-related attributes and elements. How and when *not* to do these things is as important as how and when to do them.

Finally, you can present all the features you have built into your various applications that facilitate the authors' work: markup templates, generated text, and so on.

### 13.3.2.6  Conclusion of the Lectures and Paper Exercises

Once you have finished the initial presentations and paper exercises, provide a corrected paper copy of the documents used for all the exercises so that trainees who might have skipped over a difficulty can find their way back again when they are not in training anymore.

The trainees should have all the DTD knowledge required to be excellent "taggers." Now they need to learn how to insert content and markup on their computers.

### 13.3.3  Computer Labs

The purpose of this part of the training is to ensure that your trainees not only know the DTD but that they know how to mark up document instances in the editing software and environment with which they will be supplied. This implies two steps: learning the editing software and environment, and performing markup exercises at the keyboard. This latter part breaks down into three different types of exercises that gradually build the necessary skills:

- Marking up the content of documents that have already been marked up on paper

- Marking up the content of documents never seen before

- Creating new content and simultaneously marking it up

#### 13.3.3.1  Exercises on the Editing Software and Environment

No matter what the computer platform, you must first make sure that the trainees master the usual commands, instructions, and handling of the applications in this environment. This is not the place to teach people how to use Windows. You are only supposed to teach them the editing software.

First, demonstrate the basic features of the software by using a previously prepared document instance. These will need to include the obvious SGML features such as inserting elements, changing elements, and inserting attribute values, as well as cutting, copying, and pasting.

Have the trainees start on their own with the same instance, with a list of tasks to perform. If you have built in some challenging tasks, such as inserting empty elements, making links, or declaring and referencing entities, you'll have the opportunity to explain advanced features and get the trainees to use these features immediately.

When everybody is sufficiently at ease with the software, you can move on to real exercises.

#### 13.3.3.2  Markup Exercises on Known Documents

This part of the training is based on the document you previously distributed for the paper exercises. The trainees have marked up this document on paper, and they must now apply the same markup to the content of the document, which you have made available on line. The purpose of this step is to move from a conceptual approach to a practical one. The trainees will not encounter any markup decision difficulties as such; they will just have to tame the editing software so that it does what they want.

Start by providing an electronic plain-text version of the document used for the paper exercises. Let the trainees mark it up according to what they have on paper, which should be correct since it will have been corrected at the end of the paper exercises.

When they're done, have them check the documents with a validating parser. When all problems have been resolved, print for each trainee the correct marked-up instance.

By this point, the trainees should have a feeling of achievement, because they feel confident about both using the editing software and environment and applying the appropriate markup. It is time to let them tackle both problems at once.

### 13.3.3.3  Markup Exercises on Unknown Documents

In this part of the training, the trainer's role is only to provide plain-text versions of documents that are interesting in terms of markup variety and difficulty, along with formatted versions. Then it is the trainees' turn to work; the trainer is only in the room for support.

At the conclusion of this part, the trainees will probably be feeling confident that they can carry out the task of writing and marking up SGML instances. This assessment of their abilities is not strictly accurate. What they have been doing is "post-tagging" existing documents with a formatted copy to help them. This is far from document creation, which is the next step.

### 13.3.3.4  Creation and Markup of New Documents

Only when authors are able to create new documents and deliver them with the appropriate markup can you be sure that your training has been successful and that they have mastered the DTD and the editing software.

This part of the training is difficult to deliver because it is awkward to order trainees: "Write new text!" Even if writing is their job, they usually perform it with a set goal. As a consequence, if your audience is homogenous in competence and interest, try to define a precise subject on which they must create a new document and, in the process, plan the document's structure and mark up the instance.

This is a long and costly process. You might want to have groups of trainees share the writing task to limit the time assigned to this task or, more drastically, let trainees work on this assignment outside the training session, in order to deliver the results at the beginning of the next training phase. Making the assignment this way is the perfect liaison to the training follow-up.

## 13.3.4  Conclusion of Initial Training

Now that the initial training is over, it is useful to have everybody build a synthesis of what has been learned. The trainees should now be prepared to produce real documents, and in order to move to the next phase of training they will be *required* to do so. At this point you can introduce them to the support team, and you should remind them how to get help and report problems.

← ——————————————————————————————————————— →

## 13.4  Phase 2: Training Follow-up

Compared to the initial training, the follow-up program is much shorter and more informal. Its goals are to control what knowledge is left from the previous training, to test that the concepts the trainees remember are accurate (it usually requires some tuning), and to help them solve problems they have encountered since the end of the training. Therefore, the follow-up cannot take place unless the trainees have actually been exercising at their keyboards and producing sample documents.

First, quiz the group orally to figure out what has been absorbed and correct wrong ideas. Next, gather all the problems encountered by the trainees and sort them out orally, in writing, by showing an example on the computer, or by referring to where it is explained in the user documentation. When this is done as a group, people have the feeling that they are less isolated with their problems, that it is normal to have them, and that there is a way out.

The support people should have kept a list of the problems and solutions encountered and should present them here, as most trainees usually forget what their difficulties were as soon as someone has explained how to fix the problem. You can later distribute a troubleshooting list that shows all the problems and solutions; this list should be used by the DTD maintenance team to improve the system or complete the user documentation.

Next, you can inspect particularly difficult pieces of marked-up documents together and let the group express suggestions on them. In cases where there are different markup options or where the problem cannot be easily solved, people need to know a "trick" to get around the problem or a mnemonic to help them remember the solution.

Finally, once again remind trainees how to find, fill in, and send bug report and enhancement request forms.

## 13.5  Phase 3: Refresher Course

The conclusion of the training activities is a short refresher course or "booster shot"; it takes place about three or four weeks after the training follow-up and has the same goal. However, by now the trainees have much more experience and a broader perspective, and their questions and difficulties are different.

This course often shows a division in the trainee population between the people who have made the mental jump and those who have not. You may want to separate the trainees into two groups because the learning speed and the content of the course for the two groups are going to be very different.

The slow group will want to go back to the basic concepts and to the problems they have met, and will want certainties. With them, it will be necessary to go back to what they know of the document class and to the writing standards guide if there is one in the company, and generally to keep very close to the practical side of their jobs. Inspecting the markup of a piece of document is always a favorite. Reading and explaining parts of the user documentation is less appealing but very efficient too.

The people in the fast group are the potential "power users." Typically, they have already taken the DTD and the tools to their limits and are already coming back with requests for enhancements and changes. They are avid about "tricks" and enjoy sharing how they have fixed various problems. The trainer's task here is to note what is being said and distribute it to the whole group so that everybody can share the knowledge.

At the end of the refresher course it is rewarding to gather the trainees as one group again to show how their work can be utilized. If you can show the formatted result of a document, or an online-viewable version including, for example, hyperlinks, you will give everybody a feeling of achievement, usefulness, and motivation to go on with the markup effort. A good synthesis of the course is to remind trainees about the "dos and don'ts" of markup, as listed in Section 13.3.1.

## 13.6  Phase 4: Quality Inspection of Documents

In a number of companies and organizations where the production of documents is crucial to the activity (publishers with their books, manufacturers with their product documentation, administrations with their rules), it is common to perform a review or inspection of the content and outline of the documents, similar to the computer industry's "code reviews," which are done on modules of programming code. The advent of the ISO 9000 Quality Assurance Certification process has encouraged these types of review.

After any document content inspections have been successfully passed, you should consider using the same process, if more informally, to gradually increase the quality of the markup in SGML documents.

The problem is that although the DTD is often viewed by authors as an unbearable constraint, it never obliges authors to include sophisticated and accurate markup in their documents. Often, authors try to get away with just the minimum document hierarchy, paragraphs, and lists, or they commit Tag Abuse by marking up parts of the content not for what it means but for the look it will produce on paper. Tag Abuse is just as dangerous as not marking up content, because when you want to make proper use of the content based on the markup, you end up producing absurdities.

To prevent both of these drawbacks, the quality inspection procedure provides an official framework where work is not assessed by quantity and time span but by quality. These inspections can be traumatic for some authors. Therefore, we recommend that it be done one-on-one, in the privacy of an office.

There are ways authors can assess the quality of their work before the inspection. One of these ways is to ensure a previous review with the support people. The second is to use software tools that provide statistics on the density of the markup in documents, which can indicate, in a crude way, the quality of the markup. Such tools are relatively easy to build. They are specific to each DTD and to what the editors in the company value in the documents to be published. For each instance, these tools could:

- Show the depth of the hierarchical structure used and warn if it seems abnormal.

- Print the number or percentage of each type of element and compare them with usual percentages. This can be useful for figures, examples, index entries, and so on.

- Figure out how much of the data-level information, particularly key data, has been marked up or just ignored.

Markup evaluation tools are not expected to run a formal inspection on documents; they are just meant to give clues about what might be wrong and prepare for the human inspection. Such tools have to be taken with a grain of salt. They are useless if you do not provide instructions on their proper use and the expected acceptable results. You can develop markup density benchmarks by running the tools on documents recognized for their high quality in writing and markup.

If the results of the human inspection happen to be poor, the author is supposed to fix his or her document according to the recommendations of the inspector, with the help of the support people. This process is iterative until the quality of the markup in the document is acceptable.

## 13.7  Phase 5: Information on DTD Updates

This last phase is not part of the original training or post-training program. It occurs as the DTD starts to be actively used and when no one thinks about training the users any longer. Still, when major updates of the DTD are made based on the reports and requests of the users, the first people who should be informed are the users themselves. Experience shows that it is mainly the DTD design team and implementor who know about changes, and the knowledge does not go further.

We believe that if alterations are serious enough to produce a major DTD release, short half-day training sessions should be organized for all the authors involved to:

- Describe the changes and new markup features

- Explain why they were done

- Show how to use them

- Explain and discuss how they are going to affect the authors' work

- Explain how to handle existing documents in light of the changes

Not only are these small training sessions cost effective, but they are crucial for keeping the authors' morale high: They feel they are still part of the process, their reports and requests have been heard and responded to, and they are immediately operational after an update.

If these additional training sessions cannot be organized, it's helpful to write and distribute release notes or a newsletter explaining all these points to authors.

## 13.8  Training Program Administration

This section describes how to prepare for and organize the training sessions and materials.

The sessions will need to be adapted to the population, local conditions, the complexity of the DTD, the ambition of the training, and the resources allocated to the training portion of the SGML project. Our suggestions are based on teaching complex DTDs with as many as 300 elements. We assume it is a high priority to have the trainees working productively on SGML documents as soon as possible.

### 13.8.1  Prerequisites

The trainees must meet these prerequisites:

- Know the documents covered by the scope of the DTD

  This allows you to jump right into teaching the markup model for that class of documents. If the trainees do not have this basic knowledge, then you must first teach your authors how to write the documents before they can learn how to mark them up, and the first part will take much longer than the second.

- Know the computer systems on which they will be working

  Whatever the hardware platform and the system running on it, if trainees are not familiar with it you will need to add a computer training session, which may be quite long and complex, before the DTD training session. The more you add to the amount of new concepts and new tools to learn, the steeper the learning curve will be. If the authors need training on the systems, we suggest you complete this training well beforehand and let them get used to the systems before starting the DTD training.

- Be assigned to a job related to the training in the near future

  This ensures that trainees will apply the training immediately or soon thereafter. If the training is given too early, for example, before hardware and software are available or before any documents are planned to be written in SGML, by the time they need the competence they will have forgotten everything about it. Also, if the training is given to people who have no direct motivation to achieve something with it, they will feel bored rather than challenged by the course material, and will be less receptive when they really need the information. Giving people some general SGML background before knowledge is needed for a specific project is a laudable goal, but it is a different type of training entirely.

The training session has a prerequisite of its own: The computer lab environment should be identical to the environment in which the authors will work to the greatest extent possible, because otherwise there will be a heavy loss of energy when the authors have to learn a new tool on their own. This usually militates in favor of on-site training, to benefit from the equipment, the local network, and access to common databases. Doing the training off-site has the advantage of freeing the authors completely from their daily tasks, management, and unavoidable tie-ups, but it is bound to require an environment that has differences from the future system and environment.

If you can organize a training session where all these prerequisites are met, you are well on the path to success.

## 13.8.2   Number of Participants

Defining the number of participants for a training session is always difficult because there are conflicting interests. Managers usually favor large groups of people in training sessions because the more people you put in the same room, the less expensive the session becomes and the more quickly the whole population who needs training will be trained. Trainers and trainees usually prefer small groups because the fewer people in each session, the easier it becomes to have the equipment available, trainees active at all times, and the trainer available to rectify any mistake as soon as it occurs.

As usual, the solution is probably halfway between the extremes. We have found that it is extremely effective to have two people at each computer because they discuss markup strategies, take turns in applying markup, and generally help and teach each other. Also, a group of a dozen people is lively, inventive, and representative of the most common attitudes, so discussions within the group are interesting and bring a lot to each participant. A smaller group runs the risk of being somewhat dull and also being so intimate that people feel discouraged from asking questions and expressing their worries. A much larger group is simply too big to handle; no one can get a word in edgewise, and the trainer does not have time to attend to each individual problem.

A group of 12 to 16 trainees with 6 to 8 machines seems to be an efficient compromise.

## 13.8.3   Choice of Trainers

Choosing DTD trainers is a difficult art, because when teaching a DTD the subject matter is so complex that the first reflex is to turn that training over to the person who knows the DTD best: the implementor. This can be a fatal mistake.

The implementor is often a fully trained computer scientist who has mastered the art of programming. He or she seldom has the other competencies required to teach a DTD to authors from the field: teaching skills, writing experience, and a thorough knowledge of the daily tasks of the trainees with their associated constraints and difficulties. On the other hand, it might be difficult to teach a professional trainer the world of the document class, SGML concepts, the intricacies of the DTD, and the training program itself.

We have found it effective to have several different people from the document type design team serving as trainers for different topics. They not only know the DTD by heart, but they also know the context and history, as well as the users' most common difficulties and requests. Each person will have a domain of excellence, whether in explaining the structure and the element types, in teaching a system or a tool, in knowing how to conduct an inspection, or in providing support.

This separation of tasks has two immediate benefits. First, as no one explains things the same way, it gives trainees several different opportunities to understand the contents of the training. It also adds diversity and helps break the monotony of the sessions. Second, the trainees are grateful to have been taught by people just like them, who know the trade and can understand their problems. Although this approach may not seem very orthodox, we recommend it as a way to limit the risk of producing a low-quality, ineffective training program.

## 13.8.4   Training Length and Organization

The topic of training length and organization is one of the most controversial, because the decisions you make here will determine the cost of the training, the loss of productivity of authors during the training sessions, the utilization of key resources (rooms, computers, trainers, support people, and so on), and the planning of when people will be able to deliver acceptable documents.

Unfortunately, the decisions are usually made the other way around. People in charge of training receive a budget, usually too low, and set dates for people to deliver the next batch of documents. They then start building the training program with these constraints. However, the fact that this is the current way of doing things does not mean it is the proper way. This section contains some arguments that may help you obtain training conditions that are likely to increase the success of DTD training.

The experience of people in teaching large, complex DTDs seems to show that a *a minimum of ten days per trainee* is needed.

Ten days does not mean two weeks of elapsed time, though. Most people have found out that such training is more efficient if it is stretched out over time. Thus, we suggest the following allocation of training time across the phases:

- Five days for the initial training

- One week of absorption time, then one day for the training follow-up

- Three weeks of absorption time, then two days for the refresher course

- Between one and two days of individual attention to each trainee for quality inspection of documents whenever each trainee has produced a real document

- A half-day group session for training on DTD updates at each update

Because learning a DTD usually requires real intellectual effort, the training should be intense but not so much so that it muddles people's minds. We have experienced two ways to achieve the right density: Either train people for ten half-days in a row, or train them five days in a row but alternate at least four types of activities each day. For instance, you could start with a lecture, then do a paper markup exercise, then do an exercise involving some play with an editing tool, then do an online markup exercise. With these options, trainees have time to pause and think of questions that they will have a chance to ask the trainer later. The absorption of concepts and know-how is more gradual and effective.

Ten days per trainee will mean much more for the trainers and the support people who will be part of this training. First, the trainers will need a minimum of five days to prepare the first training session. This preparation will decrease to one day for the following sessions, if they are similar. Then they must actually deliver the initial and follow-up training programs. The refresher course may require four days instead of two if the trainers decide to split the group in two to provide the "slow" and "fast" trainees with what they expect. For the document inspections, which involve individual attention, figure on an average of one and a half days per trainee. Assuming a group of 12 trainees, this results in 18 days. DTD update training will require about one more day. The total time commitment for a person who does all the training is 34 days.

If you are put off by the amount of time needed by both the trainees and the trainers, compare it with the time they needed previously to learn and relearn the use of style sheets and templates, and the effort it took to reach consensus on using them!

## 13.8.5   Training Materials

To carry out the training sessions, the training materials must be carefully planned and prepared. The material might take various forms, for example, slides and paper handouts. Some materials are meant for the trainer's use only, and some are also for the trainees. The moment when they should be introduced in the course varies.

Table 13-1 outlines a scenario for the preparation and dissemination of training materials for a typical DTD training program. Of course, this table only lists some possibilities.

The only document mentioned in this table that was not mentioned and described before is the training poster. Even when handwritten, when the training budget is on the low side, the training poster is efficient for beginners. The idea is to have a large piece of cardboard behind the computer, reminding the authors of the main hierarchical and IU structures. It nicely complements the sorted lists of elements which are defined but not explained in context. Not only is it useful during the training, but also during the author's first steps at the keyboard as a sort of large quick reference card.

The amount of training material listed here may seem huge, but believe it or not, it will all fit in a single binder (albeit a thick one!).

**Table 13-1**    Materials for a Typical DTD Training Program.

| Training Material | When to Introduce | Who | Type |
|---|---|---|---|
| Presentation of the global approach | Phase 1, introduction | Trainer, trainees | Paper, overheads |
| User documentation | Phase 1, lecture on the DTD | Trainer, trainees | Paper |
| Tree diagrams of document hierarchy and information pool (also in user documentation) | Phase 1, lecture on the DTD | Trainer | Overheads |
| Thematic list of components (IUs in one color, data-level components in another, entities, cross-references, and so on) | Phase 1, lecture on the DTD | Trainer, trainees | Cardboard or paper |
| Paper exercises: document samples | Phase 1, exercises on the DTD | Trainer, trainees | Paper, overheads |
| Paper exercises: manually marked-up corrected version (optional) | Phase 1, after finishing exercises | Trainees | Paper |
| Computer exercises 1: electronic version of document samples | Phase 1, computer lab on manually marked-up document | Trainer, trainees | Paper |
| Computer exercises 1: valid marked-up instance | Phase 1, end of computer lab on manually marked-up document | Trainer, trainees | Electronic (plain text) |

**Table 13-1**     Materials for a Typical DTD Training Program.  (Continued)

| Training Material | When to Introduce | Who | Type |
| --- | --- | --- | --- |
| Computer exercises 1: formatted file of document (optional) | Phase 1, end of computer lab on manually marked-up document | Trainees | Electronic |
| Guided tour of the editing software: instance that illustrates features | Phase 1, computer lab | Trainer, trainees | Electronic |
| Computer exercises 2: base document sample | Phase 1, computer lab on unknown documents | Trainer, trainee | Paper, electronic (plain text) |
| Computer exercises 2: valid instance (optional) | Phase 1, computer lab on unknown documents | Trainer, trainee | Electronic |
| Reference poster to paste behind the computer (optional) | Phase 1, end of computer lab | Trainer, trainees | Cardboard or paper |
| Formatted output or online document to browse (optional) | Phase 3 | Trainees | Paper or electronic |
| List of problems and solutions or workarounds | Phase 2 and Phase 3, at end | Trainer, trainees | Paper |
| Bug report and enhancement request forms | Phase 2 | Trainer, trainees | Paper, electronic |
| Markup dos and don'ts list (optional) | Phase 3, at end | Trainer, trainees | Paper |
| Reference information: articles and bibliography about SGML and its benefits (optional) | End of the course | Trainer, trainees | Paper |

## 13.9  The Learning Curve

The areas about which there is the least available data on SGML projects are their costs and duration. Unfortunately, these are the first two questions that managers ask when they are considering such a project. This section provides some figures related to training, based on our personal experience. They are likely to be inaccurate for other cases, but they may provide a useful starting point when planning a DTD training program for figuring out when trainees will be fully productive.

### 13.9.1  Time Span

As mentioned in Section 13.8.4, the learning period lasts about three months, assuming that a support team is available during the whole period, and the logistics of computer systems availability and so on have been taken care of. To be more accurate, however, authors typically admit to feeling they have mastered the whole process only when their first project has been delivered and has successfully passed the quality inspection.

Authors usually make progress as follows: After the initial training, authors enter a "crawling phase" lasting a few weeks. Then, over the next few weeks, they begin to assimilate the information. Then they often have a week where they experience a "crisis of faith." Finally, they cross the threshold of full autonomy, when they can engage in real productive work.

The date each person reaches the autonomy threshold varies with that person's learning capacity and interest.

### 13.9.2  Productivity Assessment

When trying to assess the loss of productivity, we interviewed technical writers who had to produce manuals about 250 pages long in about three months with a structured editor they did not know beforehand.

Their conclusion was that they had a drop in productivity of about 35 percent during a month and a half, which included the initial training and mastering the tool. Then this was reduced to a productivity loss of about 10 percent until the end of the first manual.

They admitted that producing the second manual was no added difficulty at all and that having to mark up their text as they created it was no overload at all. It seems that the thinking process is so important compared to the typing time that a few more tags were not significant.

Some writers even admitted that they had the tree diagrams "hardwired" in their heads and that this helped them structure their thoughts to start writing more quickly.

The interviewed writers were, of course, successful writers. To minimize productivity loss, they made the following recommendations:

- Start writing immediately during or after the initial training.

- Make sure you know the editing environment well in the first place so you're not bothered by problems unrelated to the structuring of the document.

- Choose to write a document where content is in no way a difficulty (for instance, a new revision of a document you have already written).

- Stop writing when nothing is clear in your head any longer, and start fresh after a few days.

Some tried to compare productivity when keying in the tags as they went with their structured editor to writing the contents of chapters of their manual with their favorite word processor and then importing it in ASCII form to the editor to post-tag the content. Their assessment was that it was "hell," and it amounted to a 50 percent productivity loss due to the lack of guidance in the markup. They even had to turn off the validation checking to import the source document. They recommended forgetting this solution and doing proper conversion if people want to keep using their word processors.

The unsuccessful writers could not explain their difficulties, other than that they thought the model was too complex and that you had to think of too many things at a time. This result argues in favor of even more gradual introduction of complexities.

As a conclusion, contrary to the rumor, switching to SGML seems to hinder writing productivity only slightly in the early days and not at all in normal use.

## 13.10 Training Challenges

We believe that following the suggestions in this chapter will help make the use of your DTD a success. But we do not want to paint too rosy a picture: Training is the trickiest part of an SGML project because it is the only time (other than getting buy-in on the project in the first place!) when you will be dealing with some unwilling people. And teaching a DTD and its use to people who are not enthusiastic is indeed a challenge.

We'll conclude by summarizing what the main difficulties in training are, so you can keep them in mind and overcome them at each moment of the training.

### Helping Authors Make the Effort

The authors will need to agree to make the necessary intellectual effort. Whether for reasons of intellectual comfort levels or resistance to change, this is definitely the hardest battle to win.

### Helping Authors Accept New Constraints

Particularly if you have not implemented a controlled document production environment yet, it is difficult for authors to accept the permanent constraint of the model and the permanent control of the parser. This impossibility of cheating makes some writers talk about "big brother" and the "death of creativity."

### Helping Authors Model Documents Before Writing Them

Some authors will have difficulty accepting the need for structuring their documents before they write them, and will have trouble mastering this skill. Some people naturally write in such a way, but for others, getting there is a terribly painful path.

### Cutting the Cord Between Content and Presentation

The authors will need to accept their loss of power on the presentation of their documents. The WYSIWYG years and tools have given them so much freedom and so much fun in formatting their documents that pushing them to concentrate only on the intelligence of the contents and letting the formatting be the responsibility of a formatting engine feels like extreme generosity on their part.

### Providing Support All the Way

Authors will need to be convinced to hold on as long as necessary until marking up information becomes second nature. As with all difficult situations, the temptation is great to just drop out so as not to be confronted with one's limitations. The good point of helping people to hold on, however hard it is, is the immense pleasure they feel when they finally master the use of a DTD and the editing tool.

### Getting Buy-In on the Training Program Itself

Last but not least is a difficulty that managers, rather than authors, face. The hardest part of project management is obtaining the necessary time and resources to organize a really solid training program.

If you have designed and developed a DTD using the methodology, documented it properly, delivered effective training, been vigilant in observing the difficulties encountered by the users, and helped them to overcome the difficulties, your DTD project is certain to be successful.

# DTD Implementor's Quick Reference

This appendix summarizes syntax information about the commonly used SGML markup declarations and other constructs for quick reference. The following constructs are described:

- Element declarations (Section A.1)

- Attribute definition list declarations (Section A.2)

- General and parameter entity declarations (Section A.3)

- Comments and comment declarations (Section A.4)

- Marked section declarations (Section A.5)

- Notation declarations (Section A.6)

- Processing instructions (Section A.7)

- Document type declarations (Section A.8)

- SGML declarations (Section A.9)

- Formal public identifiers and catalogs (Section A.10)

The syntax diagrams in this appendix use the following conventions:

- Curly braces ({}) surround choices from which one must be picked.

- Square brackets ([]) surround choices from which one can optionally be picked. Note that in a few cases, square brackets are actually part of the SGML markup. In these cases, the brackets are shown in boldface and an explanation is provided.

- An ellipsis (...) follows choices that are repeatable.

- *Italic* text represents portions of the markup declaration that the DTD implementor is responsible for supplying.

- Roman text and all special characters other than those mentioned above represent SGML keywords and delimiters that must be supplied as shown.

## A.1   Element Declarations

Figure A-1 shows the syntax for element declarations and content model groups.

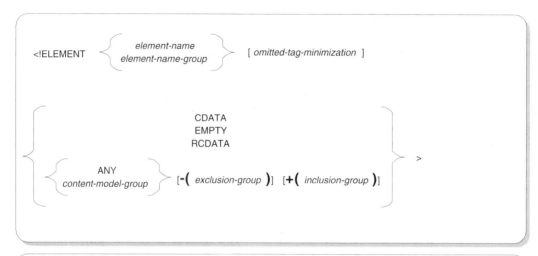

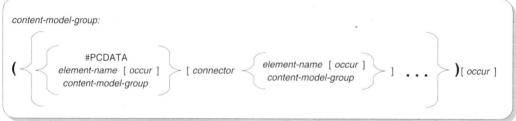

**Figure A-1**     Element Declaration Syntax.

ELEMENT

      Keyword that starts an element declaration.

*element-name*, *element-name-group*

      The names of the one or more elements being declared. If more than one name is supplied, the group must be surrounded by parentheses. Its components can be separated using any *connector*.

```
<!ELEMENT elem - - ...>
<!ELEMENT (elem1|elem2) - - ...>
```

*omitted-tag-minimization*

> Two fields separated by a space, indicating whether it is an error (–) or not (uppercase or lowercase O) for the start-tag and end-tag, respectively, to be omitted. These fields are optional if the feature OMITTAG feature is set to NO in the SGML declaration.
>
> ```
> <!ELEMENT elem - - ...>
> <!ELEMENT elem ...>
> ```

EMPTY

> Keyword indicating that the element cannot have content (and therefore cannot have an end-tag). This keyword forms an element's **declared content**.
>
> ```
> <!ELEMENT elem - O EMPTY>
> ```

CDATA

> Keyword indicating that the element's content consists solely of "character data," with no entity references or subelements allowed. This keyword forms an element's **declared content**.
>
> ```
> <!ELEMENT elem - - CDATA>
> ```

RCDATA

> Keyword indicating that the element's content consists solely of "replaceable character data," which includes entity references but not subelements (even if they are allowed with a higher-level inclusion). This keyword forms an element's **declared content**.
>
> ```
> <!ELEMENT elem - - RCDATA>
> ```

ANY

> Keyword indicating that the element's content can consist of a free mixture of parsed character data (explained below) and any of the elements available in the DTD.
>
> ```
> <!ELEMENT elem - - ANY>
> ```

*content-model-group*

> Specification of an allowable arrangement of elements and/or data characters in an element's content. Content model groups can be nested inside other content model groups. Each level of group is surrounded by parentheses.
>
> If a group contains more than one element or nested group, each component must be separated by a *connector*. Only one connector can be used inside any one level of group. The choices of connector are as follows:

,           Sequential (SEQ) connector requiring each component to appear (taking into account inner occurrence indicators) in the left-to-right order supplied.

|           Either-or (OR) connector requiring only one of the components to be chosen (taking into account inner occurrence indicators) exclusive of the others.

&           Any-order (AND) connector requiring each component to appear (taking into account inner occurrence indicators) in any order, not just the order supplied.

```
<!ELEMENT elem1 - - (elem2, elem3)>
<!ELEMENT elem1 - - (elem2|(elem3, elem4))>
```

Any group or element name in a content model can be followed with an occurrence indicator. The choices of occurrence indicator are as follows:

(no indicator)     By default, the element or group is required to occur exactly once in the content.

?           Marker indicating that the element or group is optional (OPT), that is, that it can occur zero times or one time.

*           Marker indicating that the element or group can occur any number of times (REP), including zero.

+           Marker indicating that the element or group must occur at least once and after that can occur any number of times (PLUS).

```
<!ELEMENT elem1 - - (elem2?, elem3)>
<!ELEMENT elem1 - - (elem2 & (elem3+, elem4*))>
```

#PCDATA

Keyword indicating that this location in the element's content model can contain "parsed character data," which includes characters, entity references, and any elements allowed by the current content model or by higher-level inclusions.

```
<!ELEMENT elem - - (#PCDATA)>
<!ELEMENT elem1 - - (#PCDATA|elem2)*>
```

When the keyword stands alone, whether or not an occurrence indicator is used, it still allows a free mixture of zero or more data characters.

#PCDATA should appear only by itself or in a content model containing only an optional-repeatable group, but does not generate an error if it appears in a non-recommended configuration.

*exclusion-group*, *inclusion-group*

> Exceptions to the element's content model. The exclusion group indicates one or more element names to be disallowed from the content of this element and any subelements, and the inclusion group indicates one or more element names to be freely allowed in the content of this element and any subelements.
>
> Even if only one element is supplied, the group must be surrounded by parentheses. Its components can be separated using any *connector*. An exclusion group must be preceded by a hyphen (-), and an inclusion group must be preceded by a plus sign (+).
>
> ```
> <!ELEMENT elem1 - - (elem2) -(elem3)>
> ```
>
> Exclusions take precedence over inclusions in their effect on any one content model, and any specified exclusions must appear before any specified inclusions. Elements cannot appear as both required (in the content model) and exclusions.

Following are the SGML declaration quantities related to elements.

- The number of characters in an element name cannot exceed NAMELEN, which is 8 in the reference quantity set.

- The number of nesting levels of content model groups in any one content model, including the top level, cannot exceed GRPLVL, which is 16 in the reference quantity set.

- The number of content tokens (element names, the #PCDATA keyword, and content model groups) in any one content model group cannot exceed GRPCNT, which is 32 in the reference quantity set.

- The number of content tokens in any one entire content model cannot exceed GRPGTCNT, which is 96 in the reference quantity set.

- The nesting depth of open elements cannot exceed TAGLVL, which is 24 in the reference quantity set.

- The number of characters in a start-tag, including the element name and all attribute names and values but not including the tag delimiters, cannot exceed TAGLEN, which is 960 in the reference quantity set.

## A.2  Attribute Definition List Declarations

Figure A-2 shows the syntax for attribute definition list declarations.

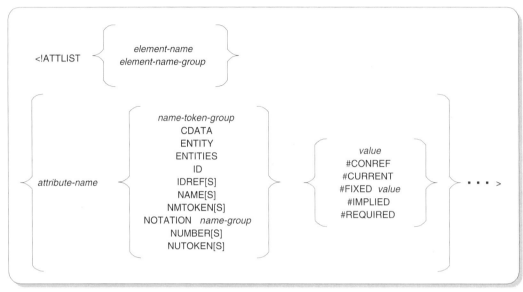

**Figure A-2**    Attribute Definition List Declaration Syntax.

ATTLIST

> Keyword that starts an element's attribute list declaration. Only one attribute list declaration can be provided for any one element. (Attribute lists can be associated with data content notations as well as with elements.)

*element-name*, *element-name-group*

> The one or more element names whose attribute list is being declared. If more than one element is supplied, the group must be surrounded by parentheses. Its components can be separated using any *connector*.

```
<!ATTLIST elem ...>
<!ATTLIST (elem1|elem2) ...>
```

*attribute-name*

> The name of the attribute being declared by the specification that follows.

```
<!ATTLIST elem
        att1 ...
        att2 ...
>
```

> Any number of attributes can be declared.

*name-token-group*

A series of one or more strings of characters from which the attribute value must be chosen, if it must be supplied at all. The group must be surrounded by parentheses. If more than one string is supplied, the strings can be separated using any *connector*. If the strings contain characters other than those allowed in SGML NAME values, each string must be surrounded by quotation marks.

```
<!ATTLIST elem
        att (val1|val2) ...
>
```

The same declared-value token can't be repeated in multiple token groups in the same attribute list declaration. The keyword values for the declared value are explained in Table A-1.

*value*

A default value for the attribute that consists of a string of characters. If the string contains characters other than those allowed in SGML NAME values, it must be surrounded by quotation marks.

```
<!ATTLIST elem
        att (val1|val2) val1
>
```

Only attributes with the declared value CDATA can have a default value consisting of an empty string (" ").

The keyword values for the default value are explained in Table A-2.

Table A-1 summarizes the rules for attribute declared values. While the examples of attribute values here are shown in double quotation marks ("), it is possible to leave off the quotation marks if the value is allowed to contain NAME characters and the actual value contains only NAME characters (even if the string is longer than NAMELEN). Also, single quotation marks (') can be used instead of double ones. If the string must itself contain quotation marks of one kind, use marks of the other kind to quote the string.

**Table A-1**    Attribute Declared Values.

| Declared Value | Lexical Constraints | Description |
|---|---|---|
| CDATA | Case-sensitive. <br><br> Maximum length: LITLEN. <br><br> All characters: any valid SGML data character. | Free-form string of character data. <br><br> If string contains any character not allowed in NAME, surround with quotes. String cannot contain element markup, but can contain entity references if it is quoted. |

**Table A-1**    Attribute Declared Values.  (Continued)

| Declared Value | Lexical Constraints | Description |
|---|---|---|
| | | Only attributes with the declared value CDATA can have a default value consisting of an empty string (""). |
| | | Examples (assuming an attribute that contains translation instructions): |
| | | Right: "This element contains a joke with no cultural referent in French" |
| | | Wrong: "\<emph>Do not\</emph> translate!" |
| ENTITY | Case-sensitive. | Reference to an entity name declared in the document, which can represent the current element's "content." |
| | Maximum length: NAMELEN. | |
| | First character: A...Z, a...z. | Do not supply the entity reference delimiters (& ; ). |
| | Subsequent characters: A..Z, a..z, 0..9, period, hyphen. | Examples: |
| | | Right: FIG06, Fig06 |
| | | Wrong: 06 |
| ENTITIES | Case-sensitive. | References to one or more entity names declared in the document, separated by spaces. |
| | Maximum length: NAMELEN. | |
| | First character: A..Z, a..z. | Do not supply the entity reference delimiters (& ; ). |
| | Subsequent characters: A..Z, a..z, 0..9, period, hyphen. | If more than one entity reference is supplied, surround the entire collection with quotes. |
| | | Examples: |
| | | Right: "Fig1a Fig1b Fig1c" |
| | | Wrong: "1a 1b 1c" |

**Table A-1**     Attribute Declared Values.  (Continued)

| Declared Value | Lexical Constraints | Description |
|---|---|---|
| ID | Case-insensitive.<br>Maximum length: NAMELEN.<br>First character: A..Z.<br>Subsequent characters: A..Z, 0..9, period, hyphen. | Symbolic identifier to be associated with the element.<br>Each value must be unique in the document instance.<br>An attribute with the declared value ID cannot appear more than once for any one element.<br>By convention, ID attributes typically have "ID" as their name, as a reminder that all ID values in an instance must be unique.<br>The default value for an ID attribute must be either #IMPLIED or #REQUIRED.<br>Examples:<br>Right: INTRO, BIKEFIG<br>Wrong: 9LIVES, CHAP_2 |
| IDREF | Case-insensitive.<br>Maximum length: NAMELEN.<br>First character: A..Z.<br>Subsequent characters: A..Z, 0..9, period, hyphen. | Reference to an element's symbolic identifier in the current document instance.<br>Examples:<br>Right: INTRO, BIKEFIG<br>Wrong: 9LIVES, CHAP_2 |

**Table A-1**    Attribute Declared Values. (Continued)

| Declared Value | Lexical Constraints | Description |
| --- | --- | --- |
| IDREFS | Case-insensitive.<br><br>Maximum length: NAMELEN.<br><br>First character: A..Z.<br><br>Subsequent characters: A..Z, 0..9, period, hyphen. | Series of one or more references to element symbolic identifiers in the current document instance, separated by spaces.<br><br>If more than one ID reference is supplied, surround the entire collection with quotes.<br><br>Examples:<br>Right: "USRINTRO ADVINTRO"<br>Wrong: "1 2 3" |
| NAME | Case-insensitive.<br><br>Maximum length: NAMELEN.<br><br>First character: A..Z.<br><br>Subsequent characters: A..Z, 0..9, period, hyphen. | Name string that can be used as an application-specific keyword.<br><br>Examples:<br>Right: ARABIC, OTHER<br>Wrong: 2PICAS |
| NAMES | Case-insensitive.<br><br>Maximum length: NAMELEN.<br><br>First character: A..Z.<br><br>Subsequent characters: A..Z, 0..9, period, hyphen. | Series of one or more name strings, separated by spaces.<br><br>If more than one name string is supplied, surround the entire collection with quotes.<br><br>Examples:<br>Right: "JOE MARY DON"<br>Wrong: "#087 #002 #296" |
| NMTOKEN | Case-insensitive.<br><br>Maximum length: NAMELEN.<br><br>All characters: A..Z, 0..9, period, hyphen. | Name string with relaxed first-character rules.<br><br>Examples:<br>Right: 9X-123-AA.1<br>Wrong: 9X_123_AA.1 |

**Table A-1**  Attribute Declared Values. (Continued)

| Declared Value | Lexical Constraints | Description |
|---|---|---|
| NMTOKENS | Case-insensitive.<br><br>Maximum length: NAMELEN.<br><br>All characters: A..Z, 0..9, period, hyphen. | Series of one or more name strings with relaxed first-character rules, separated by spaces.<br><br>If more than one name string is supplied, surround the entire collection with quotes.<br><br>Examples:<br><br>Right: `"9X-123 9X-456"`<br><br>Wrong: `"9X_123 9X_456"` |
| NOTATION | Case-insensitive.<br><br>Maximum length: NAMELEN.<br><br>First character: A..Z.<br><br>Subsequent characters: A..Z, 0..9, period, hyphen. | Reference to a notation name declared in the document, indicating the data content notation of the current element. The *name-group* that follows must contain one or more names of notations, surrounded by parentheses and separated by any *connector*.<br><br>An attribute with the declared value NOTATION cannot appear more than once for any one element.<br><br>Examples:<br><br>Right: `EPS, CGM, EQN`<br><br>Wrong: `8879` |
| NUMBER | Case-insensitive.<br><br>Maximum length: NAMELEN.<br><br>All characters: 0..9. | Whole-number string.<br><br>Examples:<br><br>Right: `0008, 620521`<br><br>Wrong: `PI, -1, .25` |

**Table A-1**    Attribute Declared Values.  (Continued)

| Declared Value | Lexical Constraints | Description |
|---|---|---|
| NUMBERS | Case-insensitive.<br><br>Maximum length: NAMELEN.<br><br>All characters: 0..9. | Series of one or more whole-number strings, separated by spaces.<br><br>If more than one number is supplied, surround the entire collection with quotes.<br><br>Examples:<br><br>Right: `"1 2 3"`<br><br>Wrong: `"F2D D7E"` |
| NUTOKEN | Case-insensitive.<br><br>Maximum length: NAMELEN.<br><br>First character: 0..9.<br><br>Subsequent characters: A..Z, 0..9, period, hyphen. | Number string with relaxed subsequent-character rules.<br><br>Examples:<br><br>Right: `950521:1400`<br><br>Wrong: `-1, .25` |
| NUTOKENS | Case-insensitive.<br><br>Maximum length: NAMELEN.<br><br>First character: 0..9.<br><br>Subsequent characters: A..Z, 0..9, period, hyphen. | Series of one or more number strings with relaxed subsequent-character rules, separated by spaces.<br><br>If more than one number is supplied, surround the entire collection with quotes.<br><br>Examples:<br><br>Right: `"0.25 0.54 0.01"`<br><br>Wrong: `"#1 #2 #3"` |

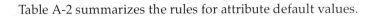

Table A-2 summarizes the rules for attribute default values.

**Table A-2**      Attribute Default Values.

| Default Value | Description |
|---|---|
| `#CONREF` | It is optional to supply a value for this attribute. If it is supplied, however, the element cannot have any content and cannot have an end-tag, as if the element were declared to be `EMPTY`. The attribute value is usually assumed to provide information that enables retrieval of the element "content," such as an entity reference. This default value cannot be used if the element requires content or if the element has a declared value of `EMPTY`. |
| `#CURRENT` | The value most recently supplied for this attribute on an element of the same type will be used as the default for the current element. "Recent" means found before this element in the linear stream of document data. The first occurrence of the element must specify a value for this attribute. |
| `#FIXED "value"` | The value that follows is the only possible value for the attribute, and it is provided as a default. |
| `#IMPLIED` | It is optional to supply a value for this attribute in the document instance; applications will need to supply their own value if one is needed for processing. Attributes with a declared value of `ID` must have a default value of either `#REQUIRED` or `#IMPLIED`. |
| `#REQUIRED` | A value must be supplied for the attribute in the document instance. Attributes with a declared value of `ID` must have a default value of either `#REQUIRED` or `#IMPLIED`. |

Following are the SGML declaration quantities related to attributes.

- The total number of name tokens, including attribute names, in the attribute definition list portion of any one attribute list declaration cannot exceed `ATTCNT`, which is 40 in the reference quantity set.

- The number of characters in an element start-tag's attribute specifications list cannot exceed `ATTSPLEN`, which is 960 in the reference quantity set.

- The number of characters in any one attribute value cannot exceed `LITLEN`, which is 240 in the reference quantity set.

## A.3  Entities

Figure A-3 shows the relationships between the functional categories of entity available to be referenced by authors and DTD implementors, and gives the SGML name for the kind of entity usually used for each.

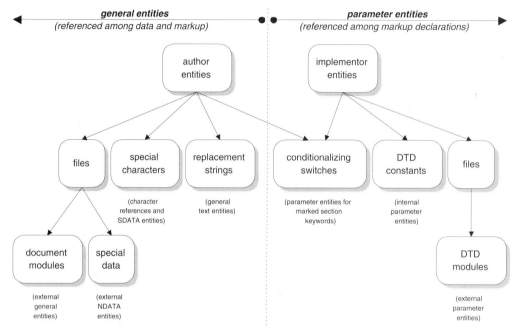

**Figure A-3**    Functional Entity Types.

Following are the SGML declaration quantities related to entities.

- The number of characters in an entity name cannot exceed NAMELEN, which is 8 in the reference quantity set. For parameter entities, the percent sign (%) delimiter must be counted as part of the name.

- The number of characters in a quoted value supplied in an entity declaration cannot exceed LITLEN, which is 240 in the reference quantity set. If the value is preceded by one of the keywords STARTTAG, ENDTAG, MS, or MD, the SGML markup delimiters for those constructs must be counted as part of the value.

## A.3.1   General Entity Declarations

General entities are used in document data and markup. Figure A-4 shows the syntax for general entity declarations.

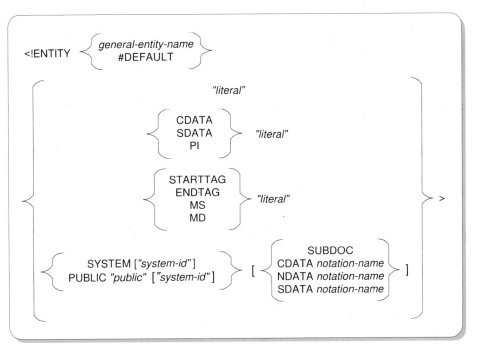

**Figure A-4**     General Entity Declaration Syntax

ENTITY

> Keyword that starts an entity declaration.

*general-entity-name*

> The name of the general entity being declared.
>
> `<!ENTITY ent ...>`

#DEFAULT

> Keyword indicating that the declaration is for the "default" entity, which will be used whenever an entity is referenced that has not been explicitly declared.
>
> `<!ENTITY #DEFAULT ...>`

*literal*

> A quoted string containing data and possibly SGML markup that serves as the replacement string for this entity when it is referenced. If it contains markup, the markup should be balanced; that is, it should close any elements it opens.
>
> `<!ENTITY ent "text">`
>
> The ISO name for this kind of declaration is an internal entity specification.

CDATA "*literal*"

> Keyword indicating that the entity's replacement string is to be treated as CDATA; that is, entity references and element markup won't be recognized. The ISO name for this kind of declaration is an internal entity specification with data text.
>
> ```
> <!ENTITY ent CDATA "chars">
> ```

SDATA "*literal*"

> Keyword indicating that the entity's replacement string is "system-specific" data containing instructions that are nonportable across computer systems. Typically, SDATA entities are used for special characters and symbols. The ISO name for this kind of declaration is an internal entity specification with data text.
>
> ```
> <!ENTITY ent SDATA "instrucs">
> ```

PI "*literal*"

> Keyword indicating that the entity's replacement string should be treated as a processing instruction. The ISO name for this kind of declaration is an internal entity specification with data text.
>
> ```
> <!ENTITY ent PI "instrucs">
> ```

STARTTAG "*literal*"

> Keyword indicating that the entity's replacement string should be interpreted as having start-tag delimiters around it, so that it can function as start-tag markup: <*literal*>.
>
> ```
> <!ENTITY ent STARTTAG "elemname att='value'">
> ```
>
> Using the STARTTAG keyword rather than including the delimiters directly in the replacement string is helpful for protecting against changes to the concrete syntax in which SGML markup is expressed.
>
> The ISO name for this kind of declaration is an internal entity specification with bracketed text.

ENDTAG "*literal*"

> Keyword indicating that the entity's replacement string should be interpreted as having end-tag delimiters around it, so that it can function as end-tag markup: </*literal*>.
>
> ```
> <!ENTITY ent ENDTAG "elemname">
> ```
>
> Using the ENDTAG keyword rather than including the delimiters directly in the replacement string is helpful for protecting against changes to the concrete syntax in which SGML markup is expressed.

The ISO name for this kind of declaration is an internal entity specification with bracketed text.

MS "*literal*"

Keyword indicating that the entity's replacement string should be interpreted as having marked section delimiters around it, so that it can function as a marked section region: `<![`*literal*`]]>` .

```
<!ENTITY ent MS "IGNORE [ignored-stuff">
```

Using the MS keyword rather than including the delimiters directly in the replacement string may not help protect against changes to the concrete syntax in which SGML markup is expressed, because the literal must actually contain the inner opening square bracket (or alternate character, if you have redefined the concrete syntax).

The ISO name for this kind of declaration is an internal entity specification with bracketed text.

MD "*literal*"

Keyword indicating that the entity's replacement string should be interpreted as having markup declaration delimiters around it, so that it can function as a markup declaration: `<!`*literal*`>` .

```
<!ENTITY ent MD "--cmt--">
```

Using the MD keyword rather than including the delimiters directly in the replacement string is helpful for protecting against changes to the concrete syntax in which SGML markup is expressed.

The ISO name for this kind of declaration is an internal entity specification with bracketed text.

SYSTEM

Keyword indicating that the entity's contents can be found on a computer system, stored separately from the entity declaration.

```
<!ENTITY ent SYSTEM>
```

*system-id*

A file name, pathname, or other specification for how to locate the entity content on the computer system.

```
<!ENTITY ent SYSTEM "file.sgm">
```

PUBLIC

> Keyword indicating that the entity's contents can be found on a computer system and that the contents can be located by mapping the supplied public identifier to location instructions that are stored outside the SGML document. An entity with a public identifier can also optionally have system location instructions stored with it.
>
> ```
> <!ENTITY ent PUBLIC "logical-name">
> ```

*public-id*

> Symbolic identifier that maps to location instructions. The mapping is done by an entity manager, often through the use of a catalog file that lists public IDs and their corresponding physical locations.
>
> If the FORMAL feature is set to YES in the SGML declaration, the public identifier must be constructed according to certain syntactic rules, described in Section A.10.

SUBDOC

> Keyword indicating that the entity contents are considered to be a separate SGML document, with its own DOCTYPE declaration pointing to a potentially different DTD.
>
> ```
> <!ENTITY ent SYSTEM SUBDOC>
> ```
>
> The SUBDOC keyword can be used only if the SUBDOC feature in the SGML declaration is set to YES.
>
> If an entity type of SUBDOC, CDATA, NDATA, or SDATA is not specified, the entity is assumed to contain SGML data and markup.

CDATA *notation-name*

> Keyword indicating that the entity contents are to be treated as CDATA; that is, entity references and element markup won't be recognized. The notation must have been declared in a NOTATION declaration.
>
> ```
> <!ENTITY ent SYSTEM CDATA notn>
> ```
>
> If an entity type of SUBDOC, CDATA, NDATA, or SDATA is not specified, the entity is assumed to contain SGML data and markup.

NDATA *notation-name*

> Keyword and value indicating that the entity contents are to be treated as non-SGML data of the specified notation. The notation must have been declared in a NOTATION declaration.
>
> ```
> <!ENTITY ent SYSTEM NDATA notn>
> ```

If an entity type of SUBDOC, CDATA, NDATA, or SDATA is not specified, the entity is assumed to contain SGML data and markup.

SDATA *notation-name*

>    Keyword indicating that the entity contents consist of data that is "system-spe-cific", that is, nonportable across computer systems. The notation must have been declared in a NOTATION declaration.

>    `<!ENTITY ent SYSTEM SDATA notn>`

>    If an entity type of SUBDOC, CDATA, NDATA, or SDATA is not specified, the entity is assumed to contain SGML data and markup.

## A.3.2   Parameter Entity Declarations

Parameter entities are used in markup declarations. Figure A-5 shows the syntax for parameter entity declarations.

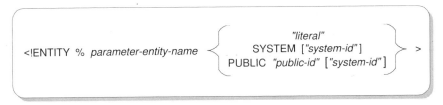

**Figure A-5**    Parameter Entity Declaration Syntax.

ENTITY

>    Keyword that starts an entity declaration.

%

>    Key letter that indicates that the declaration is for a parameter entity, an entity that can be referenced only within and among markup declarations. The per-cent sign must be surrounded by spaces.

*parameter-entity-name*

>    The name of the parameter entity.

>    `<!ENTITY % ent ...>`

*literal*

>    A quoted string containing replacement data for the parameter entity.

>    `<!ENTITY % ent "string">`

SYSTEM

> Keyword indicating that the entity's contents can be found on a computer system, stored separately from the entity declaration.
>
> ```
> <!ENTITY % ent SYSTEM>
> ```

*system-id*

> A file name, pathname, or other specification for how to locate the entity contents on the computer system.
>
> ```
> <!ENTITY % ent SYSTEM "file.dtd">
> ```

PUBLIC

> Keyword indicating that the entity's contents can be found on a computer system and that the contents can be located by mapping the supplied public identifier to location instructions that are stored outside the SGML document. An entity with a public identifier can also optionally have system location instructions stored with it.
>
> ```
> <!ENTITY % ent PUBLIC "logical-name">
> ```

*public-id*

> Symbolic identifier that maps to location instructions. The mapping is done by an entity manager, often through the use of a catalog file that lists public IDs and their corresponding physical locations.
>
> If the FORMAL feature is set to YES in the SGML declaration, the public identifier must be constructed according to certain syntactic rules, described in Section A.10.

## A.4  Comments

Figure A-6 shows the syntax for comment declarations and comments interspersed within other markup declarations. Note that comment declarations and marked section declarations are the only kinds of markup declarations that can appear directly in a document instance.

```
<!-- comment-text -- >
```

```
<! keyword  param  -- comment-text -- param ... >
```

**Figure A-6**    Comment Syntax.

For example:

```
<!DOCTYPE doc [
<!-- Here is the document element's definition.
     This document type isn't actually good for much.
-->
<!ELEMENT doc    - - (front, body)>
<!ATTLIST doc        id  ID  #REQUIRED
<!ELEMENT front - - (title) --front is for metainfo-->
<!ELEMENT title - - (#PCDATA)>
<!ELEMENT body  - - (para+)>
<!ELEMENT para  - - (#PCDATA)>
]>
<doc id="a-small-doc">
<front><title>This Is a Title<!--check: is this
an acceptable title?--></title>
<body>
<para> The first paragraph.
</para>
<para>
A second paragraph.
</para>
</body>
</doc>
```

Comments can be placed inside other markup declarations in most locations where white space must appear. However, they cannot be placed inside a content model group in an element declaration (though they can appear between a content model group and any exceptions, and between exclusions and inclusions). Whole comment declarations can be placed almost anywhere within a document instance, but can't appear inside start-tags, end-tags, or other markup.

## A.5  Marked Section Declarations

Marked sections are delimited regions of document content that should receive special attention by the parser. Each marked section is actually a markup declaration, one of only two kinds that can appear directly in a document instance (the other kind is a comment declaration). Figure A-7 shows the syntax for marked section declarations. Note that square brackets that are actually part of the SGML markup are shown in boldface, whereas brackets used to indicate the optionality of a field are not given emphasis.

**Figure A-7**    Marked Declaration Syntax.

IGNORE

> Keyword indicating that the characters in the region, other than the ones ending the marked section, should go unrecognized by parsers.
>
> `<![ IGNORE [...]]>`
>
> Often, this status keyword is stored in a parameter entity and referred to indirectly in the marked section.

INCLUDE

> Keyword indicating that the characters in the region should be treated by parsers as providing document content.
>
> `<![ INCLUDE [...]]>`
>
> Often, this status keyword is stored in a parameter entity and referred to indirectly in the marked section.

CDATA

> Keyword indicating that any characters in the region, other than the characters that end the marked section, should be interpreted not as markup or markup delimiters but as ordinary document data.
>
> `<![ CDATA [...]]>`
>
> Note that the characters ]]> cannot appear in the content of a CDATA marked section because they will be interpreted as the end of the marked section.

RCDATA

> Keyword indicating that the only kind of markup that should be recognized in the region, other than the ones ending the marked section, are entity references.
>
> `<![ RCDATA [...]]>`

Note that the characters ]]> cannot appear in the content of an RCDATA marked section because they will be interpreted as the end of the marked section.

TEMP

> Keyword indicating that the content of the region is only temporarily being provided as part of the document content.
>
> ```
> <![ TEMP [...]]>
> ```

*marked-section-content*

> Valid SGML characters making up the content of the region.
>
> ```
> The prize includes
> <![ %mice-only; [a lifetime supply
> of cheese and ]]>
> a cruise to the Bahamas.
> ```

If no keyword is supplied, INCLUDE is assumed. If multiple status keywords are supplied, they are given the following priority:

1. IGNORE

2. CDATA

3. RCDATA

4. INCLUDE

It is possible to nest marked sections, except inside CDATA and RCDATA sections, where the start of the inner marked section will be ignored and treated as ordinary data content, and the end of the inner marked section will terminate the outer marked section.

## A.6   Notation Declarations

A data notation is a descriptor for data that is in non-SGML form and therefore should be handed off by a parser to some other processor. The notation helps to identify the alternate processing that would be appropriate for the data. Figure A-8 shows the syntax for data notation declarations. The external identifier is intended to identify a "document" that specifies the particulars of the notation, which may be simply a descriptive string.

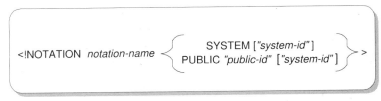

**Figure A-8**      Notation Declaration Syntax.

NOTATION

> Keyword that starts a notation declaration.

*notation-name*

> The name of the notation.
>
> ```
> <!NOTATION eps ...>
> ```

SYSTEM

> Keyword indicating that the document that specifies the notation can be found on a computer system, stored separately from the entity declaration.
>
> ```
> <!NOTATION eps SYSTEM>
> ```

*system-id*

> A file name, pathname, or other specification for how to locate the document that specifies the notation on the computer system.
>
> ```
> <!NOTATION eps SYSTEM "eps.doc">
> ```

PUBLIC

> Keyword indicating that the document that specifies the notation can be found on a computer system and that the contents can be located by mapping the supplied public identifier to location instructions that are stored outside the SGML document. A notation document with a public identifier can also optionally have system location instructions stored with it.
>
> ```
> <!NOTATION eps PUBLIC
> "+//ISBN 0-201-18127-4::Adobe//NOTATION PostScript Language Ref. Manual//EN">
> ```
>
> Many common non-SGML notations have formal public identifiers associated with them. A formal public identifier for a notation should use the NOTATION keyword.

*public-id*

> Symbolic identifier that maps to location instructions. The mapping is done by an entity manager, often through the use of a catalog file that lists public IDs and their corresponding physical locations.
>
> If the FORMAL feature is set to YES in the SGML declaration, the public identifier must be constructed according to certain syntactic rules, described in Section A.10.

## A.7   Processing Instructions

A processing instruction provides instructions to a processing application or system for how the SGML document is to be handled. Often, processing instructions are explicitly procedural. Figure A-9 shows the syntax for processing instructions.

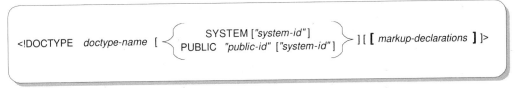

Figure A-9        Processing Instruction Syntax.

*processing-instruction*

> String intended for interpretation by a system or application besides the parser.
>
> `<?MyApp break-line-here>`

## A.8  Document Type Declarations

The document type declaration is the means by which an SGML document indicates the DTD rules to which it conforms. Figure A-10 shows the syntax for document type declarations. Note that square brackets which are actually part of the SGML markup are shown in boldface, whereas brackets used to indicate the optionality of a field are not given emphasis. Note also that after the document type name, at least one of the two fields must appear: an external identifier, actual markup declarations, or both.

```
<!DOCTYPE   doctype-name  [       SYSTEM ["system-id"]           ] [ [ markup-declarations ] ]>
                                  PUBLIC  "public-id" ["system-id"]
```

Figure A-10      Document Type Declaration Syntax.

`DOCTYPE`

> Keyword that starts a document type declaration.

*doctype-name*

> The name of the document type. This must be the same as the name of the document element (the top-level element).
>
> `<!DOCTYPE loveltr ...>`

`SYSTEM`

> Keyword indicating that the collection of some or all of the DTD's markup declarations can be found on a computer system, stored separately from the document type declaration.
>
> `<!DOCTYPE loveltr SYSTEM>`

*system-id*

A file name, pathname, or other specification for how to locate some or all of the DTD's markup declarations on the computer system.

```
<!DOCTYPE loveltr SYSTEM "loveltr.doc">
```

PUBLIC

Keyword indicating that some or all of the DTD's markup declarations can be found on a computer system and that the contents can be located by mapping the supplied public identifier to location instructions that are stored outside the SGML document. A DTD with a public identifier can also optionally have system location instructions stored with it.

```
<!DOCTYPE loveltr PUBLIC "-//Elvis Chapel//DTD Love Letter//EN">
```

*public-id*

Symbolic identifier that maps to location instructions. The mapping is done by an entity manager, often through the use of a catalog file that lists public IDs and their corresponding physical locations.

If the FORMAL feature is set to YES in the SGML declaration, the public identifier must be constructed according to certain syntactic rules, described in Section A.10.

*markup-declarations*

The **internal subset** of markup declarations, which can represent either all the necessary declarations to make a complete DTD, or a set of declarations that complement those found in a remote location. Supplying an internal subset is optional if an external identifier has been provided.

## A.9 SGML Declarations

The SGML declaration specifies setup instructions to SGML parsers and to humans. For example, it indicates the character set and the optional SGML features used in a document. If it is present, it appears in an SGML document before the document type declaration and the actual data and markup making up the document instance. (Note that it cannot be included by means of an entity reference, though some parsers allow a separate file containing an SGML declaration to be read in separately from files containing the rest of the document.) If the SGML declaration is absent, each system assumes some set of default specifications.

An SGML declaration contains a series of parameters specifying various characteristics of the DTD and instance that follow. Figure A-11 shows the order of the parameters.

<!SGML 8879:*year*

*document-character-set*

*capacity-set*

*concrete-syntax-scope*

*concrete-syntax*

*feature-use*

*application-specific-info*

\>

**Figure A-11**  SGML Declaration Syntax.

SGML

Keyword that starts an SGML declaration.

8879:*year*

The version of the standard being referenced. To date, 1986 (the year of the standard's publication) is the only value that is valid in *year*.

Note that the original ISO 8879 standard specified its own name to be ISO 8879-1986, with a hyphen (-) separating the two parts of the identifier. Amendment 1 to the standard changed the hyphen to a colon (:) to make it conform to the naming scheme used by other ISO standards. Some SGML systems accept only one character or the other, depending on when they were developed and how flexible they are. The SGML Open organization has issued Technical Resolution 9401, which specifies in part that systems should be flexible enough to accept either the hyphen or the colon in formal public identifiers.

*document-character-set*

Description of how the codes representing data characters in the document are to be interpreted as logical characters. The document character set parameter is discussed in Section A.9.1.

*capacity-set*

Declaration of the approximate computer storage capacity needed by systems to process the DTD and document instance. The capacity set parameter is discussed in Section A.9.2.

*concrete-syntax-scope*

> Indication of which parts of the SGML document adhere to the reference concrete syntax, and which to any variant concrete syntax defined. The concrete syntax scope parameter is discussed in Section A.9.3.

*concrete-syntax*

> Specification of the "concrete" (literal) characteristics of the markup used in this document, as opposed to the abstract characteristics specified by the SGML standard. This is the most complex section of the SGML declaration. The concrete syntax parameter is discussed in Section A.9.4.

*feature-use*

> Specification of the optional SGML features that this document uses. The feature use parameter is discussed in Section A.9.5.

*application-specific-info*

> Information that needs to be communicated to processors that does not appear in the document or its DTD. Documents that use HyTime and ICADD (the International Committee for Accessible Document Design) are expected to supply information here. The application-specific information parameter is discussed in Section A.9.6.

Example A-1 shows an example of an SGML declaration that uses most of the syntactic features available in the parameters; the declaration happens to be the one used for this book. There is no one "default SGML declaration," but certain collections of default values and settings are used to define conformance levels of SGML documents to the standard:

- A "basic SGML document" uses the reference concrete syntax exclusively, uses the reference capacity set, and uses only the SHORTTAG and OMITTAG features.

- A "minimal SGML document" uses the core concrete syntax, the reference capacity set, and no features.

The following sections explain these default values.

**Example A-1**   Sample SGML Declaration.

```
<!SGML   "ISO 8879:1986"
CHARSET
   BASESET
"ISO 646:1983//CHARSET International Reference Version (IRV)//ESC 2/5 4/0"
```

**Example A-1**    Sample SGML Declaration.  (Continued)

```
  DESCSET
                       0    9    UNUSED
                       9    2     9
                      11    2    UNUSED
                      13    1     13
                      14   18    UNUSED
                      32   95     32
                     127    1    UNUSED
  BASESET
"ISO Registration Number 100//CHARSET ECMA-94 Right Part of Latin
Alphabet Nr. 1//ESC 2/13 4/1"
  DESCSET
                     128   32    UNUSED
                     160   96     32
CAPACITY SGMLREF
  TOTALCAP      500000
  ATTCAP        70000
  ATTCHCAP      35000
  AVGRPCAP      35000
  ELEMCAP       35000
  ENTCAP        70000
  ENTCHCAP      35000
  GRPCAP       300000
  IDCAP         35000
  IDREFCAP      35000
SCOPE DOCUMENT
SYNTAX
  SHUNCHAR CONTROLS    0    1    2    3    4    5    6    7    8    9
                      10   11   12   13   14   15   16   17   18   19
                      20   21   22   23   24   25   26   27   28   29
                      30   31                       127  128  129
                     130  131  132  133  134  135  136  137  138  139
                     140  141  142  143  144  145  146  147  148  149
                     150  151  152  153  154  155  156  157  158  159
  BASESET   "ISO 646:1983//CHARSET
            International Reference Version (IRV)//ESC 2/5 4/0"
  DESCSET
                       0  128    0
```

**Example A-1**   Sample SGML Declaration.  (Continued)

```
    FUNCTION
       RE          13
       RS          10
       SPACE       32
       TAB SEPCHAR  9
    NAMING
      LCNMSTRT " "
      UCNMSTRT " "
      LCNMCHAR ".-"
      UCNMCHAR ".-"
      NAMECASE
        GENERAL YES
        ENTITY  NO
    DELIM
      GENERAL  SGMLREF
      SHORTREF SGMLREF
    NAMES SGMLREF
    QUANTITY SGMLREF
      ATTCNT    256
      GRPCNT    253
      GRPGTCNT  253
      LITLEN   8092
      NAMELEN    44
      TAGLVL    100
  FEATURES
    MINIMIZE
      DATATAG  NO
      OMITTAG  NO
      RANK     NO
      SHORTTAG YES
    LINK
      SIMPLE   NO
      IMPLICIT NO
      EXPLICIT NO
    OTHER
      CONCUR   NO
      SUBDOC   NO
      FORMAL   YES
  APPINFO NONE
  >
```

The SGML declaration can specify an alternative to the **reference concrete syntax**, the default set of markup delimiters and other markup characteristics that SGML assumes. (Changing the default is discussed in Section A.9.4.) For example, you can specify that curly braces should be used instead of angle brackets in markup declarations and tags. If a variant concrete syntax is defined, however, the SGML declaration itself must still use the defaults.

Within the SGML declaration, no entity references can be used except for numeric character references, since the declaration's position in a document is before the point where any normal entities can have been defined. Several parameters in the SGML declaration allow or require specification of a public identifier corresponding to an external entity, but these entities do not need to be declared in the normal way.

## A.9.1   Document Character Set

The document character set parameter contains instructions on how to interpret the numeric codes stored electronically in an SGML document as characters. Figure A-12 shows the syntax for the document character set parameter.

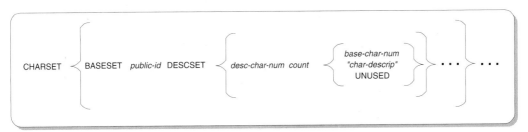

**Figure A-12**     CHARSET Parameter Syntax.

CHARSET

> Keyword for the character set parameter. This parameter is meant for human consumption. Parsers have a "bootstrapping" problem in using the CHARSET parameter to parse SGML declarations; because an SGML declaration itself is stored electronically, parsers must use a "default" understanding of the character codes within in order to read the declaration in the first place.

BASESET

> Keyword introducing the public identifier of a well-known repertoire of logical characters to which to map the actual character codes found in the document. For example, "the ABCs" is a well-known character repertoire, and it might be commonly understood to be represented by the numbers 0 to 25.
>
> Multiple BASESET/DESCSET pairs can appear here.

⟵━━━━━━━━━━━━━━━━━━━━━━━━━━━━━━━━━━━━━━━━━━━⟶

*public-id*

> Symbolic identifier that maps to a description of a character repertoire and the numeric codes representing those characters. The mapping is done by an entity manager, often through the use of a catalog file that lists public IDs and their corresponding physical locations.
>
> If the FORMAL feature is set to YES in the SGML declaration (see Section A.9.5), the public identifier must be constructed according to certain syntactic rules, described in Section A.10.

DESCSET

> Keyword introducing the "described character set," a succession of three-field entries explaining how the numeric codes found in this document should be interpreted to map to the characters represented by the base character set provided above.
>
> The simplest example might be a case where ISO 646 is both the base character set and the set actually used in the document:
>
> ```
> DESCSET
> 0 128 0
> ```

*desc-char-num*

> Numeric character code that might be found in the document.
>
> If the *count* field is greater than 1, this field serves as a starting point for a contiguous series of numeric codes corresponding to a contiguous series of the same length in the base character set.

*count*

> The number of codes, counting upwards, in succession that map exactly between the described and base character sets.
>
> If the number is 1, there is a simple mapping between the described code and the base code. If the number is greater than 1, a contiguous series of described codes corresponds to a contiguous series of base codes of the same length.

*base-char-num*

> Numeric character code in the base character set that is associated with a logical character. For example, in ISO 646, the number 65 represents the letter A.
>
> If the *count* field is greater than 1, this field serves as a starting point for a contiguous series of numeric codes corresponding to a contiguous series of the same length in the described character set.

*"char-descrip"*

>   Prose description of the logical character intended to be represented, for exam-
>   ple, "happy face." Such a description might need to be used if the character set
>   used in the document needs characters not contained in the base character set.

UNUSED

>   Indicator that this numeric code should not be found in the document. Such a
>   code is considered a non-SGML character and is not allowed to appear in the
>   document.

## A.9.2   Capacity Set

The capacity set parameter defines the maximum number of occurrences of various constructs in an SGML document, measured in terms of the number of points (characters)
needed to store information about them. Many of the capacities are related to DTDs and
thus will reflect requirements that don't change from document to document, but some
are related to information found in a particular document instance. Figure A-13 shows the
syntax for the capacity set parameter.

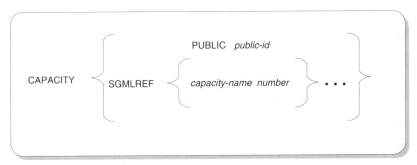

**Figure A-13**    CAPACITY Parameter Syntax.

CAPACITY

>   Keyword for the capacity set parameter.

PUBLIC

>   Keyword indicating that what follows is a public identifier for an externally
>   stored collection of capacity settings.

*public-id*

>   Symbolic identifier that maps to a collection of capacity settings. The mapping
>   is done by an entity manager, often through the use of a catalog file that lists
>   public IDs and their corresponding physical locations.

If the FORMAL feature is set to YES in the SGML declaration (see Section A.9.5), the public identifier must be constructed according to certain syntactic rules, described in Section A.10.

SGMLREF

> Keyword indicating that the reference capacity set should be used, except for any capacities provided below. The reference capacity set is explained in Table A-3.

capacity-name

> Keyword indicating the capacity whose maximum is being set. The available capacity categories are listed in Table A-3.

number

> The maximum number of computer storage points for the indicated capacity category that this SGML document needs. The default capacity points provided by the reference capacity set are listed in Table A-3.

Table A-3 lists the available capacity categories and their reference point values and explains how the number of points is derived in each case.

**Table A-3**    Reference Capacity Set.

| Capacity | Points | Description and Point Calculation |
| --- | --- | --- |
| TOTALCAP | 35000 | The total number of points required. |
| ENTCAP | 35000 | The number of entities declared, multiplied by NAMELEN (which governs the maximum length of an entity name). |
| ENTCHCAP | 35000 | The number of characters in text entities declared. |
| ELEMCAP | 35000 | The number of elements declared, multiplied by NAMELEN (which governs the maximum length of a generic identifier). |
| GRPCAP | 35000 | The number of model groups, elements, data tag groups, and reserved name keywords (such as PCDATA) mentioned in content models, multiplied by NAMELEN (which governs the maximum length of a generic identifier). |

**Table A-3**    Reference Capacity Set. (Continued)

| Capacity | Points | Description and Point Calculation |
|----------|--------|-----------------------------------|
| EXGRPCAP | 35000 | The number of exception (exclusion and inclusion) groups mentioned in element declarations, multiplied by NAMELEN (which governs the maximum length of a generic identifier). |
| EXNMCAP | 35000 | The number of names mentioned in exception (exclusion and inclusion) groups in element declarations, multiplied by NAMELEN (which governs the maximum length of a generic identifier). |
| ATTCAP | 35000 | The number of attributes that are declared in attribute definition list declarations, plus the number of attributes that occur in link set declarations, plus the number of notation names associated with entity declarations, multiplied by NAMELEN (which governs the maximum length of an attribute or notation name). |
| ATTCHCAP | 35000 | The number of characters in attribute default values, plus the number of characters explicitly specified in link set declarations and data attribute specifications. |
| AVGRPCAP | 35000 | The number of tokens defined in the name or name token groups for attribute declared values, multiplied by NAMELEN (which governs the maximum length of a token). |
| NOTCAP | 35000 | The number of data content notations declared, multiplied by NAMELEN (which governs the maximum length of a notation name). |
| NOTCHCAP | 35000 | The number of characters in notation external identifiers. |
| IDCAP | 35000 | The number of attributes with a declared type of ID that have values supplied, multiplied by NAMELEN (which governs the maximum length of an ID attribute value). |

**Table A-3**     Reference Capacity Set.  (Continued)

| Capacity | Points | Description and Point Calculation |
|----------|--------|-----------------------------------|
| IDREFCAP | 35000 | The number of attributes with a declared type of IDREF that have values explicitly supplied or have an #IMPLIED default value, multiplied by NAMELEN (which governs the maximum length of an IDREF attribute value). |
| MAPCAP | 35000 | The number of short reference maps declared, plus the number of short reference delimiters in the concrete syntax multiplied by the number of maps, with the whole multiplied by NAMELEN (which governs the maximum length of short reference delimiters). |
| LKSETCAP | 35000 | The number of link types and link sets defined, multiplied by NAMELEN (which governs the maximum length of a link type name and link set name). |
| LKNMCAP | 35000 | The number of document types or elements in a link type or link set declaration, multiplied by NAMELEN (which governs the maximum length of a document type name or generic identifier). |

## A.9.3   Concrete Syntax Scope

The concrete syntax scope parameter declares which parts of the document use the reference concrete syntax and which use a variant concrete syntax. If the reference concrete syntax is being used for the document instance, this parameter has no effect. Figure A-14 shows the syntax for the concrete syntax scope parameter.

**Figure A-14**     SCOPE Parameter Syntax.

SCOPE

> Keyword for the concrete syntax scope parameter.

DOCUMENT

> Keyword indicating that the concrete syntax defined in the SGML declaration is used everywhere in the document (except for the SGML declaration itself), including both the instance and the prologue (the markup declarations making up the one or more DTD and any link set declarations).

INSTANCE

> Keyword indicating that the concrete syntax defined in the SGML declaration is used only in the document instance, with the reference concrete syntax being used in the prolog. There are some restrictions on the variant concrete syntax if this keyword is specified, relating to ensuring that parsers can properly distinguish between the prolog and the instance and can handle both syntaxes.

## A.9.4   Concrete Syntax

The SGML standard defines many characteristics of SGML markup in terms of an **abstract syntax**; for example, it defines the ways that a "start tag open" or STAGO delimiter is used, and defines its default concrete representation separately as a left angle bracket (<). In this way, you can change the actual characters and keywords used for SGML markup if you need to. The concrete syntax parameter specifies such particulars of the markup used in the document (or just in the document instance, if the scope has been defined this way; see Section A.9.3 for more information).

Figure A-15 shows the syntax for the concrete syntax parameter. To specify a concrete syntax that is defined externally to the SGML declaration, use the first form. To specify the individual characteristics of a concrete syntax, use the second form.

SYNTAX PUBLIC *public-id* [SWITCHES [*char-num char-num* ] ... ]

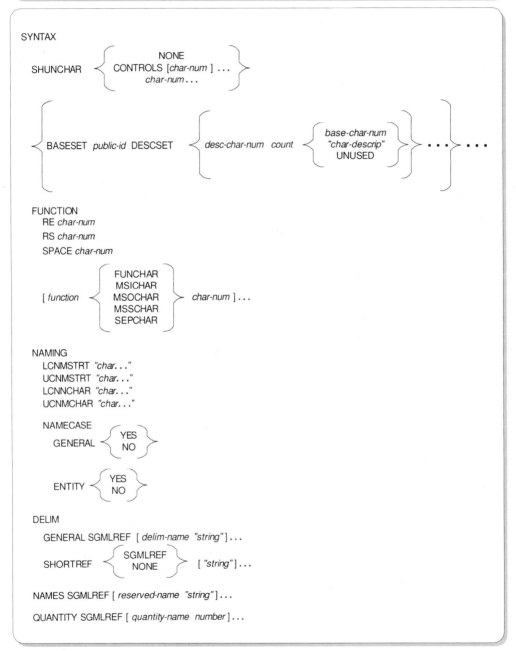

**Figure A-15**   SYNTAX Parameter Syntax.

SYNTAX

>    Keyword for the concrete syntax parameter.

PUBLIC

>    Keyword indicating that what follows is a public identifier for an externally stored description of a concrete syntax.

*public-id*

>    Symbolic identifier that maps to a description of a concrete syntax. The mapping is done by an entity manager, often through the use of a catalog file that lists public IDs and their corresponding physical locations.
>
>    If the FORMAL feature is set to YES in the SGML declaration (see Section A.9.5), the public identifier must be constructed according to certain syntactic rules, described in Section A.10.

SWITCHES etc.

>    Specification of pairs of character numbers whose logical meanings should be switched. This parameter allows a concrete syntax identified by a public ID to be used with only slight changes. An example of characters that might need to be switched is the line feed and carriage return characters, numbers 10 and 13 in the character set used by the reference concrete syntax.

SHUNCHAR etc.

>    Indication of the characters that should be prohibited from being used in markup (as opposed to data). The NONE keyword means that no characters are shunned. The CONTROLS keyword means that all "control characters" (as opposed to graphic characters) should be shunned. Any individual character numbers specified will be shunned as well.

BASESET etc.

>    Specification of the "syntax-reference character set," the mapping of numeric character codes used in markup to logical character meanings for the purpose of this subparameter. Its presence allows all specifications of character numbers and numeric character entity references in the SYNTAX parameter to be independent of the character set specified for data content in CHARSET.
>
>    See Figure A-12 for a description of how to supply BASESET/CHARSET information.

FUNCTION etc.

> Specification of the character numbers that correspond to special function character roles in SGML markup. RE identifies the record end character, RS identifies the record start character, and SPACE identifies the space character. Additional character numbers can be named and assigned special function roles as follows:
>
> - FUNCHAR names and identifies characters that have a system-specific function unrelated to SGML. Once defined in this way, such function character names can be used in character entity references (&#name).
>
> - MSOCHAR names and identifies characters that inhibit markup recognition from the point where they appear.
>
> - MSICHAR names and identifies characters that re-enable markup recognition from the point where they appear.
>
> - MSSCHAR names and identifies characters that inhibit markup recognition of the single character that appears after the point where they appear.
>
> - SEPCHAR names and identifies separator (white space) characters, such as tabs.

LCNMSTRT etc. in NAMING

> Declaration of the characters that can be used in markup names (such as generic identifiers and entity names). LCNMSTRT and LCNMCHAR specify, respectively, additional lowercase characters that can be in the first position and subsequent positions of a name. UCNMSTRT and UCNMCHAR specify, respectively, the corresponding additional uppercase characters that can be in the first position and subsequent positions of a name. If a "lowercase" character specified is a symbol that has no case, it should be specified in the same position in the character list for both the LC and UC fields. Often, an underscore (_) is added to subsequent positions.
>
> If no additional characters are specified, by default the first character must be an uppercase or lowercase letter, and the subsequent characters can be a letter or a digit. The reference concrete syntax adds a period and a hyphen to the subsequent characters. The characters specified here are not raw character numbers; they are either real typed characters or numeric character references.

NAMECASE etc. in NAMING

> Setup of the case-sensitivity of SGML markup names. GENERAL sets the case-sensitivity of all names except for entity names, and ENTITY sets the case-sensitivity of entity names. The reference concrete syntax specifies that GENERAL is NO (case insensitive) and ENTITY is YES (case-sensitive).

GENERAL etc. in DELIM

> Replaces the markup delimiters in the reference delimiter set with alternate delimiters. The SGMLREF keyword represents the specification of the reference delimiter set; the delimiter role keywords and their reference delimiters are shown in Table A-4.

SHORTREF etc. in DELIM

> Replaces the short reference markup delimiters in the reference delimiter set with alternate delimiters. The SGMLREF keyword represents the specification of the reference delimiter set (the reference delimiters for short references are not shown here). The NONE keyword means that no short reference delimiters are enabled, except any which are explicitly defined in this SGML declaration.

NAMES etc.

> Replaces the reserved name keywords in the reference set with alternate keywords. The SGMLREF keyword represents the specification of the reference set; the reference keywords are listed in Table A-5. Note that the reserved names from the SGML declaration itself are not listed here, as they must be used in their reference form.

QUANTITY etc.

> Sets the basic lengths and measurements of various SGML markup characteristics. The SGMLREF keyword represents the specification of the reference quantity set; the quantity keywords and reference values are listed in Table A-6.

Table A-4 lists the delimiter role keywords and their reference (default) delimiters. You can change these delimiters using the DELIM GENERAL subparameter.

**Table A-4**      Reference General Delimiter Set.

| Delimiter Role Keyword | Reference Delimiter | Description |
| --- | --- | --- |
| AND | & | And connector |
| COM | -- | Comment start or end |
| CRO | &# | Character reference open |
| DSC | ] | Declaration subset close |
| DSO | [ | Declaration subset open |
| DTGC | ] | Data tag group close |
| DTGO | [ | Data tag group open |

**Table A-4**      Reference General Delimiter Set.  (Continued)

| Delimiter Role Keyword | Reference Delimiter | Description |
| --- | --- | --- |
| ERO | & | Entity reference open |
| ETAGO | </ | Eng-tag open |
| GRPC | ) | Group close |
| GRPO | ( | Group open |
| LIT | " | Literal start or end |
| LITA | ' | Alternative literal start or end |
| MDC | > | Markup declaration close |
| MDO | <! | Markup declaration open |
| MINUS | – | Exclusion |
| MSC | ]> | Marked section close |
| NET | / | Null end-tag |
| OPT | ? | Optional occurrence indicator |
| OR | \| | Or connector |
| PERO | % | Parameter entity reference open |
| PIC | > | Processing instruction close |
| PIO | <? | Processing instruction open |
| PLUS | + | Required and repeatable occurrence indicator; also inclusion |
| REFC | ; | Reference close |
| REP | * | Optional and repeatable occurrence indicator |
| RNI | # | Reserved name indicator |
| SEQ | , | Sequence connector |
| STAGO | < | Start-tag open |
| TAGC | > | Tag close |
| VI | = | Value indicator |

Table A-5 lists the reserved name keywords. You can change these keywords using the NAMES subparameter.

**Table A-5**        Reference Reserved Name Set.

| | | |
|---|---|---|
| ANY | ATTLIST | CDATA |
| CONREF | CURRENT | DEFAULT |
| DOCTYPE | ELEMENT | EMPTY |
| ENDTAG | ENTITIES | ENTITY |
| FIXED | ID | IDLINK |
| IDREF | IDREFS | IGNORE |
| IMPLIED | INCLUDE | INITIAL |
| LINK | LINKTYPE | MD |
| MS | NAME | NAMES |
| NDATA | NMTOKEN | NMTOKENS |
| NOTATION | NUMBER | NUMBERS |
| NUTOKEN | NUTOKENS | O |
| PCDATA | PI | POSTLINK |
| PUBLIC | RCDATA | RE |
| REQUIRED | RESTORE | RS |
| SDATA | SHORTREF | SIMPLE |
| SPACE | STARTTAG | SUBDOC |
| SYSTEM | TEMP | USELINK |
| USEMAP | | |

Table A-6 shows the reference quantity set. You can change these quantities using the QUANTITY subparameter.

**Table A-6**     Reference Quantity Set.

| Quantity | Value | Description |
| --- | --- | --- |
| ATTCNT | 40 | The maximum number of attribute names and name tokens (for example, values in a declared value token list) in the attribute definition list of a single attribute declaration. |
| ATTSPLEN | 960 | The maximum number of characters in a start-tag's attribute specifications list, after normalization (for example, to fill in an attribute name that has been omitted through SHORTTAG minimization). |
| BSEQLEN | 960 | The maximum length of a blank sequence in a short reference string. |
| DTAGLEN | 16 | The maximum length of a data tag. |
| DTEMPLEN | 16 | The maximum length of a data tag template or pattern template. |
| ENTLVL | 16 | The maximum number of levels to which entity references have been nested inside the content of other entities. |
| GRPCNT | 32 | The maximum number of tokens in any one group (for example, a model group or a content model exclusion). |
| GRPGTCNT | 96 | The maximum "grand total" of content tokens (groups, names, and so on) at all levels of a single content model. |
| GRPLVL | 16 | The maximum number of levels to which model groups are nested in a single content model. |
| LITLEN | 240 | The maximum number of characters in a single parameter literal or attribute value literal, not including its delimiters (for example, the length of a CDATA attribute value excluding its quotation marks). |
| NAMELEN | 8 | The maximum number of characters in a markup name or token. |

**Table A-6**      Reference Quantity Set. (Continued)

| Quantity | Value | Description |
|---|---|---|
| NORMSEP | 2 | The value used to represent a "standard" number of separator characters in calculating string lengths that have been normalized. |
| PILEN | 240 | The maximum number of characters in a processing instruction, not including delimiters. |
| TAGLEN | 960 | The maximum number of characters in a start-tag, including all attribute value specification, but not including delimiters. |
| TAGLVL | 24 | The maximum number of levels to which elements can be nested inside other elements in the document instance, or, put another way, the maximum number of elements that can be open at one time. |

You can make use of two ready-made concrete syntaxes defined by the SGML standard, through either a public ID reference or a complete SYNTAX specification. Example A-2 shows the complete specification for the reference concrete syntax. Its public ID is as follows:

```
"ISO 8879:1986//SYNTAX Reference//EN"
```

**Example A-2**   Reference Concrete Syntax Specification.

```
SYNTAX
    SHUNCHAR CONTROLS    0    1    2    3    4    5    6    7    8    9
                        10   11   12   13   14   15   16   17   18   19
                        20   21   22   23   24   25   26   27   28   29
                        30   31  127  255
    BASESET
"ISO 646:1983//CHARSET International Reference Version (IRV)//ESC
2/5 4/0"
    DESCSET
                    0  128  0
    FUNCTION
        RE          13
        RS          10
        SPACE       32
        TAB SEPCHAR  9
```

**Example A-2**   Reference Concrete Syntax Specification.  (Continued)

```
NAMING
  LCNMSTRT ""
  UCNMSTRT ""
  LCNMCHAR ".-"
  UCNMCHAR ".-"
  NAMECASE
     GENERAL YES
     ENTITY  NO
 DELIM
   GENERAL  SGMLREF
   SHORTREF SGMLREF
  NAMES SGMLREF
 QUANTITY SGMLREF
```

Example A-3 shows the complete specification for the core concrete syntax, which differs from the reference concrete syntax only in that its SHORTREF delimiters are set to NONE. Its public ID is as follows:

```
"ISO 8879:1986//SYNTAX Core//EN"
```

**Example A-3**   Core Concrete Syntax Specification.

```
SYNTAX
   SHUNCHAR CONTROLS  0   1   2   3   4   5   6   7   8   9
                     10  11  12  13  14  15  16  17  18  19
                     20  21  22  23  24  25  26  27  28  29
                     30  31 127 255
  BASESET
"ISO 646:1983//CHARSET International Reference Version (IRV)//ESC
2/5 4/0"
  DESCSET
                 0 128 0
  FUNCTION
     RE          13
    .RS          10
    SPACE        32
    TAB SEPCHAR  9
```

**Example A-3**   Core Concrete Syntax Specification.  (Continued)

```
NAMING
  LCNMSTRT ""
  UCNMSTRT ""
  LCNMCHAR ".-"
  UCNMCHAR ".-"
  NAMECASE
     GENERAL YES
     ENTITY  NO
DELIM
  GENERAL  SGMLREF
  SHORTREF NONE
NAMES SGMLREF
QUANTITY SGMLREF
```

This section provides only a brief description of the SYNTAX parameter; see Appendix E for sources of more detailed information on specifying a concrete syntax.

## A.9.5   Feature Use

The feature use parameter indicates which optional features of SGML the document uses. Figure A-16 shows the syntax for the feature use parameter.

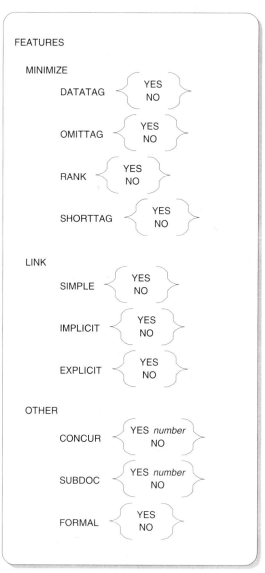

**Figure A-16**   FEATURES Parameter Syntax.

FEATURES

> Keyword for the feature use parameter.

MINIMIZE

> Keyword that groups the feature use settings for minimization.

DATATAG

> Setting indicating whether or not data characters can simultaneously serve as tags.

OMITTAG

> Setting indicating whether or not certain tags can be omitted entirely. If this setting is YES, element declarations must specify omitted-tag minimization rules. Section 8.6 discusses this kind of minimization.

RANK

> Setting indicating whether or not certain elements have several ranked incarnations, such that the rank of any one instance (indicated by a number appended to the generic identifier) can be inferred if omitted.

SHORTTAG

> Setting indicating whether or not shortened-tag minimization is used. Section 8.6 discusses this kind of minimization.

LINK

> Keyword that groups the feature use settings for the link feature. Note that the link feature is not related to hyperlinking, but rather to the association, by SGML means, of markup and content with stylesheet and other procedural computer behavior.

SIMPLE

> Setting indicating whether or not simple link process definitions are used.

IMPLICIT

> Setting indicating whether or not implicit link process definitions are used.

EXPLICIT

> Setting indicating whether or not explicit link process definitions are used.

OTHER

> Keyword that groups the feature use settings for miscellaneous features.

CONCUR

> Setting indicating whether or not an instance can conform to multiple document types concurrently. Specify the number of allowed document types in addition to the base document type in *number*.

SUBDOC

> Setting indicating whether or not an instance can contain SGML subdocument entities (which might conform to a different document type). Specify the number of allowed subdocument entities in *number*.

FORMAL

> Setting indicating whether or not public identifiers must conform to the rules for formal public identifiers (discussed in Section A.10).

## A.9.6   Application-Specific Information

Figure A-17 shows the syntax for the application-specific information parameter.

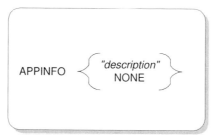

**Figure A-17**   APPINFO Parameter Syntax.

APPINFO

> Keyword for the application-specific information parameter.

NONE

> Keyword indicating that there is no application-specific information supplied.

"*description*"

> The application-specific information to be passed to an application. Documents that use HyTime must specify the value "HyTime" here.

## A.10 Formal Public Identifiers and Catalogs

Public identifiers appear in entity declarations as "logical names" that stand for the physical locations of the entity's publicly available replacement data. A public identifier can be formal or informal; only formal identifiers must conform to the constraints shown in Figure A-18.

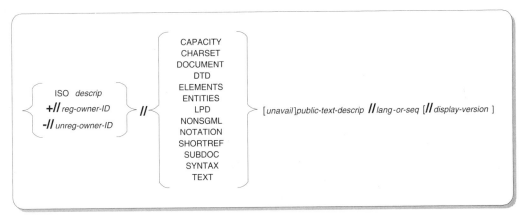

**Figure A-18**    Formal Public Identifier Syntax.

ISO *descrip*

> Indicator that the public text is owned by ISO. Public text defined by ISO 8879, such as the entity sets for characters and symbols, uses its publication number, "8879:1986," as the description. Other ISO standards use their own publication numbers.
>
> ISO 8879:1986//...
>
> Note that ISO-owned public text has only one pair of slashes before the appearance of the keyword labeling the kind of public text.

+//*reg-owner-ID*

> Indicator that the public text has an owner who is registered according to ISO 9070, the standard governing the registration of owner identifiers for SGML public text. In this case, the owner ID is composed of an assigned prefix and, optionally, one or more further fields preceded by double colons, which qualify the description of the precise owner. Currently, other than identifiers directly connected to ISO publications or other organizations duly authorized by ISO to issue prefixes, the only acceptable owner prefix is an International Standard Book Number (ISBN) preceded by the string "ISBN".
>
> +//ISBN 0-933186::IBM//...

*-//unreg-owner-ID*

>   Indicator that the public text has an unregistered owner.

>   `-//Joe's Bar and Grill//...`

`CAPACITY` etc.

>   Keywords indicating the nature of the public text. The keyword values are explained in Table A-7.

*unavail*

>   Indicator that the public text is generally unavailable, that is, its owner allows only certain users to have access to it. If the text is available, this entire field is left out. If the text is unavailable, the *unavail* field consists of a hyphen followed by two slashes.

>   `-//Ept Associates//DTD -//...`

*public-text-descrip*

>   String describing the contents of the public text. If the text is owned by ISO, the public text description must consist of the last part of the publication title.

>   `-//HyConcept Inc.//DTD Manual//...`

*lang-or-sequence*

>   String further qualifying the public text. In the case of `CHARSET` public text, it is a string containing a character set designating sequence, as defined by ISO 2022. Otherwise, it is a two-letter code in uppercase indicating the natural language used in the text, as defined by ISO 639. For example, "EN" stands for English.

>   `-//ALF Inc.//DTD Memo//EN`

*display-version*

>   String distinguishing this set of public text from others that differ only in the display device or system to which they apply.

>   `-//DEC//ENTITIES Tech chars//EN//troff`

>   The display version specification can't be used with the keywords `CAPACITY`, `CHARSET`, `NOTATION`, and `SYNTAX`.

Table A-7 explains the keywords that identify the public text referred to by a formal public identifier.

The mechanism for mapping a public identifier to a physical storage location must be recorded externally to an SGML document, which allows entity declarations to be portable across systems. Each SGML-aware software package uses some form of mapping file to record the information.

**Table A-7**      Formal Public Identifier Keywords.

| Default Value | Description |
| --- | --- |
| CAPACITY | Capacity set for use in an SGML declaration. |
| CHARSET | Character set specification for use in an SGML declaration. |
| DOCUMENT | SGML document |
| DTD | Set of markup declarations comprising a DTD (or a portion). |
| ELEMENTS | Set of element declarations and other related markup declarations for use in constructing a DTD. |
| ENTITIES | Set of entity declarations for use in adding entities to a DTD easily. |
| LPD | Entity sets, link attribute sets, and link set declarations that comprise a link type declaration. |
| NONSGML | Entity containing non-SGML data. |
| NOTATION | Public notation declaration. |
| SHORTREF | Set of short reference specifications. |
| SUBDOC | Entity containing an SGML subdocument. |
| SYNTAX | Concrete syntax specification for use in an SGML declaration. |
| TEXT | Entity containing SGML text (including data and/or markup). |

The SGML Open consortium has issued Technical Report 9401, which specifies a standard format for a "catalog file" that maps public identifiers (as well as other SGML constructs, such as whole SGML declarations) to "storage object identifiers." A storage object identifier is typically a file name or pathname, but it could also be, for example, a database query that returns the necessary data, or a World Wide Web uniform resource locator (URL). Most SGML-aware software products and public-domain packages now support the SGML Open catalog format, meaning that catalog files are becoming more portable across systems.

The catalog syntax for the mapping of a public identifier to the entity data is as follows:

```
PUBLIC "public-identifier" "storage-object-identifier"
```

Appendix E describes how to get more information on catalog files and SGML Open.

# B Tree Diagram Reference

This appendix provides a quick reference to the elm tree diagram notation.

The notation does not quite equate to "pictorial SGML." While the SGML language caters mostly to the needs of computers, tree diagrams cater mostly to humans in their modeling and markup efforts. Thus, the tree diagram that corresponds precisely to a content model in an SGML element declaration may not always be the most effective expression of the model for many purposes.

Figure B-1 summarizes the notation.

The following sections explain the notation by building up from the simpler parts to the more complex ones. Section B.8 describes how tree diagrams tend to grow and change during a DTD project.

## B.1   Elements

An element type is represented by a box containing a name. In the modeling stages, the name should be an English description. For DTD documentation purposes, element boxes might contain either descriptive names or actual generic identifiers for elements.

| paragraph | | model number |
|-----------|---|--------------|

Information on the content of a parent element appears below the box, either connected by a vertical bar to other symbols representing a particular configuration of contents (a content model group), or indicated by descriptive text. The descriptive text uses an equal sign (=) prefix to indicate either the name of another element that this element should

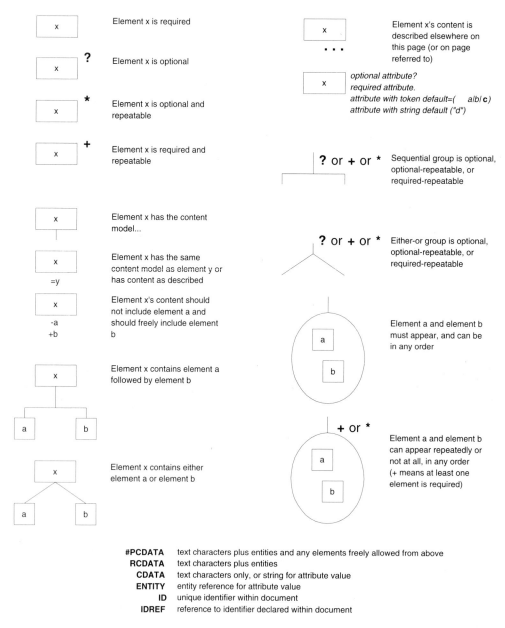

| x | Element x is required |

| x | ? | Element x is optional |

| x | * | Element x is optional and repeatable |

| x | + | Element x is required and repeatable |

| x | Element x has the content model... |

| x<br>=y | Element x has the same content model as element y or has content as described |

| x<br>-a<br>+b | Element x's content should not include element a and should freely include element b |

| x |<br>a   b | Element x contains element a followed by element b |

| x |<br>a   b | Element x contains either element a or element b |

| x | Element x's content is described elsewhere on this page (or on page referred to) |
• • •

| x | *optional attribute?*<br>*required attribute.*<br>*attribute with token default=( a|b| c)*<br>*attribute with string default ("d")* |

? or + or *   Sequential group is optional, optional-repeatable, or required-repeatable

? or + or *   Either-or group is optional, optional-repeatable, or required-repeatable

( a / b )   Element a and element b must appear, and can be in any order

+ or *   ( a / b )   Element a and element b can appear repeatedly or not at all, in any order (+ means at least one element is required)

| **#PCDATA** | text characters plus entities and any elements freely allowed from above |
| **RCDATA** | text characters plus entities |
| **CDATA** | text characters only, or string for attribute value |
| **ENTITY** | entity reference for attribute value |
| **ID** | unique identifier within document |
| **IDREF** | reference to identifier declared within document |

**Figure B-1**    Tree Diagram Notation Summary.

emulate or the kind of data-character mixture it contains. In the modeling stages, SGML keywords for declared content, such as RCDATA, may or may not be used depending on the technical knowledge of the document type design team members.

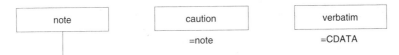

The description of the content can be adjusted through the use of inclusion and exclusion indicators, which use a minus sign (-) and plus sign (+) prefix, respectively. In the modeling stages, these symbols may or may not correspond to true SGML inclusions and exclusions.

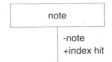

## B.2    Sequential and Either-Or Relationships

If a parent element contains two or more child elements that must appear in sequential order, the vertical bar which leads to the parent element's content branches out into a series of square brackets, each bracket point terminating in a child element. The children must appear in left-to-right order. (If right-to-left is more intuitive for the design team members because of their locale or other factors, it can be used instead, as long as the document analysis report makes this clear.) This configuration corresponds to a group that uses the SGML SEQ connector.

If a parent element contains a mutually exclusive choice among child elements, the vertical bar which leads to the parent element's content branches out into a series of angled bars, each terminating in a mutually exclusive choice. This configuration corresponds to a group that uses the SGML OR connector. Figure B-2 illustrates parent-child relationships.

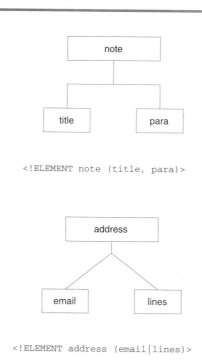

<!ELEMENT note (title, para)>

<!ELEMENT address (email|lines)>

**Figure B-2**    Parent-Child Relationships.

Two other relationships are possible; these are discussed in Section B.4.

# B.3   Occurrence Specifications

The presence of a child element is required if its box is unadorned. A symbol at the upper right indicates other occurrence requirements. A question mark (?) means the element can optionally occur. An asterisk (*) (see Figure B-3) means the element can optionally occur and can be repeated. A plus sign (+) means the element must occur at least once and can be repeated. A compact way of specifying that the minimum number of occurrences is greater than one is to precede the plus sign with that number.

These symbols correspond to the SGML occurrence indicators OPT, REP, and PLUS, respectively.

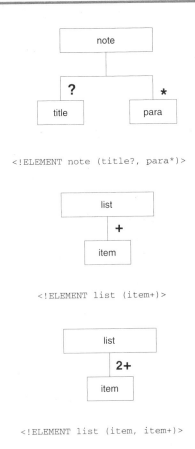

<!ELEMENT note (title?, para*)>

<!ELEMENT list (item+)>

<!ELEMENT list (item, item+)>

**Figure B-3**      Occurrence Specifications.

## B.4  Collections and Any-Order Groups

When any or all of the child elements can appear repeatedly, in an arbitrary order, they appear in an oval[1] that has either an asterisk or a plus sign occurrence indicator (showing that the contents of the collection can be chosen from repeatedly); it is shown in Figure B-4. We call this configuration a **collection**. It corresponds to a group that uses the SGML OR content model and has a REP or PLUS occurrence indicator on it. It is meaningless for the individual elements in the oval to have occurrence indicators on them.

---

1. In an early project we worked on, these ovals acquired the name **potatoes** because when hand-drawn they tend to look—how can we describe it?—much more "organic" than do the perfectly symmetrical ovals shown here. The name has stuck in several companies, and we've even seen parameter entity names that use potato as a suffix.

```
<!ELEMENT para (#PCDATA|emphasis|trademark)*>
```

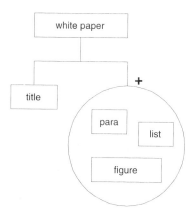

```
<!ELEMENT white-paper (title, (para|list|figure)+))>
```

**Figure B-4**    Collections.

For collections containing only elements, it is important in the modeling stages to choose an asterisk or plus sign occurrence indicator to indicate whether or not at least one element from the collection must appear. For collections of #PCDATA and elements (that is, mixed content models of the type recommended for use in ISO 8879), an occurrence indicator on the oval other than an asterisk is meaningless because an empty character string can satisfy the #PCDATA part of the content model.

Some collections that appear frequently in many contexts can be represented by a single descriptive name in an oval with an occurrence indicator on it (see Figure B-5). These common collections are often implemented in the DTD with parameter entities.

Likewise, a model consisting only of #PCDATA can be represented with a simple oval or, in shorthand, a keyword with an equal sign (see Figure B-5). #PCDATA can represent any number of data characters, including zero. Thus, an occurrence indicator is not required (and a PLUS indicator may be misleading, since the element can be entirely empty and satisfy a (#PCDATA)+ model). However, it is probably consistent and intuitive for design teams to supply occurrence indicators on #PCDATA ovals, and they can use them or not as they wish.

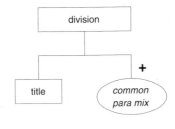

```
<!ELEMENT division (title, (%common-para-mix;)+)>
```

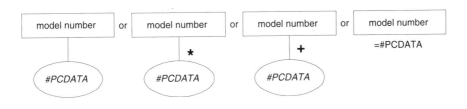

```
<!ELEMENT model-number (#PCDATA)>
```

**Figure B-5**     Additional Collection Representations.

Even though the SGML OR connector is used to implement both collections (except for simple #PCDATA collections) and either-or groups, the two configurations are fundamentally different in their effects on document authoring and processing. This is why their respective notations look different.

The design team will begin to find contexts where collections appear long before the actual contents of those locations are known. A cloud symbol represents a placeholder for a collection as shown in Figure B-6. (We show the cloud with the label "text" to distinguish it from the official ISO 8879 term.) In the specifications of the final document analysis report, no cloud symbols will remain, having been replaced by either named collections or actual lists of the contents allowed.

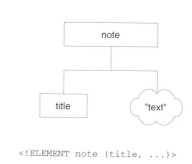

```
<!ELEMENT note (title, ...)>
```

**Figure B-6**    Collection Placeholder.

When all the child elements must appear but can appear in any order, they appear in an oval that has no occurrence indicator (showing that the elements are "required") as in Figure B-7. This configuration corresponds to a group that uses the SGML AND connector. The individual elements in the oval can have occurrence indicators on them.

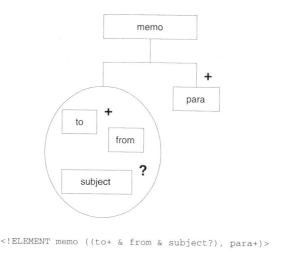

```
<!ELEMENT memo ((to+ & from & subject?), para+)>
```

**Figure B-7**    Any-Order Child Elements.

For both collections and any-order groups, it's usually impractical to define the contents of the elements inside the oval by attaching them directly. Instead, you can put an ellipsis below the boxes inside the oval, and elsewhere supply individual tree diagrams for each inner element.

## B.5   Groups

Connectors can emanate from points where an element box could have appeared, but does not. These points represent groups containing the entire model below them (see Figure B-8). Groups can have occurrence indicators, just as elements can.

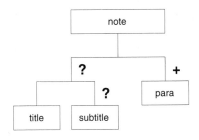

```
<!ELEMENT note ((title, subtitle?)?, para+)>
```

**Figure B-8**     Groups.

## B.6   Attributes

An element box can have lines of descriptive text on its right side, with each line indicating an attribute that the element should have, as in Figure B-9. Each line of text always includes a descriptive name for the attribute, and can also include its "data type" (declared value) and any default value. If a value is optional to supply, the line can end with a question mark. If a value is required, the line can end with a period to distinguish it from optional attributes and those for which optionality hasn't been decided. Default values can be shown underlined or in boldface.

In the modeling stages, the specifications for attributes can often be imprecise; a single descriptive word might suffice to indicate the intent. For example, "id" might be taken to mean an attribute named id with a declared content of ID. According to the technical SGML knowledge of the document type design team members, some or all of these conventions can be used to give the level of precision desired in specifying attributes.

Some examples of attribute specifications in tree diagrams, along with their possible attribute definitions in the DTD are listed in Table B-1.

**Figure B-9**    Attribute Descriptive Text.


**Table B-1**    Sample Attribute Specifications.

| Attribute Specification | Possible Declaration in DTD | | |
|---|---|---|---|
| id? | `id` | `ID` | `#IMPLIED` |
| link to entry. | `entrylink` | `IDREF` | `#REQUIRED` |
| type. | `type` | `--??--` | `#REQUIRED` |
| delim (" ") | `delimiter` | `CDATA` | `" "` |
| audience=(**novice** \| expert) | `audience` | `(novice\|expert)` | `novice` |


## B.7    Additional Notations

It is usually impractical to fit an entire markup model into a single diagram. It's better to focus each diagram on a single relevant portion of the model, and to elide unnecessary detail. This section describes parts of the notation that, like parameter entities, are unrelated to the markup model *per se* but help the model be better organized. You may find that you want to add to or change these convenience notations.

An ellipsis (...) stops the descent into lower levels of child elements and implies that a specification for the parent element can be found elsewhere. If you're preparing a package of tree diagrams as part of DTD user documentation, it can be helpful to indicate the page or section in which the desired diagram appears (see Figure B-10).

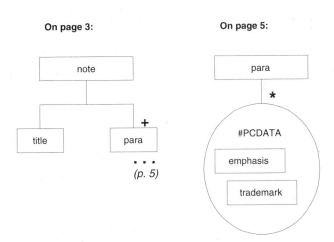

**Figure B-10**    Continuation Notation for Tree Diagrams.

To represent parent elements with many sequentially ordered child elements or many mutually exclusive choices of child elements, you can partially or wholly orient the children top-to-bottom rather than left-to-right (see Figure B-11). Unfortunately, this arrangement leaves little room for attribute information and declared content, and it appears to be less effective than the usual orientation in communicating the necessary modeling information.

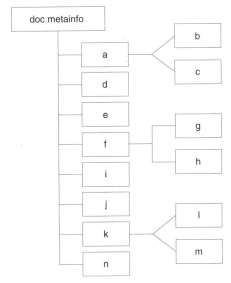

**Figure B-11**    Top-to-Bottom Representation of Parent-Child Relationship.

Alternatively, you can split the diagram into two parts and indicate a continuation with an ellipsis as shown in Figure B-12, or a page reference.

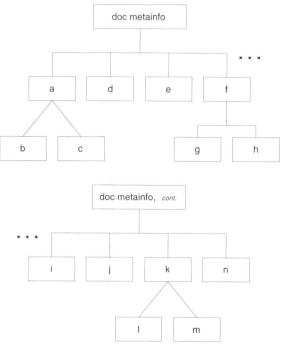

**Figure B-12**    Split-Diagram Representation of Parent-Child Relationship.

If one or more sets of common attributes are used on multiple elements, you can use a special symbol or keyword next to the relevant element boxes to stand for each set of attributes (see Figure B-13).

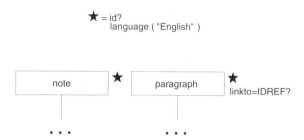

**Figure B-13**    Symbol Representation of Attribute Set.

If a group or class of elements has identical content model and attribute list characteristics and are intended to stay in synchronization, the correspondence can be shown in various ways. For example, multiple parent element boxes can be stacked on top of one another.

Alternatively, if the elements have already been identified as being part of a named class, the class can be shown in an oval as if it were the parent element. These are shown in Figure B-14. The DTD implementor can make use of this correspondence in constructing the declarations.

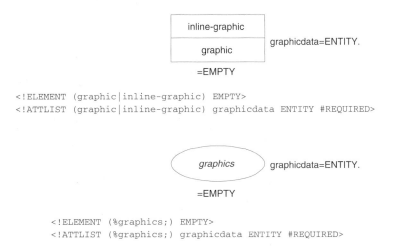

```
<!ELEMENT (graphic|inline-graphic) EMPTY>
<!ATTLIST (graphic|inline-graphic) graphicdata ENTITY #REQUIRED>
```

```
<!ELEMENT (%graphics;) EMPTY>
<!ATTLIST (%graphics;) graphicdata ENTITY #REQUIRED>
```

**Figure B-14**     Representing Synchronized Element Groups.

## B.8   Tree Diagram Building Process

The tree diagram notation can have several forms, representing modeling-in-progress, various stages of the specification work, DTD user documentation, and so on. Each design team will probably come up with its own shorthand as it develops a unique working style. Following are some examples to give you an idea of some of the shorthand forms we've used and the progression of work.

During the modeling process in a DTD design session, the notation is likely to be applied informally on a whiteboard or flipchart, with various details elided in the interest of quick communication. For example, the diagram in Figure B-15 might be produced partway through a discussion of the basic hierarchical structure of a document type. Notice that the number of levels of division is indicated, but most information about contents of those divisions and about repeatability of elements hasn't been supplied.

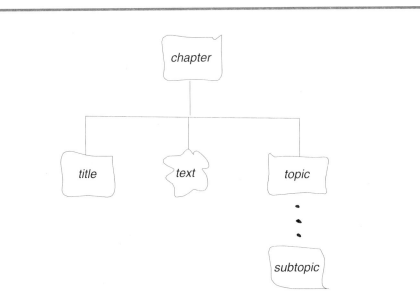

**Figure B-15**    Document Hierarchy Diagram During Modeling.

When the team is ready to commit its decision to paper (or to a graphical editor or com-puter-aided DTD development software) for a particular phase of specification work, these details must be filled in. For example, the diagram in Figure B-16 might appear in the draft document analysis report as the result of the final discussions on the document hierarchical structure, before the collections have been handled. It shows a much more sophisticated content model for each of the divisions, includes attribute information, and specifies some occurrence details even before the contents of the "text" clouds have been filled in.

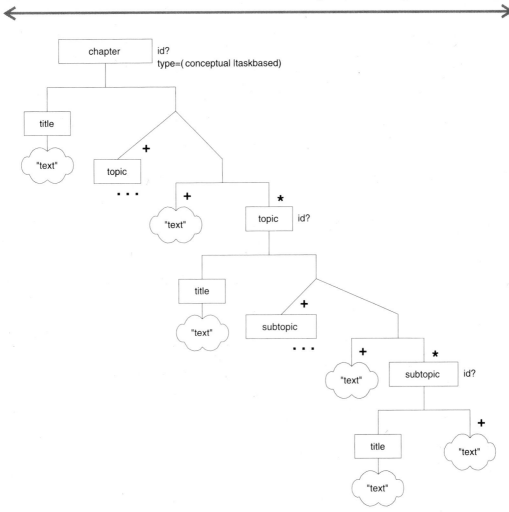

**Figure B-16**     Document Hierarchy Diagram with Empty "Text" Clouds.

When the design team is done populating the "text" clouds and has determined the occurrence requirements of those contexts, these details can be filled in. No more clouds remain in Figure B-17.

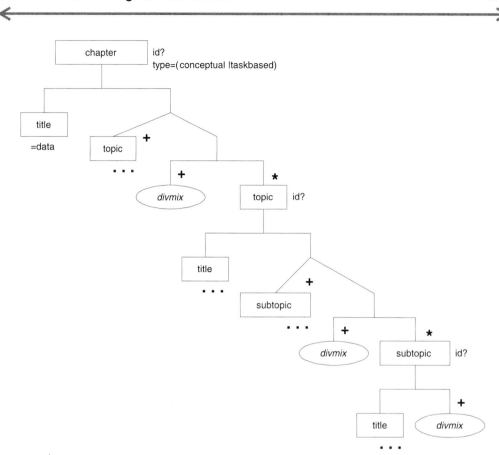

**Figure B-17**    Document Hierarchy Diagram with Details Complete.

When both the specification work and the DTD implementation and testing are done, the diagram might need changes to bring it up to date. For example, the diagram in Figure B-18 shows the result of some simplifications made to the occurrence requirements and structure and uses more precise SGML terminology.

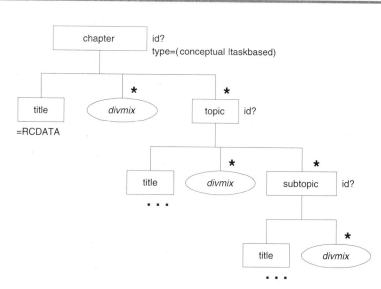

**Figure B-18**     Simplified Document Hierarchy Diagram.

In the DTD user documentation, it can be useful to excerpt various fragments of the diagrams in explaining each element, showing only the most significant or immediate levels of ancestor and descendent elements. For example, the partial diagram shown in Figure B-19 might appear in the documentation for a topic, while the whole document hierarchy might be shown elsewhere.

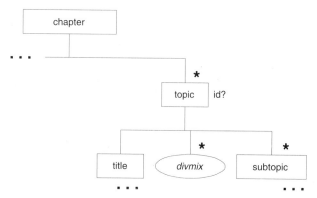

**Figure B-19**     Partial Hierarchy Diagram in User Documentation.

# DTD Reuse and Customization Sample

This appendix shows how "monolithic" DTDs can be reorganized using some of the techniques discussed in Chapters 9 and 10, resulting in modularized and parameterized versions that are considerably more scalable, manageable, and customizable. The memo, letter, and report DTDs used as examples in this appendix are used by ArborText, Inc. for introductory training purposes, and are listed with ArborText's permission.

Even though the information pools of the three DTDs are very similar, they are maintained separately so that novice DTD readers can find all the relevant information in a single file. For our reorganization scenario, we'll assume that these DTDs have, over time, also begun to be used by people to produce real memos, letters, and reports. The users have made the following enhancement requests, which suggest that a restructuring of the DTDs may be beneficial:

- From time to time, the various elements available in the information pool have gotten out of synchronization. Can the elements added to one DTD be added to the other two at the same time, and can all the information pools be as identical as possible? For example, for several months, tables in reports had a different element name from tables in letters and memos. Also, when in-line graphics were added to memos and letters, they were accidentally left out of reports.

  Keeping the elements synchronized would be convenient for authors who must write all three kinds of documents. It would also be useful in ensuring that text written for one kind of document could be reused in another kind of document. For example, the information on the proper use of the office's fax machine could be written up once, and then used in both the policy report kept on file and the memo initially sent to the staff. Finally, it would ease the development of processing applications for the common portion of all three document types.

- Rather than having to create a separate transmittal letter to accompany reports, is it possible to make the transmittal information part of the same document as a report?

- We may need to create additional types of documents, such as proposals and statements of consulting work, and for these document types we may need different document hierarchies. Can we reuse the same information pool for all of them, and to how great an extent?

A common information pool would keep those elements synchronized, and the letter model could be incorporated into the report model as a "nested DTD." Furthermore, the element classes and collections could be reorganized using the building-block method, which would make them easier to customize and control in each DTD.

## C.1  Original DTD Structure

Following are listings of the original DTDs. Example C-1 shows the memo DTD, Example C-2 shows the letter DTD, and Example C-3 shows the report DTD.

**Example C-1**   Memo DTD Before Reorganization.

```
<!-- memo.dtd for ADEPT memo sample  -->

<!-- COMMON PUBLIC DECLARATIONS  -->

<!-- Public document type definition. Typical invocation:

<!DOCTYPE document PUBLIC "-//ArborText//DTD Report//EN">
-->

<!ENTITY % atimath PUBLIC "-//ArborText//ELEMENTS Math Equation  Structures//EN">
%atimath;

<!-- ArborText equation entity refs -->
<!ENTITY % ATIeqn1 PUBLIC "-//ArborText//ENTITIES Equation1//EN">
%ATIeqn1;

<!-- ISO Character References -->
<!ENTITY % ISOpub PUBLIC
 "ISO 8879:1986//ENTITIES Publishing//EN">
%ISOpub;

<!ENTITY % ISOnum PUBLIC
 "ISO 8879:1986//ENTITIES Numeric and Special Graphic//EN">
%ISOnum;

<!ENTITY % ISOtech PUBLIC
 "ISO 8879:1986//ENTITIES General Technical//EN">
%ISOtech;
```

**Example C-1**    Memo DTD Before Reorganization.   (Continued)

```
<!ENTITY % ISOdia PUBLIC
 "ISO 8879:1986//ENTITIES Diacritical Marks//EN">
%ISOdia;

<!ENTITY % ISOlat1 PUBLIC
 "ISO 8879:1986//ENTITIES Added Latin 1//EN">
%ISOlat1;

<!ENTITY % ISOlat2 PUBLIC
 "ISO 8879:1986//ENTITIES Added Latin 2//EN">
%ISOlat2;

<!ENTITY % ISOamso PUBLIC
 "ISO 8879:1986//ENTITIES Added Math Symbols: Ordinary//EN">
%ISOamso;

<!ENTITY % ISOgrk1 PUBLIC
 "ISO 8879:1986//ENTITIES Greek Letters//EN">
%ISOgrk1;

<!ENTITY % ISOgrk3 PUBLIC
 "ISO 8879:1986//ENTITIES Greek Symbols//EN">
%ISOgrk3;

<!-- COMMON ENTITY DECLARATIONS  -->

<!ENTITY % graphics      "graphic|inline-graphic" >
<!ENTITY % tables        "table" >
<!ENTITY % equations     "inline-equation|display-equation" >

<!ENTITY % par.text      "#PCDATA|super|sub|emphasis" >
<!ENTITY % par.text.ref  "%par.text;" >
<!ENTITY % par.text.note "%par.text.ref;|footnote" >
<!ENTITY % par.list      "sequential-list|definition-list|bulleted-list" >
<!ENTITY % par.misc      "computer|asis|extract" >
<!ENTITY % par.fig       "inline-graphic|inline-equation"
>
<!ENTITY % par.all       "%par.text.note;|
                          %par.list;|
                          %par.fig;|
                            %par.misc;" >

<!ENTITY % fig.all       "graphic|%tables|display-equation" >

<!ENTITY % nonfig.all    "graphic|display-equation" >
```

Example C-1    Memo DTD Before Reorganization.  (Continued)

```
<!ENTITY % paralevel      "para|figure|%nonfig.all;" >

<!-- COMMON ELEMENT DECLARATIONS -->

<!ELEMENT para             - -     (%par.all;)* >
<!ATTLIST para id        ID      #IMPLIED >

<!ELEMENT display-equation - -   (fd) >
<!ATTLIST display-equation
            align           (left|center|right)  #IMPLIED >


<!ELEMENT inline-equation - -    (f) >

<!ELEMENT computer         - -     (#PCDATA|footnote)* >

<!ELEMENT extract          - -     (%par.text;|footnote)* >

<!ELEMENT asis             - -     (%par.text;|footnote)* >
<!ELEMENT title            - -     (%par.text.ref;)*>

<!ELEMENT figure           - -     (title,(%fig.all;)) >
<!ATTLIST figure id      ID      #IMPLIED >

<!ELEMENT super            - -     (%par.text;)*  -(super)>

<!ELEMENT sub              - -     (%par.text;)*  -(sub)>

<!ELEMENT emphasis         - -     (%par.text;)*  -(emphasis)>

<!ELEMENT footnote         - -     (%par.text;)* >

<!ELEMENT (bulleted-list|
        sequential-list)
                           - -     (title?, (item)+ ) >
<!ATTLIST (bulleted-list|
        sequential-list) id ID #IMPLIED >

<!ELEMENT definition-list      - -     (title?, (term, def)+) >
<!ATTLIST definition-list id ID #IMPLIED >

<!ELEMENT item             - -     (%par.text.note;|%par.list)* >
<!ATTLIST item  id  ID #IMPLIED >
<!ELEMENT term             - -     (%par.text.ref;)*       >
```

**Example C-1**    Memo DTD Before Reorganization. (Continued)

```
<!ELEMENT def              - -      (%par.text.note;)*        >

<!ELEMENT ( %graphics; )        - o      EMPTY >
<!ATTLIST ( %graphics; )
                 filename       CDATA       #REQUIRED
                 processor      CDATA       #REQUIRED
                 magnification  NUMBER      #IMPLIED
                 horzoffsetamt  CDATA       #IMPLIED
                 horzoffsetpct  CDATA       #IMPLIED
                 vertoffsetamt  CDATA       #IMPLIED
                 vertoffsetpct  CDATA       #IMPLIED
                 cropheight     CDATA       #IMPLIED
                 cropwidth      CDATA       #IMPLIED
                 cropllxcoord   CDATA       #IMPLIED
                 cropllycoord   CDATA       #IMPLIED
                 scalefit       NUMBER      #IMPLIED
                 scalefitheight CDATA       #IMPLIED
                 scalefitwidth  CDATA       #IMPLIED >

<!-- MORE COMMON PUBLIC DECLARATIONS -->

<!ENTITY % tblcon       "%par.text.note;|%par.fig;|%nonfig.all;" >
<!ENTITY % atitable PUBLIC "-//ArborText//ELEMENTS Table Structures//EN"
>
%atitable;
<!-- DOCUMENT STRUCTURE  -->

<!ELEMENT memo          - -      (head,body,end) >

<!-- HEAD ELEMENTS     -->
<!ELEMENT head          - -      (date, to, from, subject, cc?, (enclosure?|
                                  attachment?)) >

<!ELEMENT (date,
          subject,
          enclosure,
          attachment) - -      (%par.text;)* >

<!ELEMENT (cc,
          to,
          from)       - -      (name, jobtitle?, organization?, address*,
                                  city?, state?, zip?, phone?, fax?)* >

<!ELEMENT (name,
          jobtitle,
```

**Example C-1** Memo DTD Before Reorganization. (Continued)

```
                    organization,
                    address,
                    city,
                    state,
                    zip,
                    phone,
                    fax)          - -      (%par.text;)* >


<!--    BODY ELEMENTS       -->


<!ELEMENT body          - -      (%paralevel)* >


<!--    END ELEMENTS        -->


<!ELEMENT end           - -      (initials?, (enclosure|attachment)?,
                                 cc?) >


<!ELEMENT initials      - -      (%par.text;)* >
```

**Example C-2** Letter DTD Before Reorganization.

```
<!-- letter.dtd for ADEPT letter sample  -->


<!-- COMMON PUBLIC DECLARATIONS  -->


<!-- Public document type definition. Typical invocation:
<!DOCTYPE document PUBLIC "-//ArborText//DTD Report//EN">
-->


<!ENTITY % atimath PUBLIC "-//ArborText//ELEMENTS Math Equation Structures//EN">
%atimath;


<!-- ArborText equation entity refs -->
<!ENTITY % ATIeqn1 PUBLIC "-//ArborText//ENTITIES Equation1//EN">
%ATIeqn1;


<!-- ISO Character References -->
<!ENTITY % ISOpub PUBLIC
  "ISO 8879:1986//ENTITIES Publishing//EN">
%ISOpub;


<!ENTITY % ISOnum PUBLIC
  "ISO 8879:1986//ENTITIES Numeric and Special Graphic//EN">
%ISOnum;
```

**Example C-2**    Letter DTD Before Reorganization.  (Continued)

```
<!ENTITY % ISOtech PUBLIC
 "ISO 8879:1986//ENTITIES General Technical//EN">
%ISOtech;

<!ENTITY % ISOdia PUBLIC
 "ISO 8879:1986//ENTITIES Diacritical Marks//EN">
%ISOdia;

<!ENTITY % ISOlat1 PUBLIC
 "ISO 8879:1986//ENTITIES Added Latin 1//EN">
%ISOlat1;

<!ENTITY % ISOlat2 PUBLIC
 "ISO 8879:1986//ENTITIES Added Latin 2//EN">
%ISOlat2;

<!ENTITY % ISOamso PUBLIC
 "ISO 8879:1986//ENTITIES Added Math Symbols: Ordinary//EN">
%ISOamso;

<!ENTITY % ISOgrk1 PUBLIC
 "ISO 8879:1986//ENTITIES Greek Letters//EN">
%ISOgrk1;

<!ENTITY % ISOgrk3 PUBLIC
 "ISO 8879:1986//ENTITIES Greek Symbols//EN">
%ISOgrk3;

<!-- COMMON ENTITY DECLARATIONS  -->

<!ENTITY % graphics       "graphic|inline-graphic" >
<!ENTITY % tables         "table" >
<!ENTITY % equations      "inline-equation|display-equation" >

<!ENTITY % par.text       "#PCDATA|super|sub|emphasis" >
<!ENTITY % par.text.ref   "%par.text;" >
<!ENTITY % par.text.note  "%par.text.ref;|footnote" >
<!ENTITY % par.list       "sequential-list|definition-list|bulleted-list" >
<!ENTITY % par.misc       "computer|asis|extract" >
<!ENTITY % par.fig        "inline-graphic|inline-equation" >
<!ENTITY % par.all        "%par.text.note;|
                          %par.list;|
                          %par.fig;|
                          %par.misc;" >
```

**Example C-2**   Letter DTD Before Reorganization.  (Continued)

```
<!ENTITY % fig.all        "graphic|%tables|display-equation" >

<!ENTITY % nonfig.all     "graphic|display-equation" >

<!ENTITY % paralevel      "para|figure|%nonfig.all;" >

<!-- COMMON ELEMENT DECLARATIONS -->

<!ELEMENT para            - -    (%par.all;)* >
<!ATTLIST para id         ID     #IMPLIED >

<!ELEMENT display-equation - -   (fd) >
<!ATTLIST display-equation
                align          (left|center|right)  #IMPLIED >

<!ELEMENT inline-equation - -    (f) >

<!ELEMENT computer        - -    (#PCDATA|footnote)* >

<!ELEMENT extract         - -    (%par.text;|footnote)* >

<!ELEMENT asis            - -    (%par.text;|footnote)* >

<!ELEMENT title           - -    (%par.text.ref;)*>

<!ELEMENT figure          - -    (title,(%fig.all;)) >
<!ATTLIST figure id       ID     #IMPLIED >

<!ELEMENT super           - -    (%par.text;)*  -(super)>

<!ELEMENT sub             - -    (%par.text;)*  -(sub)>

<!ELEMENT emphasis        - -    (%par.text;)*  -(emphasis)>

<!ELEMENT footnote        - -    (%par.text;)* >

<!ELEMENT (bulleted-list|
          sequential-list)
                          - -    (title?, (item)+ ) >
<!ATTLIST (bulleted-list|
          sequential-list) id ID #IMPLIED >

<!ELEMENT definition-list      - -    (title?, (term, def)+) >
<!ATTLIST definition-list id ID #IMPLIED >
```

⟵————————————————————————————————————⟶

**Example C-2**    Letter DTD Before Reorganization.  (Continued)

```
<!ELEMENT item            - -     (%par.text.note;|%par.list)*  >
<!ATTLIST item  id   ID #IMPLIED >

<!ELEMENT term            - -     (%par.text.ref;)*        >
<!ELEMENT def             - -     (%par.text.note;)*         >

<!ELEMENT ( %graphics; )       - o     EMPTY >
<!ATTLIST ( %graphics; )
                  filename       CDATA      #REQUIRED
                  processor      CDATA      #REQUIRED
                  magnification  NUMBER     #IMPLIED
                  horzoffsetamt  CDATA      #IMPLIED
                  horzoffsetpct  CDATA      #IMPLIED
                  vertoffsetamt  CDATA      #IMPLIED
                  vertoffsetpct  CDATA      #IMPLIED
                  cropheight     CDATA      #IMPLIED
                  cropwidth      CDATA      #IMPLIED
                  cropllxcoord   CDATA      #IMPLIED
                  cropllycoord   CDATA      #IMPLIED
                  scalefit       NUMBER     #IMPLIED
                  scalefitheight CDATA      #IMPLIED
                  scalefitwidth  CDATA      #IMPLIED >

<!-- MORE COMMON PUBLIC DECLARATIONS -->

<!ENTITY % tblcon          "%par.text.note;|%par.fig;|%nonfig.all;" >
<!ENTITY % atitable PUBLIC "-//ArborText//ELEMENTS Table Structures//EN"
>
%atitable;

<!-- DOCUMENT STRUCTURE  -->

<!ELEMENT letter          - -     (head, body, end) >

<!-- HEAD ELEMENTS      -->

<!ELEMENT head            - -     (date, from?, to?, subject?, salutation? ) >

<!ELEMENT (date,
           subject,
           salutation)  - -     (%par.text;)* >

<!ELEMENT (from,
            to)          - -     (name, jobtitle?, organization?, address*,
                                  city?, state?, zip?, phone?, fax?) >
```

**Example C-2**   Letter DTD Before Reorganization.  (Continued)

```
<!ELEMENT (name,
           jobtitle,
           organization,
           address,
           city,
           state,
           zip,
           phone,
           fax)            - -    (%par.text;)* >

<!--   BODY ELEMENTS     -->

<!ELEMENT body            - -    (%paralevel;)* >

<!--   END ELEMENTS      -->

<!ELEMENT end             - -    (closing?, sender, jobtitle?, initials?,
                                  (enclosure|attachment)?, cc?, postscript?) >

<!ELEMENT (closing,
           sender,
           initials,
           enclosure,
           attachment,
           postscript)    - -    (%par.text;)* >

<!ELEMENT cc              - -    (name, jobtitle?, organization?, address*, city?,
                                  state?, zip?, phone?, fax?) >
```

**Example C-3**   Report DTD Before Reorganization.

```
<!-- report.dtd for ADEPT report sample  -->

<!-- COMMON PUBLIC DECLARATIONS  -->

<!-- Public document type definition. Typical invocation:
<!DOCTYPE report PUBLIC "-//ArborText//DTD Report//EN">
-->

<!ENTITY % atimath PUBLIC "-//ArborText//ELEMENTS Math Equation Structures//EN">
%atimath;

<!-- ArborText equation entity refs -->
```

**Example C-3**  Report DTD Before Reorganization.  (Continued)

```
<!ENTITY % ATIeqn1 PUBLIC "-//ArborText//ENTITIES Equation1//EN">
%ATIeqn1;

<!-- ISO Character References -->

<!ENTITY % ISOpub PUBLIC
 "ISO 8879:1986//ENTITIES Publishing//EN">
%ISOpub;

<!ENTITY % ISOnum PUBLIC
 "ISO 8879:1986//ENTITIES Numeric and Special Graphic//EN">
%ISOnum;

<!ENTITY % ISOtech PUBLIC
 "ISO 8879:1986//ENTITIES General Technical//EN">
%ISOtech;

<!ENTITY % ISOdia PUBLIC
 "ISO 8879:1986//ENTITIES Diacritical Marks//EN">
%ISOdia;

<!ENTITY % ISOlat1 PUBLIC
 "ISO 8879:1986//ENTITIES Added Latin 1//EN">
%ISOlat1;

<!ENTITY % ISOlat2 PUBLIC
 "ISO 8879:1986//ENTITIES Added Latin 2//EN">
%ISOlat2;

<!ENTITY % ISOamso PUBLIC
 "ISO 8879:1986//ENTITIES Added Math Symbols: Ordinary//EN">
%ISOamso;

<!ENTITY % ISOgrk1 PUBLIC
 "ISO 8879:1986//ENTITIES Greek Letters//EN">
%ISOgrk1;

<!ENTITY % ISOgrk3 PUBLIC
 "ISO 8879:1986//ENTITIES Greek Symbols//EN">
%ISOgrk3;

<!-- COMMON ENTITY DECLARATIONS  -->

<!ENTITY % par.text      "#PCDATA|super|sub|emphasis" >
<!ENTITY % par.text.ref  "%par.text;|xref" >
```

**Example C-3**   Report DTD Before Reorganization.  (Continued)

```
<!ENTITY % par.text.note "%par.text.ref;|footnote" >
<!ENTITY % par.list      "list|sequential-list|definition-list|bulleted-list" >
<!ENTITY % par.misc      "computer|asis|extract" >
<!ENTITY % par.fig       "graphic|table|inline-equation|display-equation" >
<!ENTITY % par.all       "%par.text.note;|
                           %par.list;|
                           %par.fig;|
                           %par.misc;" >


<!ENTITY % fig.all       "graphic|table|display-equation" >
<!ENTITY % paralevel     "para|figure" >


<!-- COMMON ELEMENT DECLARATIONS -->


<!ELEMENT para             - -     (%par.all;)* >
<!ATTLIST para id        ID      #IMPLIED >


<!ELEMENT display-equation - -     (fd) >


<!ELEMENT inline-equation - -      (f) >


<!ELEMENT commentary          - -      (%par.text;)* >


<!ELEMENT computer         - -     (#PCDATA | footnote )* >


<!ELEMENT extract          - -     (%par.text; | footnote )* >


<!ELEMENT asis             - -     (%par.text; | footnote )* >


<!ELEMENT title            - -     (%par.text.ref;)*>


<!ELEMENT figure           - -     (title, (%fig.all;) ) >
<!ATTLIST figure id      ID      #IMPLIED >


<!ELEMENT super            - -     (%par.text;)*  -(super)> 


<!ELEMENT sub              - -     (%par.text;)*  -(sub)>


<!ELEMENT emphasis         - -     (%par.text;)*  -(emphasis)>


<!ELEMENT footnote         - -     ((author?, title, publisher?, date?,
                                            page?)|commentary )  >


<!ELEMENT bib-entry        - -     (author?, title, publisher?, date?, page? ) >
```

**Example C-3**   Report DTD Before Reorganization.  (Continued)

```
<!ELEMENT (publisher|page)        - -       (%par.text;)* >

<!ELEMENT (list|
           sequential-list|
           bulleted-list)         - -       (title?, (item)+ ) >
<!ATTLIST (list|sequential-list|bulleted-list) id ID #IMPLIED >

<!ELEMENT definition-list         - -       (title?, (term, def)+) >
<!ATTLIST definition-list id ID #IMPLIED >

<!ELEMENT item            - -       (%par.text.note;|%par.list)*  >
<!ATTLIST item  id  ID #IMPLIED >

<!ELEMENT term            - -       (%par.text.ref;)*       >
<!ELEMENT def             - -       (%par.text.note;)*      >

<!ELEMENT graphic         - O       EMPTY >
<!ATTLIST graphic filename         CDATA      #REQUIRED
                  processor        CDATA      #REQUIRED
                  magnification    NUMBER     #IMPLIED
                  horzoffsetamt    CDATA      #IMPLIED
                  horzoffsetpct    CDATA      #IMPLIED
                  vertoffsetamt    CDATA      #IMPLIED
                  vertoffsetpct    CDATA      #IMPLIED
                  cropheight       CDATA      #IMPLIED
                  cropwidth        CDATA      #IMPLIED
                  cropllxcoord     CDATA      #IMPLIED
                  cropllycoord     CDATA      #IMPLIED
                  scalefit         NUMBER     #IMPLIED
                  scalefitheight   CDATA      #IMPLIED
                  scalefitwidth    CDATA      #IMPLIED >

<!ELEMENT xref            - O       EMPTY >
<!ATTLIST xref xrefid IDREF #REQUIRED >

<!-- MORE COMMON PUBLIC DECLARATIONS -->
<!ENTITY % tblcon         "%par.text;|graphic|inline-equation" >
<!ENTITY % atitable PUBLIC "-//ArborText//ELEMENTS Table Structures//EN" >
%atitable;

<!-- DOCUMENT STRUCTURE  -->

<!ELEMENT report          - -       (front,body,rear?) >

<!--  FRONT ELEMENTS       -->
```

**Example C-3**   Report DTD Before Reorganization.  (Continued)

```
<!ELEMENT front           - -     (title-info, author-info, contents? ) >

<!ELEMENT title-info      - -     (title, subtitle?,  version?, revision?, date)
>

<!ELEMENT author-info     - -     ((author, authloc?)+) >

<!ELEMENT contents        - O     EMPTY >

<!ELEMENT (subtitle|
           version|
           revision|
           author|
           authloc|
           date)          - -     (%par.text;)* >

<!--   BODY ELEMENTS      -->

<!ELEMENT body            - -     (section*)  >

<!ELEMENT section         - -     (title, (%paralevel;)*, topic* )>
<!ATTLIST section id   ID #IMPLIED>

<!ELEMENT topic           - -     (title, (%paralevel;)*, subtop* )>
<!ATTLIST topic  id   ID #IMPLIED>

<!ELEMENT subtop          - -     (title, (%paralevel;)* )>
<!ATTLIST subtop id   ID #IMPLIED >

<!--   REAR ELEMENTS      -->

<!ELEMENT rear            - -     (appendix*, bibliography?, glossary? ) >

<!ELEMENT appendix        - -     (title, (%paralevel)* )  >
<!ATTLIST appendix id   ID #IMPLIED>

<!ELEMENT glossary        - -     (title, (para|definition-list)+ ) >

<!ELEMENT bibliography    - -     (title, (bib-entry)+ ) >
```

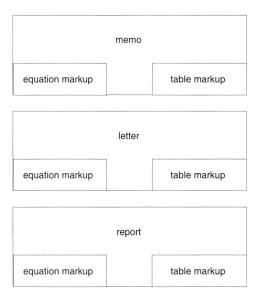

**Figure C-1**      Original Structure of the Memo, Letter, and Report DTDs.

Figure C-1 represents the structure of the original DTDs. The use of table and equation DTD fragments is done modularly, but otherwise the DTDs are separate (though large portions of them are nearly identical).

## C.2  Modified DTD Structure

Figure C-2 represents the overall structure of the DTDs as modified for the new goals. All three use an information pool module, and a module for metainformation (the elements that describe the senders and recipients of memos and letters) has been added as well. Letters can be nested within reports or created separately.

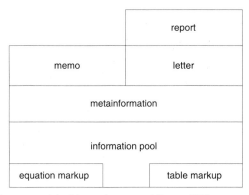

**Figure C-2**      Modified Structure of the Memo, Letter, and Report DTDs.

The following sections list and describe the new modules. The sections proceed approximately from the top down, even though the parameter entities containing the modules must be referenced from the bottom up.

Note that element name indirection hasn't been used in this reorganization. Using parameter entities to represent element names would be a good idea for maintenance reasons if any names at the lower levels are anticipated to change in the future.

## C.2.1   Main DTD Files

Figure C-2 is actually a simplified picture of the structure of the DTD modules. Each DTD needs a top-level "driver file" that pulls in all the other necessary modules, including modules for the respective document hierarchies. The hierarchy modules can't be combined with the top-level driver files because of potential problems with the letter/report nested document type: If the same file serves as the letter hierarchy module and the top-level driver file, it will need to reference all the lower-level modules that are needed. Then, when the report DTD references the single high-level letter file, it will also reference duplicates of the modules it already needs for its own structure independent of letters. Since element declarations cannot be duplicated in a DTD, errors will be reported by parsers.

If, in order to avoid the errors, the report DTD file simply relied on the modules as referenced by the letter file, it would not be possible to use different information pools for the reports and letters (if this were desired).

A more precise schematic of the module relationships is as shown in Figure C-3.

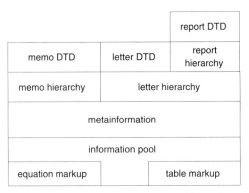

**Figure C-3**     Precise Modular Relationships of the Reorganized Memo, Letter, and Report DTDs.

Example C-4 shows the top-level memo DTD driver file that references various other modules and customizes them. In this case, no customizations are necessary. Notice that the "memo module" that is referenced contains only the overall hierarchy for memos, not any of the information pool material.

**Example C-4**   New Memo DTD Driver File.

```
<!-- ................... memo DTD ...................................... -->

<!-- ................... character entity sets ......................... -->

<!ENTITY % atimath PUBLIC "-//ArborText//ELEMENTS Math Equation Structures//EN">
%atimath;

<!-- ArborText equation entity refs -->
<!ENTITY % ATIeqn1 PUBLIC "-//ArborText//ENTITIES Equation1//EN">
%ATIeqn1;

<!-- ISO Character References -->
<!ENTITY % ISOpub PUBLIC
  "ISO 8879:1986//ENTITIES Publishing//EN">
%ISOpub;

<!ENTITY % ISOnum PUBLIC
  "ISO 8879:1986//ENTITIES Numeric and Special Graphic//EN">
%ISOnum;

<!ENTITY % ISOtech PUBLIC
  "ISO 8879:1986//ENTITIES General Technical//EN">
%ISOtech;

<!ENTITY % ISOdia PUBLIC
  "ISO 8879:1986//ENTITIES Diacritical Marks//EN">
%ISOdia;

<!ENTITY % ISOlat1 PUBLIC
  "ISO 8879:1986//ENTITIES Added Latin 1//EN">
%ISOlat1;

<!ENTITY % ISOlat2 PUBLIC
  "ISO 8879:1986//ENTITIES Added Latin 2//EN">
%ISOlat2;

<!ENTITY % ISOamso PUBLIC
  "ISO 8879:1986//ENTITIES Added Math Symbols: Ordinary//EN">
%ISOamso;
```

**Example C-4**   New Memo DTD Driver File.  (Continued)

```
<!ENTITY % ISOgrk1 PUBLIC
 "ISO 8879:1986//ENTITIES Greek Letters//EN">
%ISOgrk1;

<!ENTITY % ISOgrk3 PUBLIC
 "ISO 8879:1986//ENTITIES Greek Symbols//EN">
%ISOgrk3;

<!-- .................. customizations ................................. -->

<!--(change to INCLUDE if need to redefine info pool mixtures using classes)-->
<!ENTITY % redefine "IGNORE">

<!-- .................. lower-level modules ........................... -->

<!ENTITY % pool PUBLIC "-//ArborText//ELEMENTS Information Pool//EN">
%pool;

<!ENTITY % meta PUBLIC "-//ArborText//ELEMENTS Metainformation//EN">
%meta;

<!ENTITY % memomod PUBLIC "-//ArborText//ELEMENTS Basic Memo Module//EN">
%memomod;

<!-- .................. end of memo DTD ................................ -->
```

The main file for the letter DTD looks similar to that for the memo DTD; it is shown in Example C-5.

**Example C-5**   New Letter DTD Driver File.

```
<!-- .................. letter DTD ..................................... -->

<!-- .................. character entity sets .......................... -->

<!ENTITY % atimath PUBLIC "-//ArborText//ELEMENTS Math Equation Structures//EN">
%atimath;

<!-- ArborText equation entity refs -->
<!ENTITY % ATIeqn1 PUBLIC "-//ArborText//ENTITIES Equation1//EN">
%ATIeqn1;
```

**Example C-5**   New Letter DTD Driver File.  (Continued)

```
<!-- ISO Character References -->

<!ENTITY % ISOpub PUBLIC
 "ISO 8879:1986//ENTITIES Publishing//EN">
%ISOpub;

<!ENTITY % ISOnum PUBLIC
 "ISO 8879:1986//ENTITIES Numeric and Special Graphic//EN">
%ISOnum;

<!ENTITY % ISOtech PUBLIC
 "ISO 8879:1986//ENTITIES General Technical//EN">
%ISOtech;

<!ENTITY % ISOdia PUBLIC
 "ISO 8879:1986//ENTITIES Diacritical Marks//EN">
%ISOdia;

<!ENTITY % ISOlat1 PUBLIC
 "ISO 8879:1986//ENTITIES Added Latin 1//EN">
%ISOlat1;

<!ENTITY % ISOlat2 PUBLIC
 "ISO 8879:1986//ENTITIES Added Latin 2//EN">
%ISOlat2;

<!ENTITY % ISOamso PUBLIC
 "ISO 8879:1986//ENTITIES Added Math Symbols: Ordinary//EN">
%ISOamso;

<!ENTITY % ISOgrk1 PUBLIC
 "ISO 8879:1986//ENTITIES Greek Letters//EN">
%ISOgrk1;

<!ENTITY % ISOgrk3 PUBLIC
 "ISO 8879:1986//ENTITIES Greek Symbols//EN">
%ISOgrk3;

<!-- .................. customizations ................................. -->

<!--(change to INCLUDE if need to redefine info pool mixtures using classes)-->
<!ENTITY % redefine "IGNORE">

<!-- .................. lower-level modules ............................ -->
```

**Example C-5**   New Letter DTD Driver File.  (Continued)

```
<!ENTITY % pool PUBLIC "-//ArborText//ELEMENTS Information Pool//EN">
%pool;

<!ENTITY % meta PUBLIC "-//ArborText//ELEMENTS Metainformation//EN">
%meta;

<!ENTITY % lettermod PUBLIC "-//ArborText//ELEMENTS Basic Letter Module//EN">
%lettermod;

<!-- ................... end of letter DTD ............................. -->
```

The main file for the report DTD is a little more complex because it redefines some parameter entities in the lower-level modules in order to extend the list of available elements. While memo and letter content can be reused in reports, report text *may* not be able to be reused in memos and letters, since reports allow more elements in the information pool. The report main file contains two document hierarchy modules: one for letters (which requires that the metainformation module be included before it) and one for reports. The file is shown in Example C-6.

**Example C-6**   New Report DTD Driver File.

```
<!-- ................... report DTD ....................................... -->

<!-- ................... character entity sets ......................... -->

<!ENTITY % atimath PUBLIC "-//ArborText//ELEMENTS Math Equation Structures//EN">
%atimath;

<!-- ArborText equation entity refs -->
<!ENTITY % ATIeqn1 PUBLIC "-//ArborText//ENTITIES Equation1//EN">
%ATIeqn1;

<!-- ISO Character References -->
<!ENTITY % ISOpub PUBLIC
  "ISO 8879:1986//ENTITIES Publishing//EN">
%ISOpub;

<!ENTITY % ISOnum PUBLIC
  "ISO 8879:1986//ENTITIES Numeric and Special Graphic//EN">
%ISOnum;
```

**Example C-6**   New Report DTD Driver File.  (Continued)

```
<!ENTITY % ISOtech PUBLIC
 "ISO 8879:1986//ENTITIES General Technical//EN">
%ISOtech;

<!ENTITY % ISOdia PUBLIC
 "ISO 8879:1986//ENTITIES Diacritical Marks//EN">
%ISOdia;

<!ENTITY % ISOlat1 PUBLIC
 "ISO 8879:1986//ENTITIES Added Latin 1//EN">
%ISOlat1;

<!ENTITY % ISOlat2 PUBLIC
 "ISO 8879:1986//ENTITIES Added Latin 2//EN">
%ISOlat2;

<!ENTITY % ISOamso PUBLIC
 "ISO 8879:1986//ENTITIES Added Math Symbols: Ordinary//EN">
%ISOamso;

<!ENTITY % ISOgrk1 PUBLIC
 "ISO 8879:1986//ENTITIES Greek Letters//EN">
%ISOgrk1;

<!ENTITY % ISOgrk3 PUBLIC
 "ISO 8879:1986//ENTITIES Greek Symbols//EN">
%ISOgrk3;

<!-- .................. customizations ................................ -->

<!-- these entities are read before the modules, so take precedence -->
<!--(extend annotation class with bibliographic citation footnote)-->
<!ENTITY % local.annots        "|citation">

<!--(add new local.xrefs class)-->
<!ENTITY % local.xrefs         "xref">

<!--(define content model for citations and bibliographic entries)-->
<!ENTITY % bib.model          ."author?, title, publisher?, date?, page?">

<!--(extend list class with simple list)-->
<!ENTITY % local.lists         "|list">
<!--(extend data mixtures with local.xrefs)-->
```

**Example C-6**   New Report DTD Driver File.  (Continued)

```
<!ENTITY % local.computer.data.mix  "|%local.xrefs;">
<!ENTITY % local.normal.data.mix    "|%local.xrefs;">
<!ENTITY % local.title.data.mix     "|%local.xrefs;">
<!ENTITY % local.table.data.mix     "|%local.xrefs;">
<!ENTITY % local.para.data.mix      "|%local.xrefs;">

<!--(change to INCLUDE if need to redefine info pool mixtures using classes)-->
<!ENTITY % redefine "IGNORE">

<!-- .................. inclusion of standard modules .................. -->

<!ENTITY % pool PUBLIC "-//ArborText//ELEMENTS Information Pool//EN">
%pool;

<!ENTITY % meta PUBLIC "-//ArborText//ELEMENTS Metainformation//EN">
%meta;

<!ENTITY % letter PUBLIC "-//ArborText//ELEMENTS Basic Letter Module//EN">
%letter;

<!ENTITY % reportmod PUBLIC "-//ArborText//ELEMENTS Basic Report Module//EN">
%reportmod;

<!-- .................. new information pool elements .................. -->

<!ELEMENT citation       - - (%bib.model;)>
<!--(citation contents defined in report module, with bib-entry)-->

<!ELEMENT list           - - (%list.model;)>
<!ATTLIST list
        id             ID              #IMPLIED
>
<!ELEMENT xref           - o EMPTY>
<!ATTLIST xref
        xrefid         IDREF           #REQUIRED
>
<!-- .................. end of report DTD ............................. -->
```

## C.2.2   Hierarchy and Metainformation Modules

The document hierarchy modules for the three DTDs are relatively simple. They define only the high-level structures that make each document type unique, and leave the actual contents to the metainformation and information pool modules.

The memo hierarchy module is shown in Example C-7. Notice that it defines its own unique element collection, %memobody.mix;, by using element class entities defined in the information pool.

**Example C-7**    Memo Hierarchy Module.

```
<!-- ................... memo hierarchy module .......................... -->

<!-- ................... memo mixtures ................................ -->

<!--building blocks and mixtures are defined in information pool module -->

<!ENTITY % memobody.mix        "%paras;|%displays;|%formals;">

<!-- ................... memo structure ................................ -->

<!-- unmentioned elements are defined in metainfo module -->

<!ELEMENT memo            - - (head, body, end)>

<!ELEMENT head            - - (date, to, from, subject, cc?,
                              (enclosure|attachment)?)>
<!ELEMENT body            - - (%memobody.mix;)*>

<!ELEMENT end             - - (initials?, (enclosure|attachment)?, cc?)>

<!-- ................... memo metainformation .......................... -->

<!-- content model and other elements are defined in metainfo module -->
<!ELEMENT cc              - - (%contact.model;)*>

<!ELEMENT from            - - (%contact.model;)*>

<!ELEMENT to              - - (%contact.model;)*>

<!-- ................... end of memo hierarchy module ................... -->
```

The letter hierarchy module is shown in Example C-8. It is somewhat similar to the memo hierarchy. Notice how it uses the %contact.model; parameter entity to define slightly different content models for the cc, from, and to elements compared to the definitions in the memo module; the fact that their models are different explains why these elements aren't defined in the metainformation module. Instead, the common part of the model is in a parameter entity, which the memo and letter hierarchy modules can choose to use in defining their own versions of these elements. If letters and memos could appear in the same document (which they currently cannot), the different content models would conflict.

**Example C-8**   Letter Hierarchy Module.

```
<!-- .................... letter hierarchy module ........................ -->

<!-- .................... letter mixtures ................................ -->

<!-- building blocks and mixtures are defined in information pool module -->

<!ENTITY % letterbody.mix      "%paras;|%displays;|%formals;">

<!-- .................... letter structure ............................... -->

<!-- unmentioned elements are defined in metainfo module -->

<!ELEMENT letter          - - (head, ltrbody, end)>

<!ELEMENT head            - - (date, from?, to?, subject?, salutation?)>

<!ELEMENT ltrbody         - - (%letterbody.mix;)*>

<!ELEMENT end             - - (closing?, sender, jobtitle?, initials?,
                               (enclosure|attachment)?, cc?, postscript?)>

<!-- .................... letter metainformation ......................... -->

<!-- content model and other elements are defined in metainfo module -->
<!ELEMENT cc              - - (%contact.model;)>

<!ELEMENT from            - - (%contact.model;)>

<!ELEMENT to              - - (%contact.model;)>

<!-- .................... end of letter hierarchy module ................. -->
```

The report hierarchy module is shown in Example C-9. It mentions the `letter` element, which is why the letter hierarchy module must be included in the report DTD.

**Example C-9**   Report Hierarchy Module.

```
<!-- ................. report hierarchy module ....
................... -->

<!-- ................. report mixtures ............................... -->

<!-- building blocks and mixtures are defined in information pool module -->

<!ENTITY % reportbody.mix    "%paras;|%displays;|%formals;|%tables;">

<!-- ................. report structure ............................. -->

<!-- other elements are defined in information pool/metainfo modules -->

<!ELEMENT report           - - (letter?, front, body, rear)>
<!--     letter               (defined in letter DTD)-->


<!-- ................. front matter -->

<!ELEMENT front            - - (title-info, author-info, contents?)>
<!ELEMENT title-info       - - (title, subtitle?, version?, revision?, date)>
<!ELEMENT (subtitle,
          version,
          revision)        - - (%simple.data.mix;)*>
<!ELEMENT author-info      - - (author, authloc?)+>
<!ELEMENT (author,
          authloc)         - - (%simple.data.mix;)*>
<!ELEMENT contents         - o EMPTY>


<!-- ................. report body -->

<!ELEMENT body             - - (section*)>
<!ELEMENT section          - - (title, (%reportbody.mix;)*, topic*)>
<!ATTLIST section
       id          ID           #IMPLIED
>
<!ELEMENT topic            - - (title, (%reportbody.mix;)*, subtop*)>
<!ATTLIST topic
       id          ID           #IMPLIED
>
<!ELEMENT subtop           - - (title, (%reportbody.mix;)*)>
<!ATTLIST subtop
       id          ID           #IMPLIED
>
```

**Example C-9**   Report Hierarchy Module.  (Continued)

```
<!-- .................. rear matter -->

<!ELEMENT rear              - - (appendix*, bibliography?, glossary?)>

<!ELEMENT appendix          - - (title, (%reportbody.mix;)*)>
<!ATTLIST appendix
        id             ID              #IMPLIED
>
<!ELEMENT glossary          - - (title, (para|definition-list)+)>

<!ELEMENT bibliography      - - (title, bib-entry+)>
<!ELEMENT bib-entry         - - (%bib.model;)>

<!ELEMENT (publisher,
          page)             - - (%simple.data.mix;)*>

<!-- .................. end of report hierarchy module ................ -->
```

The memo and letter hierarchy modules have a great deal of metainformation in common, and this metainformation could be said to help define them as document types, suggesting that perhaps the metainformation "belongs" in the hierarchy modules. The reason why these elements are in a separate module is that they are shared between the two DTDs; referencing them helps to maintain them more consistently.

The metainformation module is shown in Example C-10. Notice that, for convenience of lookup, the elements are simply alphabetized, since their usage in any one document hierarchy might be in a different order from their usage in any other. Notice also that, because the content models use an element collection that is set up in the information pool (`%simple.data.mix;`), the information pool module must be referenced before the metainformation module.

**Example C-10**  Memo and Letter Metainformation Module.

```
<!-- .................. memo/letter metainformation .................... -->

<!-- .................. content models .................................. -->

<!ENTITY % contact.model    "name, jobtitle?, organization?,
                            address*, city?, state?, zip?, phone?,
                            fax?">

<!-- .................. elements ........................................ -->
```

**Example C-10**  Memo and Letter Metainformation Module.  (Continued)

```
<!-- mixtures are defined in information pool module -->

<!ELEMENT address        - - (%simple.data.mix;)*>
<!ELEMENT attachment     - - (%simple.data.mix;)*>
<!ELEMENT city           - - (%simple.data.mix;)*>
<!ELEMENT closing        - - (%simple.data.mix;)*>
<!ELEMENT date           - - (%simple.data.mix;)*>
<!ELEMENT enclosure      - - (%simple.data.mix;)*>
<!ELEMENT fax            - - (%simple.data.mix;)*>
<!ELEMENT initials       - - (%simple.data.mix;)*>
<!ELEMENT jobtitle       - - (%simple.data.mix;)*>
<!ELEMENT name           - - (%simple.data.mix;)*>
<!ELEMENT organization   - - (%simple.data.mix;)*>
<!ELEMENT phone          - - (%simple.data.mix;)*>
<!ELEMENT postscript     - - (%simple.data.mix;)*>
<!ELEMENT salutation     - - (%simple.data.mix;)*>
<!ELEMENT sender         - - (%simple.data.mix;)*>
<!ELEMENT state          - - (%simple.data.mix;)*>
<!ELEMENT subject        - - (%simple.data.mix;)*>
<!ELEMENT zip            - - (%simple.data.mix;)*>

<!-- .................. end of memo/letter metainformation .............. -->
```

## C.2.3    Information Pool Module

The information pool is used in uncustomized form for memos and letters. It is extended only for use in reports (as Example C-6 shows). All the lower-level element class and collection entities are set up in the information pool module, as well as a parameter entity for the content model of lists that was found to be useful for an extension element in reports. Table C-1 and Table C-2 show summaries of the element classes and collections.

**Table C-1**      Information Unit Classes and Collections.

| Contexts / Contents | table | body | item | para | figure |
|---|---|---|---|---|---|
| Paragraphs: <br><br> para | | X | | | |
| Lists: <br><br> bulleted-list <br><br> definition-list <br><br> sequential-list | | | X | X | |
| Blocks: <br><br> computer <br><br> extract <br><br> asis | | | | X | |
| Displays: <br><br> graphic <br><br> display-equation | X | X | | x | X |
| Tables: <br><br> table | | X | | X | X |
| Formals: <br><br> figure | | X | | | |

**Table C-2**     Data-Level Classes and Collections.

| Contexts / Contents | para | simple | computer | normal |
|---|---|---|---|---|
| #PCDATA | X | X | X | X |
| Emphasized Text: super sub emphasis | X | X | | X |
| Inline Figures: inline-graphic inline-equation | X | | | |
| Annotations: footnote | X | | X | X |

| | title | table | footnote | |
|---|---|---|---|---|
| #PCDATA | X | X | X | |
| Emphasized Text: super sub emphasis | X | X | X | |
| Inline Figures: inline-graphic inline-equation | | | | |
| Annotations: footnote | X | X | | |

The information pool module is shown in Example C-11. Notice that between the entity declarations for classes and collections, an inactive "redefinition" entity definition and reference appears. This entity is a placeholder for a file containing any entity declarations that must use existing element classes in overriding the existing element collections. (If the %local.xxx.mix; entities had not been provided on the element collection entities, the redefinition placeholder would have had to be used in order to add the xref element that appears in reports.)

**Example C-11**  Information Pool Module.

```
<!-- ................. information pool ............................... -->

<!-- ................. common entities ............................. -->

<!-- ................. classes for information units -->

<!ENTITY % local.paras          "">
<!ENTITY % paras                "para %local.paras;">

<!ENTITY % local.blocks         "">
<!ENTITY % blocks               "computer|extract|asis %local.blocks;">
<!ENTITY % local.lists          "">

<!ENTITY % lists                "bulleted-list|definition-list|sequential-list
                                %local.lists;">
<!ENTITY % local.displays       "">
<!ENTITY % displays             "graphic|display-equation %local.displays;">

<!ENTITY % local.tables         "">
<!ENTITY % tables               "table %local.tables;">

<!ENTITY % local.formals        "">
<!ENTITY % formals              "figure %local.formals;">

<!--(annots is also used in data mixtures)-->
<!ENTITY % local.annots         "">
<!ENTITY % annots               "footnote %local.annots;">

<!-- ................. classes for data-level elements -->

<!ENTITY % local.emphs            "">
<!ENTITY % emphs                "super|sub|emphasis %local.emphs;">

<!ENTITY % local.inlinefigs     "">
<!ENTITY % inlinefigs           "inline-graphic|inline-equation
                                %local.inlinefigs;">
```

**Example C-11**   Information Pool Module. (Continued)

```
<!-- .................. redefinition module -->

<![ %redefine; [
<!ENTITY % redefmod PUBLIC "-//ArborText//ENTITIES Entity Redefinitions//EN">
%redefmod;
]]>


<!-- .................. collections for information unit contexts -->

<!-- names with "iu." in them also have "data." counterparts -->

<!ENTITY % local.item.mix      "">
<!ENTITY % item.mix            "%lists; %local.item.mix;">

<!ENTITY % local.para.iu.mix   "">
<!ENTITY % para.iu.mix         "%blocks;|%lists;|%tables;|graphic
                                %local.para.iu.mix;">

<!ENTITY % local.figure.mix    "">
<!ENTITY % figure.mix          "%displays;|%tables; %local.figure.mix;">

<!ENTITY % local.table.iu.mix  "">
<!ENTITY % table.iu.mix        "%displays; %local.table.iu.mix;">

<!-- .................. collections for data-level contexts -->

<!ENTITY % local.ftnt.data.mix "">
<!ENTITY % ftnt.data.mix       "#PCDATA|%emphs; %local.ftnt.data.mix;">

<!ENTITY % local.simple.data.mix "">
<!ENTITY % simple.data.mix     "#PCDATA|%emphs; %local.simple.data.mix;">

<!ENTITY % local.computer.data.mix "">
<!ENTITY % computer.data.mix   "#PCDATA                   |%annots;
                                %local.computer.data.mix;">

<!ENTITY % local.normal.data.mix "">
<!ENTITY % normal.data.mix     "#PCDATA|%emphs;           |%annots;
                                %local.normal.data.mix;">

<!ENTITY % local.title.data.mix "">
<!ENTITY % title.data.mix      "#PCDATA|%emphs;           |%annots;
                                %local.title.data.mix;">
```

**Example C-11**  Information Pool Module.  (Continued)

```
<!ENTITY % local.table.data.mix "">
<!ENTITY % table.data.mix      "#PCDATA|%emphs;              |%annots;
                                %local.table.data.mix;">


<!ENTITY % local.para.data.mix "">
<!ENTITY % para.data.mix       "#PCDATA|%emphs;|%inlinefigs;|%annots;
                                %local.para.data.mix;">


<!-- .................. content models -->

<!ENTITY % list.model          "title?, (item+)">

<!-- .................. information unit elements ...................... -->

<!ELEMENT title           - - (%title.data.mix;)*>

<!ELEMENT para            - - (%para.iu.mix;|%para.data.mix;)*>
<!ATTLIST para
        id             ID            #IMPLIED
>
<!ELEMENT computer        - - (%computer.data.mix;)*>

<!ELEMENT extract         - - (%normal.data.mix;)*>

<!ELEMENT asis            - - (%normal.data.mix;)*>

<!ELEMENT (bulleted-list,
          sequential-list)
                          - - (%list.model;)>
<!ELEMENT item            - - (%item.mix;|%normal.data.mix;)*>

<!ELEMENT definition-list - - (title?, (term, def)+)>
<!ELEMENT term            - - (%title.data.mix;)*>
<!ELEMENT def             - - (%normal.data.mix;)*>

<!ELEMENT (graphic,
          inline-graphic) - o EMPTY>
<!ATTLIST (graphic,
          inline-graphic)
        filename      CDATA         #REQUIRED
        processor     CDATA         #REQUIRED
        magnification NUMBER        #IMPLIED
        horzoffsetamt CDATA         #IMPLIED
        horzoffsetpct CDATA         #IMPLIED
        vertoffsetamt CDATA         #IMPLIED
```

---

**Example C-11**   Information Pool Module.  (Continued)

---

```
              vertoffsetpct    CDATA            #IMPLIED
              cropheight       CDATA            #IMPLIED
              cropwidth        CDATA            #IMPLIED
              cropllxcoord     CDATA            #IMPLIED
              cropllycoord     CDATA            #IMPLIED
              scalefit         NUMBER           #IMPLIED
              scalefitheight   CDATA            #IMPLIED
              scalefitwidth    CDATA            #IMPLIED
>
<!--ELEMENT table             (declared in ATI table module, below)-->
<!--(tblcon is required to be defined by ATI table module)-->
<!ENTITY % tblcon            "%table.iu.mix;|%table.data.mix;">

<!ELEMENT display-equation - - (fd)>
<!ATTLIST display-equation
        align              (left
                           |center
                           |right)          #IMPLIED
>


<!--     fd                   (defined in ATI math module)-->

<!--(note that only one element is allowed as figure main content)-->
<!ELEMENT figure          - - (title, (%figure.mix;))>
<!ATTLIST figure
        id                 ID               #IMPLIED
>
<!ELEMENT footnote        - - (commentary)>
<!ELEMENT commentary      - - (%ftnt.data.mix;)*>

<!-- ................... data-level elements ........................... -->

<!ELEMENT super           - - (%normal.data.mix;)* -(super)>

<!ELEMENT sub             - - (%normal.data.mix;)* -(sub)>

<!ELEMENT emphasis        - - (%normal.data.mix;)* -(emphasis)>

<!--ELEMENT inline-graphic     (defined with graphic above)-->

<!ELEMENT inline-equation - - (f)>
<!--ELEMENT f                  (defined in ATI math module)-->

<!-- ................. standard DTD fragments ......................... -->
```

**Example C-11**  Information Pool Module.  (Continued)

```
<!-- these are here to catch any parameter entities defined above -->
<!ENTITY % table PUBLIC "-//ArborText//ELEMENTS Table Structures//EN">
%table;

<!ENTITY % math PUBLIC "-//ArborText//ELEMENTS Math Equation Structures//EN">
%math;

<!-- ................... end of information pool ....................... -->
```

## C.2.4   Markup Model Changes Made

This modularization and parameterization process required a few changes to the markup model:

- Footnotes in reports and the other two document types originally had different definitions. In order to make the original `footnote` element in reports consistent across all three, a `commentary` child element must now be supplied. A new child element in footnotes, `citation`, has been added to the content model of footnotes in reports to contain bibliographic citation information.

- The `body` element in letters conflicted with the element of the same name in reports, so it has been renamed `ltrbody`.

These are both backwards-incompatible changes, but they are relatively minor, and legacy documents can easily be transformed to conform to the new DTD if necessary.

# ISO Character Entity Sets

Table D-1 summarizes the available ISO entity sets. The most commonly needed sets for publishing are ISOlat1, ISOnum, ISOpub, and ISOdia.

**Table D-1**    ISO Entity Sets.

| Short Name | Full Name and Description |
|---|---|
| ISOamsa | Added Math Symbols: Arrow Relations |
| | For example, this set includes unusual arrows. (ISOnum contains simple arrows in the four directions.) |
| ISOamsb | Added Math Symbols: Binary Operators |
| ISOamsc | Added Math Symbols: Delimiters |
| ISOamsn | Added Math Symbols: Negated Relations |
| ISOamso | Added Math Symbols: Ordinary |
| ISOamsr | Added Math Symbols: Relations |
| ISObox | Box and Line Drawing |
| ISOcyr1 | Russian Cyrillic characters |
| ISOcyr2 | Non-Russian Cyrillic characters |
| ISOdia | Diacritical Marks |
| | The marks represent stand-alone characters, such as an acute accent without a character under it. |
| ISOgrk1 | Greek Letters |
| ISOgrk2 | Monotoniko Greek |

**Table D-1**   ISO Entity Sets. (Continued)

| Short Name | Full Name and Description |
|---|---|
| ISOgrk3 | Greek Symbols<br>These symbols are often used in technical publishing. |
| ISOgrk4 | Alternative Greek Symbols<br>These are emphasized versions of the symbols in ISOgrk3. |
| ISOlat1 | Added Latin 1<br>These are characters for Western European languages. For example, this set includes common letters with acute, grave, and tilde accents. |
| ISOlat2 | Added Latin 2<br>These are characters for additional languages. For example, this set includes additional letters with acute accents, letters with macron accents, and ligatures. |
| ISOnum | Numeric and Special Graphic<br>For example, this set includes some fraction symbols, currency symbols, simple arrows, and mathematical relationship symbols, including the less-than (<) and ampersand (&) that are needed for escaping SGML-significant characters. |
| ISOpub | Publishing<br>For example, this set includes fraction symbols not in ISOnum, symbols for footnotes, and various widths of spaces (such as em space). |
| ISOtech | General Technical<br>This set includes technical and scientific symbols. |

Table D-2 shows and describes each ISO character and symbol, sorted by its entity name, and indicates the entity set in which that symbol can be found. Section 8.7.2 explains how to use them.

| Symbol | Name | Set | Description |
|--------|------|-----|-------------|
| Ά | Aacgr | ISOgrk2 | =capital Alpha, accent, Greek |
| ά | aacgr | ISOgrk2 | =small alpha, accent, Greek |
| Á | Aacute | ISOlat1 | =capital A, acute accent |
| á | aacute | ISOlat1 | =small a, acute accent |
| Ă | Abreve | ISOlat2 | =capital A, breve |
| ă | abreve | ISOlat2 | =small a, breve |
| Â | Acirc | ISOlat1 | =capital A, circumflex accent |
| â | acirc | ISOlat1 | =small a, circumflex accent |
| ´ | acute | ISOdia | =acute accent |
| А | Acy | ISOcyr1 | =capital A, Cyrillic |
| а | acy | ISOcyr1 | =small a, Cyrillic |
| Æ | AElig | ISOlat1 | =capital AE diphthong (ligature) |
| æ | aelig | ISOlat1 | =small ae diphthong (ligature) |
| Α | Agr | ISOgrk1 | =capital Alpha, Greek |
| α | agr | ISOgrk1 | =small alpha, Greek |
| À | Agrave | ISOlat1 | =capital A, grave accent |
| à | agrave | ISOlat1 | =small a, grave accent |
| ℵ | aleph | ISOtech | /aleph =aleph, Hebrew |
| α | alpha | ISOgrk3 | =small alpha, Greek |
| Ā | Amacr | ISOlat2 | =capital A, macron |
| ā | amacr | ISOlat2 | =small a, macron |
| ∐ | amalg | ISOamsb | /amalg B: amalgamation or coproduct |
| & | amp | ISOnum | =ampersand |
| ∧ | and | ISOtech | /wedge /land B: =logical and |
| ∠ | ang | ISOamso | /angle - angle |
| ∟ | ang90 | ISOtech | =right (90 degree) angle |
| ∡ | angmsd | ISOamso | /measuredangle - angle-measured |
| ⊾ | angsph | ISOtech | /sphericalangle =angle-spherical |
| Å | angst | ISOtech | Angstrom =capital A, ring |
| Ą | Aogon | ISOlat2 | =capital A, ogonek |
| ą | aogon | ISOlat2 | =small a, ogonek |
| ≈ | ap | ISOtech | /approx R: =approximate |

| Symbol | Name | Set | Description |
|---|---|---|---|
| ≅ | ape | ISOamsr | /approxeq R: approximate, equals |
| ' | apos | ISOnum | =apostrophe |
| Å | Aring | ISOlat1 | =capital A, ring |
| å | aring | ISOlat1 | =small a, ring |
| * | ast | ISOnum | /ast B: =asterisk |
| ≍ | asymp | ISOamsr | /asymp R: asymptotically equal to |
| Ã | Atilde | ISOlat1 | =capital A, tilde |
| ã | atilde | ISOlat1 | =small a, tilde |
| Ä | Auml | ISOlat1 | =capital A, dieresis or umlaut mark |
| ä | auml | ISOlat1 | =small a, dieresis or umlaut mark |
| $\alpha$ | b.alpha | ISOgrk4 | =small alpha, Greek |
| $\beta$ | b.beta | ISOgrk4 | =small beta, Greek |
| $\chi$ | b.chi | ISOgrk4 | =small chi, Greek |
| $\Delta$ | b.Delta | ISOgrk4 | =capital Delta, Greek |
| $\delta$ | b.delta | ISOgrk4 | =small delta, Greek |
| $\epsilon$ | b.epsi | ISOgrk4 | =small epsilon, Greek |
| $\epsilon$ | b.epsis | ISOgrk4 | /straightepsilon |
| $\varepsilon$ | b.epsiv | ISOgrk4 | /varepsilon |
| $\eta$ | b.eta | ISOgrk4 | =small eta, Greek |
| $\Gamma$ | b.Gamma | ISOgrk4 | =capital Gamma, Greek |
| $\gamma$ | b.gamma | ISOgrk4 | =small gamma, Greek |
| Ϝ | b.gammad | ISOgrk4 | /digamma |
| $\iota$ | b.iota | ISOgrk4 | =small iota, Greek |
| $\kappa$ | b.kappa | ISOgrk4 | =small kappa, Greek |
| $\varkappa$ | b.kappav | ISOgrk4 | /varkappa |
| $\Lambda$ | b.Lambda | ISOgrk4 | =capital Lambda, Greek |
| $\lambda$ | b.lambda | ISOgrk4 | =small lambda, Greek |
| $\mu$ | b.mu | ISOgrk4 | =small mu, Greek |
| $\nu$ | b.nu | ISOgrk4 | =small nu, Greek |
| $\Omega$ | b.Omega | ISOgrk4 | =capital Omega, Greek |
| $\omega$ | b.omega | ISOgrk4 | =small omega, Greek |
| $\Phi$ | b.Phi | ISOgrk4 | =capital Phi, Greek |

| Symbol | Name | Set | Description |
|---|---|---|---|
| $\phi$ | b.phis | ISOgrk4 | /straightphi - straight phi |
| $\varphi$ | b.phiv | ISOgrk4 | /varphi - curly or open phi |
| $\Pi$ | b.Pi | ISOgrk4 | =capital Pi, Greek |
| $\pi$ | b.pi | ISOgrk4 | =small pi, Greek |
| $\varpi$ | b.piv | ISOgrk4 | /varpi |
| $\Psi$ | b.Psi | ISOgrk4 | =capital Psi, Greek |
| $\psi$ | b.psi | ISOgrk4 | =small psi, Greek |
| $\rho$ | b.rho | ISOgrk4 | =small rho, Greek |
| $\varrho$ | .b.rhov | ISOgrk4 | /varrho |
| $\Sigma$ | b.Sigma | ISOgrk4 | =capital Sigma, Greek |
| $\sigma$ | b.sigma | ISOgrk4 | =small sigma, Greek |
| $\varsigma$ | b.sigmav | ISOgrk4 | /varsigma |
| $\tau$ | b.tau | ISOgrk4 | =small tau, Greek |
| $\Theta$ | b.Theta | ISOgrk4 | =capital Theta, Greek |
| $\theta$ | b.thetas | ISOgrk4 | straight theta |
| $\vartheta$ | b.thetav | ISOgrk4 | /vartheta - curly or open theta |
| $\Upsilon$ | b.Upsi | ISOgrk4 | =capital Upsilon, Greek |
| $\upsilon$ | b.upsi | ISOgrk4 | =small upsilon, Greek |
| $\Xi$ | b.Xi | ISOgrk4 | =capital Xi, Greek |
| $\xi$ | b.xi | ISOgrk4 | =small xi, Greek |
| $\zeta$ | b.zeta | ISOgrk4 | =small zeta, Greek |
| $\overline{\overline{\wedge}}$ | Barwed | ISOamsb | /doublebarwedge B: log and, dbl bar |
| $\overline{\wedge}$ | barwed | ISOamsb | /barwedge B: logical and, bar above |
| $\backcong$ | bcong | ISOamsr | /backcong R: reverse congruent |
| Б | Bcy | ISOcyr1 | =capital BE, Cyrillic |
| б | bcy | ISOcyr1 | =small be, Cyrillic |
| $\because$ | becaus | ISOtech | /because R: =because |
| $\backepsilon$ | bepsi | ISOamsr | /backepsilon R: such that |
| $\mathcal{B}$ | bernou | ISOtech | Bernoulli function (script capital B) |
| $\beta$ | beta | ISOgrk3 | =small beta, Greek |
| $\beth$ | beth | ISOamso | /beth - beth, Hebrew |
| B | Bgr | ISOgrk1 | =capital Beta, Greek |

| Symbol | Name | Set | Description |
|--------|------|-----|-------------|
| β | bgr | ISOgrk1 | =small beta, Greek |
| ␣ | blank | ISOpub | =significant blank symbol |
| ▓ | blk12 | ISOpub | =50% shaded block |
| ░ | blk14 | ISOpub | =25% shaded block |
| ▓ | blk34 | ISOpub | =75% shaded block |
| ■ | block | ISOpub | =full block |
| ⊥ | bottom | ISOtech | /bot B: =perpendicular |
| ⋈ | bowtie | ISOamsr | /bowtie R: |
| ╗ | boxDL | ISObox | lower left quadrant |
| ╖ | boxDl | ISObox | lower left quadrant |
| ╕ | boxdL | ISObox | lower left quadrant |
| ┐ | boxdl | ISObox | lower left quadrant |
| ╔ | boxDR | ISObox | lower right quadrant |
| ╓ | boxDr | ISObox | lower right quadrant |
| ╒ | boxdR | ISObox | lower right quadrant |
| ┌ | boxdr | ISObox | lower right quadrant |
| ═ | boxH | ISObox | horizontal line |
| ─ | boxh | ISObox | horizontal line |
| ╦ | boxHD | ISObox | lower left and right quadrants |
| ╤ | boxHd | ISObox | lower left and right quadrants |
| ╥ | boxhD | ISObox | lower left and right quadrants |
| ┬ | boxhd | ISObox | lower left and right quadrants |
| ╩ | boxHU | ISObox | upper left and right quadrants |
| ╧ | boxHu | ISObox | upper left and right quadrants |
| ╨ | boxhU | ISObox | upper left and right quadrants |
| ┴ | boxhu | ISObox | upper left and right quadrants |
| ╝ | boxUL | ISObox | upper left quadrant |
| ╜ | boxUl | ISObox | upper left quadrant |
| ╛ | boxuL | ISObox | upper left quadrant |
| ┘ | boxul | ISObox | upper left quadrant |
| ╚ | boxUR | ISObox | upper right quadrant |

| Symbol | Name | Set | Description |
|--------|------|-----|-------------|
| ⌐ | boxUr | ISObox | upper right quadrant |
| ╘ | boxuR | ISObox | upper right quadrant |
| └ | boxur | ISObox | upper right quadrant |
| ‖ | boxV | ISObox | vertical line |
| │ | boxv | ISObox | vertical line |
| ╪ | boxVH | ISObox | all four quadrants |
| ╫ | boxVh | ISObox | all four quadrants |
| ╤ | boxvH | ISObox | all four quadrants |
| ┼ | boxvh | ISObox | all four quadrants |
| ╡ | boxVL | ISObox | upper and lower left quadrants |
| ╢ | boxVl | ISObox | upper and lower left quadrants |
| ╕ | boxvL | ISObox | upper and lower left quadrants |
| ┤ | boxvl | ISObox | upper and lower left quadrants |
| ╟ | boxVR | ISObox | upper and lower right quadrants |
| ╟ | boxVr | ISObox | upper and lower right quadrants |
| ╞ | boxvR | ISObox | upper and lower right quadrants |
| ├ | boxvr | ISObox | upper and lower right quadrants |
| ` | bprime | ISOamso | /backprime - reverse prime |
| ˘ | breve | ISOdia | =breve |
| ¦ | brvbar | ISOnum | =broken (vertical) bar |
| ∽ | bsim | ISOamsr | /backsim R: reverse similar |
| ⋍ | bsime | ISOamsr | /backsimeq R: reverse similar, eq |
| \ | bsol | ISOnum | /backslash =reverse solidus |
| • | bull | ISOpub | /bullet B: =round bullet, filled |
| ≎ | bump | ISOamsr | /Bumpeq R: bumpy equals |
| ≏ | bumpe | ISOamsr | /bumpeq R: bumpy equals, equals |
| Ć | Cacute | ISOlat2 | =capital C, acute accent |
| ć | cacute | ISOlat2 | =small c, acute accent |
| ⋒ | Cap | ISOamsb | /Cap /doublecap B: dbl intersection |
| ∩ | cap | ISOtech | /cap B: =intersection |
| ^ | caret | ISOpub | =caret (insertion mark) |
| ˇ | caron | ISOdia | =caron |

| Symbol | Name | Set | Description |
|---|---|---|---|
| Č | Ccaron | ISOlat2 | =capital C, caron |
| č | ccaron | ISOlat2 | =small c, caron |
| Ç | Ccedil | ISOlat1 | =capital C, cedilla |
| ç | ccedil | ISOlat1 | =small c, cedilla |
| Ĉ | Ccirc | ISOlat2 | =capital C, circumflex accent |
| ĉ | ccirc | ISOlat2 | =small c, circumflex accent |
| Ċ | Cdot | ISOlat2 | =capital C, dot above |
| ċ | cdot | ISOlat2 | =small c, dot above |
| ¸ | cedil | ISOdia | =cedilla |
| ¢ | cent | ISOnum | =cent sign |
| Ч | CHcy | ISOcyr1 | =capital CHE, Cyrillic |
| ч | chcy | ISOcyr1 | =small che, Cyrillic |
| ✓ | check | ISOpub | /checkmark =tick, check mark |
| χ | chi | ISOgrk3 | =small chi, Greek |
| ◯ | cir | ISOpub | /circ B: =circle, open |
| ˆ | circ | ISOdia | =circumflex accent |
| ≗ | cire | ISOamsr | /circeq R: circle, equals |
| ♣ | clubs | ISOpub | /clubsuit =club suit symbol |
| : | colon | ISOnum | /colon P: |
| ≔ | colone | ISOamsr | /coloneq R: colon, equals |
| , | comma | ISOnum | P: =comma |
| @ | commat | ISOnum | =commercial at |
| ∁ | comp | ISOamso | /complement - complement sign |
| ∘ | compfn | ISOtech | B: composite function (small circle) |
| ≅ | cong | ISOtech | /cong R: =congruent with |
| ∮ | conint | ISOtech | /oint L: =contour integral operator |
| ∏ | coprod | ISOamsb | /coprod L: coproduct operator |
| © | copy | ISOnum | =copyright sign |
| ℗ | copysr | ISOpub | =sound recording copyright sign |
| ✗ | cross | ISOpub | =ballot cross |
| ⋞ | cuepr | ISOamsr | /curlyeqprec R: curly eq, precedes |
| ⋟ | cuesc | ISOamsr | /curlyeqsucc R: curly eq, succeeds |

| Symbol | Name | Set | Description |
|--------|------|-----|-------------|
| ↶ | cularr | ISOamsa | /curvearrowleft A: left curved arrow |
| ⊎ | Cup | ISOamsb | /Cup /doublecup B: dbl union |
| ∪ | cup | ISOtech | /cup B: =union or logical sum |
| ≼ | cupre | ISOamsr | /curlypreceq R: curly precedes, eq |
| ↷ | curarr | ISOamsa | /curvearrowright A: rt curved arrow |
| ¤ | curren | ISOnum | =general currency sign |
| ⋎ | cuvee | ISOamsb | /curlyvee B: curly logical or |
| ⋏ | cuwed | ISOamsb | /curlywedge B: curly logical and |
| † | dagger | ISOpub | /dagger B: =dagger |
| ‡ | Dagger | ISOpub | /ddagger B: =double dagger |
| ℸ | daleth | ISOamso | /daleth - daleth, Hebrew |
| ⇓ | dArr | ISOamsa | /Downarrow A: down dbl arrow |
| ↓ | darr | ISOnum | /downarrow A: =downward arrow |
| ⇊ | darr2 | ISOamsa | /downdownarrows A: two down arrows |
| - | dash | ISOpub | =hyphen (true graphic) |
| ⊣ | dashv | ISOamsr | /dashv R: dash, vertical |
| ˝ | dblac | ISOdia | =double acute accent |
| Ď | Dcaron | ISOlat2 | =capital D, caron |
| ď | dcaron | ISOlat2 | =small d, caron |
| Д | Dcy | ISOcyr1 | =capital DE, Cyrillic |
| д | dcy | ISOcyr1 | =small de, Cyrillic |
| ° | deg | ISOnum | =degree sign |
| Δ | Delta | ISOgrk3 | =capital Delta, Greek |
| δ | delta | ISOgrk3 | =small delta, Greek |
| Δ | Dgr | ISOgrk1 | =capital Delta, Greek |
| δ | dgr | ISOgrk1 | =small delta, Greek |
| ⇃ | dharl | ISOamsa | /downleftharpoon A: dn harpoon-left |
| ⇂ | dharr | ISOamsa | /downrightharpoon A: down harpoon-rt |
| ◊ | diam | ISOamsb | /diamond B: open diamond |
| ♦ | diams | ISOpub | /diamondsuit =diamond suit symbol |
| ¨ | die | ISOdia | =dieresis |
| ÷ | divide | ISOnum | /div B: =divide sign |

| Symbol | Name | Set | Description |
|--------|------|-----|-------------|
| ✳ | divonx | ISOamsb | /divideontimes B: division on times |
| Ђ | DJcy | ISOcyr2 | =capital DJE, Serbian |
| ђ | djcy | ISOcyr2 | =small dje, Serbian |
| ↙ | dlarr | ISOamsa | /swarrow A: downward l arrow |
| ∟ | dlcorn | ISOamsc | /llcorner O: downward left corner |
| ⌐| | dlcrop | ISOpub | downward left crop mark |
| $ | dollar | ISOnum | =dollar sign |
| ¨ | Dot | ISOtech | =dieresis or umlaut mark |
| · | dot | ISOdia | =dot above |
| ⋯ | DotDot | ISOtech | four dots above |
| ↘ | drarr | ISOamsa | /searrow A: downward rt arrow |
| ⌐ | drcorn | ISOamsc | /lrcorner C: downward right corner |
| ⌐ | drcrop | ISOpub | downward right crop mark |
| S | DScy | ISOcyr2 | =capital DSE, Macedonian |
| s | dscy | ISOcyr2 | =small dse, Macedonian |
| Đ | Dstrok | ISOlat2 | =capital D, stroke |
| đ | dstrok | ISOlat2 | =small d, stroke |
| ▽ | dtri | ISOpub | /triangledown =down triangle, open |
| ▼ | dtrif | ISOpub | /blacktriangledown =dn tri, filled |
| Џ | DZcy | ISOcyr2 | =capital dze, Serbian |
| џ | dzcy | ISOcyr2 | =small dze, Serbian |
| Έ | Eacgr | ISOgrk2 | =capital Epsilon, accent, Greek |
| έ | eacgr | ISOgrk2 | =small epsilon, accent, Greek |
| É | Eacute | ISOlat1 | =capital E, acute accent |
| é | eacute | ISOlat1 | =small e, acute accent |
| Ě | Ecaron | ISOlat2 | =capital E, caron |
| ě | ecaron | ISOlat2 | =small e, caron |
| ⊜ | ecir | ISOamsr | /eqcirc R: circle on equals sign |
| Ê | Ecirc | ISOlat1 | =capital E, circumflex accent |
| ê | ecirc | ISOlat1 | =small e, circumflex accent |
| ≕ | ecolon | ISOamsr | /eqcolon R: equals, colon |
| Э | Ecy | ISOcyr1 | =capital E, Cyrillic |

| Symbol | Name | Set | Description |
|---|---|---|---|
| э | ecy | ISOcyr1 | =small e, Cyrillic |
| Ė | Edot | ISOlat2 | =capital E, dot above |
| ≐ | eDot | ISOamsr | /doteqdot /Doteq R: eq, even dots |
| ė | edot | ISOlat2 | =small e, dot above |
| Ή | EEacgr | ISOgrk2 | =capital Eta, accent, Greek |
| ή | eeacgr | ISOgrk2 | =small eta, accent, Greek |
| Η | EEgr | ISOgrk1 | =capital Eta, Greek |
| η | eegr | ISOgrk1 | =small eta, Greek |
| ≒ | efDot | ISOamsr | /fallingdotseq R: eq, falling dots |
| Ε | Egr | ISOgrk1 | =capital Epsilon, Greek |
| ε | egr | ISOgrk1 | =small epsilon, Greek |
| È | Egrave | ISOlat1 | =capital E, grave accent |
| è | egrave | ISOlat1 | =small e, grave accent |
| ⩾ | egs | ISOamsr | /eqslantgtr R: equal-or-gtr, slanted |
| ℓ | ell | ISOamso | /ell - cursive small l |
| ⩽ | els | ISOamsr | /eqslantless R: eq-or-less, slanted |
| Ē | Emacr | ISOlat2 | =capital E, macron |
| ē | emacr | ISOlat2 | =small e, macron |
| ∅ | empty | ISOamso | /emptyset /varnothing =small o, slash |
|  | emsp | ISOpub | =em space |
|  | emsp13 | ISOpub | =1/3-em space |
|  | emsp14 | ISOpub | =1/4-em space |
| Ŋ | ENG | ISOlat2 | =capital ENG, Lapp |
| ŋ | eng | ISOlat2 | =small eng, Lapp |
|  | ensp | ISOpub | =en space (1/2-em) |
| Ę | Eogon | ISOlat2 | =capital E, ogonek |
| ę | eogon | ISOlat2 | =small e, ogonek |
| ϵ | epsi | ISOgrk3 | =small epsilon, Greek |
| ϵ | epsis | ISOgrk3 | /straightepsilon |
| ε | epsiv | ISOgrk3 | /varepsilon |
| = | equals | ISOnum | =equals sign R: |
| ≡ | equiv | ISOtech | /equiv R: =identical with |

| Symbol | Name | Set | Description |
|--------|------|-----|-------------|
| ≓ | erDot | ISOamsr | /risingdotseq R: eq, rising dots |
| ≐ | esdot | ISOamsr | /doteq R: equals, single dot above |
| η | eta | ISOgrk3 | =small eta, Greek |
| Ð | ETH | ISOlat1 | =capital Eth, Icelandic |
| ð | eth | ISOlat1 | =small eth, Icelandic |
| Ë | Euml | ISOlat1 | =capital E, dieresis or umlaut mark |
| ë | euml | ISOlat1 | =small e, dieresis or umlaut mark |
| ! | excl | ISOnum | =exclamation mark |
| ∃ | exist | ISOtech | /exists =at least one exists |
| Ф | Fcy | ISOcyr1 | =capital EF, Cyrillic |
| ф | fcy | ISOcyr1 | =small ef, Cyrillic |
| ♀ | female | ISOpub | =female symbol |
| ﬃ | ffilig | ISOpub | small ffi ligature |
| ﬀ | fflig | ISOpub | small ff ligature |
| ﬄ | ffllig | ISOpub | small ffl ligature |
| ﬁ | filig | ISOpub | small fi ligature |
| fj | fjlig | ISOpub | small fj ligature |
| ♭ | flat | ISOpub | /flat =musical flat |
| ﬂ | fllig | ISOpub | small fl ligature |
| ƒ | fnof | ISOtech | =function of (italic small f) |
| ∀ | forall | ISOtech | /forall =for all |
| ⋔ | fork | ISOamsr | /pitchfork R: pitchfork |
| $\frac{1}{2}$ | frac12 | ISOnum | =fraction one-half |
| $\frac{1}{3}$ | frac13 | ISOpub | =fraction one-third |
| $\frac{1}{4}$ | frac14 | ISOnum | =fraction one-quarter |
| $\frac{1}{5}$ | frac15 | ISOpub | =fraction one-fifth |
| $\frac{1}{6}$ | frac16 | ISOpub | =fraction one-sixth |
| $\frac{1}{8}$ | frac18 | ISOnum | =fraction one-eighth |
| $\frac{2}{3}$ | frac23 | ISOpub | =fraction two-thirds |
| $\frac{2}{5}$ | frac25 | ISOpub | =fraction two-fifths |
| $\frac{3}{4}$ | frac34 | ISOnum | =fraction three-quarters |

| Symbol | Name | Set | Description |
|---|---|---|---|
| $\frac{3}{5}$ | frac35 | ISOpub | =fraction three-fifths |
| $\frac{3}{8}$ | frac38 | ISOnum | =fraction three-eighths |
| $\frac{4}{5}$ | frac45 | ISOpub | =fraction four-fifths |
| $\frac{5}{6}$ | frac56 | ISOpub | =fraction five-sixths |
| $\frac{5}{8}$ | frac58 | ISOnum | =fraction five-eighths |
| $\frac{7}{8}$ | frac78 | ISOnum | =fraction seven-eighths |
| ⌢ | frown | ISOamsr | /frown R: down curve |
| ǵ | gacute | ISOlat2 | =small g, acute accent |
| Γ | Gamma | ISOgrk3 | =capital Gamma, Greek |
| γ | gamma | ISOgrk3 | =small gamma, Greek |
| Ϝ | gammad | ISOgrk3 | /digamma |
| ⪎ | gap | ISOamsr | /gtrapprox R: greater, approximate |
| Ğ | Gbreve | ISOlat2 | =capital G, breve |
| ğ | gbreve | ISOlat2 | =small g, breve |
| Ģ | Gcedil | ISOlat2 | =capital G, cedilla |
| Ĝ | Gcirc | ISOlat2 | =capital G, circumflex accent |
| ĝ | gcirc | ISOlat2 | =small g, circumflex accent |
| Г | Gcy | ISOcyr1 | =capital GHE, Cyrillic |
| г | gcy | ISOcyr1 | =small ghe, Cyrillic |
| Ġ | Gdot | ISOlat2 | =capital G, dot above |
| ġ | gdot | ISOlat2 | =small g, dot above |
| ≧ | gE | ISOamsr | /geqq R: greater, double equals |
| ≥ | ge | ISOtech | /geq /ge R: =greater-than-or-equal |
| ⪌ | gEl | ISOamsr | /gtreqqless R: gt, dbl equals, less |
| ⋛ | gel | ISOamsr | /gtreqless R: greater, equals, less |
| ⩾ | ges | ISOamsr | /geqslant R: gt-or-equal, slanted |
| ⋙ | Gg | ISOamsr | /ggg /Gg /gggtr R: triple gtr-than |
| Γ | Ggr | ISOgrk1 | =capital Gamma, Greek |
| γ | ggr | ISOgrk1 | =small gamma, Greek |
| ג | gimel | ISOamso | /gimel - gimel, Hebrew |
| Ѓ | GJcy | ISOcyr2 | =capital GJE Macedonian |
| ѓ | gjcy | ISOcyr2 | =small gje, Macedonian |

| Symbol | Name | Set | Description |
|---|---|---|---|
| ≷ | gl | ISOamsr | /gtrless R: greater, less |
| ⪊ | gnap | ISOamsn | /gnapprox N: greater, not approximate |
| ⪈ | gnE | ISOamsn | /gneqq N: greater, not dbl equals |
| ⪈ | gne | ISOamsn | /gneq N: greater, not equals |
| ⋩ | gnsim | ISOamsn | /gnsim N: greater, not similar |
| ` | grave | ISOdia | =grave accent |
| ⋗ | gsdot | ISOamsr | /gtrdot R: greater than, single dot |
| ≳ | gsim | ISOamsr | /gtrsim R: greater, similar |
| ≫ | Gt | ISOamsr | /gg R: dbl greater-than sign |
| > | gt | ISOnum | =greater-than sign R: |
| ⪈ | gvnE | ISOamsn | /gvertneqq N: gt, vert, not dbl eq |
|  | hairsp | ISOpub | =hair space |
| $\frac{1}{2}$ | half | ISOnum | =fraction one-half |
| $\mathcal{H}$ | hamilt | ISOtech | Hamiltonian (script capital H) |
| Ъ | HARDcy | ISOcyr1 | =capital HARD sign, Cyrillic |
| ь | hardcy | ISOcyr1 | =small hard sign, Cyrillic |
| ⇔ | hArr | ISOamsa | /Leftrightarrow A: l&r dbl arrow |
| ↔ | harr | ISOamsa | /leftrightarrow A: l&r arrow |
| ↭ | harrw | ISOamsa | /leftrightsquigarrow A: l&r arr-wavy |
| Ĥ | Hcirc | ISOlat2 | =capital H, circumflex accent |
| ĥ | hcirc | ISOlat2 | =small h, circumflex accent |
| ♥ | hearts | ISOpub | /heartsuit =heart suit symbol |
| … | hellip | ISOpub | =ellipsis (horizontal) |
| — | horbar | ISOnum | =horizontal bar |
| Ħ | Hstrok | ISOlat2 | =capital H, stroke |
| ħ | hstrok | ISOlat2 | =small h, stroke |
| ▪ | hybull | ISOpub | rectangle, filled (hyphen bullet) |
| - | hyphen | ISOnum | =hyphen |
| Ί | Iacgr | ISOgrk2 | =capital Iota, accent, Greek |
| ί | iacgr | ISOgrk2 | =small iota, accent, Greek |
| Í | Iacute | ISOlat1 | =capital I, acute accent |
| í | iacute | ISOlat1 | =small i, acute accent |

| Symbol | Name | Set | Description |
|---|---|---|---|
| Î | Icirc | ISOlat1 | =capital I, circumflex accent |
| î | icirc | ISOlat1 | =small i, circumflex accent |
| И | Icy | ISOcyr1 | =capital I, Cyrillic |
| и | icy | ISOcyr1 | =small i, Cyrillic |
| ΐ | idiagr | ISOgrk2 | =small iota, dieresis, accent, Greek |
| Ϊ | Idigr | ISOgrk2 | =capital Iota, dieresis, Greek |
| ϊ | idigr | ISOgrk2 | =small iota, dieresis, Greek |
| İ | Idot | ISOlat2 | =capital I, dot above |
| Е | IEcy | ISOcyr1 | =capital IE, Cyrillic |
| е | iecy | ISOcyr1 | =small ie, Cyrillic |
| ¡ | iexcl | ISOnum | =inverted exclamation mark |
| ⇔ | iff | ISOtech | /iff =if and only if |
| Ι | Igr | ISOgrk1 | =capital Iota, Greek |
| ι | igr | ISOgrk1 | =small iota, Greek |
| Ì | Igrave | ISOlat1 | =capital I, grave accent |
| ì | igrave | ISOlat1 | =small i, grave accent |
| IJ | IJlig | ISOlat2 | =capital IJ ligature |
| ij | ijlig | ISOlat2 | =small ij ligature |
| Ī | Imacr | ISOlat2 | =capital I, macron |
| ī | imacr | ISOlat2 | =small i, macron |
| ℑ | image | ISOamso | /Im - imaginary |
| ℅ | incare | ISOpub | =in-care-of symbol |
| ∞ | infin | ISOtech | /infty =infinity |
| ı | inodot | ISOamso | /imath =small i, no dot |
| ı | inodot | ISOlat2 | =small i without dot |
| ∫ | int | ISOtech | /int L: =integral operator |
| ⊺ | intcal | ISOamsb | /intercal B: intercal |
| Ё | IOcy | ISOcyr1 | =capital IO, Russian |
| ё | iocy | ISOcyr1 | =small io, Russian |
| Į | Iogon | ISOlat2 | =capital I, ogonek |
| į | iogon | ISOlat2 | =small i, ogonek |
| ι | iota | ISOgrk3 | =small iota, Greek |

| Symbol | Name | Set | Description |
|--------|------|-----|-------------|
| ¿ | iquest | ISOnum | =inverted question mark |
| ∈ | isin | ISOtech | /in R: =set membership |
| Ĩ | Itilde | ISOlat2 | =capital I, tilde |
| ĩ | itilde | ISOlat2 | =small i, tilde |
| I | Iukcy | ISOcyr2 | =capital I, Ukrainian |
| i | iukcy | ISOcyr2 | =small i, Ukrainian |
| Ï | Iuml | ISOlat1 | =capital I, dieresis or umlaut mark |
| ï | iuml | ISOlat1 | =small i, dieresis or umlaut mark |
| Ĵ | Jcirc | ISOlat2 | =capital J, circumflex accent |
| ĵ | jcirc | ISOlat2 | =small j, circumflex accent |
| Й | Jcy | ISOcyr1 | =capital short I, Cyrillic |
| й | jcy | ISOcyr1 | =small short i, Cyrillic |
| ȷ | jnodot | ISOamso | /jmath - small j, no dot |
| Ј | Jsercy | ISOcyr2 | =capital JE, Serbian |
| ј | jsercy | ISOcyr2 | =small je, Serbian |
| Є | Jukcy | ISOcyr2 | =capital JE, Ukrainian |
| є | jukcy | ISOcyr2 | =small je, Ukrainian |
| κ | kappa | ISOgrk3 | =small kappa, Greek |
| ϰ | kappav | ISOgrk3 | /varkappa |
| Ķ | Kcedil | ISOlat2 | =capital K, cedilla |
| ķ | kcedil | ISOlat2 | =small k, cedilla |
| К | Kcy | ISOcyr1 | =capital KA, Cyrillic |
| к | kcy | ISOcyr1 | =small ka, Cyrillic |
| Κ | Kgr | ISOgrk1 | =capital Kappa, Greek |
| κ | kgr | ISOgrk1 | =small kappa, Greek |
| ĸ | kgreen | ISOlat2 | =small k, Greenlandic |
| Х | KHcy | ISOcyr1 | =capital HA, Cyrillic |
| х | khcy | ISOcyr1 | =small ha, Cyrillic |
| Χ | KHgr | ISOgrk1 | =capital Chi, Greek |
| χ | khgr | ISOgrk1 | =small chi, Greek |
| Ќ | KJcy | ISOcyr2 | =capital KJE, Macedonian |
| ќ | kjcy | ISOcyr2 | =small kje Macedonian |

| Symbol | Name | Set | Description |
|---|---|---|---|
| ⇐ | lAarr | ISOamsa | /Lleftarrow A: left triple arrow |
| Ĺ | Lacute | ISOlat2 | =capital L, acute accent |
| ĺ | lacute | ISOlat2 | =small l, acute accent |
| 𝓛 | lagran | ISOtech | Lagrangian (script capital L) |
| Λ | Lambda | ISOgrk3 | =capital Lambda, Greek |
| λ | lambda | ISOgrk3 | =small lambda, Greek |
| ⟨ | lang | ISOtech | /langle O: =left angle bracket |
| ⪅ | lap | ISOamsr | /lessapprox R: less, approximate |
| « | laquo | ISOnum | =angle quotation mark, left |
| ↞ | Larr | ISOamsa | /twoheadleftarrow A: |
| ⇐ | lArr | ISOtech | /Leftarrow A: =is implied by |
| ← | larr | ISOnum | /leftarrow /gets A: =leftward arrow |
| ⇇ | larr2 | ISOamsa | /leftleftarrows A: two left arrows |
| ↩ | larrhk | ISOamsa | /hookleftarrow A: left arrow-hooked |
| ↫ | larrlp | ISOamsa | /looparrowleft A: left arrow-looped |
| ↢ | larrtl | ISOamsa | /leftarrowtail A: left arrow-tailed |
| Ľ | Lcaron | ISOlat2 | =capital L, caron |
| ľ | lcaron | ISOlat2 | =small l, caron |
| Ļ | Lcedil | ISOlat2 | =capital L, cedilla |
| ļ | lcedil | ISOlat2 | =small l, cedilla |
| ⌈ | lceil | ISOamsc | /lceil O: left ceiling |
| { | lcub | ISOnum | /lbrace O: =left curly bracket |
| Л | Lcy | ISOcyr1 | =capital EL, Cyrillic |
| л | lcy | ISOcyr1 | =small el, Cyrillic |
| ⋖ | ldot | ISOamsr | /lessdot R: less than, with dot |
| " | ldquo | ISOnum | =double quotation mark, left |
| „ | ldquor | ISOpub | =rising dbl quote, left (low) |
| ≦ | lE | ISOamsr | /leqq R: less, double equals |
| ≤ | le | ISOtech | /leq /le R: =less-than-or-equal |
| ⪋ | lEg | ISOamsr | /lesseqqgtr R: less, dbl eq, greater |
| ⋚ | leg | ISOamsr | /lesseqgtr R: less, eq, greater |
| ⩽ | les | ISOamsr | /leqslant R: less-than-or-eq, slant |

| Symbol | Name | Set | Description |
|--------|------|-----|-------------|
| ⌊ | lfloor | ISOamsc | /lfloor O: left floor |
| ≲ | lg | ISOamsr | /lessgtr R: less, greater |
| Λ | Lgr | ISOgrk1 | =capital Lambda, Greek |
| λ | lgr | ISOgrk1 | =small lambda, Greek |
| ↽ | lhard | ISOamsa | /leftharpoondown A: l harpoon-down |
| ↼ | lharu | ISOamsa | /leftharpoonup A: left harpoon-up |
| ▄ | lhblk | ISOpub | =lower half block |
| Љ | LJcy | ISOcyr2 | =capital LJE, Serbian |
| љ | ljcy | ISOcyr2 | =small lje, Serbian |
| ⋘ | Ll | ISOamsr | /Ll /lll /llless R: triple less-than |
| Ŀ | Lmidot | ISOlat2 | =capital L, middle dot |
| ŀ | lmidot | ISOlat2 | =small l, middle dot |
| ⪉ | lnap | ISOamsn | /lnapprox N: less, not approximate |
| ⪇ | lnE | ISOamsn | /lneqq N: less, not double equals |
| ⪇ | lne | ISOamsn | /lneq N: less, not equals |
| ⋦ | lnsim | ISOamsn | /lnsim N: less, not similar |
| ∗ | lowast | ISOtech | low asterisk |
| _ | lowbar | ISOnum | =low line |
| ◊ | loz | ISOpub | /lozenge - lozenge or total mark |
| ◆ | lozf | ISOpub | /blacklozenge - lozenge, filled |
| ( | lpar | ISOnum | O: =left parenthesis |
| ⪦ | lpargt | ISOamsc | /leftparengtr O: left parenthesis, gt |
| ⇆ | lrarr2 | ISOamsa | /leftrightarrows A: l arr over r arr |
| ⇋ | lrhar2 | ISOamsa | /leftrightharpoons A: l harp over r |
| ↰ | lsh | ISOamsa | /Lsh A: |
| ≲ | lsim | ISOamsr | /lesssim R: less, similar |
| [ | lsqb | ISOnum | /lbrack O: =left square bracket |
| ' | lsquo | ISOnum | =single quotation mark, left |
| ‚ | lsquor | ISOpub | =rising single quote, left (low) |
| Ł | Lstrok | ISOlat2 | =capital L, stroke |
| ł | lstrok | ISOlat2 | =small l, stroke |
| ≪ | Lt | ISOamsr | /ll R: double less-than sign |

| Symbol | Name | Set | Description |
|--------|------|-----|-------------|
| < | lt | ISOnum | =less-than sign R: |
| ⋋ | lthree | ISOamsb | /leftthreetimes B: |
| ⋉ | ltimes | ISOamsb | /ltimes B: times sign, left closed |
| ◁ | ltri | ISOpub | /triangleleft B: l triangle, open |
| ⊴ | ltrie | ISOamsr | /trianglelefteq R: left triangle, eq |
| ◀ | ltrif | ISOpub | /blacktriangleleft R: =l tri, filled |
| ≨ | lvnE | ISOamsn | /lvertneqq N: less, vert, not dbl eq |
| ¯ | macr | ISOdia | =macron |
| ♂ | male | ISOpub | =male symbol |
| ✠ | malt | ISOpub | /maltese =maltese cross |
| ↦ | map | ISOamsa | /mapsto A: |
| ▌ | marker | ISOpub | =histogram marker |
| М | Mcy | ISOcyr1 | =capital EM, Cyrillic |
| м | mcy | ISOcyr1 | =small em, Cyrillic |
| — | mdash | ISOpub | =em dash |
| M | Mgr | ISOgrk1 | =capital Mu, Greek |
| μ | mgr | ISOgrk1 | =small mu, Greek |
| μ | micro | ISOnum | =micro sign |
| ∣ | mid | ISOamsr | /mid R: |
| · | middot | ISOnum | /centerdot B: =middle dot |
| − | minus | ISOtech | B: =minus sign |
| ⊟ | minusb | ISOamsb | /boxminus B: minus sign in box |
| … | mldr | ISOpub | em leader |
| ∓ | mnplus | ISOtech | /mp B: =minus-or-plus sign |
| ⊧ | models | ISOamsr | /models R: |
| μ | mu | ISOgrk3 | =small mu, Greek |
| ⊸ | mumap | ISOamsa | /multimap A: |
| ∇ | nabla | ISOtech | /nabla =del, Hamilton operator |
| Ń | Nacute | ISOlat2 | =capital N, acute accent |
| ń | nacute | ISOlat2 | =small n, acute accent |
| ≉ | nap | ISOamsn | /napprox N: not approximate |
| n' | napos | ISOlat2 | =small n, apostrophe |

| Symbol | Name | Set | Description |
|---|---|---|---|
| ♮ | natur | ISOpub | /natural - music natural |
|  | nbsp | ISOnum | =no break (required) space |
| Ň | Ncaron | ISOlat2 | =capital N, caron |
| ň | ncaron | ISOlat2 | =small n, caron |
| Ņ | Ncedil | ISOlat2 | =capital N, cedilla |
| ņ | ncedil | ISOlat2 | =small n, cedilla |
| ≇ | ncong | ISOamsn | /ncong N: not congruent with |
| Н | Ncy | ISOcyr1 | =capital EN, Cyrillic |
| н | ncy | ISOcyr1 | =small en, Cyrillic |
| – | ndash | ISOpub | =en dash |
| ≠ | ne | ISOtech | /ne /neq R: =not equal |
| ↗ | nearr | ISOamsa | /nearrow A: NE pointing arrow |
| ≢ | nequiv | ISOamsn | /nequiv N: not identical with |
| ∄ | nexist | ISOamso | /nexists - negated exists |
| ≩ | ngE | ISOamsn | /ngeqq N: not greater, dbl equals |
| ≱ | nge | ISOamsn | /ngeq N: not greater-than-or-equal |
| ≱ | nges | ISOamsn | /ngeqslant N: not gt-or-eq, slanted |
| N | Ngr | ISOgrk1 | =capital Nu, Greek |
| ν | ngr | ISOgrk1 | =small nu, Greek |
| ≯ | ngt | ISOamsn | /ngtr N: not greater-than |
| ⇎ | nhArr | ISOamsa | /nLeftrightarrow A: not l&r dbl arr |
| ↮ | nharr | ISOamsa | /nleftrightarrow A: not l&r arrow |
| ∋ | ni | ISOtech | /ni /owns R: =contains |
| Њ | NJcy | ISOcyr2 | =capital NJE, Serbian |
| њ | njcy | ISOcyr2 | =small nje, Serbian |
| ⇍ | nlArr | ISOamsa | /nLeftarrow A: not implied by |
| ↚ | nlarr | ISOamsa | /nleftarrow A: not left arrow |
| ‥ | nldr | ISOpub | =double baseline dot (en leader) |
| ≨ | nlE | ISOamsn | /nleqq N: not less, dbl equals |
| ≰ | nle | ISOamsn | /nleq N: not less-than-or-equal |
| ≰ | nles | ISOamsn | /nleqslant N: not less-or-eq, slant |
| ≮ | nlt | ISOamsn | /nless N: not less-than |

| Symbol | Name | Set | Description |
|---|---|---|---|
| ⋪ | nltri | ISOamsn | /ntriangleleft N: not left triangle |
| ⋬ | nltrie | ISOamsn | /ntrianglelefteq N: not l tri, eq |
| ∤ | nmid | ISOamsn | /nmid |
| ¬ | not | ISOnum | /neg /lnot =not sign |
| ∉ | notin | ISOtech | N: negated set membership |
| ∦ | npar | ISOamsn | /nparallel N: not parallel |
| ⊀ | npr | ISOamsn | /nprec N: not precedes |
| ⋠ | npre | ISOamsn | /npreceq N: not precedes, equals |
| ⇏ | nrArr | ISOamsa | /nRightarrow A: not implies |
| ↛ | nrarr | ISOamsa | /nrightarrow A: not right arrow |
| ⊳ | nrtri | ISOamsn | /ntriangleright N: not rt triangle |
| ⋭ | nrtrie | ISOamsn | /ntrianglerighteq N: not r tri, eq |
| ⊁ | nsc | ISOamsn | /nsucc N: not succeeds |
| ⋡ | nsce | ISOamsn | /nsucceq N: not succeeds, equals |
| ≁ | nsim | ISOamsn | /nsim N: not similar |
| ≄ | nsime | ISOamsn | /nsimeq N: not similar, equals |
| ∤ | nsmid | ISOamsn | /nshortmid |
| ∦ | nspar | ISOamsn | /nshortparallel N: not short par |
| ⊄ | nsub | ISOamsn | /nsubset N: not subset |
| ⊈ | nsubE | ISOamsn | /nsubseteqq N: not subset, dbl eq |
| ⊄ | nsube | ISOamsn | /nsubseteq N: not subset, equals |
| ⊅ | nsup | ISOamsn | /nsupset N: not superset |
| ⊉ | nsupE | ISOamsn | /nsupseteqq N: not superset, dbl eq |
| ⊅ | nsupe | ISOamsn | /nsupseteq N: not superset, equals |
| Ñ | Ntilde | ISOlat1 | =capital N, tilde |
| ñ | ntilde | ISOlat1 | =small n, tilde |
| ν | nu | ISOgrk3 | =small nu, Greek |
| # | num | ISOnum | =number sign |
| № | numero | ISOcyr1 | =numero sign |
|  | numsp | ISOpub | =digit space (width of a number) |
| ⊮ | nVDash | ISOamsn | /nVDash N: not dbl vert, dbl dash |
| ⊭ | nVdash | ISOamsn | /nVdash N: not dbl vertical, dash |

| Symbol | Name | Set | Description |
|--------|------|-----|-------------|
| ↯ | nvDash | ISOamsn | /nvDash N: not vertical, dbl dash |
| ↯ | nvdash | ISOamsn | /nvdash N: not vertical, dash |
| ↖ | nwarr | ISOamsa | /nwarrow A: NW pointing arrow |
| Ό | Oacgr | ISOgrk2 | =capital Omicron, accent, Greek |
| ό | oacgr | ISOgrk2 | =small omicron, accent, Greek |
| Ó | Oacute | ISOlat1 | =capital O, acute accent |
| ó | oacute | ISOlat1 | =small o, acute accent |
| ⊛ | oast | ISOamsb | /circledast B: asterisk in circle |
| ⊙ | ocir | ISOamsb | /circledcirc B: open dot in circle |
| Ô | Ocirc | ISOlat1 | =capital O, circumflex accent |
| ô | ocirc | ISOlat1 | =small o, circumflex accent |
| О | Ocy | ISOcyr1 | =capital O, Cyrillic |
| о | ocy | ISOcyr1 | =small o, Cyrillic |
| ⊖ | odash | ISOamsb | /circleddash B: hyphen in circle |
| Ő | Odblac | ISOlat2 | =capital O, double acute accent |
| ő | odblac | ISOlat2 | =small o, double acute accent |
| ⊙ | odot | ISOamsb | /odot B: middle dot in circle |
| Œ | OElig | ISOlat2 | =capital OE ligature |
| œ | oelig | ISOlat2 | =small oe ligature |
| ˛ | ogon | ISOdia | =ogonek |
| Ο | Ogr | ISOgrk1 | =capital Omicron, Greek |
| ο | ogr | ISOgrk1 | =small omicron, Greek |
| Ò | Ograve | ISOlat1 | =capital O, grave accent |
| ò | ograve | ISOlat1 | =small o, grave accent |
| Ώ | OHacgr | ISOgrk2 | =capital Omega, accent, Greek |
| ώ | ohacgr | ISOgrk2 | =small omega, accent, Greek |
| Ω | OHgr | ISOgrk1 | =capital Omega, Greek |
| ω | ohgr | ISOgrk1 | =small omega, Greek |
| Ω | ohm | ISOnum | =ohm sign |
| ↺ | olarr | ISOamsa | /circlearrowleft A: l arr in circle |
| Ō | Omacr | ISOlat2 | =capital O, macron |
| ō | omacr | ISOlat2 | =small o, macron |

| Symbol | Name | Set | Description |
|--------|------|-----|-------------|
| Ω | Omega | ISOgrk3 | =capital Omega, Greek |
| ω | omega | ISOgrk3 | =small omega, Greek |
| ⊖ | ominus | ISOamsb | /ominus B: minus sign in circle |
| ⊕ | oplus | ISOamsb | /oplus B: plus sign in circle |
| ∨ | or | ISOtech | /vee /lor B: =logical or |
| ↻ | orarr | ISOamsa | /circlearrowright A: r arr in circle |
| *o* | order | ISOtech | order of (script small o) |
| ª | ordf | ISOnum | =ordinal indicator, feminine |
| º | ordm | ISOnum | =ordinal indicator, masculine |
| Ⓢ | oS | ISOamso | /circledS - capital S in circle |
| Ø | Oslash | ISOlat1 | =capital O, slash |
| ø | oslash | ISOlat1 | =small o, slash |
| ⊘ | osol | ISOamsb | /oslash B: solidus in circle |
| Õ | Otilde | ISOlat1 | =capital O, tilde |
| õ | otilde | ISOlat1 | =small o, tilde |
| ⊗ | otimes | ISOamsb | /otimes B: multiply sign in circle |
| Ö | Ouml | ISOlat1 | =capital O, dieresis or umlaut mark |
| ö | ouml | ISOlat1 | =small o, dieresis or umlaut mark |
| ‖ | par | ISOtech | /parallel R: =parallel |
| ¶ | para | ISOnum | =pilcrow (paragraph sign) |
| ∂ | part | ISOtech | /partial =partial differential |
| П | Pcy | ISOcyr1 | =capital PE, Cyrillic |
| п | pcy | ISOcyr1 | =small pe, Cyrillic |
| % | percnt | ISOnum | =percent sign |
| . | period | ISOnum | =full stop, period |
| ‰ | permil | ISOtech | =per thousand |
| ⊥ | perp | ISOtech | /perp R: =perpendicular |
| Π | Pgr | ISOgrk1 | =capital Pi, Greek |
| π | pgr | ISOgrk1 | =small pi, Greek |
| Φ | PHgr | ISOgrk1 | =capital Phi, Greek |
| φ | phgr | ISOgrk1 | =small phi, Greek |
| Φ | Phi | ISOgrk3 | =capital Phi, Greek |

| Symbol | Name | Set | Description |
|--------|------|-----|-------------|
| φ | phis | ISOgrk3 | /straightphi - straight phi |
| φ | phiv | ISOgrk3 | /varphi - curly or open phi |
| 𝓜 | phmmat | ISOtech | physics M-matrix (script capital M) |
| ☏ | phone | ISOpub | =telephone symbol |
| Π | Pi | ISOgrk3 | =capital Pi, Greek |
| π | pi | ISOgrk3 | =small pi, Greek |
| ϖ | piv | ISOgrk3 | /varpi |
| ℏ | planck | ISOamso | /hbar /hslash - Planck's over 2pi |
| + | plus | ISOnum | =plus sign B:-- > |
| ⊞ | plusb | ISOamsb | /boxplus B: plus sign in box |
| ∔ | plusdo | ISOamsb | /dotplus B: plus sign, dot above |
| ± | plusmn | ISOnum | /pm B: =plus-or-minus sign |
| £ | pound | ISOnum | =pound sign |
| ≺ | pr | ISOamsr | /prec R: precedes |
| ⪷ | prap | ISOamsr | /precapprox R: precedes, approximate |
| ≼ | pre | ISOamsr | /preceq R: precedes, equals |
| ″ | Prime | ISOtech | =double prime or second |
| ′ | prime | ISOtech | /prime =prime or minute |
| ⪹ | prnap | ISOamsn | /precnapprox N: precedes, not approx |
| ⪵ | prnE | ISOamsn | /precneqq N: precedes, not dbl eq |
| ⋨ | prnsim | ISOamsn | /precnsim N: precedes, not similar |
| Π | prod | ISOamsb | /prod L: product operator |
| ∝ | prop | ISOtech | /propto R: =is proportional to |
| ≾ | prsim | ISOamsr | /precsim R: precedes, similar |
| Ψ | PSgr | ISOgrk1 | =capital Psi, Greek |
| ψ | psgr | ISOgrk1 | =small psi, Greek |
| Ψ | Psi | ISOgrk3 | =capital Psi, Greek |
| ψ | psi | ISOgrk3 | =small psi, Greek |
|  | puncsp | ISOpub | =punctuation space (width of comma) |
| ? | quest | ISOnum | =question mark |
| ' | quot | ISOnum | =quotation mark |
| ⟹ | rAarr | ISOamsa | /Rrightarrow A: right triple arrow |

| Symbol | Name | Set | Description |
|--------|------|-----|-------------|
| Ŕ | Racute | ISOlat2 | =capital R, acute accent |
| ŕ | racute | ISOlat2 | =small r, acute accent |
| √ | radic | ISOtech | /surd =radical |
| ⟩ | rang | ISOtech | /rangle C: =right angle bracket |
| » | raquo | ISOnum | =angle quotation mark, right |
| ↠ | Rarr | ISOamsa | /twoheadrightarrow A: |
| ⇒ | rArr | ISOtech | /Rightarrow A: =implies |
| → | rarr | ISOnum | /rightarrow /to A: =rightward arrow |
| ⇉ | rarr2 | ISOamsa | /rightrightarrows A: two rt arrows |
| ↪ | rarrhk | ISOamsa | /hookrightarrow A: rt arrow-hooked |
| ↬ | rarrlp | ISOamsa | /looparrowright A: rt arrow-looped |
| ↣ | rarrtl | ISOamsa | /rightarrowtail A: rt arrow-tailed |
| ⇝ | rarrw | ISOamsa | /squigarrowright A: rt arrow-wavy |
| Ř | Rcaron | ISOlat2 | =capital R, caron |
| ř | rcaron | ISOlat2 | =small r, caron |
| Ŗ | Rcedil | ISOlat2 | =capital R, cedilla |
| ŗ | rcedil | ISOlat2 | =small r, cedilla |
| ⌉ | rceil | ISOamsc | /rceil C: right ceiling |
| } | rcub | ISOnum | /rbrace C: =right curly bracket |
| Р | Rcy | ISOcyr1 | =capital ER, Cyrillic |
| р | rcy | ISOcyr1 | =small er, Cyrillic |
| ” | rdquo | ISOnum | =double quotation mark, right |
| " | rdquor | ISOpub | rising dbl quote, right (high) |
| ℜ | real | ISOamso | /Re - real |
| ▭ | rect | ISOpub | =rectangle, open |
| ® | reg | ISOnum | /circledR =registered sign |
| ⌋ | rfloor | ISOamsc | /rfloor C: right floor |
| Ρ | Rgr | ISOgrk1 | =capital Rho, Greek |
| ρ | rgr | ISOgrk1 | =small rho, Greek |
| ⇁ | rhard | ISOamsa | /rightharpoondown A: rt harpoon-down |
| ⇀ | rharu | ISOamsa | /rightharpoonup A: rt harpoon-up |
| ρ | rho | ISOgrk3 | =small rho, Greek |

| Symbol | Name | Set | Description |
|--------|------|-----|-------------|
| ϱ | rhov | ISOgrk3 | /varrho |
| ° | ring | ISOdia | =ring |
| ⇄ | rlarr2 | ISOamsa | /rightleftarrows A: r arr over l arr |
| ⇌ | rlhar2 | ISOamsa | /rightleftharpoons A: r harp over l |
| ) | rpar | ISOnum | C: =right parenthesis |
| ⋗ | rpargt | ISOamsc | /rightparengtr C: right paren, gt |
| ↱ | rsh | ISOamsa | /Rsh A: |
| ] | rsqb | ISOnum | /rbrack C: =right square bracket |
| ' | rsquo | ISOnum | =single quotation mark, right |
| ' | rsquor | ISOpub | rising single quote, right (high) |
| ⋌ | rthree | ISOamsb | /rightthreetimes B: |
| ⋊ | rtimes | ISOamsb | /rtimes B: times sign, right closed |
| ▷ | rtri | ISOpub | /triangleright B: r triangle, open |
| ⊵ | rtrie | ISOamsr | /trianglerighteq R: right tri, eq |
| ▶ | rtrif | ISOpub | /blacktriangleright R: =r tri, filled |
| ℞ | rx | ISOpub | pharmaceutical prescription (Rx) |
| Ś | Sacute | ISOlat2 | =capital S, acute accent |
| ś | sacute | ISOlat2 | =small s, acute accent |
| ⨿ | samalg | ISOamsr | /smallamalg R: small amalg |
| ╲ | sbsol | ISOamso | /sbs - short reverse solidus |
| ≻ | sc | ISOamsr | /succ R: succeeds |
| ⪸ | scap | ISOamsr | /succapprox R: succeeds, approximate |
| Š | Scaron | ISOlat2 | =capital S, caron |
| š | scaron | ISOlat2 | =small s, caron |
| ≽ | sccue | ISOamsr | /succcurlyeq R: succeeds, curly eq |
| ⪰ | sce | ISOamsr | /succeq R: succeeds, equals |
| Ş | Scedil | ISOlat2 | =capital S, cedilla |
| ş | scedil | ISOlat2 | =small s, cedilla |
| Ŝ | Scirc | ISOlat2 | =capital S, circumflex accent |
| ŝ | scirc | ISOlat2 | =small s, circumflex accent |
| ⪺ | scnap | ISOamsn | /succnapprox N: succeeds, not approx |
| ⪶ | scnE | ISOamsn | /succneqq N: succeeds, not dbl eq |

| Symbol | Name | Set | Description |
|---|---|---|---|
| ⋩ | scnsim | ISOamsn | /succnsim N: succeeds, not similar |
| ⋦ | scsim | ISOamsr | /succsim R: succeeds, similar |
| C | Scy | ISOcyr1 | =capital ES, Cyrillic |
| c | scy | ISOcyr1 | =small es, Cyrillic |
| · | sdot | ISOamsb | /cdot B: small middle dot |
| ⊡ | sdotb | ISOamsb | /dotsquare /boxdot B: small dot in box |
| § | sect | ISOnum | =section sign |
| ; | semi | ISOnum | =semicolon P: |
| \ | setmn | ISOamsb | /setminus B: reverse solidus |
| ✳ | sext | ISOpub | sextile (6-pointed star) |
| ς | sfgr | ISOgrk1 | =final small sigma, Greek |
| ⌢ | sfrown | ISOamsr | /smallfrown R: small down curve |
| Σ | Sgr | ISOgrk1 | =capital Sigma, Greek |
| σ | sgr | ISOgrk1 | =small sigma, Greek |
| ♯ | sharp | ISOpub | /sharp =musical sharp |
| Щ | SHCHcy | ISOcyr1 | =capital SHCHA, Cyrillic |
| щ | shchcy | ISOcyr1 | =small shcha, Cyrillic |
| Ш | SHcy | ISOcyr1 | =capital SHA, Cyrillic |
| ш | shcy | ISOcyr1 | =small sha, Cyrillic |
| - | shy | ISOnum | =soft hyphen |
| Σ | Sigma | ISOgrk3 | =capital Sigma, Greek |
| σ | sigma | ISOgrk3 | =small sigma, Greek |
| ς | sigmav | ISOgrk3 | /varsigma |
| ~ | sim | ISOtech | /sim R: =similar |
| ≃ | sime | ISOtech | /simeq R: =similar, equals |
| ∣ | smid | ISOamsr | /shortmid R: |
| ⌣ | smile | ISOamsr | /smile R: up curve |
| ь | SOFTcy | ISOcyr1 | =capital SOFT sign, Cyrillic |
| ь | softcy | ISOcyr1 | =small soft sign, Cyrillic |
| / | sol | ISOnum | =solidus |
| ♠ | spades | ISOpub | /spadesuit =spades suit symbol |
| ∥ | spar | ISOamsr | /shortparallel R: short parallel |

| Symbol | Name | Set | Description |
|--------|------|-----|-------------|
| ⊓ | sqcap | ISOamsb | /sqcap B: square intersection |
| ⊔ | sqcup | ISOamsb | /sqcup B: square union |
| ⊏ | sqsub | ISOamsr | /sqsubset R: square subset |
| ⊑ | sqsube | ISOamsr | /sqsubseteq R: square subset, equals |
| ⊐ | sqsup | ISOamsr | /sqsupset R: square superset |
| ⊒ | sqsupe | ISOamsr | /sqsupseteq R: square superset, eq |
| □ | squ | ISOpub | =square, open |
| □ | square | ISOtech | /square B: =square |
| ■ | squf | ISOpub | /blacksquare =sq bullet, filled |
| \ | ssetmn | ISOamsb | /smallsetminus B: sm reverse solidus |
| ⌣ | ssmile | ISOamsr | /smallsmile R: small up curve |
| ★ | sstarf | ISOamsb | /star B: small star, filled |
| ☆ | star | ISOpub | =star, open |
| ★ | starf | ISOpub | /bigstar - star, filled |
| ⋐ | Sub | ISOamsr | /Subset R: double subset |
| ⊂ | sub | ISOtech | /subset R: =subset or is implied by |
| ⊆ | subE | ISOamsr | /subseteqq R: subset, dbl equals |
| ⊆ | sube | ISOtech | /subseteq R: =subset, equals |
| ⊊ | subnE | ISOamsn | /subsetneqq N: subset, not dbl eq |
| ⊊ | subne | ISOamsn | /subsetneq N: subset, not equals |
| Σ | sum | ISOamsb | /sum L: summation operator |
| ♪ | sung | ISOnum | =music note (sung text sign) |
| ⊒ | Sup | ISOamsr | /Supset R: dbl superset |
| ⊃ | sup | ISOtech | /supset R: =superset or implies |
| ¹ | sup1 | ISOnum | =superscript one |
| ² | sup2 | ISOnum | =superscript two |
| ³ | sup3 | ISOnum | =superscript three |
| ⊇ | supE | ISOamsr | /supseteqq R: superset, dbl equals |
| ⊇ | supe | ISOtech | /supseteq R: =superset, equals |
| ⊋ | supnE | ISOamsn | /supsetneqq N: superset, not dbl eq |
| ⊋ | supne | ISOamsn | /supsetneq N: superset, not equals |
| ß | szlig | ISOlat1 | =small sharp s, German (sz ligature) |

| Symbol | Name | Set | Description |
|--------|------|-----|-------------|
| ⊕ | target | ISOpub | register mark or target |
| τ | tau | ISOgrk3 | =small tau, Greek |
| Ť | Tcaron | ISOlat2 | =capital T, caron |
| ť | tcaron | ISOlat2 | =small t, caron |
| Ţ | Tcedil | ISOlat2 | =capital T, cedilla |
| ţ | tcedil | ISOlat2 | =small t, cedilla |
| Т | Tcy | ISOcyr1 | =capital TE, Cyrillic |
| т | tcy | ISOcyr1 | =small te, Cyrillic |
| ⋯ | tdot | ISOtech | three dots above |
| ℘ | telrec | ISOpub | =telephone recorder symbol |
| Τ | Tgr | ISOgrk1 | =capital Tau, Greek |
| τ | tgr | ISOgrk1 | =small tau, Greek |
| ∴ | there4 | ISOtech | /therefore R: =therefore |
| Θ | Theta | ISOgrk3 | =capital Theta, Greek |
| θ | thetas | ISOgrk3 | straight theta |
| ϑ | thetav | ISOgrk3 | /vartheta - curly or open theta |
| Θ | THgr | ISOgrk1 | =capital Theta, Greek |
| θ | thgr | ISOgrk1 | =small theta, Greek |
|  | thinsp | ISOpub | =thin space (1/6-em) |
| ≈ | thkap | ISOamsr | /thickapprox R: thick approximate |
| ∼ | thksim | ISOamsr | /thicksim R: thick similar |
| Þ | THORN | ISOlat1 | =capital THORN, Icelandic |
| þ | thorn | ISOlat1 | =small thorn, Icelandic |
| ˜ | tilde | ISOdia | =tilde |
| × | times | ISOnum | /times B: =multiply sign |
| ⊠ | timesb | ISOamsb | /boxtimes B: multiply sign in box |
| ⊤ | top | ISOamsb | /top B: inverted perpendicular |
| ‴ | tprime | ISOtech | triple prime |
| ™ | trade | ISOnum | =trade mark sign |
| ≜ | trie | ISOamsr | /triangleq R: triangle, equals |
| Ц | TScy | ISOcyr1 | =capital TSE, Cyrillic |
| ц | tscy | ISOcyr1 | =small tse, Cyrillic |

| Symbol | Name | Set | Description |
| --- | --- | --- | --- |
| Ћ | TSHcy | ISOcyr2 | =capital TSHE, Serbian |
| ћ | tshcy | ISOcyr2 | =small tshe, Serbian |
| Ŧ | Tstrok | ISOlat2 | =capital T, stroke |
| t | tstrok | ISOlat2 | =small t, stroke |
| ≬ | twixt | ISOamsr | /between R: between |
| Ύ | Uacgr | ISOgrk2 | =capital Upsilon, accent, Greek |
| ύ | uacgr | ISOgrk2 | =small upsilon, accent, Greek |
| Ú | Uacute | ISOlat1 | =capital U, acute accent |
| ú | uacute | ISOlat1 | =small u, acute accent |
| ⇑ | uArr | ISOamsa | /Uparrow A: up dbl arrow |
| ↑ | uarr | ISOnum | /uparrow A: =upward arrow |
| ⇈ | uarr2 | ISOamsa | /upuparrows A: two up arrows |
| Ў | Ubrcy | ISOcyr2 | =capital U, Byelorussian |
| ў | ubrcy | ISOcyr2 | =small u, Byelorussian |
| Ŭ | Ubreve | ISOlat2 | =capital U, breve |
| ŭ | ubreve | ISOlat2 | =small u, breve |
| Û | Ucirc | ISOlat1 | =capital U, circumflex accent |
| û | ucirc | ISOlat1 | =small u, circumflex accent |
| У | Ucy | ISOcyr1 | =capital U, Cyrillic |
| у | ucy | ISOcyr1 | =small u, Cyrillic |
| Ű | Udblac | ISOlat2 | =capital U, double acute accent |
| ű | udblac | ISOlat2 | =small u, double acute accent |
| ΰ | udiagr | ISOgrk2 | =small upsilon, dieresis, accent, Greek |
| Ϋ | Udigr | ISOgrk2 | =capital Upsilon, dieresis, Greek |
| ϋ | udigr | ISOgrk2 | =small upsilon, dieresis, Greek |
| Υ | Ugr | ISOgrk1 | =capital Upsilon, Greek |
| υ | ugr | ISOgrk1 | =small upsilon, Greek |
| Ù | Ugrave | ISOlat1 | =capital U, grave accent |
| ù | ugrave | ISOlat1 | =small u, grave accent |
| ↿ | uharl | ISOamsa | /upleftharpoon A: up harpoon-left |
| ↾ | uharr | ISOamsa | /uprightharpoon A: up harp-r |
| ▀ | uhblk | ISOpub | =upper half block |

| Symbol | Name | Set | Description |
|--------|------|-----|-------------|
| ⌐ | ulcorn | ISOamsc | /ulcorner O: upper left corner |
| ⌐\| | ulcrop | ISOpub | upward left crop mark |
| Ū | Umacr | ISOlat2 | =capital U, macron |
| ū | umacr | ISOlat2 | =small u, macron |
| ¨ | uml | ISOdia | =umlaut mark |
| Ų | Uogon | ISOlat2 | =capital U, ogonek |
| ų | uogon | ISOlat2 | =small u, ogonek |
| ⊎ | uplus | ISOamsb | /uplus B: plus sign in union |
| Υ | Upsi | ISOgrk3 | =capital Upsilon, Greek |
| υ | upsi | ISOgrk3 | =small upsilon, Greek |
| ⌐ | urcorn | ISOamsc | /urcorner C: upper right corner |
| \|⌐ | urcrop | ISOpub | upward right crop mark |
| Ů | Uring | ISOlat2 | =capital U, ring |
| ů | uring | ISOlat2 | =small u, ring |
| Ũ | Utilde | ISOlat2 | =capital U, tilde |
| ũ | utilde | ISOlat2 | =small u, tilde |
| △ | utri | ISOpub | /triangle =up triangle, open |
| ▲ | utrif | ISOpub | /blacktriangle =up tri, filled |
| Ü | Uuml | ISOlat1 | =capital U, dieresis or umlaut mark |
| ü | uuml | ISOlat1 | =small u, dieresis or umlaut mark |
| ⇕ | vArr | ISOamsa | /Updownarrow A: up&down dbl arrow |
| ↕ | varr | ISOamsa | /updownarrow A: up&down arrow |
| В | Vcy | ISOcyr1 | =capital VE, Cyrillic |
| в | vcy | ISOcyr1 | =small ve, Cyrillic |
| ⊩ | Vdash | ISOamsr | /Vdash R: dbl vertical, dash |
| ⊫ | vDash | ISOamsr | /vDash R: vertical, dbl dash |
| ⊢ | vdash | ISOamsr | /vdash R: vertical, dash |
| ⊻ | veebar | ISOamsr | /veebar R: logical or, bar below |
| ⋮ | vellip | ISOpub | vertical ellipsis |
| ‖ | Verbar | ISOtech | /Vert =dbl vertical bar |
| \| | verbar | ISOnum | /vert =vertical bar |

| Symbol | Name | Set | Description |
|---|---|---|---|
| ◁ | vltri | ISOamsr | /vartriangleleft R: l tri, open, var |
| ′ | vprime | ISOamso | /varprime - prime, variant |
| ∝ | vprop | ISOamsr | /varpropto R: proportional, variant |
| ▷ | vrtri | ISOamsr | /vartriangleright R: r tri, open, var |
| ⊊̸ | vsubnE | ISOamsn | /subsetneqq N: subset not dbl eq, var |
| ⊊ | vsubne | ISOamsn | /subsetneq N: subset, not eq, var |
| ⊋̸ | vsupnE | ISOamsn | /supsetneqq N: super not dbl eq, var |
| ⊋ | vsupne | ISOamsn | /supsetneq N: superset, not eq, var |
| ⊪ | Vvdash | ISOamsr | /Vvdash R: triple vertical, dash |
| Ŵ | Wcirc | ISOlat2 | =capital W, circumflex accent |
| ŵ | wcirc | ISOlat2 | =small w, circumflex accent |
| ≜ | wedgeq | ISOtech | R: corresponds to (wedge, equals) |
| ℘ | weierp | ISOamso | /wp - Weierstrass p |
| ≀ | wreath | ISOamsb | /wr B: wreath product |
| ◯ | xcirc | ISOamsb | /bigcirc B: large circle |
| ▽ | xdtri | ISOamsb | /bigtriangledown B: big dn tri, open |
| Ξ | Xgr | ISOgrk1 | =capital Xi, Greek |
| ξ | xgr | ISOgrk1 | =small xi, Greek |
| ⟺ | xhArr | ISOamsa | /Longleftrightarrow A: long l&r dbl arr |
| ⟷ | xharr | ISOamsa | /longleftrightarrow A: long l&r arr |
| Ξ | Xi | ISOgrk3 | =capital Xi, Greek |
| ξ | xi | ISOgrk3 | =small xi, Greek |
| ⟸ | xlArr | ISOamsa | /Longleftarrow A: long l dbl arrow |
| ⟹ | xrArr | ISOamsa | /Longrightarrow A: long rt dbl arr |
| △ | xutri | ISOamsb | /bigtriangleup B: big up tri, open |
| Ý | Yacute | ISOlat1 | =capital Y, acute accent |
| ý | yacute | ISOlat1 | =small y, acute accent |
| Я | YAcy | ISOcyr1 | =capital YA, Cyrillic |
| я | yacy | ISOcyr1 | =small ya, Cyrillic |
| Ŷ | Ycirc | ISOlat2 | =capital Y, circumflex accent |
| ŷ | ycirc | ISOlat2 | =small y, circumflex accent |
| Ы | Ycy | ISOcyr1 | =capital YERU, Cyrillic |

| Symbol | Name | Set | Description |
|---|---|---|---|
| ы | ycy | ISOcyr1 | =small yeru, Cyrillic |
| ¥ | yen | ISOnum | /yen =yen sign |
| Ï | YIcy | ISOcyr2 | =capital YI, Ukrainian |
| ï | yicy | ISOcyr2 | =small yi, Ukrainian |
| Ю | YUcy | ISOcyr1 | =capital YU, Cyrillic |
| ю | yucy | ISOcyr1 | =small yu, Cyrillic |
| Ÿ | Yuml | ISOlat2 | =capital Y, dieresis or umlaut mark |
| ÿ | yuml | ISOlat1 | =small y, dieresis or umlaut mark |
| Ź | Zacute | ISOlat2 | =capital Z, acute accent |
| ź | zacute | ISOlat2 | =small z, acute accent |
| Ž | Zcaron | ISOlat2 | =capital Z, caron |
| ž | zcaron | ISOlat2 | =small z, caron |
| З | Zcy | ISOcyr1 | =capital ZE, Cyrillic |
| з | zcy | ISOcyr1 | =small ze, Cyrillic |
| Ż | Zdot | ISOlat2 | =capital Z, dot above |
| ż | zdot | ISOlat2 | =small z, dot above |
| ζ | zeta | ISOgrk3 | =small zeta, Greek |
| Z | Zgr | ISOgrk1 | =capital Zeta, Greek |
| ζ | zgr | ISOgrk1 | =small zeta, Greek |
| Ж | ZHcy | ISOcyr1 | =capital ZHE, Cyrillic |
| ж | zhcy | ISOcyr1 | =small zhe, Cyrillic |

# Bibliography
# and
# Sources

This appendix lists selected sources of SGML-related information.

The World Wide Web is an increasingly rich source of SGML information. We highly recommend *Robin Cover's SGML Web Page* at `http://www.sil.org/sgml/sgml.html`, which has links to a myriad of SGML-related topics, including information on many of the DTDs, FOSIs, and other applications widely used in the government, commercial, and academic arenas, as well as an extensive SGML bibliography. Because the list of Web sites continues to grow, search on "SGML" using your favorite search engine to get the latest information.

The following organizations and forums are organized around SGML and related topics.

- SGML Open, a nonprofit consortium of suppliers whose products and services support SGML. Contact:

    SGML Open
    910 Beaver Grade Road, #3008
    Coraopolis, PA 15108 USA
    +1 412 264 4258
    `http://www.sgmlopen.org`

- Graphic Communications Association. The GCA hosts several SGML-related conferences every year, offers publications for sale, conducts training sessions, and sponsors the GCA Research Institute. For information on services and membership, contact:

    GCA
    100 Daingerfield Road
    Alexandria, VA 22314–8160 USA
    +1 703 519 8160

- The Usenet newsgroup `comp.text.sgml`.

The following is a useful source of information on the project management methodology whose workflow notation is used in Chapter 3:

- Mallet, Robert, *La Methode Informatique*, Hermann, 1975.

The following is a useful source of information on SGML-based systems development:

- Waldt, Dale and Travis, Brian, *The SGML Implementation Guide*, Springer-Verlag, 1995, ISBN 3–540–57730–0.

The following are useful sources of information about technical SGML topics and DTD implementation:

- Bryan, Martin, *SGML: An Author's Guide to the Standard Generalized Markup Language*, Addison-Wesley, 1988, ISBN 0–201–17537–5.

- Davenport Group, *Davenport archive*, information on the DocBook DTD and DTD customization techniques, `http://www.ora.com/davenport/README.html`

- DeRose, Steven and David Durand, *Making Hypermedia Work — A Users' Guide to HyTime*, Kluwer Academic Publishers, 1994, ISBN 0–7923–9432–1.

- Goldfarb, Charles, *The SGML Handbook*, Oxford University Press, 1990, ISBN 0–19–863737–9.

- *SGML Open Technical Resolution 9401* on entity management. SGML Open contact information is listed above.

- Smith, Joan M. and Robert Stutely, *SGML: The User's Guide to ISO 8879*, Ellis Horwood, 1988, ISBN 0–7458–0221–4.

- *<TAG> The SGML Newsletter*, published by SGML Associates Inc. and the Graphic Communications Association. For subscription information, contact:

    SGML Associates, Inc.
    <TAG> The SGML Newsletter
    6360 S. Gibraltar Circle
    Aurora, CO 80016–1212 USA
    +1 303 680 0875

- Turner, Ronald C., Timothy A. Douglass, and Audrey J. Turner, *README.1ST: SGML for Writers and Editors*, Prentice Hall PTR, 1995, ISBN 0–13–432717–9.

- Van Herwijnen, Eric, *Practical SGML*, Second Edition, Kluwer Academic Publishers, 1994, ISBN 0–7923–9434–8.

- Wohler, Wayne, *SGML Declarations*, a series of articles originally published in the *<TAG>* newsletter, now available at `http://www.sil.org/sgml/wlw11.html`.

- ISO 8879:1986 and other ISO standards and technical reports, available from:

    ISO
    Case Postale 56
    CH-1211 Geneva 20
    Switzerland

See also `http://www.iso.ch/cate/d16387.html`.

# Glossary

This glossary provides definitions for SGML technical terms, as well as terms and concepts that we introduce as part of our methodology and techniques. For terms that have an ISO 8879 definition, we supply that definition with its clause reference (though without any notes that accompany the definition in the standard), along with additional explanation as appropriate.

## abstract syntax

The functional roles of pieces of SGML markup, for example, a "start-tag open" (STAGO). A concrete syntax maps actual character strings to the functional roles; for example, the reference concrete syntax maps an STAGO to the left angle bracket (<).

The ISO 8879 definition is as follows:

> Rules that define how markup is added to the data of a document, without regard to the specific characters used to represent the markup. (4.1)

See also: *concrete syntax*

## ancestor

An element that contains another element, directly or indirectly; the first is said to be an ancestor of the second.

## architectural form

A named set of rules for and constraints on the declaration and processing of an element or an attribute definition list, usually expressed as a markup declaration and accompanying documentation. A declaration conforming to an architectural form references it by supplying the form's name as the value of a certain attribute.

←——————————————————————————→

## attribute

Markup that allows further description of an element. If you think of an element as a noun, you can think of an attribute is an adjective modifying a noun. Attribute information for an element is stored in its start-tag.

The ISO 8879 definition is as follows:

> A characteristic quality, other than type or content. (4.9)

## attribute name

A label for an attribute value. Attribute information in an element's start-tag is not position-sensitive; the attribute name helps to distinguish between values for different attributes.

## attribute value

A string that provides additional description for an element. An attribute's declared value determines the rules an attribute value must follow to be valid, for example, indicating that the value must be a NUMBER (a string made up only of the characters 0–9).

See also: *declared value*

## attribute specification

The ISO 8879 definition is as follows:

> A member of an attribute specification list; it specifies the value of a single attribute. (4.15)

## authoring DTD

A variant of a reference DTD whose markup model has been optimized for use in authoring, editing, and modifying documents. Authoring DTDs are sometimes created to solve problems in specific software environments or to simplify the markup process.

See also: *conversion DTD, interchange DTD, presentation DTD, reference DTD*

## catalog

A file that maps public identifiers (primarily used in entity declarations) to objects (such as files) on a computer system, so that the contents of each object can be substituted. The format of the most commonly used catalog file was standardized by SGML Open in its Technical Resolution 9401.

## child

An element that is directly contained by another element; the first is said to be a child of the second.

## collection

A "palette" of elements from which authors can choose freely (possibly along with data characters) in a particular context, without restriction on number or order, other than potentially requiring a single element to be supplied.

An element declaration achieves this effect by using a repeatable OR group in its content model. If the optional-repeatable indicator is used or the collection allows #PCDATA, the content model can be satisfied by an absence of any content. If the required-repeatable indicator is used and the collection specifies only elements, at least one of the elements must be present to satisfy the content model.

## comment

Special markup and content that is solely for the eyes of readers of the "source" files. In a document instance, the comment is usually in its own comment declaration, surrounded with <!-- --> characters. In a DTD, comments are sometimes interspersed throughout other markup declarations.

The ISO 8879 definition is as follows:

> A portion of a markup declaration that contains explanations or remarks intended to aid persons working with the document. (4.46)

## component

See: *semantic component*

## content-based component

A semantic component that is primarily descriptive of information content, rather than structure or presentation. For example, a "mailing address" component is content-based.

See also: *presentational component, structural component*

## concrete syntax

The expression of functional roles of pieces of SGML markup in terms of character strings. For example, a "start-tag open" (STAGO) in the abstract syntax is mapped to a left angle bracket (<) in the reference concrete syntax.

The ISO 8879 definition is as follows:

> A binding of the abstract syntax to particular delimiter characters, quantities, markup declaration names, etc. (4.48)

See also: *abstract syntax*

## content model

The rules for the configuration of element and/or data content allowable in instances of an element type.

The ISO 8879 definition is as follows:

> Parameter of an element declaration that specifies the model group and exceptions that define the allowed content of the element. (4.55)

## context

The specific arrangement of document text in which a particular kind of markup or content is found (or *can be* found, if you are examining a markup model rather than a document instance).

In a document instance, context is usually understood to mean the list of element ancestors of a certain element. For example, the context of a "recipe instruction step" element might be represented as "recipe→instruction-list→step." However, other factors, such as the values of particular attributes, can also be examined. Most kinds of document utilization, such as searching and formatting, involve locating material in a certain bounded context.

## contextual markup

A markup system for which not all individual pieces of markup are allowable in all locations in a document. SGML is contextual, whereas most word-processing systems are not.

See also: *noncontextual markup*

## conversion

The process of changing a document's system-specific markup, usually permanently, to conform to an SGML DTD.

See also: *transformation*

## conversion DTD

A variant of a reference DTD that is optimized for receiving the results of converting non-SGML document sources to SGML form. Typically, conversion DTDs relax the content models and attribute rules of the reference DTD.

See also: *authoring DTD, interchange DTD, presentational DTD, reference DTD*

## data

The ISO 8879 definition is as follows:

> The characters of a document that represent the inherent information content; characters that are not recognized as markup. (4.72)

SGML distinguishes between data and markup, calling the combination of the two text.

See also: *text, data-level component, data-level element*

## data-level component, data-level element

A component or element that represents a small piece of information which needs to be processed or handled specially. A data-level element usually has a simple internal structure and would be meaningless without its surrounding context, which almost always consists of character data, usually in prose form.

See also: *information unit (IU)*

## declarative markup

A markup system that describes the document content rather than how a computer system should process that content. Markup that effectively says "This is a paragraph" is declarative, while markup that says "Wrap this region of text to fit a line length of 26 picas using 10-point Times font on 11-point leading" is procedural.

See also: *procedural markup*

## declared content

Instructions for the content of an element type that are represented with a single keyword. The three choices of element declared content are CDATA, RCDATA, and EMPTY.

## declared value

The constraints imposed by the attribute definition list declaration, which any value for that attribute must follow in a document. The declared value of an attribute serves as a kind of "data type" for the value. Table A-1 describes the available declared values.

## descendant

An element that is contained by another element, directly or indirectly; the first is said to be a descendant of the second.

## descriptive markup

See: *declarative markup*

← ————————————————————————————————————————— →

## design principle

A goal arising from the overall SGML project goals, stated specifically and unambiguously, that should be used by the document type design team and the DTD implementor in their work.

## document

The ISO 8879 definition is as follows:

> A collection of information that is processed as a unit. A document is classified as being of a particular document type. (4.96)

## document analysis report

The formal, written results of the needs analysis and document type design work performed by the document type design team. This report, along with the project documents, is the main source of information from which the DTD implementor works.

## document element

The ISO 8879 definition is as follows:

> The element that is the outermost element of an instance of a document type; that is, the element whose generic identifier is the document type name. (4.99)

## document hierarchy

The overall structure of a document type; the highest levels of markup that dictate the characteristic "shape" of the documents.

**See also:** *information pool*

## document instance

The ISO 8879 definition is as follows:

> Instance of a document type. (4.100)

The ISO 8879 definition of an "instance of a document type" is as follows:

> The data and markup for a hierarchy of elements that conforms to a document type definition. (4.160)

See also: *presentation instance*

## document type

The ISO 8879 definition is as follows:

> A class of documents having similar characteristics; for example, journal, article, technical manual, or memo. (4.102)

## document type declaration

The declaration at the top of an SGML document (after the SGML declaration, if one is present) that indicates the DTD rules to which the document instance is intended to conform.

The ISO 8879 definition is as follows:

> A markup declaration that formally specifies a portion of a document type definition. (4.103)

## document type definition

See: *DTD (document type definition)*

## DTD (document type definition)

A formal expression of the SGML-based rules that a document's markup must follow.

The ISO 8879 definition is as follows:

> Rules, determined by an application, that apply SGML to the markup of documents of a particular type. (4.105)

See also: *markup model*

## element

A named collection of document content. Most such collections can contain and/or be contained in other collections.

The ISO 8879 definition is as follows:

> A component of the hierarchical structure defined by a document type definition; it is identified in a document instance by descriptive markup, usually a start-tag and end-tag. (4.110)

See also: *element type*

## element declaration

The markup declaration that specifies the rules for an element type.

The ISO 8879 definition is as follows:

> A markup declaration that contains the formal specification of the part of an element type definition that deals with the content and markup minimization. (4.111)

### element set

A portion of a DTD, usually containing element declarations, that "travels together" and can be used easily in multiple DTDs. An element set is stored in its own parameter entity.

The ISO 8879 definition is as follows:

> A set of element, attribute definition list, and notation declarations that are used together. (4.112)

### element type

The definition of an element; an element in the abstract sense, as opposed to any instances of that element type in an actual document. Any one element declaration, even if it specifies multiple generic identifiers, defines a single element type.

The ISO 8879 definition is as follows:

> A class of elements having similar characteristics; for example, paragraph, chapter, abstract, footnote, or bibliography. (4.114)

See also: *element*

### elm tree diagram

A graphically based description of the desired markup model for part or all of a document type being designed, or a similar description of the model for an existing DTD, using the notation explained in Appendix B. "Elm" is an acronym for "enables lucid models."

### end-tag

The ISO 8879 definition is as follows:

> Descriptive markup that identifies the end of an element. (4.119)

### entity

A named fragment of document content that is stored separately from other fragments and can be included in a document one or more times by reference to its name.

The ISO 8879 definition is as follows:

> A collection of characters that can be referenced as a unit. (4.120)

### entity reference

Markup that indicates a location in a document where the content of an entity should be included.

The ISO 8879 definition is as follows:

> A reference that is replaced by an entity. (4.124)

## extended DTD

A DTD whose markup model has been modified from that of an original (usually standard) DTD, such that some or all instances conforming to the modified one can potentially be invalid according to the original one.

See also: *renamed DTD, subsetted DTD*

## external identifier

The ISO 8879 definition is as follows:

> A parameter that identifies an external entity or data content notation. (4.135)

## generic identifier

The ISO 8879 definition is as follows:

> A name that identifies the element type of an element. (4.145)

## generic markup

A markup system that is not specific to a single vendor, document producer, or computer hardware or software configuration.

See also: *system-specific markup*

## hierarchical

Arranged by means of successive levels of containment, where "lower" (or "inner") units are nested entirely within "higher" (or "outer") ones. Elements in an SGML document are arranged hierarchically.

## HyTime

The Hypermedia/Time-based Structuring Language; ISO Standard 10744. HyTime is a language, defined largely by means of architectural forms, for representing hypertext links and the scheduling and synchronization of events. To use HyTime-based processing applications, you map the relevant markup in your DTD to the architectural forms specified in the HyTime standard, following the constraints set forth by the forms.

See also: *architectural form*

## information pool

The body of markup available to authors in the contexts where they supply the "main content" of a document. These contexts typically offer great discretion in choosing and applying markup. The information pool is a kind of "supercollection" encompassing all the information units and data-level elements.

See also: *document hierarchy*

### information unit (IU)

A high-level component or element that can, to some degree, "stand alone" in order to be understood by a reader, such that it must "travel together" during information processing and assembly. An information unit typically has a complex internal structure. However, the most common information unit, the paragraph, often has a very simple content model.

See also: *data-level component, data-level element*

### instance

See: *document instance*

### interchange DTD

A DTD that has been agreed on as the standard form for document interchange by the senders and recipients of SGML documents. For example, DocBook Version 2.2.1 was the interchange DTD agreed on by the authors and publisher of this book. Reference DTDs often must use an interchange DTD as their design base.

See also: *authoring DTD, conversion DTD, presentational DTD, reference DTD*

### internal declaration subset

The portion of a DTD's markup declarations that are provided directly inside the document type declaration, between square brackets.

### International Organization for Standardization

See: *ISO (International Organization for Standardization*

### ISO (International Organization for Standardization)

ISO describes itself and explains its work as follows:

> ISO (the International Organization for Standardization) is a world-wide federation of national standards bodies (ISO member bodies). The work of preparing International Standards is normally carried out through ISO technical committees. Each member body interested in a subject for which a technical committee has been established has the right to be represented on that committee. International organizations, governmental and non-governmental, in liaison with ISO, also take part in the work.

SGML was created under the auspices of ISO/IEC JTC1/SC18/WG8—Working Group 8 of Subcommittee 18 of Joint Technical Committee 1 of the combined effort of ISO and the International Electrotechnical Commission.

See also: *SGML (Standard Generalized Markup Language)*

## IU

See: *information unit (IU)*

## key data

A data-level component or element that is highly content-based and specifically related to the information domain of the document type under discussion. For example, in software documentation, a "command name" would be key data.

## link component

A component that records the relationship of two or more pieces of information. Two common kinds of links are those that join document content to locations where that content should be reproduced, and those that constitute a suggestion to the reader to seek out additional information.

## markup, mark up

The ISO 8879 definition of markup is as follows:

> Text that is added to the data of a document in order to convey information about it. (4.183)

To mark up data is to add markup to it.

## markup declaration

A "statement" in the SGML language that defines a portion of a markup model or other markup characteristics of a document. Most markup declarations appear in DTDs, but a few (such as comment declarations) can appear in document instances.

The ISO 8879 definition is as follows:

> Markup that controls how other markup of a document is to be interpreted. (4.186)

## markup model

The markup "vocabulary" and "grammar" defined by a DTD (or some part of a DTD), which serve as the rules of the language "spoken" by documents conforming to that DTD. Many people simply use the term "DTD" for this concept, but we use a unique term for it because of the need to distinguish between the actual markup characteristics defined in a DTD and the various implementation techniques used to make the design readable, maintainable, and so on.

## metainformation

Information about information; facts about a document (or smaller piece of information) *as* a body of information. For example, a document's publication date is metainformation.

← ——————————————————————————— →

## metalanguage

A language that is used to create or define other languages. SGML is a metalanguage used to define DTDs that specify markup models; these models function as unique document markup "languages."

## modeling

The act of designing markup requirements in a way that makes the results suitable for expression in SGML markup declarations.

## noncontextual markup

A markup system that places no formal restrictions on the appearance or order of the individual pieces of markup. Most word-processing systems are noncontextual, whereas SGML is contextual.

See also: *contextual markup*

## parent

An element that directly contains another element; the first is said to be a parent of the second.

## parser

The ISO 8879 definition of "SGML parser" is as follows:

> A program (or portion of a program or a combination of programs) that recognizes markup in SGML documents. (4.285)

## potato

An oval in a tree diagram containing an element collection or any-order group. Also, an herb of the nightshade family that is widely cultivated as a vegetable crop.

## presentation instance

One form of an SGML document as presented to a user, possibly with some content changed, added, or removed compared to other presentations.

See also: *document instance*

## presentational component

A semantic component that is primarily descriptive of information appearance rather than structure or meaning. For example, a "bold font" component is presentational.

See also: *content-based component, structural component*

## presentational DTD

A variant of a reference DTD that is optimized to assist the process of transforming SGML documents into presented or otherwise processed form. Typically, presentation DTDs allow for the "augmenting" of the original document to contain generated material, such as tables of contents, and formatting-related information.

See also: *authoring DTD, conversion DTD, interchange DTD, reference DTD*

## principle

See: *design principle*

## procedural markup

A markup system that describes how a computer system should process the document content rather than what the content means. Markup that effectively says "Wrap this region of text to fit a line length of 26 picas using 10-point Times font on 11-point leading" is procedural, while markup that says "This is a paragraph" is declarative.

See also: *declarative markup*

## processing expectations

The assumptions about markup that constrain and inform its use in document authoring, management, and processing. For example, the processing expectations about a cross-reference element might include the requirement that it be replaced with generated text when it is formatted for printing. Some people use the term "semantics" or "processing semantics" for this meaning—which accounts for our use of the terms "semantic component" and "semantic extension"—but as a noun, semantics is too ambiguous for our taste.

## RE

See: *record end (RE)*

## record end (RE)

An invisible character that occurs at the end of units of stored data that are known as records or, sometimes, "lines."

The ISO 8879 definition is as follows:

> A function character, assigned by the concrete syntax, that represents the end of a record. (4.254)

## reference concrete syntax

The default concrete syntax for SGML documents, and the one used in SGML declarations.

The ISO 8879 definition is as follows:

> A concrete syntax, defined in this International Standard, that is used in all SGML declarations. (4.258)

## reference DTD

A DTD that encodes the "ideal" markup model for complete documents of a specified type. A reference DTD may be based on (that is, a variant of) an interchange DTD, but otherwise it typically provides the design base for the other variant DTDs, such as an authoring DTD.

See also: *authoring DTD, conversion DTD, interchange DTD, presentational DTD*

## renamed DTD

A DTD that is identical to another DTD, except that some or all of the element names and other markup names have been changed to be more suitable for use with authors who use a different jargon or write in a different language.

See also: *extended DTD, subsetted DTD*

## semantic component

A unit of specification representing a requirement for the design of a document type model, which corresponds to a kind of information that must be distinguished from all others. A semantic component often results in the DTD having a new element type, but can also result in other kinds of markup distinctions.

See also: *processing expectations*

## semantic extension

A technique for markup model design that allows a DTD's markup to be used for making novel distinctions among kinds of information, even if the markup didn't previously recognize the distinction. The technique is useful for DTDs that cannot be updated frequently enough to satisfy new requirements at the rate at which they are created.

## SGML (Standard Generalized Markup Language)

The ISO 8879 definition of Standard Generalized Markup Language is as follows:

> A language for document representation that formalizes markup and frees it of system and processing dependencies. (4.305)

SGML was published in 1986 as ISO Standard 8879. Amendment 1 to the standard was published in 1988.

### SGML document

See: *document*

### sibling

An element that occurs at the same level as another element which has the same parent; the two are said to be siblings of each other.

### specific markup

See: *system-specific markup*

### Standard Generalized Markup Language

See: *SGML (Standard Generalized Markup Language)*

### start-tag

The ISO 8879 definition is as follows:

> Descriptive markup that identifies the start of an element and specifies its generic identifier and attributes. (4.306)

### structural component

A semantic component that is primarily descriptive of information structure rather than meaning or appearance. For example, a "list" component is structural.

See also: *content-based component, presentational component*

### subsetted DTD

A DTD whose markup model has been modified from that of an original (usually standard) DTD, such that all instances conforming to the modified one are still valid according to the original one. Note that a subsetted DTD is unrelated to a DTD internal subset, which is a the portion of a DTD that is "local" to a document by virtue of being supplied inside the DOCTYPE declaration's square brackets ([]).

See also: *extended DTD, renamed DTD*

### system-specific markup

A markup system that is specific to a single vendor, document producer, or computer hardware or software configuration.

See also: *generic markup*

### tag

The ISO 8879 definition is as follows:

> Descriptive markup. (4.314)

← ——————————————————————————————————→

## Tag Abuse Syndrome

A condition that afflicts authors who choose inappropriate markup to get a certain formatting effect or choose markup that isn't as precise or accurate as possible. A poor DTD design often exacerbates the problem.

## text

Data and markup making up a document.

The ISO 8879 definition is as follows:

> Characters. (4.316)

Where we use the term for its colloquial meaning—the main content in the flow of a document, exclusive of the document hierarchy—we use quotation marks around it.

See also: *data*

## transformation

The process of changing the data and markup within SGML documents to make them conform to a different DTD or to another kind of markup, typically one that can be directly interpreted by printers, display devices, or further transformation software.

See also: *conversion*

## tree diagram

See: *elm tree diagram*

## validating SGML parser

The ISO 8879 definition is as follows:

> A conforming SGML parser that can find and report a reportable markup error if (and only if) one exists. (4.329)

## value

See: *attribute value*

## variant DTD

A DTD whose design is based closely on the markup model of another DTD.

See also: *reference DTD*

## WYSIWYG

"What you see is what you get." A description of word processing systems and desktop publishing systems that let authors see a representation of the formatted appearance of a document on the computer screen as they work. Most such systems also allow authors to customize the formatted appearance by manipulating the screen display dynamically.

# Index

←――――――――――――――――――――――――――――――――→